Atlas of World Development

Atlas of World Development

Edited by

TIM UNWIN

JOHN WILEY & SONS
Chichester · New York · Brisbane · Toronto · Singapore

Copyright © 1994 Developing Areas Research Group

Published 1994 by John Wiley & Sons Ltd,
Baffins Lane, Chichester,
West Sussex, PO19 1UD, England

Telephone National Chichester (0243) 779777
International + 44 243 779777

Other Wiley Editorial Offices

John Wiley & Sons, Inc., 605 Third Avenue,
New York, NY 10158-0012, USA

Jacaranda Wiley Ltd, 33 Park Road, Milton,
Queensland 4064, Australia

John Wiley & Sons (Canada) Ltd, 22 Worcester Road,
Rexdale, Ontario M9W 1L1, Canada

John Wiley & Sons (SEA) Pte Ltd, 37 Jalan Pemimpin #05-04,
Black B, Union Industrial Building,
Singapore 2057

Library of Congress Cataloging-in-Publication Data
Unwin, P. T. H.
    Atlas of world development / Tim Unwin.
        p. cm.
    Includes bibliographical references and index.
    ISBN 0-471-94991-4
    1. Human geography—Maps.   2. Social history—Maps.   3. Economic
development—Maps.   4. Historical   geography—Maps.   I. Title.
G1046.E1U5   1994 ⟨G&M⟩
911—dc20   94-6967
                                                          CIP
                                                          MAP

British Library Cataloguing in Publication Data

A catalogue record for this book is available from the British Library

ISBN 0-471-94991-4

Typeset in 10/12 pt Times from editor's disks by
Mathematical Composition Setters Ltd, Salisbury, Wiltshire.
Printed in Great Britain by Bookcraft (Bath) Ltd.
Bound in Great Britain by Hunter & Foulis, Edinburgh.

Contents

Contributors

Dr Richard Black, Lecturer in Geography, King's College London, Strand, London, WC2R 2LS, UK

Dr Gerald Blake, Director, International Boundaries Research Unit, University of Durham, Durham, DH1 3LE, UK

Dr Robert W. Bradnock, Lecturer in Geography with Special Reference to South Asia, School of Oriental and African Studies, University of London, Thornhaugh Street, Russell Square, London, WC1H 0XG, UK

Dr Michael J. Bradshaw, Lecturer in the School of Geography and Associate Member of the Centre for Russian and East European Studies, University of Birmingham, Edgbaston, Birmingham, B15 2TT, UK

Dr John Briggs, Senior Lecturer in Geography, University of Glasgow, Glasgow, G12 8QQ, UK

Mr Paul Brignall, Research Scientist, Environmental Change Unit, University of Oxford, Oxford, OX1 3TB, UK

Juliette Brown, Visiting Researcher, Applied Population Research Unit, University of Glasgow, Glasgow, G12 8QQ, UK

Professor Graham Chapman, Department of Geography, University of Lancaster, Lancaster, LA1 4YW, UK

Martin Cottingham, Information Officer, Christian Aid, P.O. Box 100, London, SE1 7RT, UK

Cecile Cutler, Associate Lecturer in Geography, Flinders University, GPO Box 2100, Adelaide, Australia 5001

Dr Ian Davison, Lecturer, Department of Geology, Royal Holloway, University of London, Egham, Surrey, TW20 0EX, UK

Dr John Dickenson, Senior Lecturer, Department of Geography, University of Liverpool, Liverpool, L69 3BX, UK

Professor Chris Dixon, Department of Geography, London Guildhall University, Old Castle Street, London, E1 7NT, UK

Elizabeth Dowler, Lecturer, Centre for Human Nutrition, Department of Public Health and Policy, London School of Hygiene and Tropical Medicine (University of London), Keppel Street, London, WC1E 7HT, UK

Professor David Drakakis-Smith, Department of Geography, University of Keele, Keele, Staffordshire, ST5 5BG, England

Dr Jennifer A. Elliott, Senior Lecturer, Division of Geography, Staffordshire University, Leek Road, Stoke-on-Trent, Staffordshire, ST4 2DF, UK

Professor Allan M. Findlay, Department of Geography, University of Dundee, Dundee, DD1 4HN, UK

Professor Dean Forbes, Professor of Geography, Flinders University, GPO Box 2100, Adelaide, Australia 5001

Dr Roddy Fox, Senior Lecturer, Department of Geography, Rhodes University, Grahamstown, South Africa 6140

Dr Peter Furley, Reader in Tropical Soils & Biogeography, Department of Geography, University of Edinburgh, Drummond Street, Edinburgh, EH8 9XP, UK

Professor Alan Gilbert, Department of Geography, University College London, 26 Bedford Way, London, WC1H 0AP, UK

Professor Bill Gould, Department of Geography, University of Liverpool, Liverpool, L69 3BX, UK

Ms Paula Harrison, Research Scientist, Environmental Change Unit, University of Oxford, Oxford, OX1 3TB, UK

Dr David Hilling, Senior Lecturer in Geography, Royal Holloway, University of London, Egham, Surrey, TW20 0EX, UK

Dr J.E. Hossell, Research Scientist, Environmental Change Unit, University of Oxford, Oxford, OX1 3TB, UK

Dr Mike Hulme, Senior Research Associate, Climatic Research Unit, School of Environmental Sciences, University of East Anglia, Norwich, NR4 7TJ, UK

Dr Jörg Janzen, Zentrum für Entwicklungsländer-Forschung, Freie Universität Berlin, FB Geowissenschaften, WE 02, Grunewaldstr. 35, D-12165 Berlin 41, Germany

Dr Gareth A. Jones, Lecturer in Geography, University College of Swansea, Singleton Park, Swansea, West Glamorgan, SA2 8PP, UK

Professor Huw Jones, Department of Geography, Dundee University, Dundee, DD1 4HN, UK

Professor Russell King, Professor of Geography, School of European Studies, University of Sussex, Falmer, Brighton, BN1 9QN, UK

Eileen Maybin, Journalist, Asia/Pacific Group, Christian Aid, P.O. Box 100, London, SE1 7RT, UK

Dr Duncan McGregor, Senior Lecturer in Geography, Royal Holloway, University of London, Egham, Surrey, TW20 0EX, UK

Dr Jørgen S. Nielsen, Director, Centre for the Study of Islam and Christian-Muslim Relations, Selly Oak Colleges, Birmingham, B29 6LQ, UK

Dr Lewis A. Owen, Lecturer, Departments of Geography and Geology, Royal Holloway, University of London, Egham, Surrey, TW20 0EX, UK

Professor Robert B. Potter, Centre for Developing Areas Research, Department of Geography, Royal Holloway, University of London, Egham, Surrey, TW20 0EX, UK

Dr David Preston, Director of the Centre for Development Studies, University of Leeds, Leeds, LS2 9JT, UK

Dr Sarah A. Radcliffe, Lecturer in Geography, Royal Holloway, University of London, Egham, Surrey, TW20 0EX, UK

Dr Jonathan Rigg, Lecturer in Geography, Department of Geography, University of Durham, South Road, Durham, DH1 3LE, UK

Dr James D. Sidaway, Lecturer in Geography, School of Geography, University of Birmingham, Edgbaston, Birmingham, B15 2TT, UK

Dr David Simon, Director, Centre for Developing Areas Research, Department of Geography, Royal Holloway, University of London, Egham, Surrey, TW20 0EX, UK

Dr Michael Stocking, Reader in Natural Resource Development, School of Development Studies, University of East Anglia, Norwich, NR4 7TJ, UK

Dr Jeffrey Stone, Senior Lecturer, Department of Geography, University of Aberdeen, Aberdeen, AB9 2UF, Scotland

Dr John Tarrant, Deputy Vice-Chancellor, University of East Anglia, Norwich, Norfolk, NR4 7TJ, UK

Professor Peter J. Taylor, Professor of Political Geography, Department of Geography, The University, Newcastle upon Tyne, NE1 7RU

Dr Brian Turton, Senior Lecturer in Geography, University of Keele, Keele, Staffordshire, ST5 5BG, UK

Dr Tim Unwin, Reader in Geography, Royal Holloway, University of London, Egham, Surrey, TW20 0EX, UK

Ms Josephine Vespa, Ph.D. student, Centre for Human Nutrition, Department of Public Health and Policy, London School of Hygiene and Tropical Medicine (University of London), Keppel Street, London, WC1E 7HT, UK

Dr Peter Vujakovic, Senior Lecturer in Geography, Anglia Polytechnic University, Cambridge, CB1 1PT, UK

Professor Malcolm Wagstaff, Professor of Geography, University of Southampton, Highfield, Southampton, SO17 1BJ, UK

Dr Gordon Walker, Principal Lecturer in Geography, Staffordshire University, Stoke on Trent, Staffordshire, ST4 2DF, UK

Douglas Webb, Department of Geography, Royal Holloway, University of London, Egham, Surrey, TW20 0EX, UK

Professor Colin Williams, Professor of Geography, Division of Geography, Staffordshire University, Leek Road, Stoke-on-Trent, Staffordshire, ST4 2DF, UK

Dr Stephen Wyn Williams, Principal Lecturer, Division of Geography, Staffordshire University, Leek Road, Stoke-on-Trent, Staffordshire, ST4 2DF, UK

Preface

This atlas has been produced on behalf of the Developing Areas Research Group (DARG) of the Institute of British Geographers, and all of the authors have agreed to donate their royalties to support the Research Group's activities. These currently include the publication of research monographs on the developing areas of the world, the award of prizes to undergraduate and postgraduate students for work in developing countries, and the convening of conferences and symposia on development issues. Most of the authors are members of DARG, and the atlas therefore in part reflects the current research being undertaken by British geographers on issues of economic and social change in the poorer countries of the world. Where members of DARG could not be found to write sections, other authors were invited to contribute, and several of them add an important international flavour to the atlas. Members of the DARG Committee in 1989–90 acted as an advisory body in the early stages of the planning of the atlas, and I am particularly grateful for the advice and assistance of Robert Potter, David Drakakis-Smith, Sarah Radcliffe, Chris Dixon, Allan Findlay and Iain Stevenson in the various stages of production that have ensued. Don Shewan and Gareth Owen at London Guildhall University have designed and produced the world maps, building on the work of numerous other cartographers in institutions throughout the world, and without their very significant contribution the atlas would never have been completed. Kathy Roberts in the Department of Geography at Royal Holloway, University of London, prepared the typescript with her usual high speed, accuracy and good humour. Finally, I am grateful to all of the authors who have found the time to produce their contributions, and through the donation of their royalties to support the continuing research work of DARG.

ACKNOWLEDGEMENTS

The authors and publisher are grateful to the following for their assistance in making material available: Swiss Reinsurance Company, Zurich, and Petroconsultants SA London. The kind permission of Routledge to reproduce Figures 6.11a and 6.11b is hereby acknowledged.

Tim Unwin

Introduction

TIM UNWIN

The early 1990s have seen enormous transformations in global geopolitics, and yet the life experiences of the world's poor remain very little different from those experienced by their predecessors half a century, or even longer, ago. Despite the global recession, the collapse of the Soviet Union has heralded an apparent new era in the fortunes of the capitalist world economy. Yet this economy is built fundamentally on preconditions of difference: for there to be rich, there have to be poor; for there to be free, there have to be unfree. This atlas is centrally concerned with these issues of difference, and with the reasons why they continue to prevail.

Choosing a title that conveyed the atlas's central concern with difference and with inequality was not easy. Other options considered involved the phrases 'Third World' and 'Developing Areas', but neither of these quite captured the core focus of the present work. The term 'Third World' is now more widely used than ever before to refer to the poorer or less developed states of the world (Drakakis-Smith, 1993), and it has already been used in the title of two important atlases, one published by the Open University (Crow and Thomas, 1983) and the other by Facts on File (Kurian, 1992). However, as the Open University atlas illustrated, it is impossible to understand the processes creating poverty in the Third World without analysing the richer states as well. Thus most of the maps in the *Third World Atlas* (Crow and Thomas, 1983) were actually of the whole world, and not just of the 'Third World'. A title including the phrase 'Developing Areas' would closely have reflected the origin of the atlas as a co-operative venture produced by the Developing Areas Research Group of the Institute of British Geographers, but as with the use of the 'Third World' it could have suggested a work purely on the poorer areas of the world. Once again, to understand this poverty, and to be able to gain an appreciation of the extent of the differences between so-called 'developing' and 'developed' areas, it is essential to illustrate the rich alongside the poor. More importantly, though, the use of the word 'areas' would have suggested an excessive orientation to places rather than people. In most areas of the world, rich and poor live together in close proximity.

The term 'development' itself is not, though, unproblematic (Sachs, 1992). It is all too often taken to mean linear progress along a continuum, from poverty to wealth, and is still most usually defined in largely economic terms (Unwin, 1983; Esteve, 1992). It was in this sense, for example, that the concept was used by Rostow (1960) in his influential, but subsequently much criticised, model of stages of economic growth. Such a conceptualisation is built upon the belief that it is possible for all countries and people to improve their economic condition, and that there can be in effect a total increase in global economic affluence. However, it is in marked contrast to more 'radical' models, focusing on inequality, which suggest that increases in economic wealth of one group of countries or people can only be at the expense of another political or social group (Frank, 1969; Harriss and Harriss, 1979). Over a decade ago Mabogunje (1980) drew attention to four other uses of the term 'development': as modernisation, as distributional justice, as socio-economic transformation, and as socio-spatial process. By the mid-1980s, it had thus become apparent that socio-economic change was very much more complex than many economic theorists in the 1950s and 1960s had believed, and this was recognised in much broader conceptualisations of 'development' to include 'cultural and social as well as economic and technological change' (Crow and Thomas, 1983: 8). More recent critiques (Sachs, 1992; Drakakis-Smith, 1993) illustrate that although 'development' continues most frequently to be used as an abbreviation for 'economic development' associated with 'modernity', this need not necessarily always be so.

For the purposes of the title of the present atlas, the word 'development' has been chosen to reflect two meanings. On the one hand it is used to refer to the processes of economic and social change that have taken place over the last century, and more specifically over the last two decades. These have centrally been associated with the increasing global dominance of capitalism, grounded in the *economic* conditions to which Marx (1976) drew attention well over a century ago (Howard and King, 1976), and more recently embedded within the label of *modernity* (Watts, 1993). On the other hand, 'development' is also used in the sense of 'progress' to suggest a hope for the future: that *social* and *political* changes may one day take place that will provide the preconditions for a fairer sharing of the world's resources, and that present inequalities at all levels from the global economy to the household may be reduced. Development is thus seen as being something very different from simple economic advancement in the context of global capitalism. No attempt, however, has been made to constrain the authors of the present atlas in their own use of terminology. Indeed, the diversity of phrases used within this atlas, such as 'Less Developed Countries', 'developing areas', 'poorer states', and 'underdeveloped countries', is seen as providing a richness indicative of the differing conceptual backgrounds used by the authors.

If the theme of this book is concerned with the processes giving rise to contrasts in the life experiences of people living in different places, its format is overtly that of an atlas. Geography and cartography have for centuries been closely related (Crone, 1968; Dilke, 1985), and with the recent development of Geographical Information Systems this relationship has been re-established on a new footing (Rhind, 1993). Maps serve many purposes. They were thus central to the European voyages of 'discovery' in the 15th and 16th centuries, with every new coastline or island eagerly being plotted by Italian, Iberian or Dutch cartographers. Maps and exploration went hand in hand, with new discoveries enabling increasingly accurate maps to be drawn, which in turn opened up opportunities for yet further exploratory voyages. Maps and 'geographies' have been central to military campaigns, from the days of classical antiquity, when Strabo (1949: 31) argued that 'geography as a whole has a direct bearing upon the activities of commanders', to the military origins of national mapping agencies such as the Ordnance Survey in Britain, and the highly sophisticated use of digitised spatial information associated with today's missile systems. However, it must be remembered that all maps are constructs, and abstractions from reality. They represent selective images, which can be manipulated in a variety of ways to convey particular themes and ideas. Frequently, they have been used by dominant groups of people as a way of reinforcing their positions of power, albeit often unconsciously. Thus the widespread use of Mercator's projection developed in the 16th century, which placed a disproportionately large Europe in the centre of the upper half of the map, is generally seen as having promoted an excessively Eurocentric view of the world. However, it must be noted that for its original use as a guide to navigation it was essential that it maintained the true directions between points, and the sacrifice in accuracy of areas and shapes towards the poles was therefore one that was crucially necessary.

In this atlas maps have been used for two main purposes. First, they provide illustrations of the themes addressed by the authors. They therefore convey images which are designed to be persuasive, and to draw attention to the particular phenomena and processes being investigated. This combination of both text and maps thus provides an important contrast to atlases such as that edited by Kurian (1992), which concentrate primarily on the presentation of maps with little, if any, interpretative text. However, secondly, the maps are also part of a research exercise. The juxtaposition of information in a spatial context generates a wide range of research questions. Tables of data thus often appear to have little shape or form until they are plotted on maps or graphs, when patterns emerge that provide the basis for subsequent investigation and analysis. Moreover, it is an intention of this atlas to provoke its readers to examine new research issues; to draw their attention to patterns of inequality with which they might not otherwise have been familiar.

Having summarised the reasons for the atlas's title and commented on the role of cartography in general, this introductory chapter is designed to serve three further purposes: to outline the research framework within which the atlas has been prepared; to justify the cartographic style and conventions used; and to provide a brief introduction to the way in which information is presented within it.

The research framework

This atlas seeks to be different from its predecessors (see for example Crow and Thomas, 1983; Seager and Olson, 1986; Freeman, 1991; and Kurian, 1992) in three main ways: in its theoretical framework, through its process oriented research context, and by its incorporation of three main scales of analysis. Fundamentally, the atlas is not just about economic development, and it thus differs markedly in orientation from, for example, Freeman's (1991) *Atlas of the World Economy*. Instead, it builds on a conceptualisation which sees all groups of people as having four main types of activity: economic, social, political and ideological. While these categories are not necessarily always mutually exclusive, they encompass concepts that are sufficiently different to warrant their separation into distinct entities. Social activity is thus concerned with the interpersonal relations between people, economic activity focuses on production and exchange, political action is associated with the establishment and maintenance of power relationships, and ideological activities are concerned with the maintenance of legitimation. Through time these activities are codified into particular structures (Giddens, 1979; Gregory and Urry, 1985), more often than not reproduced through the everyday lived experiences of people, but sometimes formalised into written laws and constitutions. These structures then provide the framework within which future generations work out their own lives through a constant interplay between lived experience and inherited structure.

Most of the material in this atlas is therefore divided into four main sections on the social, economic, political and ideological structures of development. While this broad conceptualisation does not give primacy to any one structural component, such as the economic base (Althusser, 1969; Althusser and Balibar, 1970), the order in which these categories are presented is not entirely arbitrary. Social relationships, involving personal contacts between people, their births, illnesses and deaths, are treated first since above all the atlas is about people, their lived experiences and how these might be changed. Economic issues are addressed next, since they largely determine the material well-being of different groups of people, and these are followed by an examination of political activities concerned with the creation of states, elections and the practice of war. The final section of the atlas then addresses ideological issues mainly associated with the legitimation and justification of the various aspects of 'development' addressed previously. These activities and interactions between people, however, do not take place in isolation; rather, they happen in particular places and at specific moments in time. The first two sections of the atlas therefore explore the historical and environmental contexts of contemporary development.

A second aspect of the research framework is its concern with processes of change. The historical introduction provides an overall temporal framework to the atlas, but within each section authors have generally sought not only to illustrate the contemporary position with respect to their subjects of enquiry, but also to provide an analysis of the processes giving rise to the observed phenomena and patterns. Thus, while many of the maps present cross-sections of information at given points in time, the text addresses critical research issues designed to develop an interpretation of the processes giving rise to these phenomena. This concern with process is also reflected in the atlas's concentration on interactions, linkages and flows between different places (Potter and Unwin, 1989). To understand the problems of farmers in Bangladesh, for example, it is insufficient to concentrate exclusively on Bangladesh; instead it is essential to take into account the way in which that state is incorporated into the global economy. It is only through understanding such processes that effective action can be developed to change the circumstances giving rise to the inequalities observed.

Thirdly, the framework is designed to illustrate and provide an interpretation of processes as they operate at different scales. Most atlases concerned with development issues, such as Crow and Thomas's (1983) *Third World Atlas* and Seager and Olson's (1986) *Women in the World: an International Atlas*, concentrate almost exclusively at the global scale, including at most a few maps of specific phenomena at a regional scale. However, not only do processes have different effects at different scales, but different processes also tend to dominate at different scales. Moreover, maps at one scale invariably hide important differences in the distribution of phenomena at another scale. Typically, for example, people from urban and rural areas have markedly different levels of access to health and education facilities, but these are masked by general global maps of the provision of such facilities based simply on data at the scale of individual countries. Likewise, gender differences are generally hidden in most global maps, unless specific attention is drawn to them as in Seager and Olson's (1986) atlas which focuses overtly on women. Consequently, the present atlas includes maps at three main scales: the global, the regional or national, and the local.

The global maps provide the overall framework for the atlas, highlighting the inequalities between different parts of the world as a whole. A central problem with the preparation of such maps, though, is the difficulty of obtaining information on many processes at a world scale, and much reliance therefore has had to be placed on the data collated by international bodies such as the World Bank, the World Health Organisation (WHO) and the various agencies of the United Nations. These data are, however, selectively created, reflecting the priorities of those responsible for their compilation, and they are in any case usually based on information provided by national governments, which can vary greatly in reliability. The maps at a regional or national scale are designed to illustrate processes in more detail than is possible at a global scale, and focus on issues of particular pertinence to specific areas of the world. Thus, for example, detailed analyses are undertaken of vegetation change in Amazonia, of wildlife exploitation in the African savannas, of political and economic reorganisation in the former Soviet Union, and of the legacy of apartheid in South Africa. The local scale maps reflect much more directly the primary research undertaken by their authors, and unlike the global or regional maps they rely much less on data provided by national governments. In general they focus on detailed case studies of processes as they affect relatively small groups of people, and rather than being seen as typical of any particular broad themes they have been included to reflect the diversity of experiences and complexity of development processes. The choice of the location of regional and local case studies has been designed to be as representative as possible of different parts of the world, although it has also been determined to some extent by the particular research experiences of the authors (Potter and Unwin, 1988), and not all areas of the world have therefore been equally covered.

Cartographic style and conventions

Maps, like any work of art, piece of poetry, or manuscript, reflect the style and intentions of their designers. Not only do different topics frequently warrant contrasting cartographic conventions, but different cartographers will approach the same subject in a variety of ways. Given this inherent diversity, a key aim of this atlas was therefore to allow individual authors and their cartographers quite a large degree of freedom in their choice of cartographic representation, with the main constraints being the size and format of the pages, the use of black and white rather than colour, and general recommendations concerning minimum line thickness (0.2 mm) and font size (minimum 6 point).

It was, however, decided that, for consistency and ease of interpretation, most of the maps at a world scale should be depicted uniformly. This meant that a series of decisions had to be made concerning the projection to be used and the cartographic conventions to be adopted. The most crucial decision concerned the projection, and the choice eventually adopted was the Eckert IV. This has been widely used by the World Bank, and was also the preferred choice of Crow and Thomas (1983) in their Third World Atlas. Its main advantages are that it is an equal area projection, depicting regions of the globe of equal area by equal areas on the map, and that it distorts shape to a much lesser extent than do, for example, the Peters' and Mollweide's projections. Moreover, the curved lines of longitude help to give the impression of a spherical globe. However, as with most projections it retains the position of Europe in an upper central location, which some commentators have suggested lays it open to the criticism of being Eurocentric (Saarinen, 1988). Against such arguments, though, it can be noted that Africa, in terms of many criteria the poorest continent of the world, is given central prominence, unlike the choice in Seager and Olson's (1986) atlas, for example, where the central ground is taken by Australia and the Pacific Ocean.

All maps at the world scale suffer from difficulties associated with the depiction of small states, and in particular small islands. This is a marked problem in the Caribbean and the Pacific Ocean, but it is hoped that by focusing on these regions in specific case studies the disappearance of their small island states from the global maps will to some extent be compensated for. A further serious difficulty results from the political instability following the collapse of the former Soviet Union and the fragmentation of eastern Europe over the period in which this atlas has been produced. Numerous new states, such as Estonia, Tajikistan and Slovenia, have thus been created for which comprehensive data are as yet unavailable. The atlas in general therefore uses political boundaries extant at the date for which the data is presented. Moreover, a special section has been included to cover the political and economic reorganisation that has taken place in the former Soviet Union, and in order to provide as up-to-date a political overview as possible, Figure 0.1 provides a reference map for the state names and boundaries pertaining in July 1993 and used subsequently in the text.

The choice of shading types to be used in the choropleth and isopleth maps (Monkhouse and Wilkinson, 1963) was also problematic. Most of the global maps are choropleth maps, indicating average values of variables, usually per unit of area, in the various political units depicted. Without the use of colour, the maximum number of shading categories that can satisfactorily be reproduced at the scale of this atlas is approximately seven, although where possible authors were restricted to five or six categories. Initially it had been intended to use a specific symbol for cases where data were not available, but the small size of many of the political units precluded this possibility. Consequently, unshaded areas have consistently been used to indicate the absence of data on all of the global maps. Where possible, solid black shading has also been avoided, but where authors have insisted on using seven categories it has been necessary to represent the densest of these by an 80% black infill. Following several experimental designs, it was found that varying densities of diagonal shading in combination with state boundaries represented by $-\cdot-\cdot-$ provided the clearest method of differentiating the categories on the maps. To distinguish them from choropleth maps, the isopleth maps, based on data in the form of lines of equal value, have been depicted using different densities of dot shading.

The use of dots for the isopleth maps rather than for the choropleth maps was predicated on the observation that whatever type of line was used for state boundaries, which were of central importance to the choropleth maps, these boundaries tended to become invisible when overlain by dot shading.

In general, keys have all been placed at the bottom left corner of the world maps in the conveniently largely empty area of the Pacific Ocean, although where insets have been necessary this is the location where they have also had to be placed. The graticule shows lines of longitude and latitude at every 15°, but with the exception of Figure 0.1 they have remained unlabelled.

Structure and presentation

The atlas is divided into six main chapters, each of which commences with a short introductory essay designed to present an overview of the material presented. Within each chapter the sections are numbered consecutively (1.1, 1.2, 1.3 etc.) with all Figures and Tables within each section being referred to by the same numbers. Thus Section 4.7 includes Figures 4.7a, 4.7b, 4.7c and Tables 4.7a, 4.7b, 4.7c. Sources for all Figures and Tables are listed at the end of the atlas, following the bibliography which gives publication details of all of the references cited in the text. At the end of each

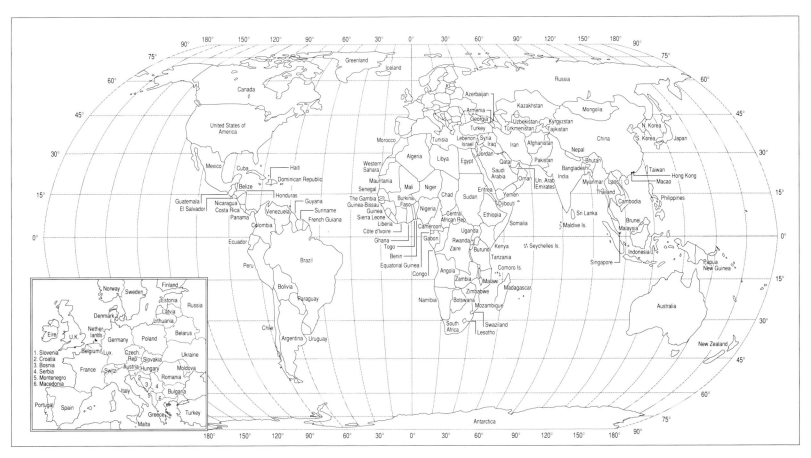

Figure 0.1   State names and boundaries, July 1993

section there is a guide to further reading on the subject covered, and an index provides a quick source of reference to the places and key themes addressed in the text.

In conclusion, this atlas is overtly the work of geographers. It looks at themes of difference and inequality, and in its combination of text and cartography it seeks to provide an interpretation of the world at the end of the 20th century. This interpretation reveals the very great complexity of social, economic, political and ideological change, and also the fundamental interaction between people and the physical world that creates the particular lived experiences of people in different places.

1 Definitions of Development and Historical Context

TIM UNWIN

As was stressed in the overall introduction to this atlas, it is impossible satisfactorily to understand the present circumstances of difference and poverty within the world without some comprehension of the past processes that have operated to bring these about. Moreover, a survey of the use of different kinds of projections, and an analysis of the varying ways in which 'development' can be interpreted are central to any atlas seeking to represent development cartographically. This first chapter of the atlas therefore considers these three broad themes in order to provide a more detailed conceptual overview of the issues associated with the concept of world development.

First, two sections contrast the ways in which traditional and alternative projections of the world have been used to illustrate global phenomena. These are then followed by an examination of the way in which the world was represented cartographically towards the end of the 16th century, at a time of critical economic and political change when cartographers and geographers played an important role in opening up 'new' lands to European influence and exploitation.

The next six sections examine aspects of the historical context of contemporary development issues. In the medieval period western Europe was a relatively backward part of the world, economically and culturally very different from the empires of China and the Ottoman Turks. In order to emphasise this difference, Section 1.4 therefore begins by noting the highly advanced organisation of the Ottoman Empire in the 16th century. At a very general level it is possible to see the subsequent development of an integrated world economy as being a process whereby Europeans, from a position of relatively obscurity, came to dominate the rest of the world. This was achieved in the context of the emergence of a particular economic system, namely capitalism. The creation of this modern world system, and the associated processes of colonialism and imperialism at a global level are then examined in the following three sections, with a regional case study of the 19th century struggle for Africa being included in Section 1.8. This is followed by an account of the decolonisation movements that have led to the break up of European political imperialism during the 20th century.

The final part of the chapter turns to an examination of different concepts of 'development', and the ways in which these have been measured and represented. Section 1.10 thus addresses terminological issues associated with the use of phrases such as the Third World and the North–South debate, and this is followed by an analysis of different measures of development, from purely economic indicators to indices associated with more overtly social characteristics. These amply illustrate the great complexities associated with questions of social, economic and political change, but they also emphasise the importance of adopting a spatially and temporally integrated approach to an understanding of the processes that influence variations in human welfare in different parts of the world.

1.1 CONVENTIONAL PROJECTIONS OF THE WORLD

Peter Vujakovic and Russell King

For centuries, cartographers have grappled with the challenge of mapping the globe, but no world map is entirely accurate. The process of transferring information from the globe to a sheet of paper inevitably involves distortion, whether of distance, direction, area or shape. During recent years the debate concerning map projections has shifted from the geometrical to the ideological plane. World maps like the famous Mercator (Figure 1.1) are egocentric from a national viewpoint, and inevitably influence the personal geographies of their 'readers'. The German historian Arno Peters (1983: 24) argues that traditional projections have played a fundamental role in the preservation of the 'ideology of continued global exploitation of the Third World by the industrial nations'. This ideology perpetuates a *Eurocentric world concept* in order to survive (*see* Saarinen, 1988).

Peters (1983) focuses his attack on the Mercator projection. He argues that this projection supports a European sense of superiority by placing Europe centrally and by artificially enlarging the *apparent* area of high latitude land masses (compare Greenland and South America; in reality the latter is about eight times the area of the former). However, this limitation of Mercator has been recognised for many years (Robinson, 1990) and its use has now greatly declined. In most instances equal-area maps now replace the Mercator in atlases and other publications. Equal-area projections are the best alternatives, especially where real comparisons are being made.

However, Peters also criticises these conventional equal-area maps, claiming that they too maintain a Eurocentric bias – curved meridians focus the eye on Europe at top centre – and he stresses that they abandon the rectangular graticule and fidelity of angle.

In response, Peters developed his own projection (Figure 1.1), which maintains both fidelity of area and a rectangular graticule (although directions are only true along meridians and parallels). These features, together with a range of other supposed innovations, form the basis of his *New Cartography*, which he and his supporters regard as the foundation for an objective, egalitarian global concept. However, the map's validity as an equal area projection has been questioned, as has its originality. It is thus often regarded as a 'reinvention' of the Gall Orthographic of 1885, and its supposed universal applicability can also be questioned (King and Vujakovic, 1989; Maling, 1974; Robinson, 1990).

The Peters debate has caused a re-examination of the importance of other projections (Vujakovic, 1989). In reality, there is a wide range of equal-area projections which are much less distorting of continental shapes than the Peters, whilst the use of curved meridians may actually be an advantage in maintaining an image of the world as a sphere. Examples of equal-area projections which are acceptable to most cartographers include the Mollweide's Projection (long used in many world atlases), Winkel's 'Tripel' (used in Kidron and Segal's *The State of the World Atlas*), and the Eckert IV, chosen for this volume. Alternative projections have been created by adapting pre-existing forms. A very successful

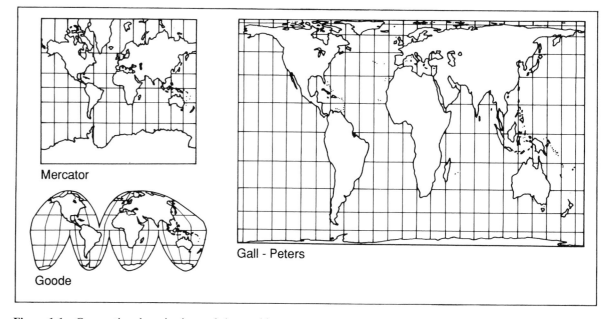

Figure 1.1 Conventional projections of the world

example is Goode's Homolosine (Figure 1.1): this uses one projection (the Sanson Sinusoidal) for the region between 40° north and south, then switches to another equal-area projection (the Mollweide) for the higher latitudes. By this means, and the use of interruption (the 'orange peel' effect), the continental shapes are extremely well preserved.

In reality, of course, no projection is perfect. Only through exposure to a large range of projections can we be released from the tyranny and misunderstanding caused by partial and prejudiced global concepts.

Further reading

King, R. (1990), *Visions of the World and Language of Maps*, Dublin: Department of Geography, Trinity College Dublin, Trinity Papers in Geography, 1.
Peters, A. (1983), *The New Cartography*, New York: Friendship Press.

1.2 ALTERNATIVE MAPS OF THE WORLD
Peter Vujakovic

Equal-area projections are generally regarded as providing a fair and objective base for thematic world maps. However, these maps give prominence to large continental land masses which may be relatively sparsely populated, such as Africa and the Americas, at the expense of densely populated regions, such as southern Asia, and island states like Indonesia and the Philippines. It can be argued that population distribution is a more important criterion by which to view development issues than land area (Figure 1.2). One of the main ways of expressing such 'alternative' views is by the construction of *cartograms*, hybrid map-diagrams in which countries or regions are drawn in proportion to some criterion other than land area. Total population is often used as the basis for such maps, although a large number of other social and economic criteria have been employed. Contrasts in international living conditions and economic relations can be very effectively displayed using cartograms (*see* Kidron and Segal, 1984). Cartograms and 'unfamiliar' representations of the world also have other advantages over conventional maps. Their very unfamiliarity can be used to generate interest and to challenge accepted viewpoints. On the other hand their novelty value means that they are more open to abuse for propaganda purposes.

Another criticism of conventional projections has focused on the centring of these maps on Europe (and Africa). Eurocentric (or Afrocentric) maps dominate the majority of atlases, even those produced by authors such as Arno Peters (1989) who are critical of Eurocentrist representations (see for instance *Peters' Atlas of the World*).

When other centres are used, they tend to be reserved for specific themes rather than being used to subvert established global concepts. One of the few Western thematic atlases to use a different centre (Sinocentric) throughout is the *Women in the World* (Seager and Olson, 1986) atlas; this iconoclastic work seeks to dispel myths concerning the roles of women worldwide and to raise questions about authority, '... who has power and who does not, who is on top and who is at the bottom' (Seager and Olson, 1986: 8). In such circumstances, the authority of traditional cartography must itself be questioned.

Map orientation is also important to perception of global issues; associations between North-South, rich-poor, top-bottom, developed-undeveloped, white-black, may be entrenched by the almost invariable orientation of world maps with north at the top (Figure 1.2). Murray (1987: 241) argues that this orientation '... and the symbolic connotations a "higher" placement has with "dignity" and "superiority" have had adverse effects on notions of the southern hemisphere'. Symbols such as the arbitrary Brandt 'North-South Divide' line, used in association with Eurocentric maps, such as Gall-Peters, help to perpetuate adverse notions of the 'place' of developing countries in the global context. A few attempts have been made to alter such conventional world views, as with the publication of a 'turn-about' map of the Americas in the 1980s (Murray, 1987).

Once it is accepted that fidelity of area is just one of many important factors in the choice of

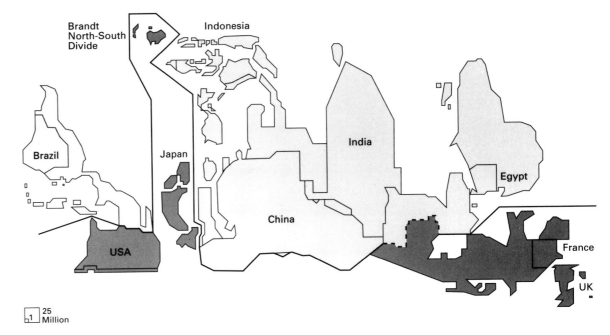

Figure 1.2 Sino-centric 'turnabout' cartogram of world population 1991

maps it may be possible to rehabilitate global projections which are not equal-area, but which offer other advantages (Vujakovic, 1989). One such is the Buckminster Fuller Dymaxion Projection, created by the segmentation of the globe into a mesh of squares and triangles (all with sides equal to 60° of arc or 3600 nautical miles). This allows the globe to be unwrapped in a way which retains a feeling for its spherical nature, and with no dominant orientation. The mesh is extremely adaptable and can be rearranged in numerous ways to emphasise different global relationships, or even folded to create a simplified 'globe'.

Further reading

Vujakovic, P. (1989), Mapping for world development, *Geography*, **74**(2): 97–105.

1.3 A RENAISSANCE VIEW OF THE WORLD
Jeffrey Stone

Rumold Mercator's double hemispherical map of the world, first published in 1587, was widely circulated over some five decades (Figure 1.3). The author was the son of Gerard Mercator, famous for his projection published in 1569. However, the new projection did not gain immediate acceptance as a practical aid to navigation and perhaps for this reason, or possibly because a hemispherical map was more intelligible to the public (Crone, 1978: 78), Rumold adopted a stereographic equatorial projection. Unlike Mercator's projection, Rumold's choice of projection retains correct representation of shape at any point. It also avoids the great inequality in the depiction of area which is inherent in Mercator's projection, whose alleged abuse for the political purposes of the countries of the North has recently made it the subject of controversy.

Europe's view of the world in the late 16th century was, in part, the product of recent journeys and voyages of exploration, but true to the Renaissance, the influence of classical models is apparent. The content of the map, as opposed to its projection, draws heavily on Gerard Mercator's world chart of 1569, which has been described as one of the most significant Renaissance scientific accomplishments (Nebenzahl, 1990: 126). The Mercators incorporated the concept of an extensive continent in the southern hemisphere counter-balancing the inhabited world. The descriptions of Marco Polo written in 1298 are usually assumed to be the main source of inland information on eastern Asia. More recent sources were used in the American continent, as seen in the name of Magellan who sailed into the south Pacific in 1502 and whose Strait was appearing on maps by 1515. However, Mercator continued the error of depicting Tierra del Fuego as a promontory of the southern continent and it was not until Drake's voyage of 1578 that the major error in the form of the quadrilateral shape of the southern part of the continent was corrected. There was a wide range of English, French, Spanish and Portuguese sources for northeast America, including Cartier's voyage of 1534 into the St Lawrence. However, it is in the depiction of Africa that the fusion of classical and contemporary sources is most apparent. The shape of the continent is relatively accurate, mainly as a consequence of Portuguese voyages of exploration, including the rounding of the Cape of Good Hope by Vasco da Gama in 1498, but inland the influence of Ptolemy is still evident in the sources of the Nile. Africa was a 'barrier continent' (Bridges, 1985: 17) on the trade route to India and the east, a Eurocentric view of Africa which is in keeping with the Renaissance attitude to the world beyond Europe.

The cartographic image of the world from Renaissance Europe is sometimes seen as the product of the conflicting interests of the European powers, so that, for example, the maritime discoveries of the Portuguese were so jealously guarded from rivals that they were not available to commercial cartographers. The conflict of interests and the secrecy which supposedly resulted has, perhaps, been exaggerated, as this map suggests in its variety of sources. Information did eventually disseminate and, once published, it was common knowledge. Even the Portuguese penetration of the Zambezi basin in the late 16th century was published in France in maps by 1678. Cartographers were more at a loss in obtaining access to non-European sources, for example the Chinese and Arab navigators who knew the east African coast. Rumold's map is the result of an informal process of pooling of knowledge, which was to form the basis of a collaborative European imperial relationship with Africa and elsewhere spanning five centuries (Hargreaves, 1984).

Further reading

Bridges, R.C. (1985), Africa, Africans and the Sea, in: Stone, J.C. (ed.), *Africa and the Sea*, Aberdeen: Aberdeen University African Studies Group, 14–26.

Crone, G.R. (1978), *Maps and their Makers* (5th edition), Folkestone: Dawson.

Hargreaves, J.D. (1984), The Berlin West Africa Conference. A timely centenary? *History Today*, **34** (Nov): 16–22.

Nebenzahl, K. (1990), *Maps from the Age of Discovery: Colombus to Mercator*, London: Times Books.

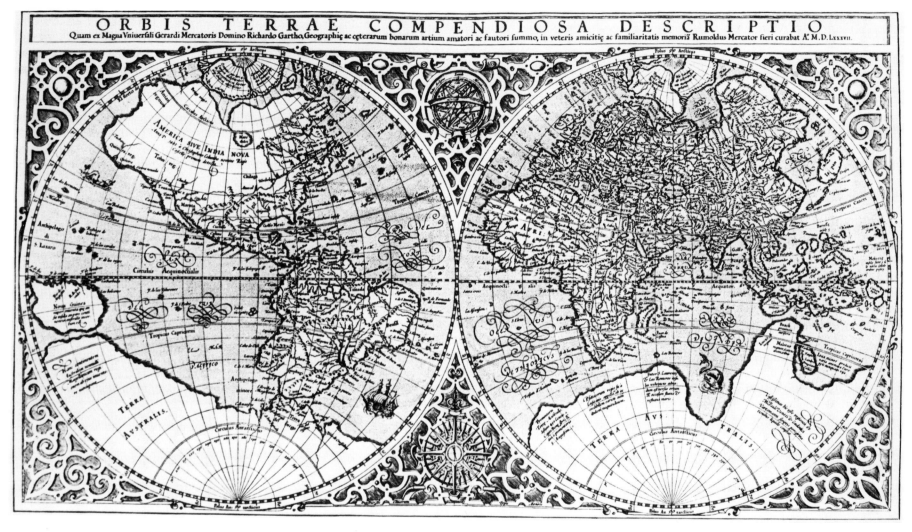

Figure 1.3   Rumold Mercator's 2-hemisphere map of the world, 1587

1.4 THE OTTOMAN EMPIRE
c. 1520
Malcolm Wagstaff

Within seventeen years of the first Portuguese commercial voyage to India (March–August, 1500) and the consequent opening up of the Indian Ocean trade to European shipping, the western terminals of the historic caravan routes which tied India and China to Europe across the Middle East were in the hands of an expansionist Muslim state already in control of the Balkans. This was the Ottoman Empire, the largest and most integrated state in the Muslim world. The Mughal conquests, which imposed a measure of unity on much of India, had yet to begin (1526). Accordingly, the Ottoman Empire's rivals in terms of size and power at the beginning of the 16th century were China, unified under the Ming (1366–1644), and the diversified state of the Holy Roman Emperor, Charles V (1519–56).

By contrast with a divided India and a fragmented Habsburg state, the Empire inherited in 1520 by the Ottoman Sultan Suleyman (called in the West, 'The Magnificent') was powerful, stable and united. It seemed poised to absorb the rest of central and eastern Europe, as well as the whole of the Middle East and north Africa. Ottomans and Habsburgs were soon in conflict by land and water, in the Red Sea as well as the Mediterranean.

Ottoman wealth was immense: in the mid-16th century the annual tribute of Egypt alone was 33% greater than the yield of the entire Spanish New World. Farming was market-oriented, with significant amounts of industrial crops, such as cotton and silk, produced in particular regions. Manufacturing industry was highly developed and widely distributed. The core of the Ottoman Empire lay in the triangle between the old imperial capitals of Bursa (population 34 930 c. 1520) and Edirne (population 22 335 c. 1520) and the new one (since 1453) of Istanbul (population >400 000 c. 1520). Here lay the ancient Ottoman lands which contained the imperial mosques, as well as the dynastic tombs. Istanbul itself was the *locus* of the court (>8000 people) and the full-time element of the army (>27 000 troops) with their immense absorptive capacity. Demand was met through the 'tributary-distributive system' of the classic Ottoman organisation, the state-controlled tentacles of which embraced the entire Empire. The wealth and population concentrated at the heart of the state made it the centre of a world economy well before such a core had emerged in northern Europe (Figure 1.4). The Ottoman world economy embraced the Black Sea region, extended into Persian domains, reached to the Caucasus and central Asia, stretched far along the Nile, and connected with the Indian Ocean trading system through the Gulf and the Red Sea. Cairo, the main entrepot in the 16th century, though described as dilapidated, still retained a population similar in size to that of Venice (about 150 000), whilst the desert ports of Aleppo (56 881) and Damascus (57 726) were at least as large as London (about 60 000) and bigger than Amsterdam (about 11 000).

If later conditions also prevailed in the 16th century, the Ottoman Empire was probably in deficit on its trade with the East. This was covered by a net outflow of specie, derived not only from Ottoman mines, but also as payments for cereals exported to the hungry cities of Italy and Spain and in exchange for the spices and luxury items forwarded to Europe. As late as 1600, western Europe still obtained 60% of its pepper and 52% of its other spices and drugs from the Ottoman-controlled Levant. European agents and factors were active in several Ottoman cities, but the only items of European origin which interested Ottoman subjects were woollen cloth and basic raw materials, such as base metals. Ottoman superiority in the balance of trade with western Europe allowed the Sultans to grant the first Capitulations to the ambitious infidels (the first were negotiated with France in 1536 but not ratified). These privileges, however, eventually helped to undermine the Ottoman world-economy in subsequent centuries.

Further reading

Cahen, C. (1970), Quelques notes sur le déclin commerciale du monde musulman à la fin du moyen age, in: Cook, M.A. (ed.), *Studies in the Economic History of the Middle East*, Oxford: Oxford University Press, 31–36.

Hess, A.C. (1970), The creation of the Ottoman seaborne empire in the age of oceanic discoveries, 1453–1525, *American Historical Review*, **75**: 892–919.

İnalcık, H. (1973), *The Ottoman Empire: the Classical Age 1300–1600*, London: Weidenfeld and Nicolson.

Islamoğlu, H. and Faroqhi, S. (1979), Crop-patterns and agricultural production trends in sixteenth-century Anatolia, *Review*, **2**: 401–436.

Mantran, R. (ed.) (1989), *Histoire de l'Empire Ottoman*, Paris: Fayard.

Steensgard, N. (1974), *The Asian Trade Revolution of the Seventeenth Century*, Chicago: Chicago University Press.

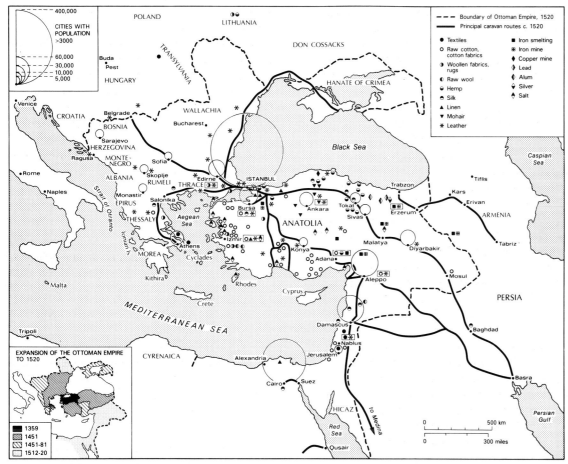

Figure 1.4   The Ottoman Empire, *c.* 1520

1.5 THE DEVELOPMENT OF A MODERN WORLD SYSTEM
Malcolm Wagstaff

Although contacts existed within and between different parts of the world during, and even before, the first millenium and a half of the Common Era, they were short-lived and discontinuous. Relations were characterised by episodic warfare and the sporadic movements of emissaries and missionaries, as well as the handing-on over long distances of high-value, low-bulk goods such as amber, lapiz-lazuli, gold, silk, spices, furs and slaves. Virtually no contacts existed between the Americas and the 'Old World' after 20 000 BP. Australia and Oceania, including New Zealand, were worlds apart until the 17th and 18th centuries.

The so-called 'Geographical Discoveries' of European seamen in the 15th to 18th centuries destroyed the relative separation of these economies. They led to their replacement by an ever widening and increasingly integrated world economy created by demand generated in western Europe. Mediated through such port-cities as Amsterdam, Cadiz, Lisbon and London, the demand was met by joint-stock companies, characterised by large amounts of investment capital and organisational continuity. Examples include the Hudson's Bay Company in England and the Verenigde Oostindische Compagnie (VOC) in the Netherlands. Building on bulk trades in salt, fish, wine and grain developed during the later Middle Ages along the Atlantic coast of Europe and around the North Sea and the Baltic, the basic foundations of the integrated world economy were created during the 16th and 17th centuries. They were well established by the end of the 18th century. The development of steam ships and the building of railways in the 19th century extended the system still further, provided better integration and increased the amount of activity within the system.

The vital elements in the world economy around 1780 were the great sea routes. These are represented on Bartholomew's Nordic Projection (Figure 1.5), which stresses both the centrality of England and the Netherlands in the system and also the importance of the northern hemisphere. Whilst planetary winds drove the system, silver powered it. Mined on a large scale in Mexico and the Andes, silver was moved to the Caribbean for shipment to Cadiz (until 1778). From Spain it flowed out to purchase the goods demanded by Europe. These included the sugar, coffee, rice and cotton introduced to the New World from western Asia and produced on slave-worked plantations around the Caribbean, on the coast of Brazil and along the rivers of the southern states in an emergent USA. The indigenous crops, tobacco and cacao, were also brought into extensive systems of production to meet the demand created in Europe. Slaves, brought from Africa to replace exterminated populations, were fed and clothed by small farmers and artisans in the largely self-sufficient colonies of North America and along the River Plate. Supplies were constantly replenished for guns, cheap cloth, spirits and chandlery in West Africa, where slave-raiding became rife.

India and the Far East supplied Europe with spices, drugs and luxury textiles. Tea and porcelain from China became fashionable. Production began to be organised, in part, to supply the European market and to suit European taste. Large consignments of goods were moved in the bulk-carrying East Indiamen (500–800 tons). They were paid for in silver since European manufactured goods held little attraction in the East at the time. Woollen cloths and metal wares were often hard to sell, sometimes remaining for years in the warehouses of the European coastal and island 'factories'.

From the entrepots in Europe, colonial and East India goods were dispersed either to the ports' hinterlands or to overseas markets. These included the remoter parts of northern Europe, which supplied naval stores, iron and grain to the dynamic core. They also extended to the eastern Mediterranean. In the 18th century the Ottoman Empire was an important source of industrial raw materials (cotton, silk, valonia and olive oil) and foodstuffs (wheat, dried fruits), though Europe ran a deficit on this trade which was covered by the export of specie.

European manufactures, which found markets in the Ottoman Empire as well as the New World, were increasingly mass-produced by a growing workforce whose diet came to include potatoes (introduced from South America) and whose capacity to consume gradually expanded. Much of the improvement in European standards of living, however, came to depend upon colonies in the Americas and Africa and the expansion of European political control in India and the East Indies.

Further reading

Chaudhuri, K.N. (1985), *Trade and Civilisation in the Indian Ocean*, Cambridge: Cambridge University Press.

Davis, R. (1979), *The Industrial Revolution and British Overseas Trade*, Leicester: Leicester University Press.

Dermigny, L. (1964), Le Commerce à Canton au XVIIIe Siècle, 1719–1833, Paris: SEVPEN.

Nitz, H.-J. (ed.) (1993), *The Early Modern World-System in Geographical Perspective*, Stuttgart: Franz Steiner Verlag.

Stavrianos, L.S. (1981), *Global Rift: the Third World Comes of Age*, New York: William Morrow.

Wallerstein, I. (1974, 1980, 1989), *The Modern World System*, New York and London: Academic Press, 3 volumes.

ELEMENTS OF THE WORLD ECONOMY c.1780

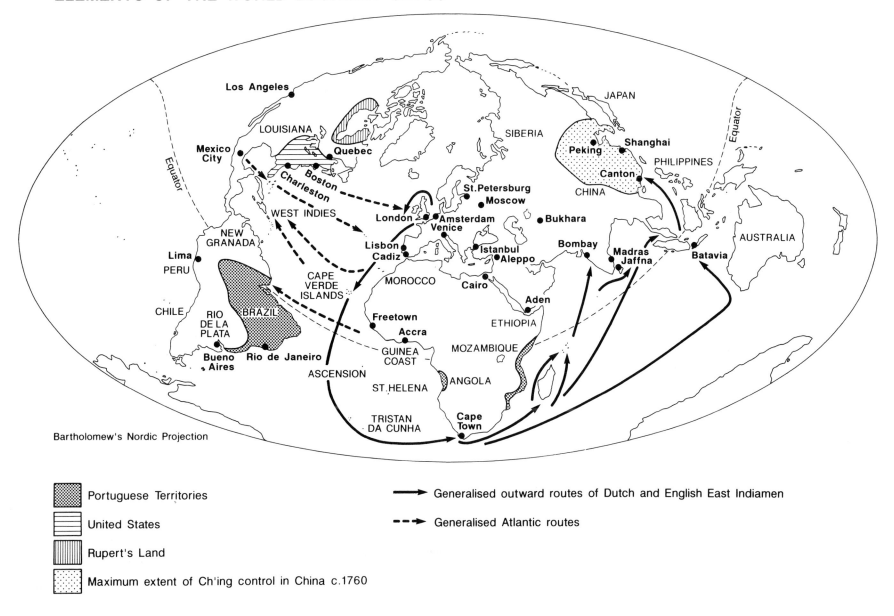

Bartholomew's Nordic Projection

Portuguese Territories

United States

Rupert's Land

Maximum extent of Ch'ing control in China c.1760

Generalised outward routes of Dutch and English East Indiamen

Generalised Atlantic routes

Figure 1.5 Elements of the world economy, *c.* 1780

1.6 THE 'OLD' IMPERIALISM
Peter J. Taylor

Imperialism has been an integral component of our modern world. Beginning with the initial probes of the Portuguese and Spanish in the late 15th century, European states were able to dominate the peoples of other continents bringing them all into a single world-economy by about 1900. This imperialism has taken many forms but the most direct has been the political control of extra-European lands by European states. This involves the despatching of a 'governor' (exact title varies) as the political authority in an overseas territory (Henige, 1970). Using the appointment of a governor by the metropolitan power to define the existence of a colony (Taylor, 1993b), the number of colonies can be traced over time (Figure1.6a). Of these two very distinct cycles of political imperialism we will consider the first cycle – the 'old' imperialism – here, leaving the second cycle to Section 1.7.

In the 16th century there were just two European imperial powers, the original Iberian exploration centres of Portugal and Spain. With a division of the extra-European world brokered by the Papacy, these two states developed their colonies without outside pressures. All this changed in the 17th century with the entry into the field of three new predatory imperial powers, the Netherlands, France and England. Colonies and colonial development now became part of the intense European state competition, political and economic, that is the age of mercantilism. Originally attracted by the possibility of intercepting Spanish bullion en route to Europe, the newcomers captured some Portuguese islands in the Caribbean but also set up completely new island colonies making this region the focus of extra-European

mercantilist competition. In addition new colonies were set up to the north in what is today the USA and to the south the Dutch battled the Portuguese for control of what is today the north-east coast of Brazil. This zone from north-east Brazil to Maryland became a crucial production zone in the growing world economy, providing new commodities, sugar and also tobacco, grown in plantations for the European market. The dearth of local labour for this highly intensive production stimulated the Atlantic slave trade which transported Africans to all parts of the 'Greater Caribbean' (Figure 1.6b). This infamous triangular trade – guns from Europe to west Africa, people from west Africa to the Greater Caribbean, sugar from the Greater Caribbean to Europe – necessitated some minor European colonies in Africa to oversee that corner of the trade.

Coinciding with development of this Atlantic economy, European states also developed an eastern trade with the East Indies (Figure 1.6b). Unlike in the Caribbean, the Europeans did not develop new production but concentrated on transferring luxury items such as exotic spices to the European market. Hence their colonies here were insubstantial, since their function, as in

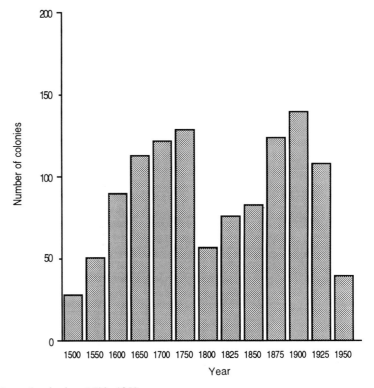

Figure 1.6a Number of colonies, 1500–1950

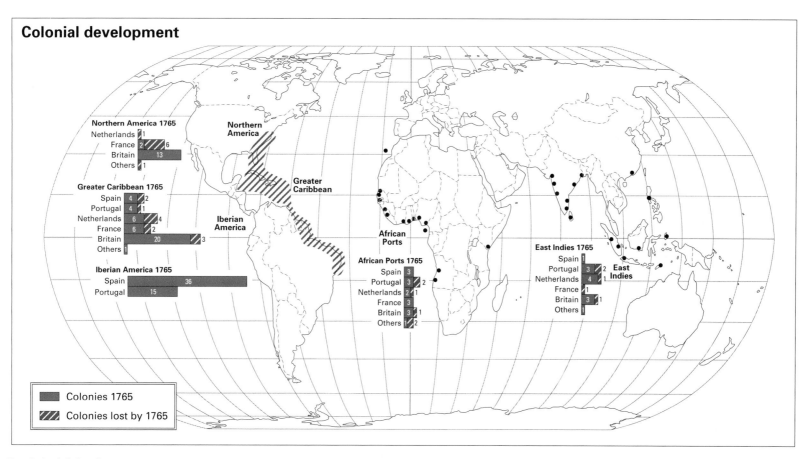

Figure 1.6b Colonial development

Africa, was only to oversee and defend trade not organise production.

The international competition of mercantilism was resolved by the Seven Years War between France and Britain (1756–63), which ended French ambitions in north America and India. With the post-war rearrangement of territories the pattern of colonies in 1765 left Britain as indisputably the leading European world power, as indicated in Figure 1.6b. If Britain was the final 'winner' of the 'old' imperialism, the map also shows the relative importance of the Greater Caribbean as the key extra-European focus of the early world-economy.

Further reading

Bergesen, A. and Schoenberg, R. (1980), Long waves of colonial expansion and contraction, 1415–1969, in: Bergesen, A. (ed.), *Studies of the Modern World-System*, London: Macmillan, 231–77.

Richardson, B.H. (1992), *The Caribbean and the Wider World, 1492–1992*, New York: Cambridge University Press.

1.7 THE 'AGE' OF IMPERIALISM
Peter J. Taylor

With the successful revolt of thirteen north American colonies against the British Empire and the subsequent disintegration of the Spanish and Portuguese American empires (*see* Section 1.9), political imperialism became much less important in the world economy by the middle decades of the 19th century. The Caribbean 'sugar' islands remained colonies but were no longer the focus of European attention. Political imperialism continued in a small way but with none of the competition that characterised the mercantilist period. In this respect the imperialism was similar to the non-competitive expansion of the imperial powers in the 16th century; Britain expanded its political influence in India and France did likewise in Indo-China, both with no outside interference. Given this relative lull in political imperialism it is not surprising that when new competition between European powers spilt over into non-European areas in the final decades of the 19th century, it was seen as essentially a new phenomenon. Historians have subsequently dubbed the period from 1870 to 1914 'the age of imperialism' although by taking a longer perspective (*see* Section 1.6) we can see that this was really the second of two cycles of imperialism (Taylor, 1993b).

This 'new imperialism' was the product of a changing balance of power in Europe that led to a challenging of Britain's global supremacy. Both in 1870 and 1914 Britain was the leading imperial power but between these two dates other imperial powers joined the search for colonies and the whole world was finally divided up between European states, with Japan and the USA joining in as late and minor imperialists. The major exception to direct political imperial control was China but even here the sovereignty of the state was severely curtailed by the 'unequal treaties' it was forced to sign by the Europeans and its territory was divided into spheres of influence instead of colonies, which remained coastal enclaves. 1914 represents the acme of European political dominance of the world which was hurt by World War I, shattered by World War II, and its final vestiges disposed of by post-war decolonisation (*see* Section 1.9).

The political world map of 1914 depicts a European world organised economically as a global functional region centred on northern Europe. As can be seen in Figure 1.7 the new imperialism was largely focused on Africa and Asia with three major imperialist powers, the old-stagers Britain and France joined by the newcomer Germany. The latter was the trigger for the new competition and its colonies define the new imperial arena. Basically Germany in 'finding its place in the sun' carved out for herself a colony in each zone of competition: Togo in west Africa, Kamerun in central Africa, Southwest Africa in south Africa, Tanganyika in east Africa, New Guinea in the East Indies, Samoa in the Pacific and the Chinese port of Kiaochow. In contrast to this scattering, France's imperial strategy was to concentrate resources on where she was already strong, producing, for instance, the large contiguous swath of African territory from the equator to the Mediterranean under the French flag. Britain's strategy was somewhere between these two spatial extremes. In Africa, Britain pursued a policy of trying to consolidate contiguous territories – Cecil Rhodes' dream of British colonies from 'Cairo to the Cape' – but globally it acquired colonies throughout the world. These included islands in all oceans and major seas to facilitate the operations of the Royal Navy. The three colonies of Gibraltar, Malta and Cyprus guarding the Mediterranean-Suez route to India epitomise this aspect of imperial policy.

All other imperialist powers can be fairly designated minor and each one had their colonies largely restricted to one region. The old imperialist powers of Spain, Portugal and the Netherlands entered the new imperialism like Britain and France with some longstanding colonies. In 1898 Spain lost the Philippines and Puerto Rico to the USA, and Cuba became independent so that this imperial power is almost missing from the map of 1914. Portugal had consolidated its old African colonies into something somewhat larger in the 'scramble for Africa' (*see* Section 1.8) and the Netherlands did the same in the East Indies. Of the new imperial powers the most significant was Italy with its attempts to emulate France with a consolidated north African empire (foiled in part by Ethiopia in 1896). Belgium, in the guise of King Leopold, obtained a single large colony to dominate central Africa and Japan had begun its expansion in east Asia, notably in Korea and Formosa (Taiwan).

Imperialism was not only a matter of European politics, of course. Non-European peoples did not just meekly wait for their incorporation into this European world. They resisted. European powers were fighting wars of oppression throughout the so-called 'long peace', the name historians give to the 19th century. Although sometimes denigrated as minor skirmishes – 'Queen Victoria's little wars', for instance – in reality many were major wars of resistance. The two most well-known are the Indian Mutiny (Sepoy) and the Zulu War but these are ranked only tenth in terms of severity (Table 1.7).

The estimated deaths in Table 1.7 are *for the imperial armies only* (Small and Singer, 1982) since we have no way of knowing how many died resisting the European expansions. Despite the

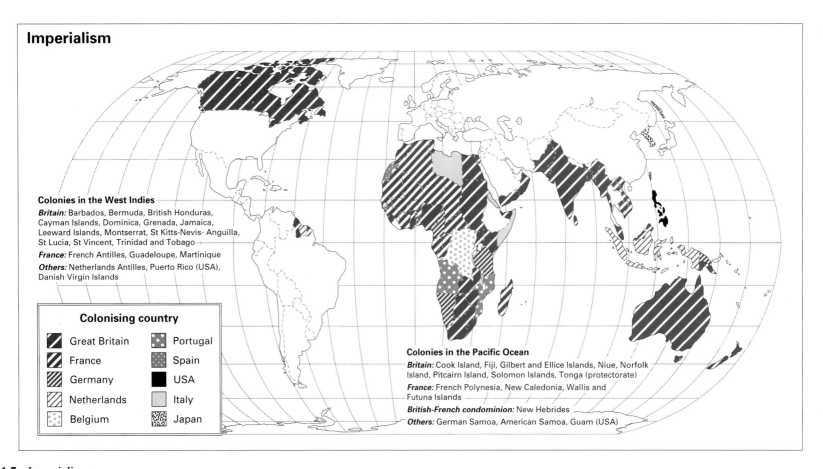

Figure 1.7 Imperialism

Table 1.7 Resistance to imperialism in the 19th century

War	Years	Number of war deaths
1 First British-Afghan	1838–42	20 000
British-Mahdist (Sudan)	1882–87	20 000
3 First British-Burmese	1823–26	15 000
Dutch-Javanese	1925–30	15 000
French-Algerian	1839–47	15 000
6 Italian–Ethiopian	1895–96	9000
7 Dutch-Achinese	1873–79	6000
8 French-Indochinese	1882–84	4500
9 Second British-Afghan	1878–80	4000
10 British-Indian (Sepoy)	1857–59	3500
British Zulu	1878–79	3500

Source: derived from Small and Singer (1982)

technological superiority of the Europeans, imperialism was never easy.

Further reading

Foeken, D. (1982), Explanation for the partition of sub-Saharan Africa, 1881–1900, *Tijdschrift voor Economische en Sociale Geografie*, **73**: 138–148.

Hobsbawm, E.J. (1987), *The Age of Empire, 1875–1914*, London: Guild.

Wallerstein, I. (1980), Imperialism and development, in: Bergesen, A. (ed.), *Studies of the Modern World-System*, London: Macmillan, 128–145.

1.8 IMPERIALISM: THE STRUGGLE FOR AFRICA
David Simon

Africa was the last inhabited continent to fall under European imperial control and also the last to decolonise during the death throes of empire in the 1950s and 1960s. Despite its relatively short duration of between 80 years and a century in most cases, formal European hegemony proved both intense and extremely traumatic for Africa and its people. The roots of the continent's current crisis of maldevelopment, poverty and misgovernment lie firmly in that experience and the rather longer period of European exploitation which pre-dated it.

This is not to suggest that all Africa's problems can be blamed on colonialism, or to imply that the continent was a peaceful paradise prior to the arrival of predatory Europeans. Long-distance migrations and associated demographic changes,

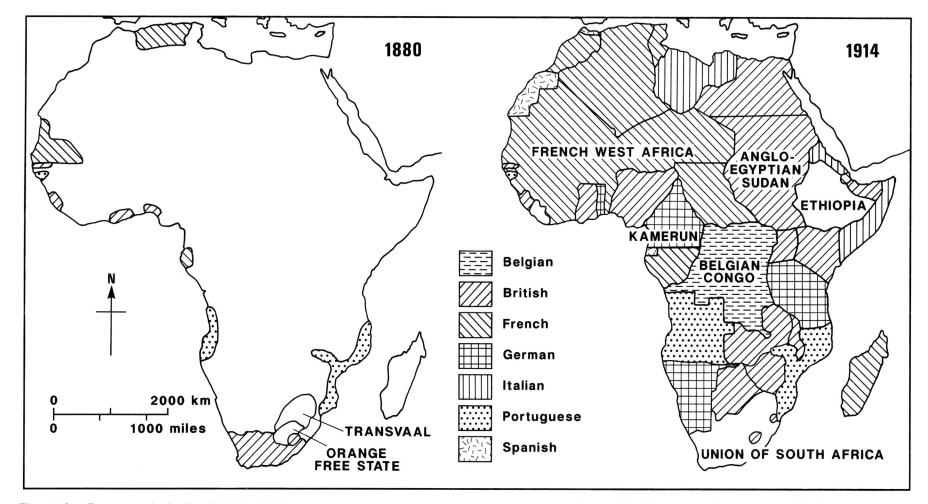

Figure 1.8a European colonisation of Africa, 1880

Figure 1.8b The extent of European colonisation in Africa, 1914

political struggles, and conflicts over territory and resources have no shorter or less brutal a history than elsewhere. One of the most violent and profound pre-European transformations was wrought by the spread of Islam from the Arabian Peninsula across much of north Africa and the Sahel by the early 12th century, and the ensuing trans-Saharan slave trade. In addition, Arab traders plying the east African coast over many centuries had established flourishing ports and settlements and developed a sophisticated slave trade network from the eastern-central interior to supply Arabia.

Sustained European interest in Africa dates from the so-called voyages of discovery in search of the East Indies by the Portuguese in the 15th and early 16th centuries. Gradually refreshment stations and trading posts were established at various points along the often rugged coast, especially in west Africa and what are today Angola and Mozambique. Gold, ivory and 'free' labour proved the most attractive commodities. The Gulf of Guinea soon became the focus of the Atlantic slave trade, initiated and for long controlled by the Portuguese in order to supply the settler economy in Brazil. The trade precipitated innumerable conflicts and untold suffering among the peoples of the interior and a haemorrhage of some 11.7 million surviving Africans to the 'New World' by 1900 (Coquery-Vidrovitch, 1988: 19–29). In other words, the process of profound disruption and transformation whereby Africa was incorporated into the emerging world system had been under way since the mid-15th century.

The Dutch refreshment station founded at the Cape of Good Hope in 1652 provided the genesis of the first permanent European settlement colony on the continent. The area and intensity of European conquest expanded steadily following the displacement of the Dutch by Britain in 1806. The French first settled along the Algerian coast during the 1830s and established a West African base at Dakar in 1857.

The process of annexation and colonisation accelerated after about 1880 (Figure 1.8a) as industrialisation in Europe created sustained demand for increasing supplies of both new and existing raw materials and required the penetration of new markets for its products. The entrenchment of industrial capitalism consequently promoted a new imperialism as rivalry between Britain, France, Germany, Portugal, Belgium, Spain and Italy was extended into the pursuit of new subject territories and the associated

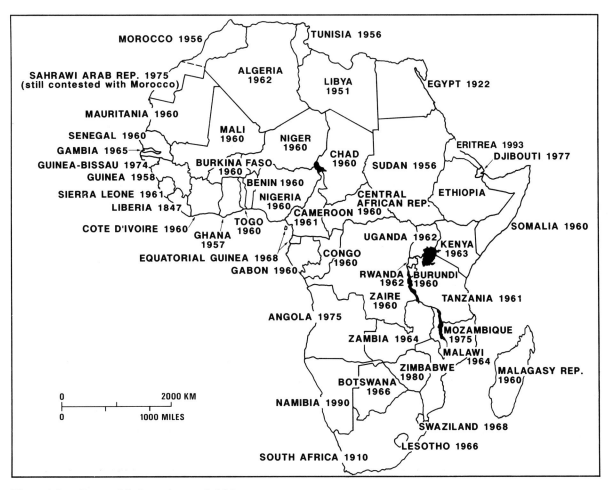

Figure 1.8c Dates of independence of African states

aggrandisement. Where conditions proved suitable, as in Algeria, Morocco, Senegal, South Africa, German South West Africa, Rhodesia and Kenya, the establishment of settlement colonies to absorb displaced 'surplus' European populations proved an efficient way of satisfying all these objectives simultaneously. Against the background of increasing competition and the consequent risk of conflict, the Berlin Conference of 1884/5 sought to systematise the respective powers' territorial claims. Since these had to be backed up by effective occupation, the ensuing two decades witnessed unparalleled expansion of European control by conquest, deception and dubious treaties, the content and implications of which were beyond the imagination of most indigenous leaders. By the outbreak of World War I in 1914, virtually the whole of Africa had become a European 'possession'. The principal exceptions were Ethiopia, an indigenous empire which, apart from Eritrea, successfully resisted permanent colonisation; Liberia, an independent state since its creation by freed slaves with American assistance in 1847; and South Africa, which gained independence from Britain under minority white rule in 1910 (Figure 1.8b). Egypt gained independence in 1922, while former German colonies were parcelled out to the victors, or as League of Nations Mandates, in the wake of World War I.

Throughout the continent, today's political boundaries were demarcated in line with imperial needs and convenience and usually in ignorance of local conditions, indigenous affiliations and political boundaries, transhumance or migration routes, or economic interactions. Herein lies one cause of many post-colonial problems. Local resources were extracted, and the indigenous population subordinated and their land and labour commoditised, primarily for European profit rather than local development. Forms of rule differed markedly, but everywhere the tide of nationalism spawned by the Second World War precipitated independence struggles. Most of Africa's contemporary states emerged during the 1950s and 1960s, although the Portuguese empire collapsed only in 1975, Zimbabwe gained independence only in 1980 and Namibia ten years later (Figure 1.8c).

Further reading

Coquery-Vidrovitch, C. (1988), *Africa: Endurance and Change South of the Sahara*, Berkeley: University of California Press.

Hallett, R. (1970), *Africa to 1875*, Ann Arbor: University of Michigan Press.

Hallett, R. (1974), *Africa since 1875*, Ann Arbor: University of Michigan Press.

Oliver, R. (ed.) (1977), *The Cambridge History of Africa*, Cambridge: Cambridge University Press.

Rodney, W. (1972), *How Europe Underdeveloped Africa*, Dar es Salaam: Tanzania Publishing House.

1.9 DECOLONISATION
Peter J. Taylor

The two cycles of imperialism (*see* Section 1.6) both concluded with an initial phase of limited decolonisation which then led to a rapid collapse of empires in a seemingly irresistible movement for political independence (Taylor, 1993b).

The first successful challenge to the 'old' imperialism came from Britain's North American colonies, declaring their independence in 1776 and finally forming the USA in 1789. Britain was successful in containing the revolution and kept its colonies to the north (Canada) and south (Caribbean islands). In the aftermath of the Napoleonic War upheavals in Europe, which exposed the weaknesses of both Spain and Portugal, independence movements prospered throughout central and South America. Imitating the politics of their northern neighbours in the USA, the European settlers from Mexico to Chile rebelled and expelled their imperial masters. The result was the total elimination of the Spanish and Portuguese empires in mainland America by 1825, bringing to an end the first cycle of imperialism.

In the 115 years to World War II decolonisation was not a major world political force. Apart from Cuba's belated independence from Spain (as a result of the Spanish-USA war of 1898), decolonisation occurred in just two small and distinct groups of British colonies. First, colonies dominated by white settlers (Canada, Australia, New Zealand and South Africa) were given internal autonomy and finally full sovereignty in 1931. Second, two Arab states, Egypt and Iraq, were deemed ready to run their own affairs. Iraq is interesting because it was a mandate given to Britain by the League of Nations after World War I. The disposal of imperial spoils after World War I revealed a crack in imperial practice and politics. Both German colonies and the Arab provinces of the Ottoman Empire were reallocated to the victorious imperial powers as mandates envisaging future self-government rather than simply as new colonies. In effect decolonisation was back on the political agenda and the Indian independence movement grew rapidly in the period up to World War II.

World War II spelt the death-knell for European political imperialism. Self-determination became a war aim as in World War I, but this time it was clearly meant to include non-European peoples. In the aftermath of the war, as well as the end of Britain's Indian empire, the Philippines achieved independence from the USA, Indo-China from France, and Indonesia from the Netherlands, along with the remaining Arab mandate territories (Syria, Jordan and Palestine/Israel). This set up a decolonisation movement that proved to be unstoppable. The independence of Ghana in 1957 as the first black African state was a key event precipitating an avalanche of imitators – 17 African colonies achieved independence in 1960 alone. In 1962 Jamaica and Trinidad became the first two Caribbean islands to become independent in the 20th century. In the 1970s and 1980s, remaining African colonies and island colonies joined the world community of states, the final success being Namibia in 1990. The result was that in the post-World War II period over a hundred new states were created before the demise of the USSR and eastern European communist states began another round of state-making.

Independence was gained in many different ways. Sometimes it was the result of negotiations between colony and imperial power, as for instance with Ghana, but very often decolonisation only came after military pressure. Britain fought independence movements in Malaya, Cyprus, Aden (Yemen) and Kenya, but the country resisting decolonisation most was France. In Indo-China (Vietnam, Laos and Kampuchea) between 1945 and 1954 France lost 95 000 troops before moving on to Algeria where another 18 000 troops were lost (Small and Singer, 1982). Both imperial campaigns failed, as did similar large-scale Portuguese campaigns in Africa (Angola, Mozambique and Guinea-Bissau) in the early 1970s. Imperial chickens were finally coming home to roost: these military failures led to the overthrow of the existing imperial states themselves (France in 1957, Portugal in 1974) symbolically bringing to an end the era when European states could dominate the world.

Further reading

Bergesen, A. and Schoenberg, R. (1980), Long waves of colonial expansion and contraction, 1415–1969, in: Bergesen, A. (ed.), *Studies of the Modern World-System*, London: Macmillan, 231–277.

Chamberlain, M.E. (1985), *Decolonization*, Oxford: Blackwell.

Grimal, H. (1978), *Decolonization: the British, French, Dutch and Belgian Empires 1919–1963*, London: Routledge and Kegan Paul.

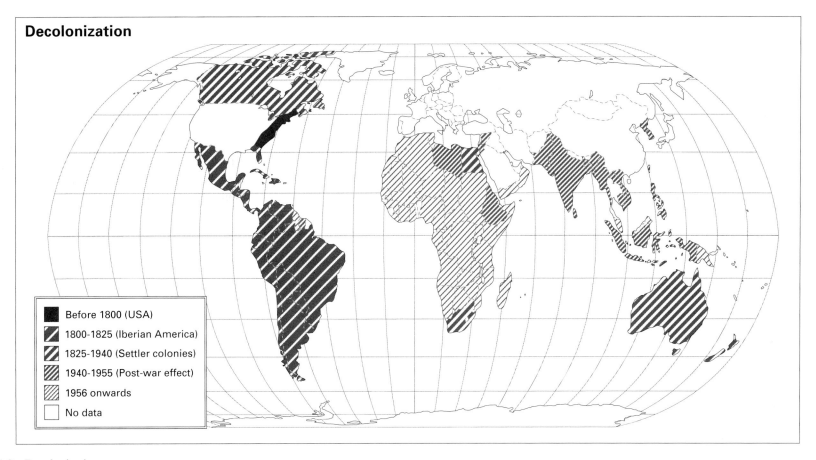

Figure 1.9   Decolonisation

1.10 ONE WORLD OR MANY WORLDS
David Drakakis-Smith

The Czech educator Comenius (Merriam, 1988: 18) once stated 'we are all citizens of one world . . . let us have but one end in view, the welfare of humanity'. These sentiments have often been repeated by politicians over the years but such universalist rhetoric has worn thin. We may all be in the same boat but few are on the upper deck and fewer still are steering. Despite the wave of independence that came to many former colonies from the 1940s onwards, the development gap has widened in the second half of the 20th century. As these disparities became too obvious to ignore, both theorists and popular commentators alike have sought to conceptualise the divisions within the world.

Over the last few decades the most common phrase used to describe the developing countries has been the Third World. The term came into popular use in the 1950s largely in a political context, being used to describe an alternative third way, or third force, to the communist-capitalist dichotomy of the cold war era. The term is essentially Eurocentric, with the First World referring to the advanced capitalist nations, the Second World to Eastern Europe and what was the USSR, and the Third World to the remainder (Figure 1.10).

The sociologist Peter Worsley (1964, 1979) played an important role in popularising the term in his book *The Third World*. Although he emphasised the political common denominators of the Third World (its colonial past and attempts to avoid a neo-colonial future), Worsley also expanded the meaning of the term to encompass the poverty with which it is usually associated today. By the 1970s the term had been adopted by a wide range of external observers and also by representatives of its constituent countries in international fora. However, there were also many critics.

Some felt that the term Third World was derogatory, implying 'third place'. Others pointed out that it was conceptually weak since the socialist developing countries were often excluded, falling as they did across the Second and Third Worlds. By the mid-1970s, however, it was also clear that economic gaps were beginning to widen within the Third World itself. The oil-rich OPEC states were the first to begin to undermine assumptions on economic commonality followed by the select band of Newly Industrialising Countries (NICs).

This growing diversity led to attempts to divide the Third World into subdivisions largely on economic well-being. The academic debate intensified in the pages of journals such as *Area* (Auty, 1979) and *Third World Quarterly* (Mountjoy, 1980) in the late 1970s and even reached the popular press. *Newsweek*, for example, identified Four Worlds and *Time* Five Worlds in which the Third comprised the resource-rich developing countries, the Fourth contained the NICs, whilst the Fifth constituted the 'basket cases'. Not to be outdone, one academic produced nine divisions including, at the lower end of the scale, the better-off poor, the middling poor, the poor and the poorest. Such refinements of poverty were of little comfort to those under such detailed scrutiny.

The reaction of the 1980s to this scholastic dancing on pin-heads was two-fold. First, there was a reaction away from economic data, particularly GNP, as indicators of development. Development became identified with more than economic growth and a whole range of social and political variables became absorbed into the measurement and classification process. These are discussed more extensively in Section 1.13.

The second reaction was a return to a simpler conceptualisation, into two groups of nations – the developed and the developing. This dualistic interpretation was given a considerable boost by the report of the Brandt Commission in 1981 which divided the world into a wealthy North and a poor, underdeveloped South. The associated line of division has become a very common addition to most world maps (Figure 1.10). This dividing line is, however, geographically unsound including, as it does, many states from the Northern Hemisphere in 'the South', whilst classifying Australasia as part of 'the North'. The contorted line of division also conveniently ignores many small Pacific Island states, generously but incorrectly ascribing them developed status.

It must be admitted that the Third World is not an homogeneous collection of states, but then some regions are best defined or distinguished by their diversity. The term Third World is not merely a semantic or geographical device but it is a conceptual reference to a persistent process of exploitation. Its unity lies in processes rather than patterns – the process of colonial and neo-colonial exploitation of its physical and human resources that has given rise to continuous and grinding poverty. It is a western arrogance to think that the world and its differences are shrinking because of new informational technologies. It may now be possible to transfer investment funds almost instantaneously in this post-modern world but only between certain points on the globe. Within many parts of the world the bicycle is still the fastest and most reliable form of transport. There is little point in enthusing about the fax machine to an Ethiopian or Bangladeshi peasant!

In this context, the concept of the Third World is 'an extremely useful figment of the human

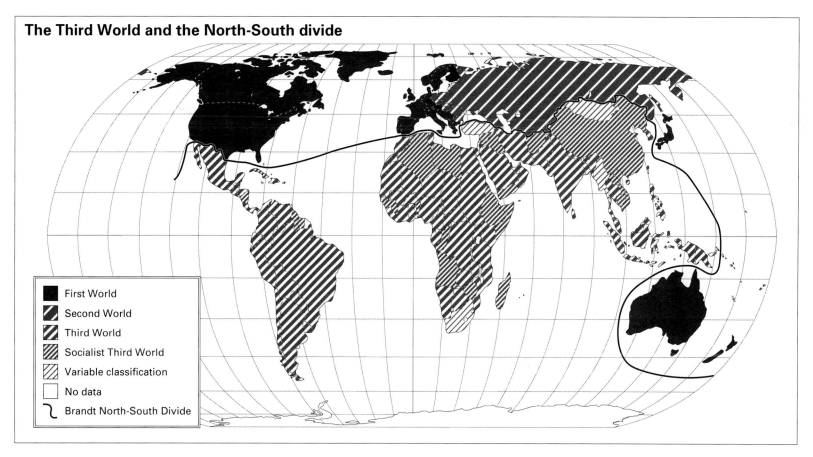

Figure 1.10   The Third World and the North-South divide

imagination ... The Third World exists whatever
we choose to call it. The more difficult question is
how can we understand it' (Norwine and
Gonzalez, 1988: 2–3) and change it.

Further reading

Auty, R. (1979), Worlds within worlds, *Area*, **11**:
    232–235.
Drakakis-Smith, D. (1993), Is there still a Third
    World?, *Choros*, **1**: 1–21.
Mountjoy, A. (1980), Worlds without end, *Third World
    Quarterly*, **2**(4): 753–757.
Sachs, G. (1992), One world, in: Sachs, G. (ed.), *The
    Development Dictionary*, London: Zed Books,
    102–115.

1.11 NATIONAL INCOME AND THE MEASUREMENT OF DEVELOPMENT
Chris Dixon

Per capita Gross National Product (GNP) and Gross Domestic Product (GDP) are the most widely used measurements of development, largely because of their ready availability and appearance of precision (Figure 1.11a). However, the shortcomings of these statistics are all too often glossed over. There are significant differences in national accounting and demographic reporting systems as well as in statistical coverage and reliability. In addition, the conversion of measures of national income into a standard currency unit, usually US dollars, is heavily influenced by the exchange rate used (World Bank, 1992b: 286–289). Particular problems are associated with the very poorest countries and the so-called 'socialist' group. The GNP figures for the latter are often estimates based on a variety of other measures (Forbes and Thrift, 1987; Drakakis-Smith *et al.*, 1987).

The World Bank ranks countries by per capita GNP, and has prepared a number of subdivisions. In 1992 a fourfold division was used:

Income Group	Per Capita Income
Low	less than US$ 610
Lower middle	between US$ 611 and US$ 2490
Upper middle	between US$ 2491 and US$ 7619
High	more than US$ 7620

This contrasted with the five-fold classification used between 1981 and 1988 which separated the more wealthy countries into 'High income oil exporters' and 'Industrial market economies'.

There is some overlap between the per capita GNP of the wealthier Third World countries and the poorer developed economies. In 1992 Hong Kong (US$11 100) and Singapore (US$11 490) were classed as less-developed, while Spain (US$11 020), Ireland (US$9550) and New Zealand (US$12 680) were considered developed. Similarly, the United Arab Emirates was classed as less-developed despite a per capita GNP of US$19 866, little short of that of the USA (US$21 790).

The World Bank has repeatedly refined the basis on which national income has been calculated, most notably in 1989. In addition, the United Nations International Comparison Programme (ICP) has produced an alternative set of per capita GDP figures. These are regarded as provisional, and the methodology is still being refined. However, they do in many cases depart radically from the World Bank calculations, particularly for the lower income countries.

Both the World Bank and ICP procedures reflect attempts to overcome the deficiencies and inconsistencies of national level statistical reporting. However, it cannot be stressed too strongly that considerable caution should be exercised in making comparisons between countries and over time. These difficulties lend weight to the argument that national income is an inadequate measure of the level of development. There has been increasing interest in the production of alternative indicators, most notably the Index of Human Progress produced by the United Nations Development Programme (UNDP).

Despite the deficiencies of national income measures there is little doubt that disparities between countries have increased. Only a very small number of Third World countries have managed to narrow the gap between their per capita GDP or GNP and those of the OECD group. These gains are more than offset by the relative deterioration of large numbers of low income countries, particularly those in Sub-Saharan Africa.

At the sub-national level, income data is even more deficient. However, all the evidence points to widening spatial, including rural-urban, disparities, and, even where the incidence of poverty appears to have declined, in most cases the ownership of wealth has become increasingly polarised. This is particularly apparent in Thailand, where high rates of economic growth (GDP grew at an annual average of 10.1% between 1985 and 1989) have been accompanied by an increasing concentration of development in the Bangkok Metropolitan Region (Figure 1.11b). The data on poverty and income distribution reveal a more complex pattern. Recession and government austerity measures during the early 1980s resulted in an increasing incidence of poverty, particularly in rural areas, and a marked rise in income disparities (Table 1.11). Rapid economic growth since 1986 has been accompanied by a sharp decrease in poverty but only a marginal decrease in the polarity of income distribution (Table 1.11).

Further reading

Drakakis-Smith, D., Doherty, J. and Thrift, N. (1987), Socialist development in the Third World, *Geography*, **72**: 333–362.

Gilbert, A. and Goodman, D.E. (1976), Regional income disparities in development, in: Gilbert, A. (ed.), *Development Planning and Spatial Structure*, New York: Wiley, 113–142.

Sundrum, R.M. (1990), *Income Distribution in Less-developed Countries*, London: Routledge.

United Nations Development Programme (annual), *Human Development Report*, Oxford: Oxford University Press.

World Bank (annual), *World Development Report*, Oxford: Oxford University Press.

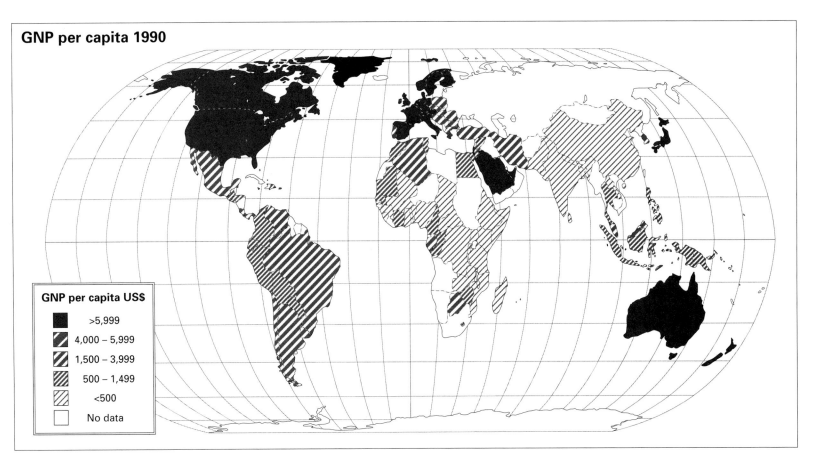

Figure 1.11a   GNP per capita, 1990

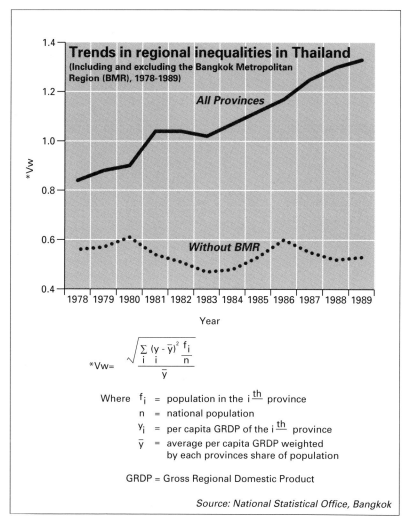

Figure 1.11b Trends in regional inequalities in Thailand. Note: BMR = Bangkok Metropolitan Region

Table 1.11 Poverty and income distribution in Thailand

(a) Incidence of poverty (per cent of total population)

Region	1975/76	1980/81	1985/86	1988/89
North	33.2	21.5	25.5	23.2
Northeast	44.9	35.9	48.2	37.5
Central	13.0	13.6	15.6	16.0
South	30.7	20.4	27.2	21.5
Bangkok Metropolitan	7.8	3.9	3.5	3.4
Whole Kingdom	30.0	23.0	29.5	23.7

(b) Income share by population quintile group (per cent of total income)

Quintile	1975/76	1980/81	1985/86	1988/89
1st	49.26	51.47	55.63	54.62
highest top 10%	33.40	35.44	39.15	37.50
second top 10%	15.86	16.04	16.48	17.13
2nd	20.96	20.64	19.86	20.42
3rd	14.00	13.38	12.09	12.31
4th	9.73	9.10	7.87	8.07
5th	6.05	5.41	4.55	4.56
second bottom 10%	3.62	3.28	2.75	2.78
lowest bottom 10%	2.43	2.13	1.80	1.78
TOTAL SHARE	100.00	100.00	100.00	100.00
Gini Coefficient	0.426	0.453	0.500	0.489

Source: data from National Statistical Office, Thailand

1.12 THE SPATIAL DIMENSIONS OF THE DEVELOPMENT PROCESS: CORE, SEMI-PERIPHERY AND PERIPHERY

David Drakakis-Smith

The notion of cores (or centres) and peripheries is not new and is an analytical device which has been employed by all political shades of development strategists, including the dependency and world-system schools who employed the idea as a framework to illustrate the permanent disequilibrium in the global economy.

For many critics this simple bipolarisation contained too many contradictions to be analytically useful. The overemphasis on unequal exchange between a dynamic core and a passive periphery ignored not only the global movement of finance and production capital, but also the fact that internal social, political, and economic structures, together with their articulation with international capital (colonial or neo-colonial), have strongly shaped the nature of specific social formations in even the remotest corners of the Third World.

A consequent criticism of the simple dichotomy of dependency and world-system theory was that it failed to recognise and account for variations from the polarised core and periphery, such as the Newly Industrialising Countries (NICs) of Taiwan, Singapore, and the like, or the 'developed periphery' of countries such as Australia and New Zealand (Browett, 1981; Smith, 1982). To counter this criticism, writers such as Galtung (1971) and Wallerstein (1976) introduced the 'go-between' or 'semi-periphery' as an intermediary stage of development, suggesting that this comprised nations on the way up or down in the world economic system. They particularly highlighted the importance of periods of economic stagnation (as at present) in changing the economic ranking of nations.

Arrighi and Drangel (1986) undertook a detached analysis which confirmed this element of constant adjustment (Figure 1.12a). The results apparently verify the existence of a stable group of some twenty countries 'capable of selectively exploiting the peripheralizing tendencies of the world economy so as to prevent downgrading of their mix of core-peripheral activities but not sufficiently to attain core status' (Arrighi and Drangel, 1986: 41). In seeking to explain a changing world situation, information about mobility and its causes is clearly valuable, producing a division of the world into three categories that is substantially different from that noted in Section 1.10 (Figure 1.12b).

One of the most vigorous attempts to characterise the semi-periphery was by Vayrynen (1983) who not only compiled a list of the major characteristics of expanding semi-peripheral nations, but also classified them into four main types (Table 1.12). Vayrynen's work is important because it introduces non-economic variables into the classification system, although it does not go far enough in recognising the importance of social movements in the generation of change. It is on these grounds above all that the system fails to incorporate some of the more developed

Table 1.12 Vayrynen's semi-periphery

	Regional powers	NICs	Pariahs	Oil exporters
Economic				
Strong internal markets	*		*	
Middle income GNP	*	*	*	*
Rapid expansion of manufacturing exports		*		
Indebtedness	*	*		
Balance of payments deficit	*	*		
High level of state investment		*	*	
Social				
Continuing social crisis	*	*	*	*
Growing gap between rich and poor	*			*
Political				
Unstable	*	*	*	*
Strong central government controls	*	*	*	*
Strongly nationalist	*	*	*	*
High military expenditure			*	*
Examples	Brazil India	Hong Kong Spain	South Africa Israel	Saudi Arabia Venezuela
			←————— Iran —————→	
	←——————————— Taiwan ———————————→			

Source: after Vayrynen (1983)

semi-peripheral states, such as Australia and New Zealand. Vayrynen's classification is also limited in that, like many aspects of development theory, it does not seek to establish those characteristics of the periphery which persist in the semi-periphery (or begin to appear in declining core nations?). The concept of the semi-periphery has always contained a contradiction in that whilst the label itself emphasises the 'periphery', it is always the features of the 'core' which are used to characterise it. Such is the Eurocentric logic of even radical development theory. It would be equally facile to identify a 'semi-core' by using only the characteristics of the periphery.

It is not surprising in these circumstances that there has been no clear agreement on a list of nations or features that represent the 'semi-periphery'. In many ways this must be expected, for the notion is more symbolic than real, representing as it does the full range of features between the 'crude buckets' of conceptual dualism. However, the discussion on the existence of a qualitatively, if not quantitatively, recognisable semi-periphery does serve a useful purpose in drawing attention towards the processes which gave rise to social formations that were neither core nor periphery. In this sense, it still features

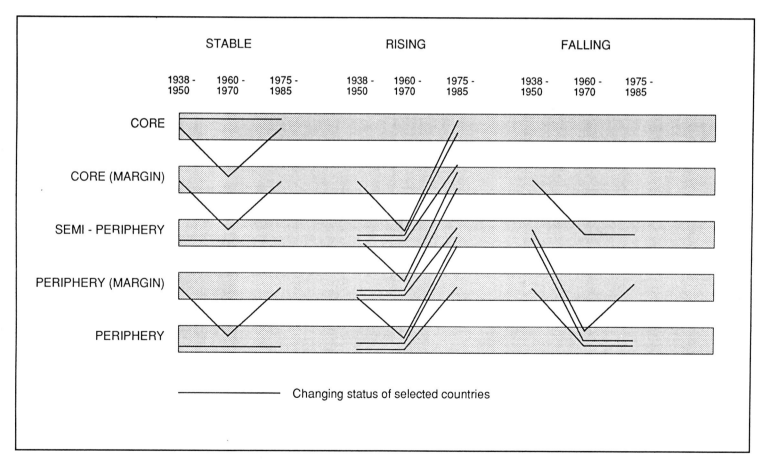

Figure 1.12a The stability of countries in the core, semi-periphery and periphery

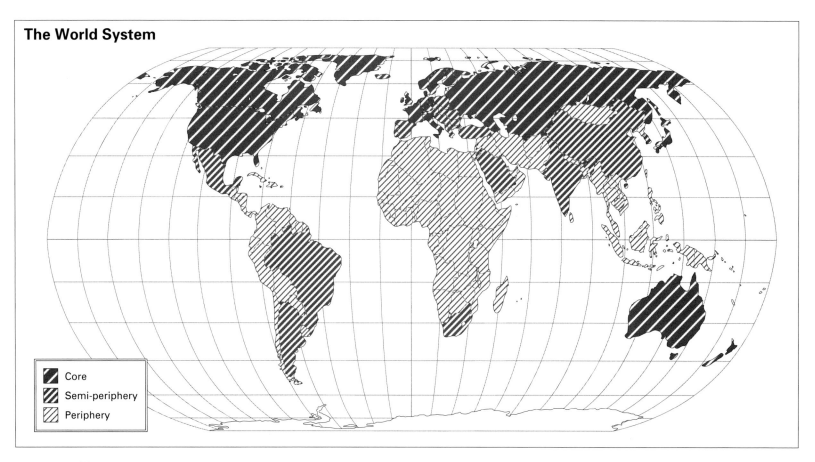

Figure 1.12b   The world system

in the debates of geographers investigating the broader question of the varying spatial dimensions of development.

Further reading

Doherty, J. (1983), Beyond dependency, *Professional Geographer*, **35**(1): 81–83.
Knox, P. and Agnew, J. (1989), *The Geography of the World Economy*, London: Routledge.

1.13 HUMAN DEVELOPMENT INDICATORS

David Drakakis-Smith

Economic growth as measured by GNP per capita is a poor indicator of human development. Inequality in income distribution compounds the effect of low overall levels of economic development to give rise to widespread poverty which is reflected in access to a range of basic needs, such as education, health care, adequate levels of nutrition and the like.

Several attempts have been made to devise a quality of life index which incorporates information on multiple measurements of human development. One of the first to receive widespread attention was the Physical Quality of Life Index (PQLI) developed at the Overseas Development Council in Washington. This comprised data on three factors, namely life expectancy, infant mortality and literacy, which were transformed into a common score base with equal weighting.

The resultant spatial pattern of scores is shown on Figure 1.13a and its lack of correlation with the map of GNP per capita (Figure 1.11a) confirms that very different aspects of development are being measured. Other indices were more statistically complex. Gonzalez's (1988) Socio-Economic Development Index (SEDI), for example, used seven measures to cover four basic factors of income, health, diet and education. Estes (1988) went even further and his Index of Social Progress (ISP) incorporated 44 items within 11 clusters encompassing fields such as political stability, political participation and defence effort! Ginsburg *et al.* (1986) similarly cover 42 variables in their World Standard Distance Scales.

Whilst these indices are useful in constructing general views on world development which are much broader than GNP alone, they have been widely criticised. Often, despite the sophisticated massaging of data, the end set of scores seems to be almost arbitrarily carved up into two or three sections for mapping purposes (*see* Tata and Schultz, 1988). Perhaps this does not matter given the very dubious quality of the data which is fed into the system in the first place. Even apparently reliable measurements such as the urban:rural proportions of total population can vary widely in the criteria used. In Peru, for example, an urban centre is one with 100 dwellings; in Senegal it has to have 10 000 inhabitants. In the light of comments such as these, it is perhaps not surprising that the most recent attempts to measure and map human welfare have returned to a simpler and easier to compile index. The Human Development Index of UNDP (1991) thus only contains measurements for income, life expectancy and literacy, and yet is just as useful as the ISP.

However, there is substantial variation between these major indices. Whilst some countries, such as Switzerland and Sweden are consistently high on the scales, and others, such as Ethiopia or Bangladesh, consistently low, there are many

Table 1.13 Socio-economic development indices for selected countries

Per Capita GNP Ranking 1990	Human Development Index		Physical Quality of Life Index		Index of Social Progress		Socio-Economic Development Index	
Switzerland	Japan	993	Sweden	97	Netherlands	190	USA	90
Japan	Canada	983	Netherlands	96	Sweden	189	Switzerland	85
Sweden	Sweden	982	Japan	96	New Zealand	186	Canada	82
USA	Switzerland	981	Canada	95	Australia	184	Sweden	82
Germany	USA	976	Switzerland	95	Belgium	178	France	77
Canada	Netherlands	976	USA	94	Germany	174	Netherlands	77
France	Australia	973	New Zealand	94	Canada	170	Japan	77
Belgium	France	971	UK	94	Switzerland	170	Germany	76
Netherlands	UK	976	France	94	Poland	168	Australia	74
Italy	Germany	959	Australia	93	France	165	Belgium	73
UK	New Zealand	959	Germany	93	Czechoslovakia	163	New Zealand	71
Australia	Belgium	958	Belgium	93	Italy	158	UK	70
Israel	Italy	955	Czechoslovakia	93	Japan	149	Italy	68
New Zealand	Spain	951	Italy	92	UK	143	Spain	65

Table 1.13 (*Continued*)

Per Capita GNP Ranking 1990	Human Development Index		Physical Quality of Life Index		Index of Social Progress		Socio-Economic Development Index	
Spain	Israel	950	USSR	91	Cuba	141	Israel	64
Saudi Arabia	Czechoslovakia	920	Spain	91	Yugoslavia	137	Czechoslovakia	63
Taiwan	USSR	908	Poland	91	Venezuela	137	Poland	60
South Korea	Yugoslavia	893	Israel	89	Brazil	137	USSR	57
Czechoslovakia	South Korea	884	Taiwan	86	Colombia	130	Yugoslavia	57
Iran	Chile	878	Argentina	85	Spain	129	Argentina	56
Yugoslavia	Poland	863	Yugoslavia	84	Argentina	124	Taiwan	53
Brazil	Argentina	854	Cuba	84	Mexico	121	Cuba	53
South Africa	Venezuela	848	South Korea	82	USA	116	South Korea	51
Venezeuela	Mexico	838	Venezuela	79	USSR	113	Saudi Arabia	51
Algeria	Malaysia	802	Chile	77	Turkey	112	Venezuela	50
Malaysia	South Africa	766	Mexico	73	South Korea	107	Chile	49
Argentina	Brazil	759	Colombia	71	Thailand	99	Mexico	46
Mexico	Colombia	757	Philippines	71	South Africa	98	Philippines	44
Cuba	Cuba	754	Brazil	68	Algeria	96	Malaysia	42
Poland	Thailand	713	Thailand	68	Israel	92	Turkey	42
USSR	Saudi Arabia	697	Malaysia	66	Malaysia	92	Colombia	41
Chile	Turkey	694	Peru	62	Philippines	91	Thailand	41
Turkey	Peru	644	Turkey	55	Chile	90	South Africa	40
Thailand	China	614	Vietnam	54	Egypt	81	Brazil	39
Colombia	Philippines	613	South Africa	53	Peru	76	Egypt	39
Peru	Iran	534	Burma	51	Morocco	73	Iran	38
Morocco	Indonesia	499	Indonesia	48	Indonesia	71	Peru	37
Philippines	Vietnam	498	Egypt	43	Burma	71	Algeria	36
Egypt	Algeria	490	Iran	43	Iran	69	Burma	35
Indonesia	Burma	437	India	43	Sudan	60	China	34
Ghana	Morocco	431	China	43	Kenya	56	Vietnam	34
Pakistan	Kenya	399	Morocco	41	Vietnam	53	Morocco	33
Kenya	Egypt	394	Algeria	41	India	53	Indonesia	32
Sudan	Pakistan	311	Uganda	40	Zaire	52	Tanzania	31
China	Ghana	311	Kenya	39	Ghana	39	India	28
India	India	308	Pakistan	38	Nigeria	33	Nigeria	28
Zaire	Zaire	299	Sudan	36	Pakistan	31	Kenya	27
Uganda	Tanzania	266	Bangladesh	35	Tanzania	29	Sudan	27
Nigeria	Nigeria	242	Ghana	35	Uganda	21	Pakistan	27
Burma	Uganda	204	Zaire	32	Ethiopia	−12	Ghana	26
Vietnam	Bangladesh	186	Tanzania	31	Taiwan*		Uganda	25
Bangladesh	Ethiopia	166	Saudia Arabia	29	China*		Ethiopia	25
Tanzania	Sudan	164	Nigeria	25	Bangladesh*		Zaire	24
Ethiopia	Taiwan*		Ethiopia	20	Saudi Arabia*		Bangladesh	23

* Not evaluated by this index

Sources: Drakakis-Smith (1993), UNDP (1991), World Bank Development Report (1990)

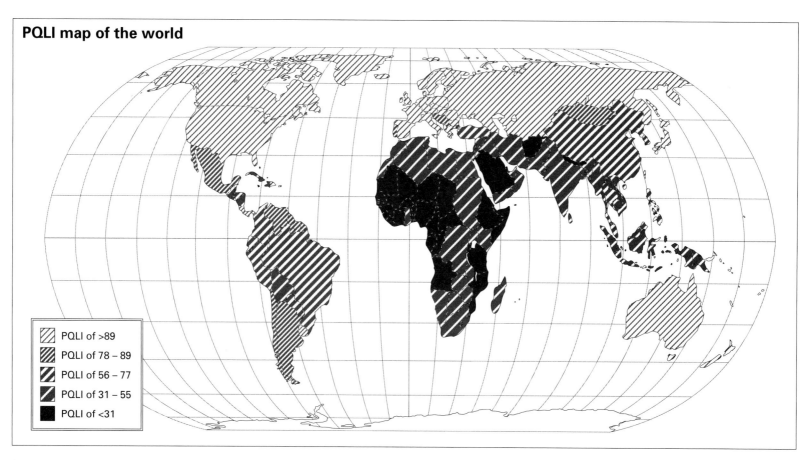

Figure 1.13a   PQLI map of the world

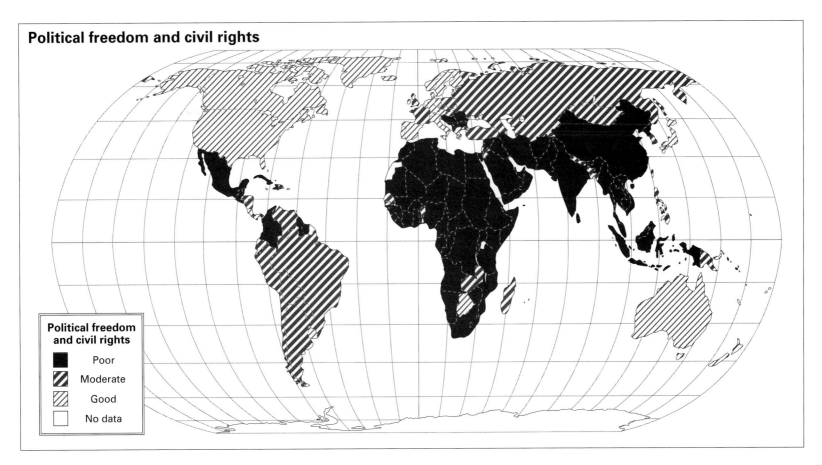

Figure 1.13b   Political freedom and civil rights

countries whose position fluctuates enormously depending on what data have been incorporated (Table 1.13). More recently, the Population Crisis Committee (1992) has produced an index of the human suffering which, in addition to the usual variables reflecting economic or physical well-being, included measurements on civil rights and human freedoms. If these are abstracted and mapped on their own (Figure 1.13b) the poor correlation between economic growth and human rights is clearly seen, particularly in Pacific Asia. The Vienna conference on Human Rights debated whether this reflects different conceptualisations of individual rights and freedoms between different cultures. As yet no consensus on this issue has emerged.

Perhaps the greatest criticism that can be levelled at development indices is that they have no explanatory dimension. They simply describe in various ways world inequality. As such, they must not be seen as an end in themselves, but rather as a starting point for deeper examination and analysis of the development process. We need to be able to explain the inequality that we see on our maps.

Further reading

Loh, C. (1993), The rights stuff, *Far Eastern Economic Review*, July 8:15

Population Crisis Committee (1993), *An Index of Human Suffering*, Washington D.C.: Population Crisis Committee.

UNDP (1991), *Human Development Index*, Oxford: Oxford University Press.

2 The Environment of Development

TIM UNWIN

Geographers have long been concerned with the relationships between people and the physical environments in which they live (Glacken, 1967; Unwin, 1992). However, the precise balance between the effects that people have on the environment, and the physical environment's influences on human activity has been much disputed. Thus while contemporary climatic change is now widely seen as being the result of 'damaging' human influences, and therefore indicative of increasing human domination of 'nature', we are also periodically shocked by the devastating power of the physical world, as with the loss of life and destruction associated with such 'natural' disasters as earthquakes and floods. Humanity might increasingly like to think that it controls the environment, but the physical world still provides not only violent reminders of its power, but also the very varied conditions existing in different parts of the world with which societies have to interact for their survival.

This chapter therefore addresses some characteristics of the physical environment which have been important in influencing the varied distribution of economic activity across the surface of the globe, as well as certain aspects of direct human influence on the environment. It begins with surveys of global geology, climate and vegetation, which provide the overall physical context against which the processes of development examined in the ensuing chapters can be assessed. The importance of the spatially discrete location of mineral resources, and the distribution of varying levels of tectonic activity at a global scale are thus, for example, analysed as indicators of the ways in which geology can have a significant influence on human activity. Issues associated with climatic variability, seasonality and change are then examined in Sections 2.4 to 2.9, before a broad summary of global vegetation types is described in Section 2.10.

The final sections of the chapter address issues more directly associated with human interactions with the environment. After the summary of global vegetation types, there is therefore a more detailed regional analysis of vegetation change in the Amazon basin, and this is followed by an examination of environmental management at a variety of scales, from the global level to detailed case studies of the humid tropics and a small community in Zimbabwe. The last two sections contrast positive and negative aspects of human interaction with the physical environment, through an examination of the development of irrigation projects in India, Pakistan and Bangladesh and a survey of levels of air pollution in Asia.

2.1 GLOBAL GEOLOGY AND WORLD DEVELOPMENT
Lewis A. Owen

Figure 2.1 illustrates the distribution of the major groups of rocks based on lithology, age and geological structure. This distribution reflects both past and present tectonic settings (*see also* Section 2.2). An understanding of this map is important in assessing tectonic hazard, and the distribution of geological resources such as fossil fuels, minerals, groundwater and geothermal energy (*see also* Section 2.3). On a local and regional scale the geology determines the ground conditions which are important for building and engineering design and construction, as well as agricultural activities. In addition, development in all these regions is governed by topography, which to a large extent is governed by the rock types and the tectonic setting. Topography in turn influences the accessibility of raw resources which themselves are functions of the particular geology. Although the gross geology is known reasonably well in most developing regions detailed geological mapping is often crude, based on remote sensing and reconnaissance surveys. The utilisation of geological information is essential to socio-economic development throughout the globe. Global geology can be crudely divided into six main regions:

(1) The young ocean floors which have formed during the last 100 million years and are presently forming at ocean ridges and hot spots. In some areas, hot fluids rich in metals are emitted in association with the formation of ocean crust, providing ores such as manganese nodules. These may be economically viable to exploit in the future.

(2) The young mountain ranges which include: the Alpine-Himalaya belt formed by the collision of continental plates; and the Andes and North American Western Cordillera, and the New Zealand Alps formed by the subduction of oceanic plates under continental plates. These regions contain large reserves of strategic metals and valuable minerals. They are also regions where active tectonism and high magnitude geomorphological processes constitute major hazards.

(3) The young islands of the Eastern Pacific where oceanic crust is being subducted beneath oceanic crust leading to the formation of volcanic island arcs. Earthquakes, volcanic eruptions and associated phenomena such as tsunami constitute a major hazard, seriously retarding development, as was exemplified by the recent volcanic eruptions in the Philippines (Mt Pinatubo in 1991 and Mt Mayon in 1993).

(4) Rift valleys such as the East Africa, Dead Sea, Rhine, Icelandic, and submarine rifts as in the North Sea and the Red Sea represent areas of young crustal extension. These are regions of high geothermal heat flow which may provide abundant geothermal energy. In many areas sedimentary deposits associated with rifting contain abundant oil and gas reserves, which have been important for the development of regions such as the Arabian Peninsula.

(5) The old continental interiors of Canada, Africa and Central Asia. Important resources such as iron ore, uranium and gold are associated with these regions, which are generally considered tectonically stable, though large earthquakes have been experienced as with the Hyderabad earthquake of October 1993.

(6) Sedimentary basins associated with all the above where the deposition of eroded rock or the precipitation of minerals and rocks such as carbonates and iron ores provide important sedimentary mineral deposits and source rocks for fossil fuels.

Further reading

Larson, R.L., Pitman, III, W.C., Golovchenko, X., Cande, S.C., Dewey, J.F., Haxby, W.F. and LaBrecque, J.L. (1985), *The Bedrock Geology of the World*, New York: W.H. Freeman.

UNESCO (United Nations Economic, Social and Cultural Organisation) Commission for the Geological Map of the World (1976), *Atlas Géologique du Monde*, Paris: United Nations Economic, Social and Cultural Organisation.

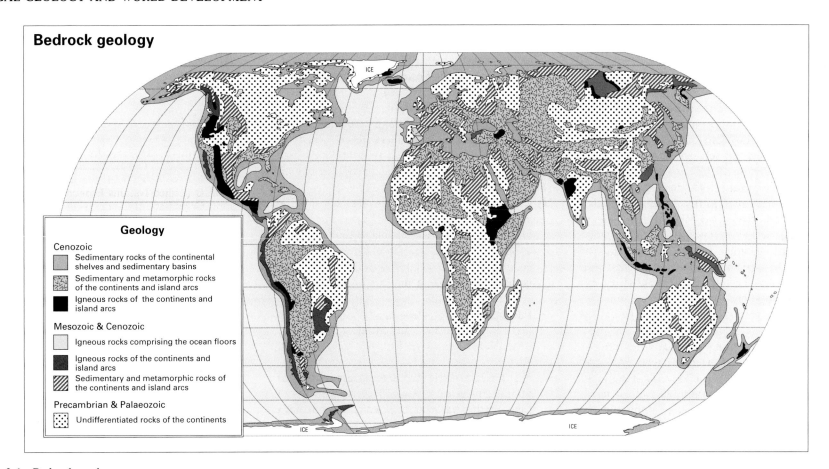

Figure 2.1 Bedrock geology

2.2 PLATE TECTONICS AND WORLD DEVELOPMENT

Ian Davison

Plate tectonic theory describes the behaviour of the outer rigid shell (lithosphere) of the Earth which is divided into a small number of plates moving relative to each other at rates of 1–18 cm per year. The lithosphere is about 100 km thick and overlies the viscous hotter asthenosphere. The plates are part of a convective cycle, where upwelling of the asthenosphere produces new lithospheric plate at mid-ocean ridges and plates fall into the asthenosphere at subduction zones (Figure 2.2a). Most of the deformation (folding and faulting) which results from this constant motion is produced along the edges of the plates and each continent has at least one major mountain belt which has been produced by plate crumpling in the last 100 million years (Figure 2.2b).

Mountain belts have a dramatic effect on world development because of their impact on climate and agriculture (Figure 2.2b). For example, the harsh Tibetan Plateau has an average altitude of 5400 m and covers an area of 3 million km^2 (Figure 2.2b). It developed about 15 million years ago in response to collision between the Eurasian and Indian plates, and this has been linked to dramatic cooling and increased precipitation over Asia since that time (Ruddiman and Kutzbach, 1991). In contrast, mountains are also responsible for rain shadow deserts such as the Gobi and Atacama.

Most earthquakes and volcanoes occur along plate boundaries (interplate events), with the largest and most destructive activity located along subduction zone boundaries (Figure 2.2b). Many large earthquakes occur in the oceanic plates producing tsunami waves, which travel thousands of kilometres across deep oceans without energy loss, and cause enormous damage to coastal development; sedimentary deposits produced by a tsunami wave have been found up to 300 m above sea level on Lanai (Hawaii) (Tilling and Lipman, 1993). Less frequently, earthquakes can also occur within plates (intraplate events; Figure 2.2b). These are equally violent, and shock waves can travel for long distances through cold rigid continental plates affecting unprepared cities which are distant from known high risk areas. Hence, it is difficult to quantify earthquake risk, and the zones on Figure 2.2b are only a general guide.

Direct volcanic damage is usually more localised than earthquake effects; nevertheless, it is estimated that over 260 000 lives have been lost due to volcanic activity in the last 400 years (Rampino, 1992). More importantly, large volcanic events can produce global changes in the climate, which affect agriculture, transportation, energy consumption and health. Sulphur dioxide aerosol clouds in the stratosphere are the main volcanic agent of climate change. Observation and theoretical modelling suggest that relatively small volcanic events (0.5 km^3 of erupted magma) can change the average surface temperature by several tenths of a degree Celsius. This is enough to change the growing season by one week in northern Europe. Probably the best example of a volcanically-controlled climatic effect on development was produced by a very large volcanic ash eruption in Tambora, Eastern Java in 1815 when darkness lasted for two days up to 600 km from the volcano. This led to a cool and wet climate in western Europe in the following year with crop failure and ensuing famine and social unrest.

Despite increased knowledge of areas at risk, the world's largest (China), and most rapidly growing populations (Pacific 'Ring of Fire', Middle East) live within these areas (Figure 2.2b).

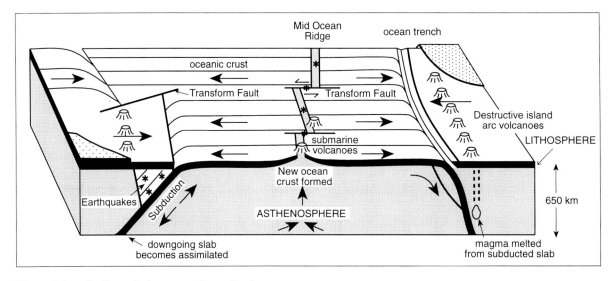

Figure 2.2a Outline of plate tectonic mechanism

It is estimated that about 55 cities with populations over one million lie in high risk zones. There is an urgent need to improve hazard monitoring to avoid disasters such as the Tangshan earthquake in China (350 000 deaths). However, this requires much larger long-term investments and more effective international co-operation than current levels.

Further reading

Bolt, B.A. (1988), *Earthquakes, a Primer*, New York: Freeman.

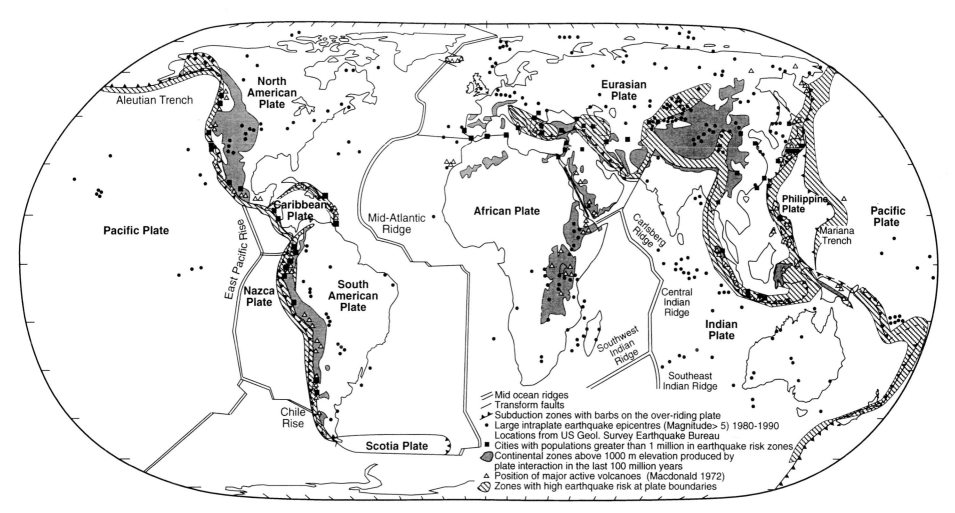

Figure 2.2b Simplified distribution of major tectonic plates and their relationship to earthquakes, volcanoes and zones of elevated topography

2.3 GEOLOGY, RESOURCES AND HYDROCARBONS

Ian Davison and Tim Unwin

Geology plays a central role in determining the global distribution of physical resources, and this is nowhere more strikingly revealed than in the location of hydrocarbon reserves. If coal drove the 'industrial revolution' of the 19th century, then oil has been the key source of energy and raw materials that has provided the basis for the transformation of the global economy of the 20th century. However, the world's oil and gas reserves are found in sedimentary basins many of which are far from the main areas of demand in north America, Europe and Japan (Figure 2.3 and Table 2.3). Not only has this necessitated the long-distance transport of oil by tanker and pipeline, but it has also been the cause for considerable political involvement by states such as Britain and the USA in the Middle East. Moreover, long distance transport has led to many recent ecological disasters where large oil tanker spills have devastated marine wildlife. A less well-known source of pollution is the escape of methane gas from pipelines. Of the total global methane emissions of about 500 million tons a year, roughly 83 million tons comes from the natural gas industry. Major emissions come from the former Soviet Union, and it is possible that part of the reason for the fall in global atmospheric methane in 1992–93 is a reduction in natural gas emissions from Russia (E. Nesbit, 1993, pers. comm.).

The location of hydrocarbon reserves is controlled by the distribution of good source rocks, which are generally marine organic-rich black shales. These source rocks are laid down in deep waters (more than 500 m) where lack of oxygen in the bottom waters allows preservation of green and blue-green algae, which are most abundant at higher latitudes. The source rocks must be buried to at least 1.5 km beneath other sedimentary deposits in a subsiding basin so that the consequent temperature increase (to 100°C) drives molecular reactions to produce hydrocarbons. Most of the world's hydrocarbon reserves are concentrated in the northern hemisphere in the Tethyan realm which contains two-thirds of the reserves and occupies only one-quarter of the world's landmass (Figure 2.3). Ninety % of the world's reserves are sourced from rocks laid down during six short time periods spread over the last 500 million years, with the Late Jurassic and Middle Cretaceous periods accounting for over 54% of known reserves (Ulmishek and Klemme, 1990) (Figure 2.3). These periods were characterised by different geological conditions, and do not represent a cyclical phenomenon.

Hydrocarbons are trapped by impermeable rock horizons which drape over porous and permeable reservoir rocks (such as sandstones and limestones). The most effective seals are evaporite salt horizons which trap approximately 35% of world reserves (Ulmishek and Klemme, 1990). Evaporitic salt horizons are also used by the US government for strategic fuel storage and nuclear waste disposal in underground caverns, where they are cheaply excavated by dissolving the salt with fresh water.

As Table 2.3 indicates, the bulk of the world's oil reserves are found in the countries of the Middle East and the former Soviet Union. Until the early 1970s most of these were exploited under traditional concession agreements, by which companies were given exclusive rights for exploration, production and ownership of oil, with the governments receiving a rental and either a share of profits or a fixed royalty. Thereafter, the oil producing countries either nationalised foreign companies or took increasingly large stakes in them, and the growing strength of the Organisation of Petroleum Exporting Countries (OPEC) led to rapid price increases in 1973–4 and 1978–9.

Table 2.3 Global hydrocarbon reserves and production

Region	Estimated proved oil reserves January 1993 (1000 barrels)	Estimated proved gas reserves January 1993 (bcf)	Estimated 1992 oil production (1000 barrels per day)	Ratio 1993 oil reserves:1992 oil production per annum
Asia-Pacific	44 572 328	341 013	6484.3	18.83
Western Europe	15 828 836	191 770	4485.9	9.66
Eastern Europe and former Soviet Union	59 192 880	1 963 306	9181.0	17.66
Middle East	661 791 002	1 520 140	17 420.6	104.08
Africa	61 872 424	346 865	6319.3	26.82
North America	81 271 630	333 696	11 503.4	19.31
South America and Caribbean	72 512 674	188 572	4607.9	43.11

Source: derived from *Oil and Gas Journal* (1993) **91**(52): 44–45

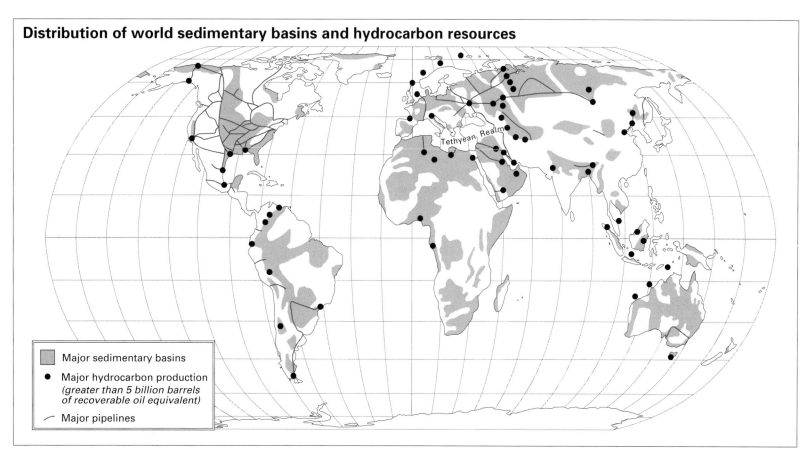

Figure 2.3 Distribution of world sedimentary basins and hydrocarbon resources

These created serious problems for all oil importing countries, leading to global recession and balance of payments difficulties. Indeed, it was only the recycling of OPEC's oil revenues through the international banking system that enabled the world economy to revive and restructure itself during the 1980s. One result of the nearly sevenfold increase in crude oil prices between 1973 and 1980 was a considerable increase in hydrocarbon exploration and the exploitation of new reserves, particularly of gas, in areas such as the North Sea. As Table 2.3 illustrates, though, at current rates of production the presently known resources of most parts of the world will be depleted within well under fifty years. Thus, while new reserves may well be exploited, the essentially limited supply of fossil fuels is likely to lead to considerable further tensions in the world economy and political order in the future.

Further reading

North, F.K. (1985), *Petroleum Geology*, London and Sydney: Allen and Unwin.

2.4 GLOBAL CLIMATE
Paula Harrison and Paul Brignall

The climate is the average character of weather in a region over many years. It consists of an array of climatic elements, such as temperature, precipitation, sunshine, atmospheric humidity and wind velocity. These principal climatic variables are observed at specific times throughout the day at numerous meteorological stations dispersed about the globe on land masses and on ships. These detailed statistics are summarised temporally, in terms of monthly and annual means and totals, and spatially across regions. At the regional scale climates are greatly influenced by continental, oceanic and topographical considerations. However, at the global scale broad patterns of climate can be identified.

The mean annual surface air temperature of the globe is around 15°C. Temperatures are unevenly distributed about the Earth's surface due to differences in amount of solar radiation received (Figure 2.4a). In general, temperatures are highest at the equator and decrease towards the poles. This latitudinal temperature gradient is the critical driving force of the global climate system. Mean annual surface air temperatures between the two Tropics range from 20°C to 30°C, with highest temperatures occurring in the southern Sahara, north-eastern portion of South America, India, south-east Asia, Indonesia and northern Australia. In the mid-latitude regions, between the Arctic and Antarctic Circles and the Tropics, they range from −10°C to 20°C, the coldest temperatures occurring in northern Russia where the effects of continentality are strongest. In the polar regions mean annual temperatures are less than −10°C and on a monthly scale may be as cold as −90°C in Antarctica. Oceanic (warm and cold coastal currents) and topographic (mountain and plain) features influence this latitudinal temperature gradient. Warm currents, such as the Gulf Stream, Kuroshio and the Brazil Current, increase local surface temperatures, whilst cold currents, such as the California, Peru, Benguela and Canaries Currents, decrease local surface temperatures and weaken north-south air temperature gradients. Also, since temperature decreases with altitude, low temperatures are found in high altitude regions, such as the Andes, Himalayas, Alps and Rocky Mountains and over the high plateaus of Tibet, Iran, Ethiopia and Brazil.

Mean annual precipitation is heaviest along the Inter-Tropical Convergence Zone (ITCZ) and generally decreases towards the poles (Figure 2.4b). Heavy annual precipitation (greater than 8 mmday^{-1}) occurs over large areas of the equatorial Pacific and over the rain forests of South America, Africa and Asia. The ITCZ is a low pressure zone where the north-east and south-east trade winds meet and warm moist air rises. The two Tropics are high pressure zones with descending air and low rainfall. These include the hot desert regions of the Sahara, Gobi, Kalahari, Atacama, American south-west and Australian Outback. Winds blow from this high pressure zone towards the low pressure zone of the mid-latitudes. In this zone the weather is determined by depressions (low pressure centres) which are generally rain-bearing or anti-cyclones (high pressure centres) which are generally dry. The polar regions (north and south of the Arctic and Antarctic circles), which include the cold deserts, are characterised by low precipitation. These are high pressure areas with descending cold air, which hold little water vapour.

Oceanic and topographic features also influence precipitation patterns. Air masses passing across warm ocean currents take up large quantities of water leading to high precipitation on land masses in their path. On the other hand, air masses passing across cold currents remain relatively dry. Regional relief has a significant effect on the spatial distribution of precipitation. Precipitation is relatively homogeneous over level terrain, such as the Australian Outback, the Tibetan Plateau and central North America, whilst it varies dramatically in mountainous regions, such as the Rockies and the Alps.

Further reading

Barry, R.G. and Chorley , R.J. (1990), *Atmosphere, Weather and Climate*, London: Routledge, 6th ed.

Henderson-Sellers, A. and Robinson, P.J. (1986), *Contemporary Climatology*, New York: Longman Scientific and Technical.

Legates, D.R. and Willmott, C.J. (1990a), Mean seasonal and spatial variability in global surface air temperatures, *Theoretical and Applied Climatology*, **41**: 11−21.

Legates, D.R and Willmott, C.J. (1990b), Mean seasonal and spatial variability in gauge-corrected global precipitation, *International Journal of Climatology*, **10**: 111−127.

Martyn, D. (1992), *Climates of the World*, Amsterdam: Elsevier, Developments in Atmospheric Science 18.

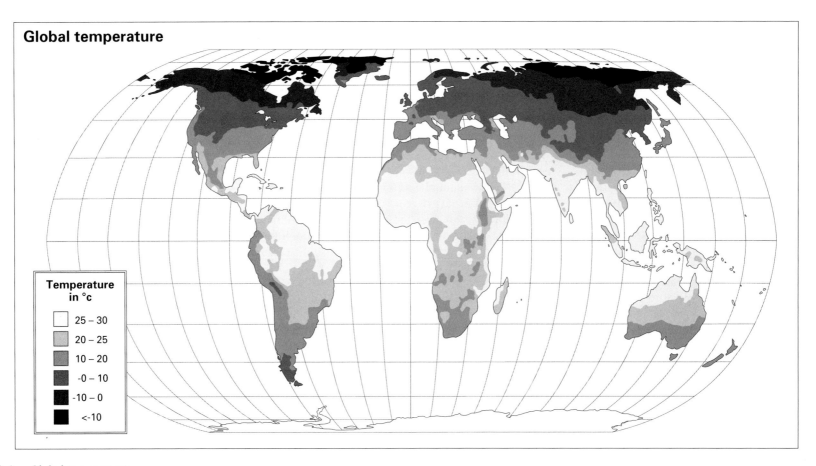

Figure 2.4a   Global temperature

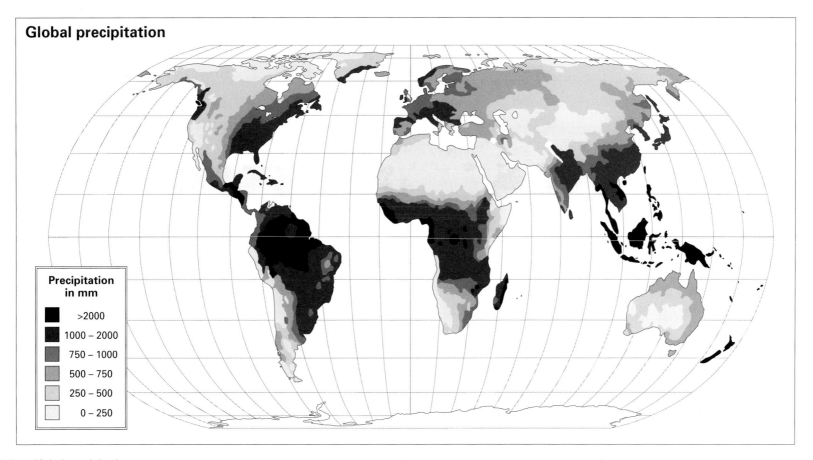

Figure 2.4b   Global precipitation

2.5 CLIMATIC VARIABILITY
Mike Hulme

Large regional differences exist in the interannual variability of both temperature and precipitation. This mode of climatic variability may be regarded as describing the 'reliability' of a given climatic regime and is of major significance for a wide range of planning purposes. In regions of low variability, natural and social systems can evolve which have little need for adaptability to climatic extremes, as in the UK where there is no large-scale regional transfer of water resources owing to the reliability of precipitation. In regions where large interannual variability exists for either temperature or precipitation, then for natural and social systems to be robust, they have to be able to adapt to a wide range of possible climates, as with the response of nomadism in semi-arid regions where precipitation variability is high. These latter regions are sometimes referred to as possessing 'marginal climates' (Parry *et al.*, 1988).

Figure 2.5 shows an index of precipitation variability using data for the period 1951–80. The standardised decile range is defined as the difference between the annual precipitation expected in the wettest and driest 10% of years, expressed as a percentage of the median precipitation. Regions of greatest reliability in precipitation have the lowest index values and these regions are generally found in mid-latitudes of the Northern Hemisphere and within 5° north or south of the Equator. The region of lowest precipitation variability (index values less than 20%) is western equatorial Africa – the countries of the Cameroons, Gabon and Congo. High variability regions (index values greater than 100%) are generally associated with drier climatic regimes, such as the Sahara Desert and its margins, western South America

and the Middle East. Regions with highly variable precipitation generally coincide with regions of highly seasonal precipitation (Section 2.6) and often are regions which are sensitive to ENSO-related precipitation anomalies (Section 2.7).

Table 2.5 shows this index of reliability for three selected locations which illustrate regions of low, moderate and high precipitation variability. Although Brazzaville and Calcutta receive similar median annual precipitation totals (1400–1500 mm), the year-to-year variability around this total is much greater at Calcutta than at Brazzaville. At In Salalah in Oman the relative variability is greater still, indicating much more uncertainty about the amount of precipitation received each year.

Further reading

Glantz, M.H. and Katz, R.W. (1986), Drought as a constraint to development in sub-Saharan Africa, *Ambio*, **6**: 334–339.
Parry, M.L., Carter, T.R. and Konijn, N.T. (eds) (1988), *The Impact of Climatic Variations on Agriculture, Vol. 2: Assessments in Semi-Arid Regions*, Dordrecht: Kluwer Academic Publishers.

Table 2.5 Examples of annual precipitation variability for three selected stations illustrating low, moderate and high precipitation variability regimes

	Brazzaville (Congo)	Calcutta (India)	In Salalah (Oman)
Lowest decile	1112 (−25%)	1125 (−24%)	36 (−50%)
Median	1395	1484	72
Highest decile	1551 (+11%)	2062 (+39%)	208 (+188%)
SDR index value	31%	63%	239%

Note: Precipitation totals are in millimetres. The lowest and highest deciles are the precipitation expected, respectively, in the driest and wettest 10% of years; the values in parentheses are the percentage differences from the median precipitation. The standardised decile range (SDR index) is shown for each station. Data are for the period 1951–80.
Source: author

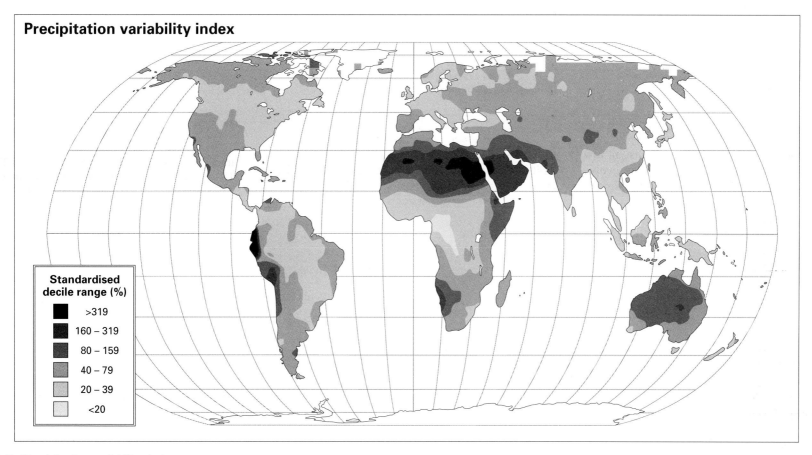

Figure 2.5 Precipitation variability index

2.6 THE SEASONALITY OF CLIMATE
Mike Hulme

Differences in the annual cycle of climate are one of the most important determinants of regional differences in agricultural and cultural characteristics of ecosystems and societies. The response of natural vegetation to climate and the evolution of agricultural and cultural systems are constrained by the seasonality of temperature and precipitation. Changes in the seasonality of climate may consequently have profound influences upon human activity. The development of potential agricultural domesticates, such as annual grasses, legumes and geophytes, between 12 000 and 8000 BP may partly have been stimulated by increases in the seasonality of precipitation and temperature (Byrne, 1992).

Two maps of seasonality are shown, one for temperature (Figure 2.6a) and one for precipitation (Figure 2.6b). The temperature seasonality index is defined according to the amplitude of the annual cycle, which ranges from close to zero in the equatorial regions to well over 20°C in high northern latitudes. The strongest temperature seasonality is reserved for interior areas of the great land masses of Asia and North America, reflecting the continentality of the climate of these regions. Nearly all of the tropical regions of the world have a temperature amplitude of less than 5°C.

The precipitation seasonality index (Figure 2.6b) is similarly calculated by fitting a sine curve to the annual cycle of precipitation, although in this case the amplitude is expressed as a percentage of the mean monthly precipitation. In the case of precipitation there are some regions which display a strong bimodality in precipitation, with two wet seasons and two dry seasons. Such regions are not well-defined using the above index, and are found notably in equatorial Africa, the Rockies of North America, and parts of eastern USA and southern Europe.

Figure 2.6c contrasts three regions of Africa in terms of precipitation seasonality. Niamey and Harare both have a strongly unimodal regime, although with contrasting phase, whereas Nairobi is bimodal – wet seasons occur between March and May and again between November and December.

Further reading

Byrne, R. (1992), Climatic change and the origins of agriculture, paper presented to the IBG Annual Conference, Swansea, 7–10 January 1992.

Mazrui, A.A. (1986), In search of self-reliance: capitalism without winter, in: Mazrui, A.A. (ed.), *The Africans: a Triple Heritage*, London: Guild Publishing, 213–239.

Barry, R.G. and Chorley, R.J. (1987), Climatic classification, in: Barry, R.G. and Chorley, R.J., *Atmosphere, Weather and Climate* (5th edition), London: Routledge, 411–427.

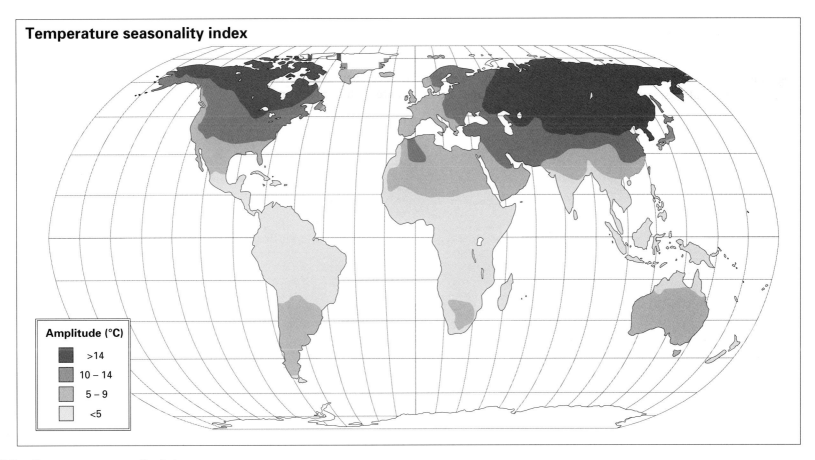

Figure 2.6a   Temperature seasonality index

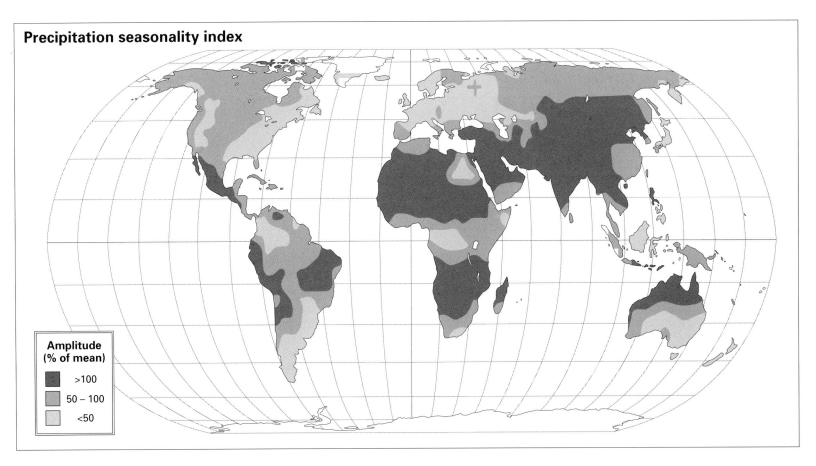

Figure 2.6b   Precipitation seasonality index

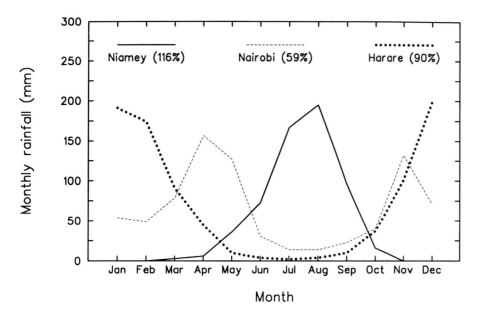

Figure 2.6c Annual cycle of precipitation at three contrasting African stations: Niamey (Niger), Nairobi (Kenya) and Harare (Zimbabwe), 1951–80. Note: The precipitation seasonality index for each station is shown in parenthesis

2.7 NATURAL DROUGHT AND FLOOD EVENTS
Mike Hulme

Many adverse influences of climate variability are related to regional or local precipitation anomalies whether these occur on short (e.g. intense rainstorms causing localised flooding), medium (e.g. seasonal drought leading to extensive crop failure), or long (e.g. sequences of successive years of below average rainfall as occurred from the late-1960s into the 1990s in the African Sahel) timescales. The most significant known natural cause of medium-term climate variability is the El Niño/Southern Oscillation (ENSO) which develops every three to seven years in the Pacific Ocean. ENSO events are characterised by a warming of sea surface temperatures (SSTs) in the eastern Pacific of up to several degrees Celsius and this large area of excess surface heat alters the circulation of much of the tropical atmosphere. Figure 2.7a displays regions of the world where negative (drought) and positive (flood) seasonal precipitation anomalies are most likely to occur during, or shortly after, ENSO events. Most of the well-identified regional precipitation anomalies associated with ENSO events are restricted to the tropics.

ENSO events have been recorded as far back as the 15th century (Enfield and Luis, 1991) and within the present century have recurred every three to seven years. The most severe ENSO event of recent decades occurred in 1982/83 and caused billions of dollars of damage both to the Australian economy, owing to prolonged drought, and to the Pacific states of South America owing to flooding and disruption of marine-related industries (Glantz *et al.*, 1991). Other recent ENSO episodes have occurred in 1986/87 and 1991/92, with the latter causing substantial agricultural damage in southeastern Africa owing to severe seasonal drought.

Rainfall in the Sahel of Africa is only slightly affected by ENSO events, yet this region has experienced the most substantial and long-term drought recorded since continuous instrumental observations began in the 19th century. Figure 2.7b shows the historical time series of annual rainfall anomalies from 1900 to 1992 for the Sahel region stretching from the Atlantic coast in Senegal and Mauritania to eastern Sudan and the Red Sea. The prolonged 25-year period of low rainfall totals commenced in the late-1960s and is in contrast to the two or three decades of relatively abundant rainfall which occurred towards the end of the colonial era in Africa. The three driest years recorded have been, in order of severity, 1984, 1983 and 1990. Although rainfall in the Sahel is only marginally related to ENSO events, recent work has shown the strong dependence of Sahel rainfall on SSTs in other regions of the world's oceans. In particular, when the southern oceans (South Atlantic, Indian and South Pacific Oceans) are warm relative to the northern oceans then drought conditions are experienced in the Sahel. This pattern of contrasting hemispheric sea surface temperature anomalies has persisted, with only small year-to-year changes, since the 1960s and is now widely believed to be a major cause of the persistence of the Sahel drought (Rowell *et al.*, 1992).

Further reading

Glantz, M.H., Katz, R.W. and Nicholls, N. (1991), *Teleconnections: linkages between ENSO, Worldwide Climate Anomalies and Societal Impacts*, Cambridge: Cambridge University Press.
IUCN (1989), *The IUCN Sahel Studies 1989*, Gland: IUCN.

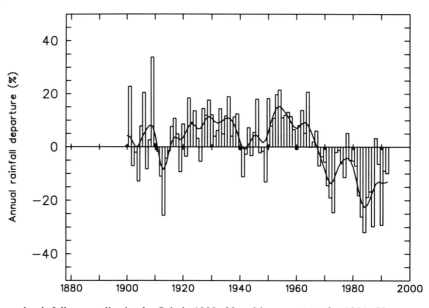

Figure 2.7b Annual rainfall anomalies in the Sahel, 1900–92, with respect to the 1951–80 mean

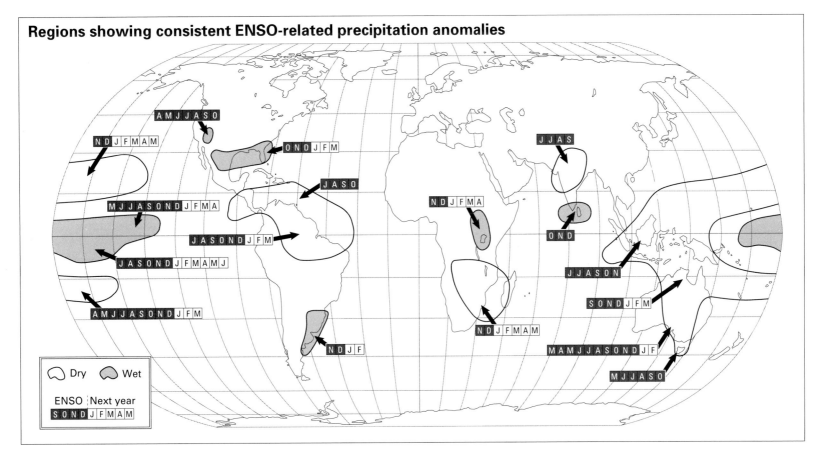

Figure 2.7a Regions showing consistent ENSO-related precipitation anomalies. Note: Letters indicate months

2.8 CLIMATIC CHANGE
Mike Hulme

Climates change on all timescales. The earth has experienced substantial changes in global-mean temperature during its history and the glacial and interglacial cycles of the Quaternary era (the last two million years) have been associated with fluctuations of up to 4° or 5°C in annually averaged global temperature. More recent changes have not been as substantial as these and the last 1000 years have produced fluctuations of perhaps ±0.3°C.

Recent compilations of historical records of both land and marine temperature data have enabled global-mean surface air temperature to be estimated quantitatively only since the mid-19th century. The longest and most carefully compiled global time series is shown in Figure 2.8a and covers the period 1854 to 1992 (Jones *et al.*, 1991). This record shows that the world has warmed by 0.45 ± 0.15°C since the late-19th century (Bloomfield, 1992), although this warming has not been continuous either through time or in space. Two periods of sustained warming have occurred – in the period from 1920 to 1940 and again since the mid-1970s. Indeed, the six warmest years in the record have all occurred since 1980, with 1990 being the single warmest year.

The variations in the spatial pattern of this temperature change are illustrated in Figure 2.8b. This shows the change in mean annual temperature from 1931–60 to 1961–90. The map indicates a substantial difference between the southern (warming) and northern (both warming and cooling) hemispheres. Certain land areas (e.g. central Africa and eastern USA) have cooled between these two 30-year periods, while other regions (most notably interior Asia) have warmed by more than 0.5°C.

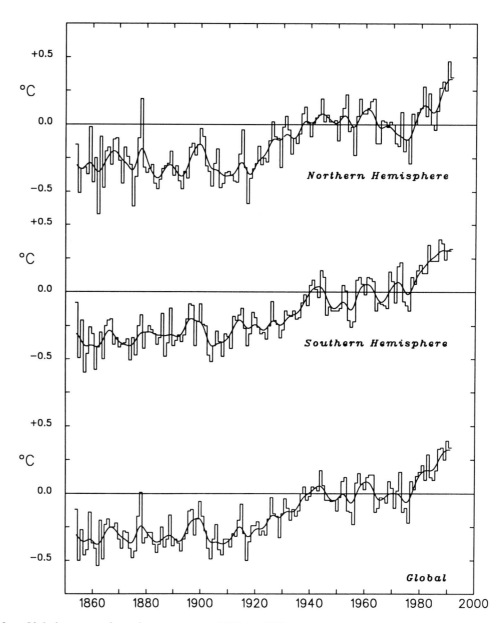

Figure 2.8a Global-mean surface air temperature, 1854 to 1992

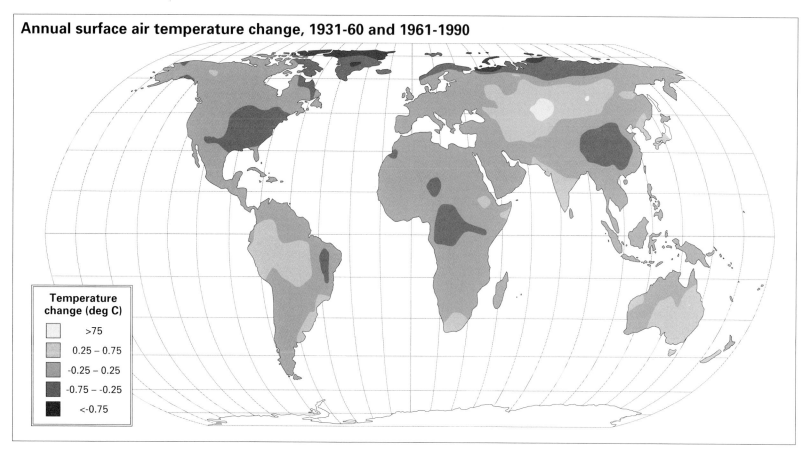

Figure 2.8b Annual surface air temperature change, 1931–1960 and 1961–1990

What do these changes in surface air temperature imply for climate change and, particularly, for the possibility of greenhouse-gas-induced warming? The warming of the earth over the last 13 or 14 decades of $0.45°C$ provides strong observational evidence of a genuine warming of global climate. Attributing the cause of this low-frequency variation unequivocally to the increasing global concentration of greenhouse gases nevertheless remains difficult. Recent work has attempted to quantify the effect on global temperatures of other known forcing mechanisms such as solar variability (both short and long-term), volcanic eruptions, ENSO events (Section 2.7), and the internal variability of the ocean-atmosphere system (Wigley and Raper, 1991). Although none of these mechanisms would, individually, appear sufficient to account for a $0.45°C$ warming, two problems continue to prevent us from determining the exact magnitude of the enhanced greenhouse effect.

First, the uncertainty in the observed warming of the global temperature series is $±0.15°C$. If the low end of this range is correct (i.e. a 1854–1992 warming of only $0.3°C$), then this magnitude of warming could yet be due to some combination of 'natural' forcing mechanisms. The other problem of course is that there may be other mechanisms at work forcing global climate, including feedbacks within the climate system, about which we currently have little knowledge. Statistical detection of the greenhouse effect from the observational record requires us to know clearly, and with some confidence, how such a forcing of *global* climate will manifest itself in *local and regional* characteristics.

Further reading

Houghton, J.T., Callendar, B.A. and Varney, S.K. (eds), (1992), *Climate Change 1992: the Supplementary Report to the IPCC Scientific Assessment*, Cambridge: Cambridge University Press.

Jones, P.D. and Briffa, K.R. (1992), Global surface air temperature variations: part I, the instrumental period, *Holocene*, 2: 174–188.

2.9 SEA LEVEL RISE AND GLOBAL WARMING
Mike Hulme

Natural variations in mean sea level are evident over a large range of time and space scales, from the diurnal pulse of tides to variations in global-mean sea level occurring over many millennia. With the prospect of future global warming as a result of human alteration of the composition of the atmosphere, there is an increased likelihood of future rises in global sea level which will be rapid by geological standards. There are four potential contributors to such a rise:

(1) *Thermal expansion of sea-water.* The oceans will expand as they warm. Even without the addition of more water, the ocean volume will increase as the temperature of the existing water mass is raised.

(2) *Mountain glaciers.* There are thousands of glaciers located in the mountains of the mid- and high-latitudes. Although such glaciers represent a tiny fraction (less than 1%) of all land ice in the world, they would still raise mean sea level by 30–60 cm if completely melted.

(3) *Greenland ice sheet.* By far the majority of the world's land-based ice is found in Greenland and Antarctica. In Greenland, a climate warming would be expected to increase the area of the ice sheet subject to melting, increase melt rates and slowly decrease the total ice mass.

(4) *Antarctic ice sheets.* In Antarctica, where about 90% of the world's land ice is located, the climate is much colder. Relatively speaking, very little direct melting and runoff to the sea occurs. Antarctic ice is lost primarily through calving (the breaking off of icebergs).

For the Antarctic ice sheet as a whole, changes in the rate of accumulation of ice are likely to be more important than ice losses. The extreme cold over Antarctica limits precipitation. Many glaciologists believe that a warmer climate would increase precipitation rates, and thus ice accumulation, over the ice sheets which would decrease sea level.

What about the future? The past provides some clues. Since global-mean temperature over the last 130 years has risen by about 0.5°C, one might expect that sea level has also been rising. Analyses of tide gauge records from all over the world suggest that this is indeed the case: 10–20 cm over the last 100 years (or 1.0 to 2.0 mm per year) (Figure 2.9a). Various studies suggest that this rise has been due largely to oceanic thermal expansion and retreating mountain glaciers. This finding supports the idea of a global climate–sea level connection.

Predicting the future is far more difficult than explaining the past. There are two substantial sets of uncertainties: those associated with global warming itself, and those associated with relationships between climate and each of the four contributions to sea level rise noted above. By systematically choosing the set of assumptions most likely to give small changes, sea level is projected to rise only 6 cm by 2050 – a rate of rise similar to that observed over the last 100 years. If, however, assumptions at the other end of the range are chosen, sea level by 2050 will be about 42 cm higher than today – an implied rate of

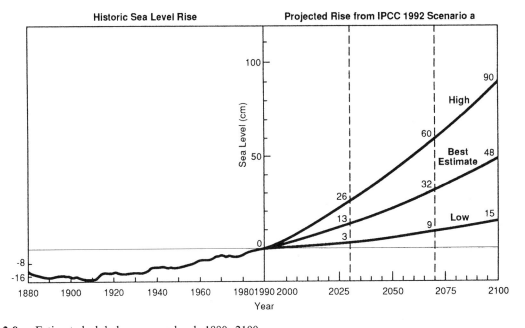

Figure 2.9a Estimated global-mean sea level, 1880–2100

change about seven times faster than in the recent past. Both of these possibilities should be considered extreme scenarios.

The best estimate is that global-mean sea level will be about 22 cm higher than today by 2050 (and around 50 cm higher by 2100). As shown in Figure 2.9b, this rise would be caused largely by thermal expansion of the oceans and by diminishing mountain glaciers. For the reasons

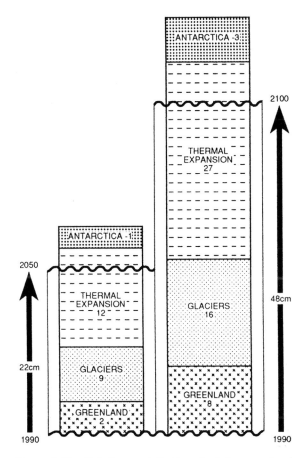

Figure 2.9b Relative contributions to future sea level rise (numbers are in cms)

suggested above, there is likely to be a net gain of ice in Antarctica, although this is more than cancelled out by the positive contribution from Greenland. The total rise in global-mean sea level implies a rate of change nearly four times faster than that which the world has been recently experiencing. Some of the impacts of such a sea level rise can be illustrated through the examples of the Nile and Ganges deltas.

The Nile Delta Over 3.2 million people and 70% of Egypt's industry are located in Alexandria below the one metre mean sea level mark. The Nile delta, including Alexandria, is particularly vulnerable to the increased storm surges and flooding that would result from a rise in sea level. Coastal erosion along the Nile delta resulting from a one metre rise in mean sea level would cause the loss of about 100 km^2 of land. Parts of the delta and Alexandria would be inundated, seriously affecting about five million people (10% of Egypt's population).

The Ganges Delta Over 110 million people in Bangladesh live in an area of 144 000 km^2. Two of the country's major ports are on the coast, as are the major tourist beach at Cox's Bazaar, the world's largest mangrove swamp (the Sundarbans), a number of islands, extensive shrimp farms and other agricultural areas. While all of these are likely to be at risk from a sea level rise, the impacts will not be restricted to the coastal zone. Over 10% of the nation's land would be lost through a one metre rise in sea level. Retreat from the coastal zone is not a practical solution because of the high population density. Levees could be built along the river banks, although this would starve the fertile agricultural flood plains of needed nutrients. More substantial coastal protection for the major industrial and commercial areas would require substantial external finance and technical assistance.

Further reading

Coastal Zone Management Subgroup (1992), *Global Climate Change and the Rising Challenge of the Sea*, The Hague: Ministry of Transport, Public Works and Water Management.

Milliman, J.D., Broadus, J.M. and Gable, F. (1989), Environmental and economic implications of rising sea level and subsiding deltas: the Nile and Bengal examples, *Ambio*, **18**: 340–345.

Warrick, R.A., Barrow, E.M. and Wigley, T.M.L. (1993), *Climate and Sea Level Change*, Cambridge: Cambridge University Press.

2.10 POTENTIAL NATURAL VEGETATION
J.E. Hossell

At a global scale, climate is one of the key factors which determine the distribution of natural ecosystems. Climate has long been recognised as an important influence on vegetation location, both directly through its effects on plant growth and reproduction and, indirectly, through the effects on soil formation and the breakdown of organic matter in soils. Each plant species has associated with it a particular combination of climatic factors most favourable to its growth, as well as certain extremes of heat, cold, drought or moisture beyond which it cannot survive. Hence, at the broad-scale the distribution of major vegetation types or biomes is roughly in equilibrium with the present climate, though locally it has been extensively disturbed by human actions.

The concept of the determination of vegetation patterns by climate forms the basis for a number of classifications of global biomes (Holdridge, 1964; Whittaker, 1975; Woodward, 1987). One such distribution, a modified Holdridge Life Zone Classification, is illustrated in Figures 2.10a and 2.10b (Leemans, 1990). It provides an indication of the potential vegetation types and their distributions under undisturbed conditions and is based on the assumption that the climax vegetation of a region can be defined objectively by its climate. For the Holdridge Classification the variables used are based on a combination of three readily available climatic parameters: biotemperature, mean annual precipitation, and a potential evapotranspiration ratio.

Biotemperature is the sum of daily mean temperatures between $0°C$ and $30°C$, which is divided by the number of days in the year. Height zones are also included to account for the influence of altitude on temperatures and, hence, vegetation. Biotemperature, thus, delimits the latitudinal or altitudinal bands of the life zones by providing an indication of the growing season length and intensity. For example, in tropical areas the classification delimits areas where there is no end to the growing period, as with Tropical Rain Forest, from areas where cooler temperatures caused by variation in the height of the sun's path during the year, result in a seasonal influence on growth patterns, as with Tropical Seasonal Forest or Temperate Forest.

Annual precipitation and potential evapotranspiration provide an indication of the moisture and humidity levels in an area and enable areas of drought tolerant species, such as Tundra or Hot Desert, to be delimited from areas where the flora has higher moisture requirements, such as Tropical Rain Forest or Warm Temperate Forest.

The name given to each of the life zones is designed to indicate the vegetation associations within it. The Life Zone Model can provide an accurate indication of tropical vegetation, mediterranean zones and boreal zones. It also accurately reflects the life zones of mountainous areas, but is less accurate where soil and soil-moisture conditions provide a strong limit to vegetation type.

Further reading

Carter, R.N. and Prince, S.D. (1985), The effect of climate on plant distributions, in Tooley, M.J. and Sheail, G.M. (eds), *The Climatic Scene*, London: George Allen and Unwin, 234–254.

Holdridge, L.R. (1947), Determination of world plant formations from simple climatic data, *Science*, **105**: 367–368.

Holdridge, L.R. (1964), *Life Zone Ecology,* San José, Costa Rica: Tropical Science Centre.

Leemans, R. (1990), Possible changes in natural vegetation patterns due to global warming, Laxenburg, Austria: International Institute for Applied Systems Analysis, Biosphere Dynamics Project (Publication No. 108).

Whittaker, R.H. (1975), *Communities and Ecosystems*, New York: Macmillan, 2nd ed.

Woodward, F.I. (1987), *Climate and Plant Distribution*, Cambridge: Cambridge University Press.

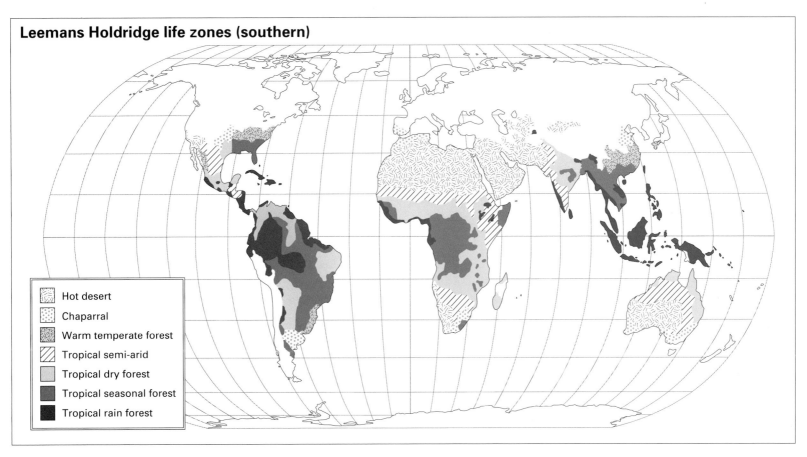

Figure 2.10a Holdridge Life Zones, southern

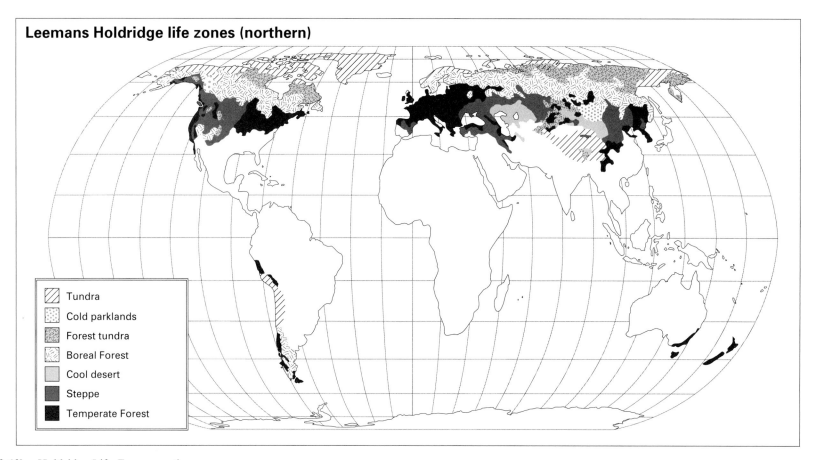

Figure 2.10b   Holdridge Life Zones, northern

2.11 VEGETATION CHANGE: THE AMAZON FOREST
Peter Furley

The Amazon Basin contains by far the largest stretch of tropical forest, representing around one third of existing world resources. Although, for much of the area, Amazonia is not amongst the most biologically diverse of forests, its sheer size means that a high proportion of global biodiversity lies within its borders.

The Amazon forest is shared by nine countries dominated by Brazil (Figure 2.11a). Although the extent of destruction is less than some other parts of the world, the rate is accelerating and the processes responsible appear unstoppable (Figure 2.11b). A recent satellite study indicates total deforestation of *c.* 400 000 km^2, whilst the average annual loss is estimated at *c.* 21 218 km^2.

Discussion of tropical forest issues tends to make the false assumption that the biome is fairly uniform. Many people equate tropical forest with tropical rain forest, but continuous purely evergreen tracts are rare, since there are many inclusions of semi-deciduous forest in drier tracts, or on more fertile soils. Equally, there are patches of wet forest – ranging from semi-permanent wetlands such as the Pantanal, swamp forest and flooded riverine plains to brackish and saline coastal mangroves. Similarly there are coastal forests of great beauty and diversity, such as the Atlantic forest in Brazil, which survives only in fragments. These and the remaining patches of deciduous forest are far more endangered than the mass of evergreen forest. All forests are being inexorably consumed by processes which seem, at present, irreversible.

The forest disturbance includes both government directed schemes and spontaneous occupation. Most governments are well aware of the issues of deforestation, particularly since UNCED in Rio, 1992, but look on the forests as a major resource to be developed. In Brazil, until recently, tax concessions were given for forest clearance as a means of furthering 'development' – allowing greater political control, opening up of isolated areas and mineral resources or, misguidedly, hoping for commercial returns from agropastoral expansion. Most deforestation in the Brazilian Amazon has been for cattle ranching or for mining.

Most of the land use strategies adopted so far appear to be unsustainable. Pastures degrade rapidly and require capital inputs for re-seeding, fertilisation, weed control, animal welfare as well as transport to markets. Commercial cultivation, except in small patches of more fertile soil with consistent water supplies, has not been demonstrated to be economic without subsidies. Smallholder agriculture, either through the government colonisation agency INCRA or spontaneous squatter occupation, hangs precariously at a near-subsistence level. Although the best option for the peasant farmer, it has been shown to devour forest constantly.

Even slight disturbances can affect the regenerative capabilities of tropical forests. Whereas shifting cultivation, at small scale and at infrequent intervals, reproduces the gap ecology of natural forests and is relatively quickly absorbed, increases in the clearing intensity and frequency result in the drying of land surfaces often forming impermeable crusts and increasing runoff. Organic matter oxidises, losing nutrient and water storage capacity; short lived seeds cease to be viable and the potential for regeneration progressively decreases. Since the rainfall of humid tropical areas is frequently derived from the evapotranspiration of adjacent tracts of forest, deforestation reduces water availability.

The impact on indigenous societies is profound. From possibly five to ten million Amazonian indians at the time of the Conquest, the numbers have been reduced to less than quarter of a million. The knowledge and management skills of indigenous people are only just beginning to be appreciated.

The current status of tropical forest is critical. It will take more than political gestures, such as those at UNCED, to protect such areas. Better methods of valuing the tropical forest, better understanding of the knowledge possessed by native people, better knowledge of the complexity and possibilities of resource management, and, above all, a real commitment by governments will be necessary to prevent the constant attrition of the world's richest biological resource.

Further reading

Cleary, D. (1991), *The Brazilian Rainforest: Politics, Finance, Mining and the Environment*, London: Economist Intelligence Unit, Special Report 2100.

Eden, M.J. (1990), *Ecology and Land Management in Amazonia*, London: Belhaven Press.

Furley, P.A. (1993), Tropical moist forests: transformation or conservation?, in: Roberts, N. (ed.), *The Changing Global Environment*, Oxford: Basil Blackwell.

Goodman, D. and Hall, A. (eds) (1990), *The Future of Amazonia: Destruction or Sustainable Development?*, London: Macmillan.

Hecht, S. and Cockburn, A. (1990), *The Fate of the Forest*, London: Penguin.

Peters, C.M., Gentry, A.H. and Mendelsohn, R.O. (1989), Valuation of an Amazonian rainforest, *Nature*, **339**: 655–656.

Posey, D. and Balee, W. (eds) (1989), Resource management in Amazonia: indigenous and folk strategies, *Advances in Economic Botany*, **7**: 1–240.

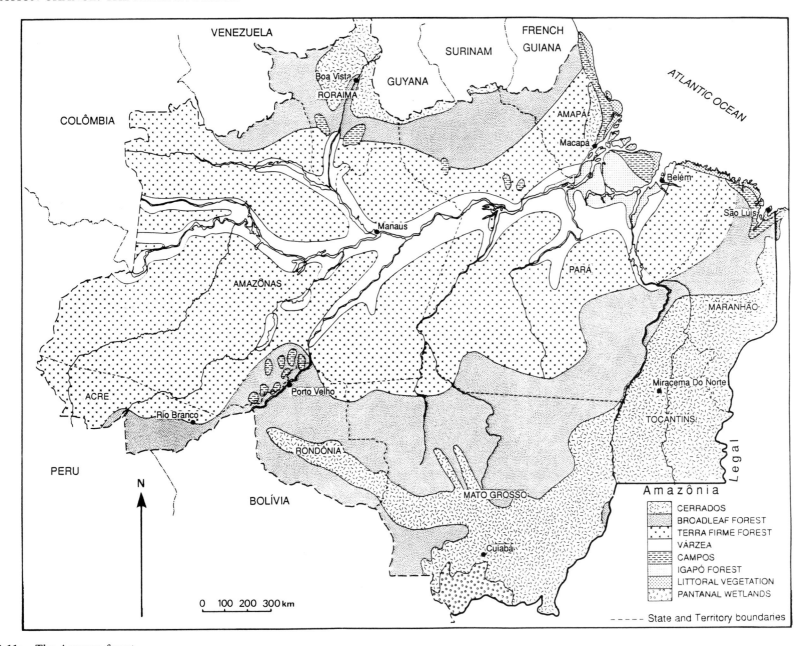

Figure 2.11a The Amazon forest

DEFORESTATION RATES

Ivory Coast	15.6%
Nigeria	14.3%
Madagascar	8.3%
Thailand	8.1%
Vietnam	5.8%
Philippines	5.4%
Mexico	4.2%
Ecuador	4.0%
Central America	3.7%
Burma	3.3%
Malaysia	3.1%
Colombia	2.8%
India	2.4%
Brazil	2.3%
Bolivia	2.1%
Indonesia	1.5%
Laos	1.5%
Cameroon	1.2%
Papua New Guinea	1.0%
Congo	0.8%
Kampuchea	0.75%
Peru	0.7%
Venezuela	0.4%
Zaire	0.4%
Gabon	0.3%
Guyanas	0.12%

Biome Average 1.8%

Rate (%)

TROPICAL DEFORESTATION: 10 LEADING COUNTRIES

Brazil
Burma
Colombia
India
Indonesia
Malaysia
Mexico
Nigeria
Thailand
Zaire

106,300 sq. kms.,
77% of total

OtherCountries
32,300 sq. kms.,
23% of total

Figure 2.11b   Rates of deforestation

2.12 ENVIRONMENTAL CRISIS
Michael Stocking

'Environmental crisis' goes by many names – drought, famine, desertification, soil degradation, erosion. It is an emotive term, redolent of images of the collapse of human society, of starving children, of desperate people caught up in environmental tragedy exacerbated by crime, war and corruption. The message to the developed world is 'do something'; 'here is a situation you have created – colonialism, the debt burden, unequal terms of trade, exploitation of natural resources'. It is enhanced environmental blackmail. Most blackmail, however, has a kernel of truth. For the developing world, environmental crisis is part of the reality of a struggle for existence; a struggle between an environment that is fast deteriorating and a people who have no choice but to utilise that environment in a damaging way.

In this environment of development, with confusing messages and sometimes deliberate distortions, it is essential to identify key indicators of environmental change and to consider how they might be measured in practical, unambiguous and comparatively accurate ways:

(1) *Land degradation* – the term most commonly used to describe the central process of environmental degradation. Defined as the loss of the productive capacity of the land to sustain life. Impossible to measure in a single variable.

(2) *Desertification* – a term grossly misused; refers primarily to land degradation in drylands caused by human agency. Again, impossible to measure simply.

(3) *Soil degradation* – a reduction in soil quality caused by any one or a combination of wind and water erosion, salinisation and sodicity, chemical change, physical and structural deterioration or biological change. FAO (1979) specifies sets of measurements for each of these processes.

(4) *Soil productivity loss* – productivity is the potential for future production; it is very close to the concept of 'sustainability', indicating an assurance that the quality of the resource base is maintained and the necessary inputs can continue to be provided. Loss in soil productivity occurs through any of the processes of soil degradation. It may be reversible, given time. A number of proxy measures are possible: historical and current crop yield or biomass production are useful indicators;

measures of nutrient loss or particular soil variables such as infiltration, rooting volume, soil depth are also relevant.

Estimates of the extent of soil or land degradation must be treated with extreme caution. Consistent data are unavailable or unverifiable. FAO (1990) estimates that between 50 000 and 70 000 km^2 go out of production through land degradation in sub-Saharan Africa every year. WRI (1990) reckons that 10% of the world's land surface has been transformed from productive use to desert and up to 25% more is at risk. However, the maps of suspended sediment yield from

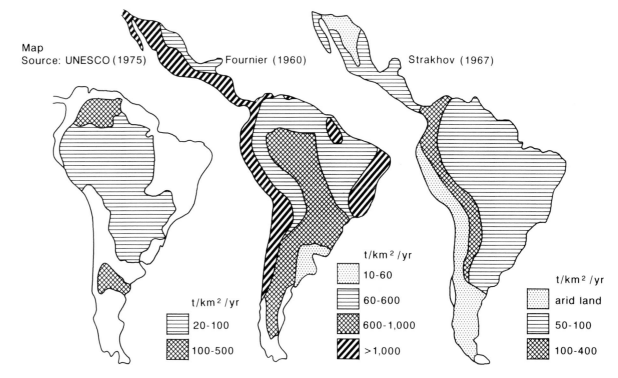

Figure 2.12a Suspended sediment yields in South America: a comparison of published estimates by three authors

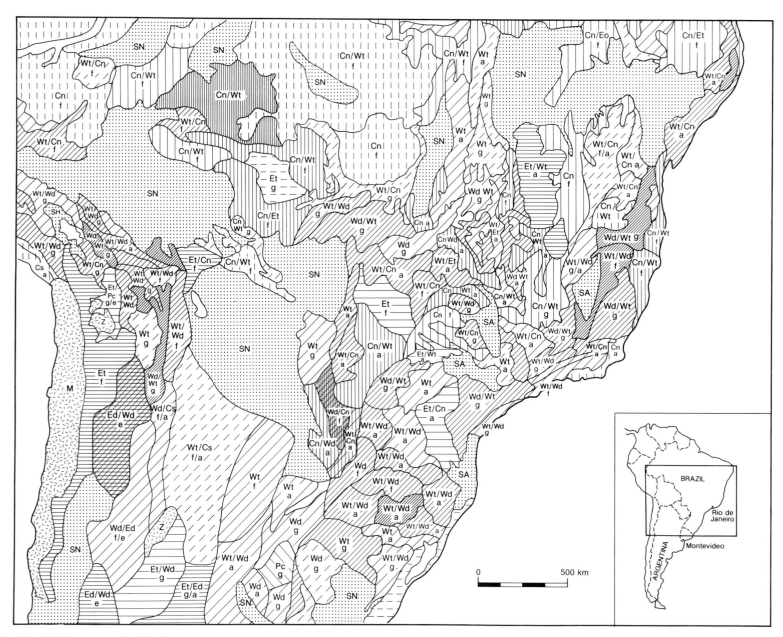

Figure 2.12b   Simplified extract of Global Assessment of Soil Degradation map for South America

DEGRADATION SEVERITY

	LOW	MEDIUM	HIGH	VERY HIGH

WATER EROSION

WIND EROSION

CHEMICAL DETERIORATION

PHYSICAL DETERIORATION

STABLE TERRAIN   NON-USED WASTELAND

SOIL DEGRADATION TYPES

WATER EROSION
Wt loss of topsoil
Wd terrain deformation/
        mass movement

CHEMICAL DETERIORATION
Cn loss of nutrients/
              organic matter
Cs salinization
Ca acidification
Cp pollution

WIND EROSION
Et loss of topsoil
Ed terrain deformation
Eo overblowing

PHYSICAL DETERIORATION
Pc compaction/crusting
Pw waterlogging
Ps subsidence of organic
        soils

STABLE TERRAIN
SN stable under natural conditions
SA stable with permanent agriculture
SH stabilized by human intervention

NON-USED WASTELAND
D active dunes
Z salt flats
R rock outcrops
A deserts
G ice caps
M arid mountain regions

CAUSATIVE FACTORS

f deforestation and removal of the natural vegetation
a agricultural activities
e overexploitation of vegetation for domestic use

g overgrazing
i (bio)industrial activities

Figure 2.12b (*continued*)

erosion in South America (Figure 2.12a) — all derived from essentially the same information — are an important lesson in showing the variable interpretations of 'crisis'. The patterns of erosion and the orders of magnitude, because of different ways of analysing the data, are quite different.

Two international co-operative efforts have been undertaken to estimate soil degradation at a regional scale. The first, completed in 1979, by the UN Food and Agriculture Organization was the only attempt to measure, map and integrate into degrees of seriousness the various processes of soil degradation. Although there are some fundamental flaws in the methodology, it was a pioneering effort. The more recent attempt, known as GLASOD (Global Assessment of Soil Degradation), uses an 'expert-system' approach where over 250 soil and environmental scientists co-operated with 21 regional correlators to prepare a set of world maps on the status of human-induced soil degradation. At this scale, the GLASOD objective is to 'strengthen the awareness of policy-makers and decision-makers of the dangers resulting from inappropriate land and soil management, leading to a basis for the establishment of priorities for action programmes' (Figure 2.12b shows a simplified extract for South America).

The missing ingredient in such assessments is how degradation translates to the most important crisis indicator in the minds of rural land users: immediate production and longer-term productivity. Trends in the relationship between soil erosion and crop growth are being researched worldwide. Most tropical and subtropical soils are known to be extremely susceptible to declining yields with only mild levels of soil degradation. This information is yet to be systematically collected. What we do know is that the environment of the developing world and the people who live in it are critically dependent upon maintaining the quality and performance of the natural resource base.

Further reading

Blaikie, P. and Brookfield, H. (1987), *Land Degradation and Society*, London: Methuen.

FAO (Food and Agriculture Organization) (1979), *A Provisional Methodology for Soil Degradation Assessment. FAO/UNEP/UNESCO Report with Mapping of Soil Degradation of Africa North of the Equator and the Middle East*. Rome: Food and Agriculture Organisation.

IFAD (International Fund for Agricultural Development) (1992), *Soil and Water Conservation in Sub-Saharan Africa. Towards Sustainable Production by the Rural Poor. A Report Prepared by the Centre for Development Cooperation Services, Free University, Amsterdam*, Rome: International Fund for Agricultural Development.

Oldeman, L.R., Hakkeling, R.T.A. and Sombroek, W.G. (1990), *World Map on the Status of Human-Induced Soil Degradation. At a Scale of 1:10 Million with Explanatory Note*, Wageningen: International Soil Reference and Information Centre.

Warren, A. and Khogali, M. (1992), *Assessment of Desertification and Drought in the Sudano-Sahelian Region, 1985–1991*, New York: United Nations Sudano-Sahelian Office, UNDP.

2.13 ENVIRONMENTAL CHANGE AND SMALL ISLAND ECOSYSTEMS
Duncan McGregor

Small islands are particularly sensitive to environmental change. Biological vulnerability is high, as specialised habitats may be very small in area and may be unique to one or two locations. A relatively high degree of endemism is common, particularly as the limited range of habitats may discourage incoming species. MacArthur (1972) demonstrates effectively the influence of island size on species diversity (Figure 2.13a). Thus, disturbance or habitat destruction may more easily affect or destroy particular populations than in larger land masses. Dispersal is also limited, the surrounding sea acting as a barrier to most organisms. Not only is the small size of the island area critical, but the effects of human interference are disproportionately higher than within a continental area. The small island has limited capacity for freshwater storage, small and short catchments (leading to higher environmental sensitivity), and a relatively high vulnerability to extreme natural events which may affect much or all of the island (such as hurricane, volcanic eruption or tsunami).

Human-induced environmental change has radically affected island ecosystems in the past. For example, Watts (1987) demonstrates how the introduction of plantation monoculture has impoverished the native fauna and flora in the West Indies, and has led in many instances to severe land degradation. Forest removal has also been shown (Lugo, 1990) in the case of St Vincent to have a significantly reducing effect on stream fauna.

For the immediate future, a particular problem is potential sea level rise, forecast by global warming scenarios. Recent estimates (IPCC 1990, 1992) forecast significant rises in sea levels throughout the 21st century, which would lead to the partial or total submergence of many tropical small islands and the destruction of many habitats. In particular, significant rises in sea level would inundate low-lying areas, drown coastal wetlands, erode shorelines (perhaps by hundreds of metres in extreme cases of gently-shelving beach), increase coastal flooding, and raise the salinity of rivers, bays and aquifers in coastal areas. Also, by drowning fringing reefs, the potential for storm surge damage would be significantly increased. The inundation of coastal wetlands will be particularly significant, as these form an important resource for wildlife and plantlife, including mangrove, and also act as a sediment trap, preventing much eroded material being lost out to sea. As such, they are often drained and converted to agricultural land. Inundation and salinisation may destroy this resource, particularly as in many small islands there is no possibility of the wetland migrating inland.

Island groups particularly at risk include (in the Indian Ocean) the Maldives, the Seychelles and adjacent island groups such as the Amorantes, the Cocos and Keeling Islands; (in the Pacific) the Marshall Islands, Tokelau, Kiribati and Tuvalu; and (in the Caribbean) the Bahamas, the Turks and Caicos Islands and the Caymans. Grand Cayman serves as an example (Figure 2.13b). All but the eastern end of the island is at risk from a combination of a rise in sea level and reef drowning. The area at risk includes the majority of human settlement and significant concentrations of mangrove forest (*c.* 11 000 ha). The reefs

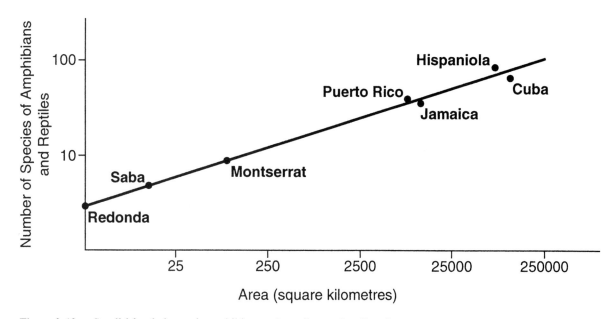

Figure 2.13a Small island size and amphibian and reptile species diversity

which fringe Grand Cayman have already been significantly damaged by cruise ship anchorage, and are as a result less likely to be able to respond to the effects of environmental change, such as sea level rise.

Coral reefs and atolls are particularly vulnerable to environmental change. Ecologically, they are areas of high biological activity, important in food chains and as support structures for marine life. Environmentally, they protect the shoreline from storm-driven high-energy ocean swell and waves. The reduction in productivity or destruction of live coral occurs by a wide variety of sources, but typically by onshore environmental changes inducing siltation or pollution. If, critically, the rate of sea level rise is greater than the growth of coral, fringing reefs will be drowned progressively, and the landward area will be increasingly susceptible to storm damage. In extreme cases of low-lying islands, complete obliteration of the land area may result unless expensive protective measures are implemented. In some coastal areas, for example the Caribbean, IPCC estimates indicate that this may be accentuated by changes in storm patterns and an increased risk of extreme events damaging these fragile ecosystems.

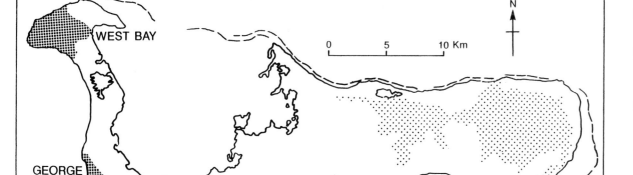

Further reading

IPCC (Intergovernmental Panel on Climatic Change) (1990), *Climatic Change: the IPCC Scientific Assessment*, Cambridge: Cambridge University Press.

IPCC (Intergovernmental Panel on Climatic Change) (1992), *Climatic Change 1992: the Supplementary Report to the IPCC Scientific Assessment*, Cambridge: Cambridge University Press.

Lugo, A.E. (1990), Development, forestry, and environmental quality in the eastern Caribbean, in: Beller,W., d'Ayala, P. and Hein, P. (eds), *Sustainable Development and Environmental Management of Small Islands*, Carnwath: Parthenon Publishing, 317–342.

MacArthur, R.H. (1972), *Geographical Ecology*, New York: Harper & Row.

Watts, D. (1987), *The West Indies: Patterns of Development, Culture and Environmental Change Since 1492*, Cambridge: Cambridge University Press.

Figure 2.13b Grand Cayman, Caribbean: land below six metres at risk from sea level rise and increased storminess

2.14 ENVIRONMENTAL MANAGEMENT OF HUMID TROPICAL HILLSIDES
Duncan McGregor

Humid tropical hillsides are notoriously suscept-ible to degradation. Accelerated soil erosion and the accompanying impoverishment of soil through nutrient losses is the natural consequence of clearing natural vegetation. Land degradation may become extreme, as illustrated by the case of Haiti (Paskett and Philoctete, 1990). A wide vari-ety of environment management schemes is avail-able, a number of which have been applied in the case of Jamaica (Sheng, 1972, 1981). However, the Jamaican case also illustrates the pitfalls which attend such management schemes (Figure 2.14a).

Over 200 years of inappropriate land use, a combination of coffee monoculture and intense subsistence cropping, had led by the 1940s to chronic land degradation and entrenched rural poverty. A number of land authority schemes were initiated in 1951, of which that in the Yallahs Valley, on the southern flank of the Blue Moun-tains, is the best documented. As reported in McGregor and Barker (1991), the land authority schemes were initially successful. However, despite a well thought out scheme of integrated rural development planning and 20 years of finan-cial input, the situation on rural hillsides in the Yallahs Valley is little better today than in the 1940s. The agricultural system is in such decline that it is unable to withstand extreme natural events. Hurricane Gilbert, in September 1988, dis-rupted domestic agriculture to a significant extent (Table 2.14a). The reasons for this failure are complex, but undoubtedly partly financial – ending of funding for the installation of structures, lack of funding for the upkeep of

Table 2.14a Environmental management of humid tropical hillsides

	1987	1988	1989	1990	1991
(i) Jamaica – volume of major agricultural export (tonnes)					
Sugar	133 549	153 024	132 332	146 359	157 181
Banana	33 778	28 050	41 628	61 066	75 290
Citrus	8307	10 870	5676	11 918	9985
Coffee	911	946	827	771	912
Coconut	21 176	21 729	9276	9373	12 569
(ii) Jamaica – output of selected domestic food crops (tonnes)					
Yam	175 592	166 831	133 255	161 428	186 104
Other tubers	43 781	39 437	32 236	35 049	34 336
Plantain	28 161	26 167	9914	27 562	26 692
Rice	2257	1731	516	219	562
Overall Total	437 603	387 989	351 600	411 150	415 416

Source: Planning Institute of Jamaica (1992)

structures, and the subsequent inability of farmers to generate sufficient funds to pay for new instal-lations. With the removal of financial incentives, the inducement for individual farmers to con-tribute finance or labour to the upkeep of integrated structures covering larger areas that might contain several properties is largely, if not entirely, negated.

Part of the problem also lies in the necessity for implementation of measures and strategies which the farmer understands and is prepared to operate, and which are consistent with the chronic labour shortages experienced in many Jamaican farming communities. The work of Sheng (1972, 1981), continuing to date at the Smithfield Experimental Station in northwest Jamaica, has demonstrated the effectiveness of a wide range of strategies for integrated soil conservation (*see* Figure 2.14b and Table 2.14b for examples). Yet the diffusion of this knowledge to farmers in the

east of Jamaica has been relatively minimal. Tra-ditional practices such as fire clearance and clean-weeding continue, and farmers' perception of the nature of soil erosion is poor. Relatively few farmers consider erosion to be a problem, and many feel that there is little they can do about it (McGregor and Barker, 1991). Yet surveys show that most farmers use at least one form of erosion

Table 2.14b Average mean dry soil loss, yams under soil conservation treatments

Treatment	Soil loss (tonnes/ha)
Bench terrace and continuous mounds	17.30
Hillside ditches and continuous mounds	27.18
Hillside ditches and individual mounds	39.54
No conservation structures	133.43

Source: data derived from unpublished statistics, Soil Conservation Division, Kingston, Jamaica control, inherited from the Land Authority schemes, and now being passed on to the next generation of farmers.

As Sheng (1972, 1981) suggests, almost any form of cultivation is likely to be uneconomical on these steep slopes. He quotes a threshold of 25° for any form of agriculture other than permanent tree crops. This immediately poses a dilemma as, typically, these watersheds are dominated by slopes above this threshold. As stated above, coffee monoculture has led to severe land degradation, while plantations such as eucalyptus have not proved to be economically successful in the Jamaican context. Food forest appears to be a practical management tool for the protection of

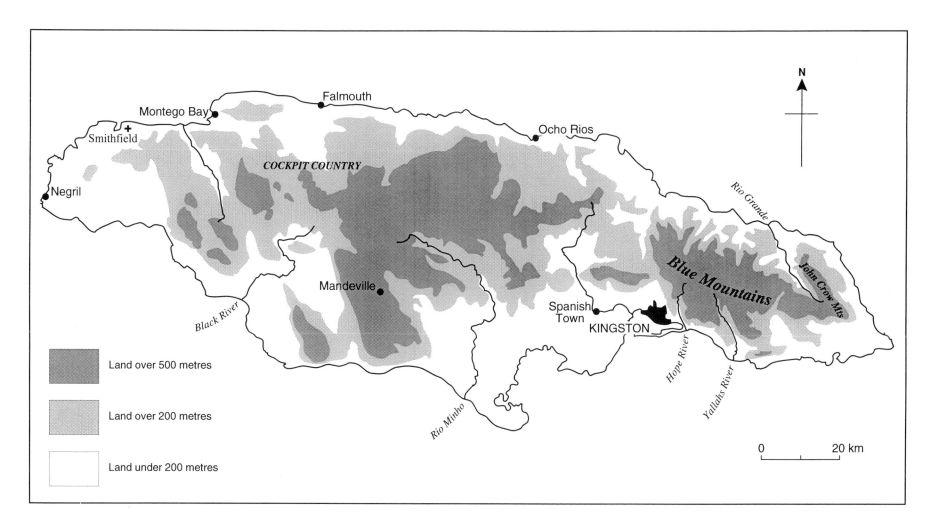

Figure 2.14a Jamaica

these vulnerable watersheds, since it effectively reduces runoff and soil loss on steep slopes compared with other types of cultivation. Food forest is a term used in the Caribbean to describe a particular agronomic practice whereby a large number of food-bearing plants are grown together in a multi-stratified manner. This is almost certainly an adaptation of the African agronomic practice of kitchen compound farming. In Jamaica, stratification commonly comprises tall trees such as coconut, mango and breadfruit;

bushes and tall grasses such as coffee, cocoa, cane and corn; and ground storey plants such as dasheen, beans, sweet potato, pumpkin, herbs and spices. Yet the potential of food forest as an environmental management technique remains to be researched properly. It is a technique which small farmers are familiar with, and understand intimately.

Perhaps the most significant conclusion regarding continuing environmental degradation is the difficulty of maintaining a mixed farming

system of any kind on steeply sloping terrain in the humid tropics. The exceptions worldwide to this are few – if spectacular. The installation even of fully integrated soil conservation systems offers little economic return. Bench terracing is the most effective single method of erosion control, but is not necessarily the most cost effective. The steeper the slope, the more land is lost in the terrace riser, and the more expensive and time-consuming upkeep becomes. At present, the Jamaican hillside farmer's choices of cropping systems are severely constrained, and are little more than survival strategies. The principal research need is to identify and encourage practical and effective techniques and cropping systems, and to discourage those with negative environmental impacts. The elusive problem is to mobilise the political will, through comprehensive development planning, to attempt to produce a more enduring solution.

Further reading

McGregor, D.F.M. and Barker. D. (1991) Land degradation and hillside farming in the Fall River Basin, Jamaica, *Applied Geography*, **11**: 143–156.

Paskett, C.J. and Philoctete, C.-E. (1990), Soil conservation in Haiti, *Journal of Soil and Water Conservation*, **45**: 457–459.

Sheng, T.C. (1972), A treatment-oriented land capability classification scheme for hilly marginal lands in the humid tropics, *Journal of the Science Research Council of Jamaica*, **3**: 93–112.

Sheng, T.C. (1981), The need for soil conservation structures for steep cultivated slopes in the humid tropics, in: Lal, R. and Russell, E.W. (eds), *Tropical Agricultural Hydrology*, Chichester: John Wiley, 357–372.

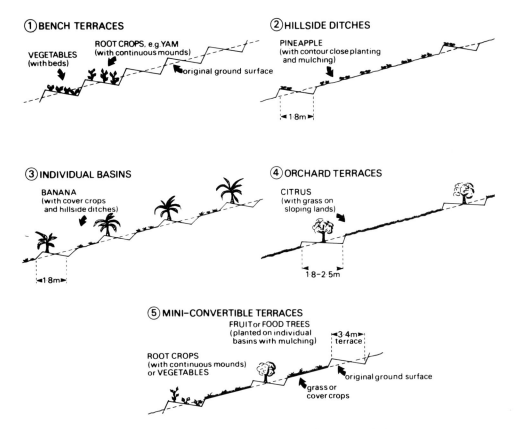

Figure 2.14b Integrated soil conservation strategies for steeply-sloping tropical hillsides

2.15 LOCAL PATTERNS OF EROSION CHANGE: SVOSVE COMMUNAL AREA, ZIMBABWE

Jennifer A. Elliott

Patterns of soil erosion can be studied at various scales. In Zimbabwe, much information is at the national level. In 1987, it was found from aerial photographs that 60% of the country experienced soil erosion of varying degrees. The African farming (communal) areas were identified as suffering much more severe levels than the large scale commercial sector. But ultimately, soil erosion is a problem in specific places and for particular people. Even within a community, some people will have the knowledge, power and resources to cope with soil erosion, whereas others will not. In order to understand the national pattern of erosion in Zimbabwe, it is necessary to pay greater attention to this complexity at the local level. In particular, it is necessary to identify the underlying processes operating and how these have changed over time.

Contemporary patterns of soil erosion are a product of a complex interaction of physical and human factors. These operate over a variety of spatial as well as temporal scales. Explanation of soil erosion at any one time in a specific location rests on an understanding of such diverse factors as rainfall erosivity, land tenure and conservation policies. Some of these factors may operate over very short time periods with an immediate influence on erosion status; others operate over much longer timescales. In addition, some are very site-specific, whilst others refer to wider regional or even international scales. All are factors which influence the land user in his or her decision-making and are therefore fundamental determinants of whether soil erosion occurs at the local scale.

Svosve communal area is situated 80 kms southeast of Harare. It has a population of around 5500. In 1944, the Native Commissioner for the region stated that due to the rocky and fragmented terrain, Svosve was quite useless for the 'advancement of the native today'. In the following year, he reported that he had seen gullies in Svosve big enough to hide trains in.

Today, these aspects of the physical environment continue to challenge administrators and farmers alike. Figure 2.15a shows the nature and extent of soil erosion in Svosve identified from air photography flown in 1947, just after the period for which the Native Commissioner was reporting. Gullying is seen to be prevalent, especially in the grazing areas. Figure 2.15b is a similar map based on photography for 1981. Many of the same scars of erosion can be identified. Table 2.15 quantifies the area subject to erosion for the two time periods. The overall extent of erosion in Svosve is seen to have been very stable despite significant changes in the contribution of erosion by type to the total.

Closer examination of Figures 2.15a and 2.15b shows that certain areas of Svosve have been subject to continued erosion, whilst some have shown regeneration. This confirms the spatial and temporal specificity of soil erosion in Svosve; it is not a ubiquitous problem, nor is it irreversible. In addition, some areas of Svosve which were in cultivation in 1947, were no longer classified as such in 1981. The explanation of these patterns lies in aspects of the historical, political-economic and cultural environment of Svosve which cannot be identified from air photography. For example, the Native Land Husbandry Act of 1951 led to a limited number of rights to cultivation being allocated to individual farmers in Svosve. In addition,

Table 2.15 Change in the nature and extent of soil erosion (hectares) in Svosve 1947–81

Type	1947	1981
Croplands		
Gully	89	42
Sheet/rilling	276	319
Grazing		
Gully	264	256
Sheet/rilling	313	326
Streambank	25	47
Dambo	98	71
Total	1065	1061

Source: Elliott, J.A. (1989)

any such explanation of the patterns of soil erosion at the local level, and indeed any proposed solution to the problem, requires an analysis which extends beyond the parochial boundaries.

Further reading

Blaikie, P. (1985), *The Political Economy of Soil Erosion in Developing Countries*, London: Longman.
Sill, M. (1992), Cultivating a new system, *Geographical Magazine*, **64**(5): 45–50.

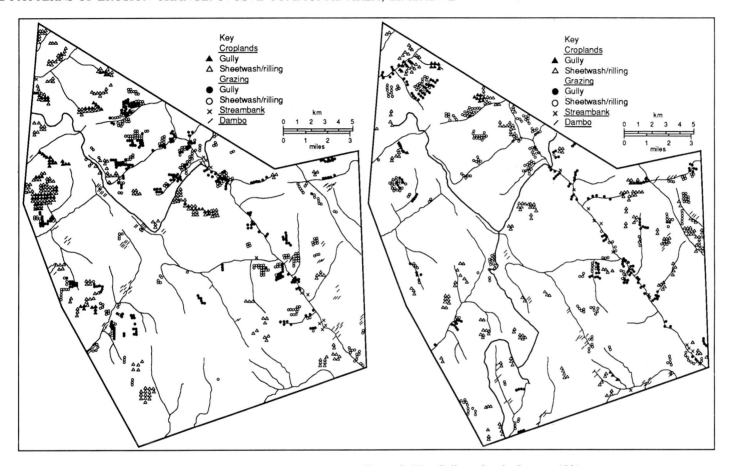

Figure 2.15a Soil erosion in Svosve, 1947   **Figure 2.15b** Soil erosion in Svosve, 1981

2.16 IRRIGATION IN SOUTH ASIA
Graham P. Chapman

The shaded area of Figure 2.16a shows the command areas (areas to which water *can* be distributed) of major irrigation schemes in India (note: Pakistani and Bangladeshi command areas are not shown on this map). There are many smaller local reservoirs, particularly in the hilly hard-rock areas of the Deccan, and in many areas there are in addition tube-wells and open wells. The major areas covered by large schemes are in the upper parts of the Ganges Valley. There was some slight development of canals here before the British period, but it is mostly in the last 100 or so years that these schemes have been implemented and continuously enlarged and developed. The climate in the upper parts of the valley is drier and less reliable than in the lower parts, such as Bengal and Bihar, and large tributaries of the Ganges and the main river itself offer obvious barrage off-take points as they flow from the Himalayas on to the plains. The flow is augmented by snow-melt throughout the low (non-monsoon season). It is ironic that the alluvial deposits of the Ganges Valley also contain substantial ground-water reserves, so that in a sense there is less need of major canal systems here than elsewhere. Rising water tables are, however, causing increasing problems of salinisation. Modern thinking stresses the need to use tube-wells in canal areas to help keep water tables lower. In peninsula India most of the water in the very seasonal east-flowing rivers has been tapped. Only the major west-flowing Narmada and Tapti lack much utilisation. Current plans for a massive project on the Narmada are in abeyance as environmentalists and local political movements battle with the State and Central Governments about the

environmental and human costs of the project, which could nevertheless bring huge benefits to Gujarat, Maharashtra and parts of Madhya Pradesh. In some parts of the drier interior Deccan tube-wells are effectively mining water – taking it out at greater rates than natural replenishment.

Figure 2.16b illustrates the irrigation schemes in the Punjab (meaning 'five rivers') now divided into Pakistani Punjab and Indian Punjab, which were started over 100 years ago by the British, when the Upper Bari Doab Canal was commissioned. Most of the initial development stressed the eastern three of the five rivers, the Sutlej, Beas and Ravi. But most of the water was in the western

rivers, the Chenab and the Jhelum. Link canals were built to ship water from the west to the east and by the time of independence in 1947 this was the world's largest integrated irrigation area. However, the new international frontier split the system in two, and hostility between India and Pakistan has meant that the scheme has had to be rent asunder – so note some canals are shown as no longer irrigating parts of Pakistan. Because of this and increased water demand and because of new technology, new storage dams have been built in the Himalayas on a massive scale (Tarbela is the world's largest rock-fill dam), and the Indus has now been linked with the rest of the system. The dams are also used for power generation and there is sometimes conflict of the timing of water releases for power and water for agriculture, which do not always coincide. Moreover, the longevity of the dams is in doubt because of the very high siltation rates of the rivers. Perhaps Tarbela will last as little as 50 years, certainly less than 100.

Further reading

Michel, A.A. (1967), *The Indus Rivers*, New Haven: Yale University Press.

Paranjpye, V. (1990), *High Dams on the Narmada*, New Delhi: India National Trust for Art and Cultural Heritage (Intach).

Rao, K.L. (1979), *India's Water Wealth*, New Delhi: Orient Longman.

Sinha, B. and Bhatia, R. (1984), *Economic Appraisal of Irrigation Projects in India*, New Delhi: Agricole Publishing.

Stone, I. (1984), *Canal Irrigation in British India*, Cambridge: Cambridge University Press.

Figure 2.16a The command areas of major irrigation schemes in India

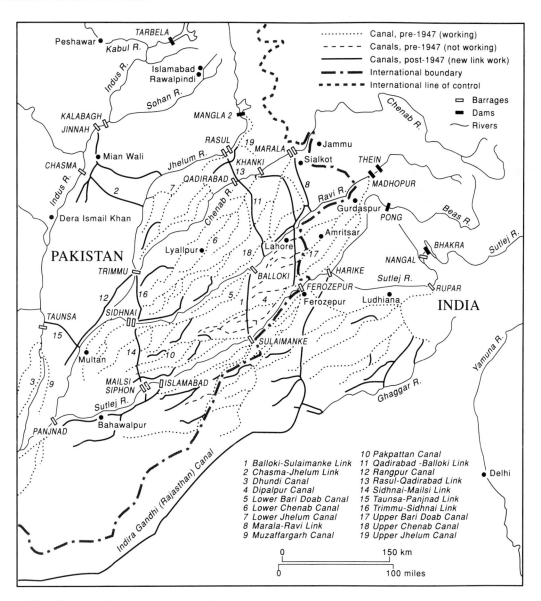

Figure 2.16b The irrigation schemes in the Punjab

2.17   URBAN AIR POLLUTION IN ASIA

Gordon Walker

Air quality is one of the many aspects of the environment which suffers from processes of economic development. Activities such as electricity generation from coal or oil, the movement of people and goods by road and rail, domestic heating and cooking and industrial processes, all generate a range of atmospheric pollutants. Concentrated in densely populated urban areas these pollutants can lead to a deterioration in air quality and to potentially serious impacts on the health of millions of people.

The rapidly growing and industrialising cities of Asia provide examples of some of the most severe of current urban air pollution problems. Figure 2.17 draws on recent data from the Global Environment Monitoring System (UNEP, 1991) for two pollutants: suspended particulate matter (SPM) and sulphur dioxide (SO_2). Both are chiefly associated with the combustion of fossil fuels and are often referred to as 'traditional' air pollutants. Independently and in combination SO_2 and SPM affect the respiratory tract, worsening respiratory illness and increasing respiratory symptoms (including chronic bronchitis) with short-term and long-term exposure.

The graphs in Figure 2.17 show average annual levels of SPM at a total of 41 monitoring stations in 12 of the largest cities in Asia. At 35 of these monitoring stations, World Health Organisation (WHO) guidelines for ambient SPM concentrations (indicated by the shading on the graphs) are exceeded. Cities in China, where heavily polluting coal is the most widely used domestic and industrial fuel, consistently show some of the worst levels of urban SPM pollution in the world. For

example, in Xian all four stations in the city exceed the WHO upper limit of 90 μgm^{-3} by over 500%. At one station in a residential part of the city centre an annual average of 658 μgm^{-3} was recorded with a massive peak value of 2574 μgm^{-3}. Cities in India also show high concentrations of SPM. This is in part due to the widespread domestic use of coal, but, for example, in Bombay much of the blame is also laid at the door of chemical, petrochemical and power production plants using inadequate, outdated or inefficient pollution control technology

(Centre for Science and Environment, India, 1989).

Results for the monitoring of SO_2 also show that WHO guidelines are being exceeded although less consistently and in fewer locations (the 12 stations marked with an 'x' in the bar diagrams on Figure 2.17). In cities such as Delhi and Beijing both SPM and SO_2 levels are high, potentially leading to acute health impacts through the synergistic effects of combined exposure. Such impacts will be felt hardest by the urban poor within these cities, who typically spend long periods 'outside',

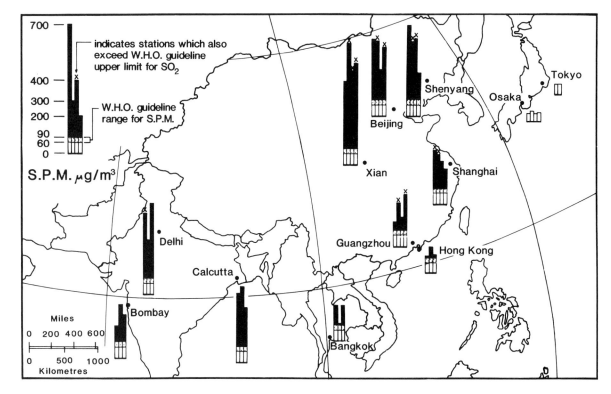

Figure 2.17   Average annual suspended particulate matter (SPM) concentrations at monitoring stations within selected cities

are more vulnerable due to generally poor health and live in marginal environments often associated with the close proximity of sources of pollution (Hardoy and Satterthwaite, 1989).

In stark contrast to the high pollution levels measured in the cities of China and India, are those of the more prosperous cities of Tokyo and Osaka in Japan, where, as in most of the cities of the developed world, SPM and SO_2 levels are consistently well under WHO guidelines. This suggests a relationship between poverty and pollution levels at a macro level, leading some to the conclusion that the best way to reduce pollution is to increase the rate of economic growth (*The Economist*, 1992a). Greater prosperity enables pollution control to be 'afforded' and given a higher priority within government programmes. However, this simplistic interpretation effectively condemns millions of city dwellers to breathe increasingly polluted air, until, in the long term, improvements can be afforded. It also ignores other less traditional forms of pollution (particularly those associated with traffic emissions) which show a positive rather than an inverse relationship with prosperity.

Further reading

Elsom, D. (1991), *Atmospheric Pollution – a Global Problem*, Oxford: Blackwell.
UNEP (United Nations Environment Programme) (1991), *Urban Air Pollution. UNEP/GEMS Environment Library No. 4*, Nairobi: UNEP.
UNEP (United Nations Environment Programme) (1992), *Urban Air Pollution in Megacities of the World*, Oxford: Blackwell.
World Resources Institute and International Institute for Environment and Development (1988), *World Resources 1988–89*, New York: Basic Books.

3 Population, Class and Education: the Social Structure of Development

TIM UNWIN

Demographic change is widely seen as one of the most important factors influencing development (Harrison, 1993). On the one hand neo-Malthusians have argued that increasing levels of famine and disease are a direct result of population increase, whereas others, such as Boserup (1965, 1981), have suggested in contrast that population growth often leads to technological changes enabling higher levels of population to be supported. This chapter therefore begins by a broad examination of global population change, concentrating on population densities, doubling times, fertility rates and family planning policies. Attention then shifts to an interpretation of evidence more overtly on the lived experiences of people, and the factors influencing their chances of survival. These are examined in sections on life expectancy and child survival rates, with Section 3.7 then pursuing the place of children at a regional level in Latin America. 'Development' is often seen as being closely synonymous with a rapid increase in urbanisation, and the implications of major urban population growth in many of the poorer countries of the world are therefore explored in Section 3.8.

In recent years there has been a growing awareness, not only among academics but also increasingly in international bodies such as the United Nations, that the benefits of capitalist economic growth have not been distributed equally. Consequently, greater attention is now being paid to the basic needs of people in poorer parts of the world, and this agenda is examined in three sections on immunisation programmes, access to safe water, and nutrition. Poverty itself is extremely hard to define and equally difficult to measure. However, Section 3.12 seeks to grapple with the distribution of poverty in order to help to identify the states and people in greatest need of such assistance.

There is widespread agreement that the concept of 'class' is a key category in understanding the way in which societies are structured. However, as with poverty it is an elusive concept. In particular, the idea of 'class' not only has social and economic attributes, but it is also centrally concerned with political and ideological expressions. One surrogate measure of class is provided by data on income, and Sections 3.13 and 3.14 examine income distribution at a global scale and then within the context of a single state, namely Indonesia. Closely related to definitions of class are concerns over employment and tenure, and these issues are therefore addressed in the ensuing three sections, drawing contrasts not only between rural and urban areas, but also between the richer and poorer parts of the world.

Human decision making is closely influenced both by people's perceptions and by the constraints within which they act. Sections 3.18 and 3.19 thus focus on two examples of perception, one in the context of a study of residential desirability in the Caribbean and the other drawn from research on pastoralists' perceptions of environmental resources in south-eastern Egypt. These both indicate a need for greater understanding between different groups of people involved in 'development', and the way in which education can serve to reduce the many misconceptions that frequently prevent the introduction of beneficial change. Another example of the way in which social factors can play an important part in determining the success of innovation adoption is provided by the analysis in Section 3.20 of the use of new rice technology by different groups of people in Asia. Education is central to the successful propagation of change, and the next three sections therefore examine the global distribution of educational provision in terms of basic literacy, school enrolment and higher education, revealing stark contrasts between levels of education in rich and poor countries.

The final sections of Chapter 3 explore other aspects of the social structure of development not fully addressed elsewhere. Section 3.24 thus focuses on an area of Cuzco department in southern Peru, illustrating how the structure of rural settlement and peasant lifestyles there result from a complex interaction between indigenous pre-Colombian social structures and the subsequent incorporation of the region into the global capitalist economy. Section 3.25 explores the influence of ethnic plurality on development in the context of Myanmar, and the final section of the chapter explores the social factors influencing the spread of the Human Immuno-deficiency Virus in a small region of Namibia.

3.1 GLOBAL POPULATION DENSITY
Tim Unwin

The balance between population levels and the capacity of the environment to support them lies at the heart of many theories of social and economic change (Grigg, 1982). However, it is extremely difficult to produce meaningful indices of this relationship. Population density by itself is widely used as an indicator of the actual carrying capacity of different parts of the world, but it takes no account of the quality of life of the people concerned. Moreover, maps of global population density, based on data at the scale of individual countries, fail to illustrate the very large variations in population density that can occur within particular states.

Malthus (1798), writing at the end of the 18th century, argued that the potential for human populations to expand was far greater than the potential for increases in agricultural production, and that both preventive and positive checks served to curb population growth once a ceiling, determined by the level of food production, had been reached. As global population levels have soared in the 20th century, and images of starving children have filled the television screens of those living in Europe and north America, such arguments have taken on a new poignancy. In particular, during the 1960s and 1970s a series of publications by neo-Malthusians, such as the Ehrlichs (1969) and Meadows *et al.* (1972), sought to show that unless dramatic measures were taken to reduce the level of population increase, very large numbers of people would imminently die from famine and disease. Despite such predictions, and an increase in global population from some 3.7 billion in 1970 to 5.5 billion in 1992,

levels of agricultural production have so far managed to keep pace. This evidence would, to some extent, seem to support critics of the neo-Malthusians, most notably Boserup (1965, 1981), who have argued that increases in population density, rather than being curtailed by the ability of the environment to support them, have actually been the main factor determining technological innovation and agrarian change (Unwin, 1988). This has, though, been at the cost of considerable environmental change, illustrated all too clearly by the destruction of forests, increased levels of pollution, depletion of renewable resources, and the complete transformation of food producing systems in many parts of the world (Harrison, 1993).

Despite the problems of interpreting global maps of population density, Figure 3.1 provides a basic overview of the considerable variations in density to be found in different parts of the world. At the extremes, there is frequently a negative relationship between the size of a country and its population density. Many of the world's largest states, such as the former Soviet Union, Canada, Brazil, and Australia, thus have relatively low overall population densities, although these frequently mask areas of high urban population density because of their inclusion of extensive tracts of very low density in deserts and mountainous regions. A clear exception to this generalisation is China with an area of some 9.6 million km^2 and yet a population density in 1991 of around 120 people per km^2. In contrast, those states with the highest population densities are almost all very small in size, such as Macão, Singapore, Hong Kong, Malta and Bahrain, where a particular economic niche has enabled a very high urban population density to be maintained. Again, an exception to this generalisation is Bangladesh, with a population density of about 810 people per

km^2, and yet an area of some 144 000 km^2. In terms of regional variation, Figure 3.1 indicates that in general Africa and the Americas have much lower population densities than south and east Asia and Europe. In part, this emphasises the very high absolute populations of China and India which between them have 37% of the world's population. However, the relatively dense populations of Europe also reflect the high levels of technology and inputs applied to its agricultural production, and the way in which European populations have for the past 500 years sought to exploit and then maintain a competitive advantage over those living in other parts of the world.

Further reading

Findlay, A. and Findlay, A. (1987), *Population and Development in the Third World*, London: Routledge.

Harrison, P. (1993), *The Third Revolution: Population, Environment and a Sustainable World*, Harmondsworth: Penguin.

Jones, H. (1990), *Population Geography*, London: Paul Chapman.

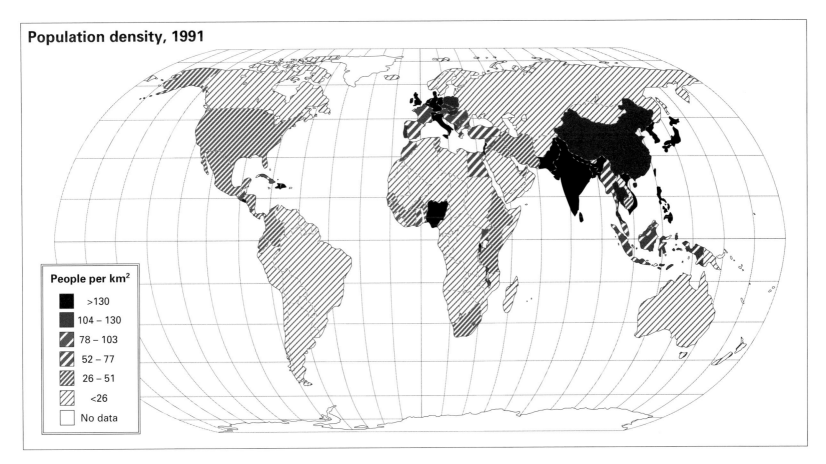

Figure 3.1 Population density, 1991

3.2 POPULATION DOUBLING TIME

Allan M. Findlay

Population doubling time can be defined as the number of years until a population will double assuming a constant rate of natural increase. It is not intended to forecast the actual doubling time of a given population, but provides an interesting indicator which highlights the very varied demographic trajectories of different populations. It indicates the potential growth associated with a given rate of natural increase (the birth rate minus the death rate expressed as a percentage). The measure takes no account of migration.

At the beginning of the 1990s the Palestinian population of Gaza had the world's highest doubling rate (just 16 years) followed by the population of Jordan (17 years). These extraordinary rates of potential population growth arose because of the combination of very high crude birth rates (in Jordan 46 births per 1000 population) and very low death rates (in Jordan only five deaths per 1000 population). By contrast the more aged structure of populations in most west European countries combined with low fertility rates to produce very low population doubling times. In Britain, it would take 330 years, at current rates of natural increase, to double the population. In Denmark the equivalent statistic is a remarkable doubling period of over 1700 years. These contrasts in doubling times between states show that contemporary concern about the rate of world population growth needs to be qualified by a more profound understanding of the demographic mechanisms responsible for producing such varied patterns of population change.

Concern about the global level of population growth is based, amongst other factors, on the awareness that while it took all of human history up to 1800 AD for the world's population to reach one billion persons (or a thousand million), it took only a further 130 years to reach two billion (by 1930) and a mere 45 years to double again by 1975. Currently a billion extra people are being added to the world population total every 11 years.

Figure 3.2a, which maps population doubling times for individual states, illustrates some striking regional contrasts. The first feature which should be noted is that the rate of natural increase is not directly associated either with the overall level of economic development or the pace of economic growth. The wealthier countries of the world fall into three groups when mapped in terms of their doubling times.

(1) The older industrial nations of western Europe, which experienced rapid population growth in the last century, are now growing very slowly in demographic terms. Some such as Germany face demographic decline were it not for net immigration.
(2) The two former superpower rivals, the USA and Soviet Union, have younger and more diverse populations than those of western Europe, and continue to have higher crude birth rates. Canada and Australia also belong to this same group of wealthy countries whose populations are set to double in a period of between 80 and 100 years. It is of interest that Japan is more like western Europe than North America in its demographic behaviour.
(3) The oil rich states of the Arab world have amongst the most rapidly growing populations of the world. Cultural factors play a strong role in these Islamic states, favouring high fertility, while at the same time the wealth of these countries has been diverted in part to producing much improved health services.

This, along with improved nutrition and better health education has facilitated a strong downward shift in death rates amongst the young, and a considerable improvement in life expectancies.

Just as the wealthier states of the world face very different demographic futures, so too do the developing countries of Africa, South America and Asia. It is noticeable from the world map that parts of Asia such as Sri Lanka, Thailand and Indonesia have low rates of population growth. Thailand for example, with low crude birth and death rates, has a population doubling time of 53 years. By contrast, nine African states have population doubling times of 20 years or less. To provide for the needs of their very rapidly growing populations, countries such as Côte d'Ivoire or Zambia clearly face a difficult if not impossible challenge, with any gains in economic growth being rapidly wiped out by the effects of population growth. Zambia, for example, would have to sustain economic growth at a level of 3.8% per annum even to match its pace of population increase.

A final feature of Figure 3.2a which should be noted is that national boundaries have in some cases become very significant demographic divides. For example, the US/Mexican frontier is a key boundary between an area of extremely high population growth in Central America and the lower population growth rates of North America. The contrast between the high population growth situation in Africa and the low population growth of southern Europe is another stark juxtapositioning of demographic regimes. These sharp demographic divides have become of particular concern to the wealthier countries afraid of mass immigration (both legal and clandestine). The result has been the introduction of very strict

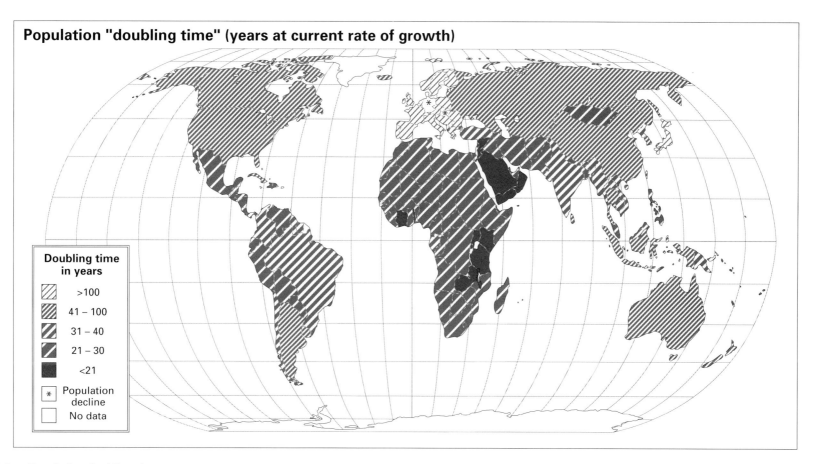

Figure 3.2a   Population doubling times

immigration policies to many of the wealthier countries.

Figure 3.2b attempts to show what rapid population growth means in absolute terms for one country, namely India. India's population growth rate accelerated from 0.01% per annum at the start of the 20th century to 2.25% in the 1980s. The increased pace of population growth and the doubling of the Indian population between 1941 and 1981 was the result of a dramatic reduction in death rates at a time when crude birth rates remained high. Death rates have fallen because of steps taken to reduce the impact of famine and the gradual control of epidemics through the improvement of medical standards, better nutrition and improvements in food distribution mechanisms. Furthermore, the rapid rate of population increase has not outpaced India's ability to feed its

population. Contrary to Malthusian claims, India has been able to increase foodgrain production in line with population growth. It would therefore be wrong to conclude that rapid population growth and short population doubling times inevitably imply economic disaster for developing countries. This view needs to be balanced against the recognition that many problems remain to be solved in developing countries and that rapid population growth may slow progress or make it more difficult. One example will suffice to illustrate this. Population growth either directly or indirectly has contributed to India's problem of environmental crisis. The effort which has been made over-rapidly to expand the arable area is in part responsible for the fact that an estimated 60% of arable land suffers from environmental degradation.

Further reading

Findlay, A. and Findlay, A. (1987), *Population and Development in the Third World*, London: Routledge.

Jones, H. (1990), *Population Geography*, London: Paul Chapman.

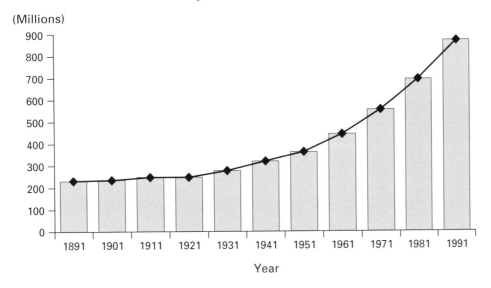

Population in India

Figure 3.2b   Population in India

3.3 TOTAL FERTILITY RATES 1990
Allan M. Findlay and Juliette Brown

The Total Fertility Rate (TFR) is perhaps the most useful general indicator of fertility behaviour since it is not affected by the size or age composition of a population. The TFR is the summation of cohort specific fertility rates (the number of children born per 1000 women in a cohort) in a particular year. The Population Reference Bureau interprets the TFR as the average number of children born to a woman during her lifetime. This interpretation is easy to grasp, but rests on a number of major assumptions which lie beyond the scope of this analysis.

Variations in TFRs around the globe are very great. In 1990 Rwanda and Malawi had the highest TFRs at 8.1 and 7.7 respectively. Other clusters of high fertility were found in the former French territories of west Africa and in the Arabian peninsula. Although most of the industrial market economies have low TFRs, so too does China with its low levels of GNP per capita. Inversely, high fertility is not a characteristic associated only with 'poor' countries, since oil states such as Saudi Arabia and Oman have TFRs of over 7.0. Having noted that sweeping generalisations about the causes of high or low fertility are not possible, it remains evident from Figure 3.3a that fertility levels and economic development are geographically associated. Poorer families in developing countries have quite understandable reasons for having large families. These include the higher infant mortality rates of these countries, the labour value of having children to work the land or to earn income as street hawkers in the city, and the dependence of parents on their children for support in old age. The high TFRs of many developing countries should therefore be seen in many ways as a logical response of poorer families to their uncertain and vulnerable situations.

Demographers have identified a small number of 'intermediate' determinants of fertility which account for much of the variation in fertility behaviour between populations (Bongaarts, 1985). These determinants include the proportion of married females, contraceptive use and effectiveness, the prevalence of abortion, and the length of post-partum infecundability. Age at marriage is a major influence on the proportion of married women in a population at any point in time. In a country such as India where age at marriage at the turn of the century was only 13.2 years, TFRs were inevitably high, given the large number of years over which married women were at risk of childbearing. Age at marriage is only one of the many underlying factors, including levels of social and economic development and a wide range of cultural factors, which affect the intermediate determinants and produce spatial and temporal variations in fertility.

Figure 3.3b shows the pattern of age-specific fertility for Jordan for 1976 and 1990. Like many Islamic countries Jordan sustains a high TFR, but reductions in fertility have been taking place over time. Peak fertility in both years is found in the 25–29 age cohort. Reductions in fertility between the two dates are evident for women in the 20–24 age cohort. This reflects both an increase in the average age of marriage (affecting the percentage

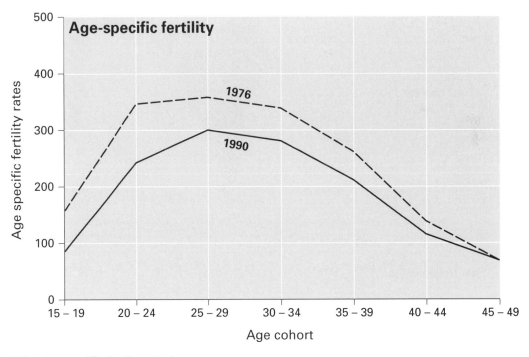

Figure 3.3b Age-specific fertility, Jordan

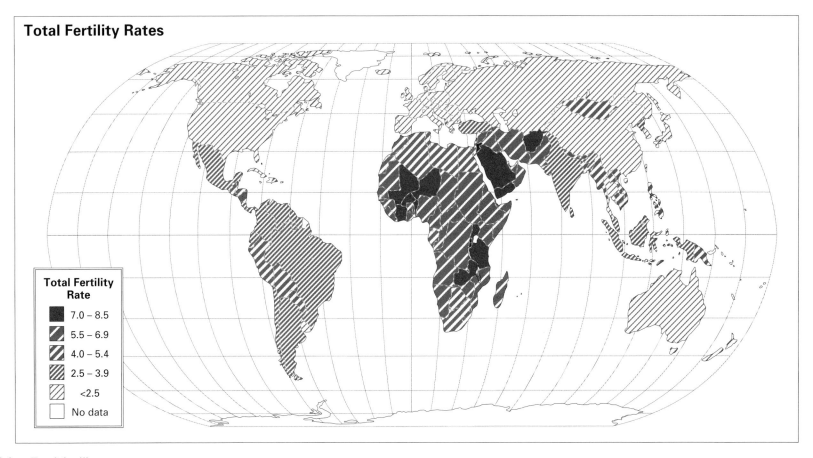

Figure 3.3a   Total fertility rates

of women married) and increased use of contraceptives, particularly in urban areas. A major factor producing both changes is the increased involvement of women in secondary and tertiary education in Jordan.

One of the greatest difficulties in commenting at a global level on fertility trends and differentials is that fertility behaviour does not seem to respond in a unilinear fashion to other development influences (Cleland and Hobcroft, 1985). For example, while nearly every society has found that women with higher levels of education have fewer children than those with only limited education, TFRs vary greatly between one country and another for women sharing the same levels of education. This situation arises because cultural and societal factors operate strongly to set norms about childbearing, family formation and the woman's role in society. For example, in Islamic countries polygamy and purdah (female seclusion) have been just two culturally significant influences

amongst many others which have meant that fertility rates have remained much higher than might otherwise have been expected given levels of economic development (Fargues, 1989).

Government attitudes to fertility vary depending on whether the dominant perception is of people as mouths to feed or hands to work. Table 3.3 summarises current perspectives at a regional level. While a majority of developing countries believe that fertility is too high and support family planning programmes (Section 3.4), there are some which for cultural or economic reasons wish fertility to rise. For example, Singapore and Malaysia both support selective pronatalist positions. The ability of countries to affect fertility levels through family planning measures has been much debated. The weight of evidence suggests that anti-natalist policies are less effective in the least developed countries, but that in middle and high income countries the pace of fertility reduction is accelerated by government

policy. China, with its one child per couple family planning policy, is an extreme, but fascinating, example of a country which has very forcefully moved to reduce fertility (Jowett, 1989).

Further reading

Bongaarts, J. (1985), The fertility inhibiting effects of the intermediate fertility variables, in: Shorter, F. et al. (eds), *Population Factors in Development Planning in the Middle East*, Cairo: Population Council, 152–169.

Cleland, J. and Hobcroft, J. (eds) (1985), *Reproductive Change in Developing Countries*, Oxford: Oxford University Press.

Fargues, P. (1989), The decline of Arab fertility, *Population*, **44**: 147–174.

Jowett, A.J. (1989), *China's One Child Programme*, Glasgow: University of Glasgow, Applied Population Research Unit Discussion Paper 89/3.

Table 3.3 Government views of fertility levels in developing countries

		Fertility		
	TFR	Too high	Satisfactory	Too low
North Africa	5.0	4	2	0
Western Asia	4.9	3	8	3
Southern Asia	4.4	7	2	0
South East Asia	3.4	4	3	2
East Asia	2.2	2	4	0
Central America	4.1	6	2	0
Caribbean	3.2	9	4	0
South America	3.3	3	8	1
West Africa	6.4	12	4	0
East Africa	6.8	12	4	0
Central Africa	6.0	4	2	3

Note: numbers relate to the number of countries in each category
Source: calculated from data in Population Reference Bureau (1991)

3.4 FAMILY PLANNING POLICIES
Huw Jones

The first government to support a family planning (FP) programme with the explicit aim of reducing national fertility was India in 1952, but it was not until the mid-1960s that there was a surge internationally in fertility regulation policies. This was a response to the 1960s round of censuses, which revealed much higher rates of population growth than had been anticipated. In addition, the development at the time of the oral contraceptive pill and intra-uterine devices encouraged development planners for the first time to believe that Third World fertility rates could be regulated by intervention policies. Accordingly, by 1976 as many as 63 countries in the less developed world, embracing 92% of its population, had launched their own FP programmes or endorsed those of private groups like the International Planned Parenthood Federation.

In about half of current programmes, the explicit aim is to reduce fertility in the interest of national development planning, while in the others FP is supported essentially on grounds of health, human rights and family welfare, regardless of any national demographic impact. Figure 3.4 demonstrates that programme strength varies from country to country, for two major reasons. First, some governments are ideologically resistant to fertility reduction, notably Islamic, Catholic and some socialist countries. Second, since strong programmes are dependent on an infrastructural capability, including roads, media and health centres, it is clear that there is a functional link between development and programme effectiveness.

There are major regional patterns of programme strength evident in Figure 3.4. In eastern and southern Asia, under conditions of very large populations and high densities, the great majority of governments have long been committed to a reduction in population growth rate. The only exceptions are Bhutan, Burma, Laos, Cambodia and Papua New Guinea, reflecting combinations of introversion, low population density and war disruption.

In western Asia and the Middle East, the growth of Islamic fundamentalism has led to contraception being widely seen as a threat to the traditional power structures of the family, especially male domination of wives and daughters. In addition, many countries in the region have very small populations, labour shortages and a perceived need for military strength – all conditions that weaken any FP programmes. Indeed, the Iraqi and Saudi Arabian governments are strongly pronatalist, restricting access to modern contraceptives and providing substantial financial benefits to large families.

Islam is also dominant in north Africa, but higher population densities and Western influence there have led to significant FP programmes in Egypt, Morocco and especially Tunisia, where ex-President Bourgibba played a key role in enhancing the status of women. Elsewhere in Africa, high death rates, international and tribal conflicts, and low development levels deter the adoption, let alone implementation, of anti-natalist policies.

Latin America has remarkably few governments prepared to back strongly FP policies. One potent cause is the widespread cult of *machismo*. Another is the large expanse of sparsely peopled 'outback' of perceived development potential. Then there has been the suspicion that United States imperialism was imposing birth control as a means of limiting the emerging power of Latin America. Finally, the Roman Catholic Church continues to exert a powerful conservative influence on the governments of these former Spanish and Portuguese territories.

In the 'strong programme' countries shown in Figure 3.4 there was a substantial overall fall in total fertility rate of 33% between 1975 and 1990. In countries with 'moderate programmes' the decline was 24%, but in those with weaker programmes only 6% (Mauldin and Ross, 1991). It must be said, however, that programme effort interacts with development level in determining fertility levels. Both determinants matter, so that fertility decline is sharpest when they reinforce each other.

Further reading

Donaldson, P. and Tsui, A. (1990), The international family planning movement, *Population Bulletin*, **45**(3): 1–46.

Mauldin, W.P. and Ross, J. (1991), Family planning programs, efforts and results, 1982–89, *Studies in Family Planning*, **22**: 350–367.

Ross, J. and Frankenberg, E. (1993), *Findings from Two Decades of Family Planning Research*, New York: Population Council.

Ross, J., Mauldin, W.P., Green, S. and Cooke, E. (1992), *Family Planning and Child Survival Programs*, New York: Population Council.

UN Population Division (1990), *Global Population Policy Data Base 1989*, New York: United Nations, Population Policy Paper 28, ST/ESA/SER.R/99.

Figure 3.4 Strength of family planning programmes in less developed countries, 1989

3.5 LIFE EXPECTANCY
Allan M. Findlay

Mortality may be measured in many different ways. The most often used indicator is the crude death rate (CDR), which expresses the number of deaths in a given year per 1000 persons in a population at mid-year. Although frequently cited, it is not a particularly useful indicator in making international comparisons since it is strongly affected by the age composition of a population. For example, the populations of north European countries have a high proportion of elderly persons and consequently have moderately high CDRs by comparison with those found in developing countries. For example, in 1990/91 Sweden had a CDR of 11 per thousand, while Kenya boasted only seven deaths per thousand population.

Age specific death rates, and a measure known as life expectancy at birth, are more sensitive indicators of the true life chances of a population. Life expectancy at birth measures the average numbers of years that a cohort of people born in a particular year are likely to live, given the age-specific death rates existing at that time (Newell, 1988). Figure 3.5a shows that while the industrial market economies of Europe, Japan and North America had achieved very high life expectancies (Sweden, 78 years; Canada, 77 years), life expectancies of over 70 years were also enjoyed in states which had followed a socialist development path (in eastern Europe, Cuba and the former Soviet Union) as well as in some oil states (United Arab Emirates, Venezuela, Brunei) and a range of developing countries such as Sri Lanka, Panama, Chile, Jordan and South Korea. By contrast, extremely poor life chances remained in large parts of Africa as well as at locations which had suffered in the 1980s from superpower conflicts such as Afghanistan and Cambodia (with life expectancies of 41 and 49 respectively).

Until the 20th century extremely low life expectancies existed in most of the developing countries. High death rates were sustained by, amongst other features, periodic epidemics. For example, one cholera epidemic in southern India in the late-19th century is believed to have contributed to a ten-fold increase in death rates. Although most developing countries continue to have life expectancies which are much poorer than in other parts of the globe, significant health risks have been eradicated in recent decades and life expectancies have risen. For example, at the time of the first Yemeni census in 1975, life expectancy at birth was still only 39 years, compared with 50 years by 1990/91. Rapid gains in life expectancies in developing countries over recent decades have dominantly been attributed to the diffusion of western medical knowledge and the introduction of state organised health programmes. The eradication of smallpox as a result of sustained efforts by the World Health Organisation in the 1960s and early 1970s is just one example of how the application of western medical knowledge helped to avoid the unnecessary early deaths of millions of people. Vaccination programmes, inoculations and vector control have undoubtedly increased life expectancies, but so too have the effects of improved maternal education, through the reduction of infant and child mortality. It has been shown in Cairo that the chances of a child dying before the age of two are three times as great if it is born to an illiterate mother as opposed to a university graduate (Tecke, 1985).

The trend towards lower early death rates and towards increased life expectancies encouraged predictions that the mortality regimes of less developed countries would soon converge with those of Europe and North America. Omran (1971) for example, has identified what he describes as an epidemiological transition in which not only do life expectancies rise during the demographic development of a population, but the causes of death also change. In countries such as Hong Kong there is clear evidence that infectious diseases have declined very rapidly as a cause of death, while the so-called diseases of old age have become more important in proportional terms (Phillips, 1988). For most developing countries, however, demographic convergence has not occurred. This is because sickness and mortality are linked in part at least to standards of living. Malnutrition remains widespread in Africa. In circumstances where most of the world's poorest states are still unable to adequately feed their populations, it is not surprising that their populations are more susceptible to 'poverty related' diseases. The poor in the developing world have not the means to improve their life expectancies, since they cannot afford to live in adequate housing, nor to achieve the necessary nutrition levels (Section 3.11) to avoid infectious diseases, nor to reach the standards of education to be able to provide the best health care for themselves and their children.

The ultimate cause of the differential patterns of life expectancy shown in Figure 3.5a are therefore complex, but relate to some extent to standards of living and levels of economic development. Johnston (1989: 222) has used international differentials in life expectancy as an indicator of the human consequences of the core-periphery structure of the world economy in terms of the way in which 'the life chances of the population of the periphery are subordinated to those of the population of the core'.

One particularly sensitive indicator of human welfare is the infant mortality rate. This measures

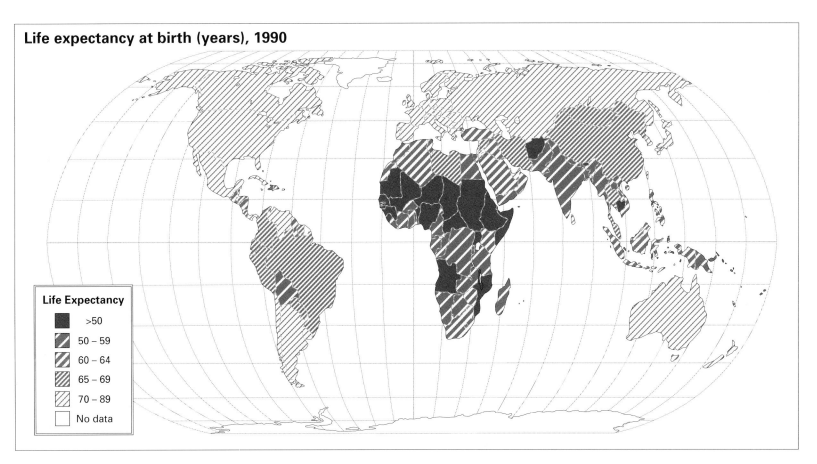

Figure 3.5a   Life expectancy at birth (years), 1990

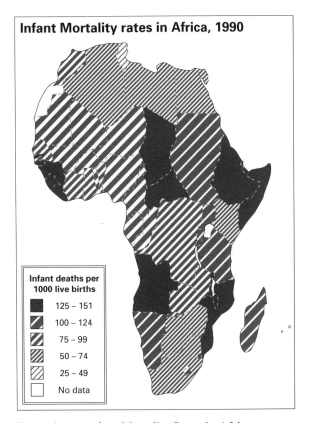

Figure 3.5b Infant Mortality Rates in Africa

infant mortality rates in many African countries were higher in 1990 than they were in 1980.

Further reading

Johnston, R. (1989), The individual and the world economy, in: Johnston, R. and Taylor, P. (eds), *World in Crisis*, Oxford: Blackwell, 205–226.

Newell, C. (1988), *Methods and Models of Demography*, London: Belhaven.

Omran, A. (1971), The epidemiologic transition, *Millbank Memorial Fund Quarterly*, **19**: 509–538.

Phillips, D. (1988), *The Epidemiological Transition in Hong Kong*, Hong Kong: University of Hong Kong, Centre for Asian Studies Occasional Papers, 75.

Tecke, B. (1985), Determinants of child survival, in: Shorter, F. *et al.* (eds), *Population Factors in Development Planning in the Middle East*, Cairo: Population Council, 137–150.

the life chances of the most vulnerable element of any population, by considering the number of deaths in a particular year of babies under one year of age per thousand live births. Figure 3.5b shows that political and economic circumstances in Africa remain highly threatening to the continent's most vulnerable population growth. In Guinea and Guinea-Bissau, babies had a three in twenty chance of dying before their first birthday, while across Africa infants had on average a one in ten chance of dying within the first year. Sadly,

3.6 CHILD SURVIVAL RATES
Tim Unwin

Pictures of mutilated and dying children, suffering from the ravages of war, disease and malnutrition, regularly fill television screens and newspaper columns in the richer countries of the world. However, despite the observation that a quarter of a million of the world's children die every week, and millions more suffer from malnutrition and permanent ill health, surprisingly little effort has gone into the alleviation of such problems. This is largely because they mainly affect the poor and the powerless (UNICEF, 1992).

The emphasis of most child oriented health programmes that have been implemented is generally placed on a reduction of the numbers of children dying, rather than on an improvement in the quality of life of those that survive. This is well indicated by the standard statistical information provided by organisations concerned with child welfare, such as the United Nations Children's Fund (UNICEF) (1992), which regularly provide data on infant mortality rate (IMR) or the mortality rate of children under five years of age (U5MR). A good illustration of the use of IMR, for example, is given for Africa in Figure 3.5b. However, Myers (1992) has argued cogently that such negative approaches to childhood should be replaced by a more positive emphasis on child survival. As he argues 'Accepting this positive reconceptualization of child survival – as a process of seeking a healthy state at birth and in the early months and years of life – requires looking beyond the analysis of causes of mortality and beyond programmes that reduce mortality' (Myers, 1992: 36–37). Instead, he suggests that more attention needs to be placed on ways of moving children towards the healthy end of the death-sickness-health spectrum, and that there should be a reorientation of programmes towards those that will improve health rather than simply reduce mortality.

Figure 3.6 presents information on under-five survival rates in 1990. This shows the stark contrast in the survival chances of children born in different parts of the world. Whereas in most of the countries of western Europe, north America, Japan, Australia and New Zealand, more than 980 children out of every 1000 live births survive until the age of five, the figure in 1990 was less than 800 for some 15 countries, almost all of which were in Africa. Moreover, in two countries, Mozambique and Angola, the decade 1980–1990 had actually seen a worsening of this position. Not only do these figures vary between countries, but it should be emphasised that within countries other factors such as race, class, income and place of residence also have a significant influence on child survival rates.

In general, the last two decades have seen a considerable improvement in child survival, with states such as Oman, Hong Kong, Greece and Egypt, all having an annual rate of increase of under-five survival rates of 7% or over in the decade 1980–1990. Sadly, though, the countries with the lowest survival rates are also those which in general have seen least improvement. In recognition that much more needed to be done, in September 1990 the World Summit for Children brought together leaders of over 150 countries, who made a commitment to make the resources available to achieve 27 child-related goals by the year 2000, all of which were seen as being feasible. Among the most important of these were 'a one–third reduction in child deaths, a halving of child malnutrition, a halving of deaths among women during pregnancy and childbirth, universally available family planning, safe water and sanitation for all, and basic education for all children' (UNICEF, 1992: 6). Whether there is the will for these to be achieved in practice remains, however, to be seen. Moreover, the complexity of the cultural, social and economic role of children in different parts of the world means that no single package of measures will be appropriate in all circumstances, and organisations involved in improving childhood survival rates must be careful to recommend culturally appropriate measures.

Further reading

Myers, R. (1992), *The Twelve who Survive: Strengthening Programmes of Early Childhood Development in the Third World*, London: Routledge in cooperation with UNESCO for The Consultative Group on Early Childhood Care and Development.

UNICEF (United Nations Children's Fund) (1990), *Children and Development in the 1990s: a UNICEF Sourcebook*, New York: UNICEF.

UNICEF (United Nations Children's Fund) (1992), *The State of the World's Children*, New York: Oxford University Press for UNICEF.

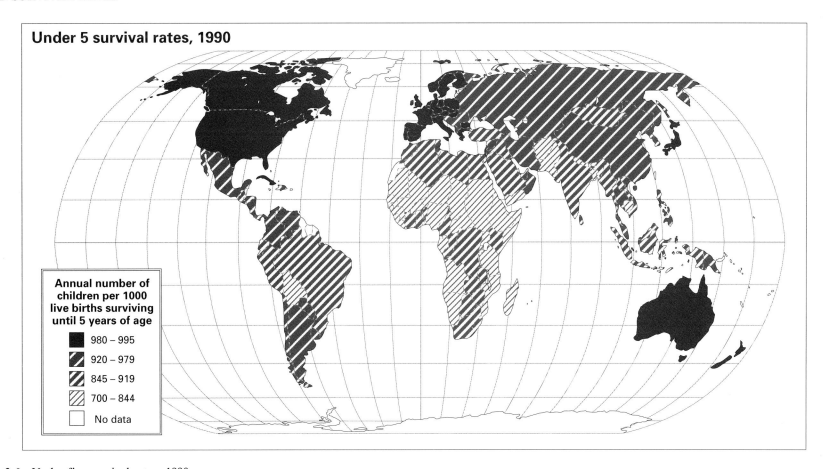

Figure 3.6 Under-five survival rates, 1990

3.7 THE PLACE OF CHILDREN IN LATIN AMERICA
Sarah A. Radcliffe

The notion of 'childhood' in Latin America has a complex history (UNICEF, 1990b). Until the late 18th century, children were treated as small adults, but by the 19th century the figure of the minor (*menor*) emerged. Perceived as requiring state intervention, a 'minor' in Latin America designated a child or adolescent potentially or actually institutionalised.

The place of children in Latin America is highly differentiated at a range of scales. At a national level, children's health indicators (such as infant mortality rates [IMR], life expectancy) and education provision vary from poor in Bolivia (IMR in 1990, 102/1000) to good in Cuba (IMR of 11/1000), with the other countries falling between these extremes (Figure 3.7). Countries' abilities to provide adequate health and educational provision for populations depends upon political will and resource allocation. Compared with other developing areas, Latin America has highly uneven wealth distributions: in Colombia, the poorest 40% of households control 13% of income, compared with 53% controlled by the top fifth. Wealthy decision-makers place low priority on social provision: in 1988 in Colombia, Brazil, Chile and Argentina, the wealthiest Latin countries, under 15% of government expenditures were spent on primary health care and primary education. This is reflected in health indicators, such as Brazil's, with an IMR of 60/1000, and 7% of children under four years moderately or severely underweight. Other countries make children's

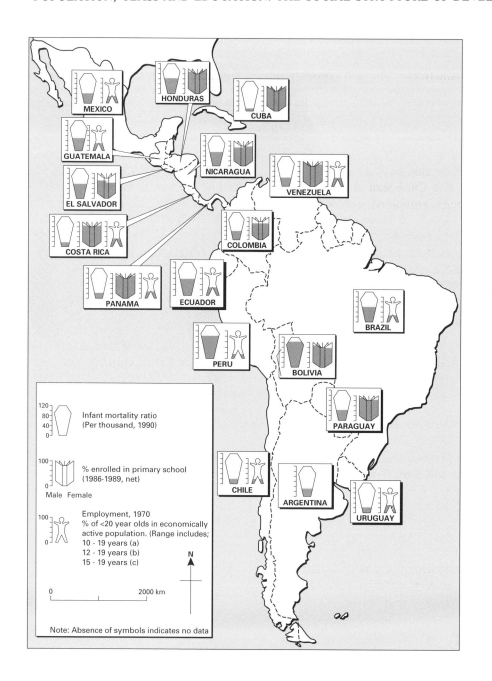

Figure 3.7 The place of children in Latin America

futures a greater priority: in 1990, Mexico adopted UNICEF's goals on reducing mortality. Action in the field of health care provision is a high priority in many Latin American countries, especially in under-resourced rural areas and poor urban neighbourhoods.

Literacy and general educational provision is fundamental to children's welfare. However, numbers of children in education are low compared with other developing areas. Some 70% of Latin American and Caribbean children reached grade 2 in 1986–89, compared with higher rates elsewhere (except southern Asia), and those reaching 3rd and 4th grade were consistently lower (61% and 55% respectively). Gender ideologies which value male education over female education are noticeable and literacy rates are higher for men (except Venezuela [UNICEF, 1992: 78–79]).

Within countries, children's experiences are highly differentiated according to gender, 'race', class and location, although the majority live in urban areas. Gender ideologies affect children from birth in every sphere of their lives (Harris, 1980; Ennew, 1986). In poor rural and urban areas, female children assist in childcare, cooking and washing, while boy children begin to herd animals, collect firewood, run errands and start an apprenticeship. Throughout Latin America, racisms result in differing lives for 'white' and lighter mixed race (*mestizo*) children, compared with children of amerindian and black heritage. Most children killed by gangs in urban Brazil during the early 1990s were black. Racisms are not always so violent: other children are discriminated against in work opportunities. Class too makes for different lives among children, where being wealthy means taking foreign holidays and having servants, while being poor means starting waged work at 10 years.

As children often work in family farms or domestic informal enterprises, their contributions to family income go unrecorded (also countries do not generally collect regular data on children's unemployment). On the basis of scanty evidence, in 1970 rates of economic activity among under-20s ranged from 31.8% in Costa Rica to 15.4% in Peru (PREALC, 1985). Street children are often the most visible working children. Located largely in urban centres swollen by rapid rural-urban migration, street children are a common sight in Latin America. Between 40 and 50 million street children live in Latin America and the Caribbean. While 60% of street children retain close contacts with their families and only work on the street, the remainder are dependent upon the street for shelter, food and companionship, and 7% are abandoned, forced to live on the street (MacPherson, 1987: 204–05). During recessions such as the 'lost decade' of the 1980s, children entered labour markets in larger numbers and at younger ages (Gonzalez de la Rocha, 1988: 214).

Wars in Latin America affect children in particular ways through disruption of families, and breaks in education and work. While children have become combatants in civil-military conflicts, as in El Salvador, Nicaragua and Peru, they are usually recipients rather than initiators of violence. However, actions to protect children continue during conflicts. Thus, during El Salvador's civil war, children were immunized over three days of cease–fire agreed annually by both sides.

Further reading

Ennew, J. (1986), *Mujercita y mamacita*: girls growing up in Lima, *Bulletin of Latin American Research*, **5**(2): 49–66.

Ennew, J. and Milne, B. (1989), *The Next Generation: Lives of Third World Children*, London: Zed.

MacPherson, S. (1987), *Five Hundred Million Children: Poverty and Child Welfare in the Third World*, Sussex: Wheatsheaf Books.

UNICEF (1990), *Infancia, Adolescencia y Control Social en América Latina, Primer informe Proyecto de investigación Desarrollo de los Tribunales de Menores en Latinoamérica: Tendencias y perspectivas*, Buenos Aires: Ediciones Depalma.

3.8 URBAN POPULATION
Allan M. Findlay

The industrial revolution in Britain and other west European countries in the 18th and 19th centuries required the spatial concentration of capital in new centres of industrial activity, such as the coalfield regions. It also required a concentration of population, with net transfers of people into the rapidly growing industrial cities. By the end of the 20th century, it was taken almost for granted that the majority of people in these countries were urban dwellers. De-industrialisation, improved transportation systems and the search for a better quality of life have led to only a limited reversal of this trend.

For the developing countries the 20th century was the century of major urban growth. Unlike the older industrial societies of western Europe, urbanisation in developing countries has not generally followed industrialisation, but has often preceded it. The process of rural to urban migration has transferred large numbers of people from the relative poverty of the countryside to the large cities of the Third World. Rapid rates of natural increase have added to other economic problems in rural areas, making rural out-migration the chosen option for many people in developing countries. Neither the labour nor housing markets of the large cities of these countries are well placed to receive these migrants, who are often forced to survive through insecure forms of employment in the so-called 'informal sector', and occupy illegally constructed dwellings in the shanty towns which encircle the mushrooming cities of developing countries.

Gilbert and Gugler (1982: 25) have vividly compared the lot of the urban poor in developed and developing countries: 'Urban poverty in the Third World is on a scale quite different to that in developed countries ... In the Third World city the relative poverty of the black Baltimore slum dweller is accentuated by absolute material deprivation. Some poor people in the United States suffer from malnutrition, most of the poor in Indian cities fall into this category. Overcrowded tenement slums and too few jobs are abhorrent, but the lack of fresh water, medical services, drainage, and unemployment compensation adds to the problem in most Third World cities'.

The locations of urban growth in developing countries have usually been the former colonial capitals and port cities, whose origins were linked with the colonial export economy of cash crops and raw materials. For example, three quarters of the population growth of Lagos in the 1950s was due to migration, while in São Paulo the equivalent figure for the 1960s was 68%. In the 1970s 80% of the populations of the Saudi Arabian cities of Dammam, Jeddah and Riyadh were migrants. It has been estimated that if current urban growth rates are maintained, then there will be 25 cities of ten million inhabitants or more by the year 2000. Of these 20 will be in the Third World.

Figure 3.8 shows that the extent of urbanisation is highly variable around the globe. As one would anticipate, western Europe has a strong concentration of population in urban areas, while Africa and South Asia remain strongly rural. The effects of rural to urban migration are however evident in Latin America, north Africa and the Middle East in making the majority of people in these regions urban dwellers by 1990.

It should, though, be noted that the data source used for Figure 3.8 is problematic, since no agreed standardised definition of what is considered 'urban' exists, and the map is based on each country's own definition. Another important caveat which should be attached to Figure 3.8 is the distinction between urbanisation and urbanism. The map offers an overview of the level of urbanisation in 1990 (i.e. the proportion of people living in urban areas), but it does not distinguish between city dwellers who have adopted an urban way of life and those who remain essentially rural even though they are living in the city. The map does not measure the sociological concept of 'urbanism'. Many of the cities of the Third World have been described by researchers as large villages, because of the tendency of rural in-migrants to bring many of their ways of life with them, and because of the very limited degree of integration which they achieve in these large overcrowded cities. There are therefore very great differences between the developed and developing world in terms of what is signified by a country having a highly urban population. These distinctions stem from the varied development contexts within which cities have emerged and evolved within the world economy.

Further reading

Gilbert, A. and Gugler, A. (1982), *Cities, Poverty and Development*, Oxford: Oxford University Press.

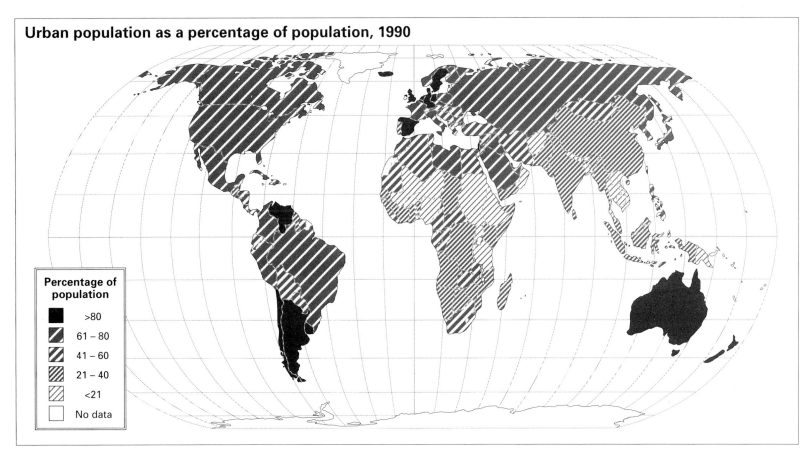

Figure 3.8   Urban population as a percentage of population, 1990

3.9 IMMUNISATION PROGRAMMES: THE EXAMPLE OF DPT
Tim Unwin

Aid agencies and national governments involved in improving the lived experiences of the world's poor are usually concerned to reach as many people as possible within the constraints of available resources. In recent years this has led to a growing interest in the issue of scale, and with the failure of many small-scale pilot projects to move to the full implementation stage, international development organisations are increasingly seeking to scale up many of their initiatives. As Myers (1992: 370) has commented, 'thinking big and setting large-scale targets have become part of a methodology. They are part of a process of mobilizing resources, of convincing people that the impossible (or difficult) is possible. Once a target … has been set, for instance, and public agreement on this goal has been obtained by governments and international organisations, it forces actions that would otherwise not have been taken'.

One set of health and nutrition technologies that has been associated with this increase in the scale of activity has been that encapsulated in the acronym GOBI, which stands for 'growth monitoring', 'oral rehydration', 'breastfeeding' and 'immunization'. Of these, immunisation is the most demanding in terms of organisation and expense, and has also received most attention. In the late 1970s, immunisation programmes reached only about 10% of the children in what the United Nations Children's Fund (UNICEF) called the 'developing world'. However, by the mid-1980s most governments had committed themselves to an 80% immunisation rate by the end of 1990. As

a result, 'over 500 million separate contacts are now being made each year between modern health services and children. The result of this effort – the largest international operation ever mounted in peacetime – is that *the lives of almost 9000 children are being saved every day*' (UNICEF, 1992: 11). This initiative has so far focused on four main types of immunisation, against tuberculosis, polio, measles, and DPT (diptheria, pertussis and tetanus). In 1990 the Children's Vaccine Initiative launched by the World Health Organisation (WHO), the United Nations Development Programme (UNDP) and UNICEF involved a commitment to extend this range to include affordable vaccines against malaria, certain respiratory diseases, meningitis, various diarrhoeal diseases, hepatitis B and A, and a number of other fatal diseases. This involves great investment in the development of appropriate vaccines, but until now the emphasis of research has been driven primarily by the demands of the rich nations. An important challenge for the global community is thus whether sufficient investment can be attracted to the greater needs, but much less financial power, of the world's poorer states and peoples.

Figure 3.9 illustrates the extent of immunisation of one-year-old children against diptheria, pertussis (whooping cough) and tetanus (DPT) in 1989–90. WHO and UNICEF (1992) estimates suggest that immunisation against DPT in 'developing countries' had risen from a figure of only about 28% of all children under one in 1981 to some 83% by 1990. As Figure 3.9 indicates, though, this increase was by no means uniform throughout the world. While most of the richer states have rates of DPT immunisation well over 90%, it is interesting to note that some European countries such as Spain (73%), the United Kingdom (75%), and Ireland (77%) had very

much lower rates, putting them on a par with states such as Peru (72%) and Kenya (74%). Of much more significance, though, is the very low rate of immunisation in many of the central and southern African countries, a pattern which closely reflects the much higher child mortality to be encountered there (*see* Figure 3.5b). In general, it can be noted that at a global scale the overall pattern of immunisation against polio and measles is broadly similar to that against DPT, but that rates of immunisation against TB are usually much higher.

While immunisation programmes have undoubtedly proved to be a success in reducing childhood mortality, they should not simply be seen as an end in themselves. Such programmes in part appear successful because it is easy to count the number of vaccines distributed, and relatively easy to arrange for children to be vaccinated in regular campaigns. It is much harder, though, to provide the social and economic conditions for the poor to achieve a lasting improvement in their life conditions. Enhancement of health is much more than simply a matter of immunisation, and great strides need to be taken in health education and primary health care in rural areas. War and famine remain as potent killers as any disease.

Further reading

Gray, A. (ed.) (1993), *World Health and Disease*, Buckingham: Open University Press.

Howe, G.M. (ed.) (1977), *A World Geography of Human Diseases*, London: Academic Press.

McGlashen, N.D. and Blunden J.R. (eds) (1983), *Geographical Aspects of Health*, London: Academic Press.

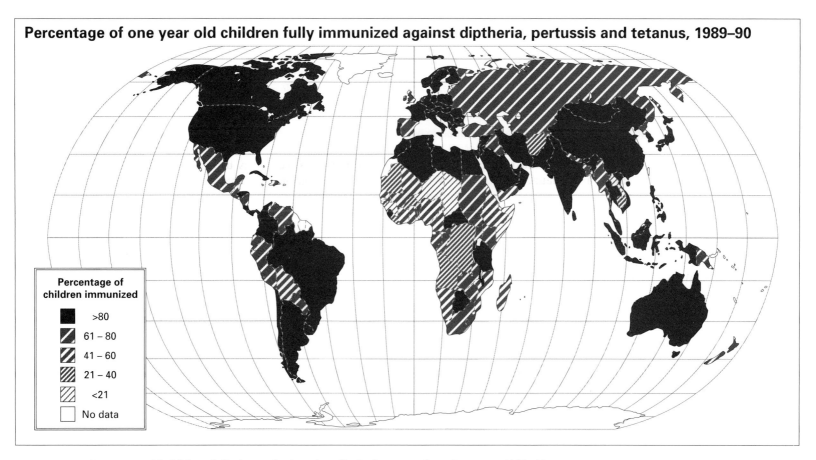

Figure 3.9 Percentage of one-year-old children fully immunised against diptheria, pertussis and tetanus, 1989–90

3.10 ACCESS TO SAFE WATER
Tim Unwin

Definitions of what are seen as basic human needs vary (Stewart, 1985), but access to safe water is generally considered to be one of the most important human requirements, alongside primary health care provision, education, and shelter. Basic needs, however, do not always receive the funding support that they warrant. Thus, the twelve industrialised countries for which information is available only give about 9% of their aid to meet directly the primary health care, primary and secondary education, family planning, and rural water supply and sanitation needs of people in the developing world (UNICEF, 1992).

Water is essential for human survival, both in terms of its direct consumption as drinking water and through its use for agriculture, industry and energy production, although the balance in its use varies appreciably between countries. Thus, in India, Mexico and Bulgaria most water is used for agricultural purposes, whereas in the United Kingdom, Poland and Germany water supplies are directed principally to the supply of industry (Redclift, 1984).

In general, the quality of drinking water is closely associated with the incidence of disease. Not only are poor water and sanitation one of the main causes of diarrhoea, which kills about four million children under five in developing countries every year (UNEP/UNICEF, 1990), but water conditions are a major factor in the distribution of other diseases such as malaria, schistosomiasis, and cholera. Consequently, the provision of safe drinking water has attracted increasing global attention in recent years, with the period 1981–90 being termed by the United Nations the International Drinking Water Supply and Sanitation

Decade. As a result, it is estimated that between 1980 and 1988, approximately 535 million people were given access to safe water supplies, with 325 million people receiving adequate sanitation facilities. However, this still leaves over 1130 million without a satisfactory water supply (UNEP/UNICEF, 1990). Moreover, it is estimated that 80% of the global expenditure on water supply systems is spent on providing facilities for the relatively rich, at an average cost of around $600 per person, whereas only 20% goes on public wells and standpipes serving the poor, at a cost of between $30 and $50 per person served (WHO, 1990).

Figure 3.10a indicates the global provision of safe water at the end of the 1980s based on data provided by the World Health Organisation (WHO) and the United Nations Children's Fund (UNICEF). This indicates marked differences between safe water provision in the poorer states of the world, with central and southern African states in general having higher percentages of their populations without access to safe water than was the case in Latin America and Asia. While there are substantial variations between states, it is also important to note that urban areas are usually much more likely to have safe drinking water than are rural areas. This is portrayed graphically in Figure 3.10b. Although this Figure excludes most of the countries of Europe and North America for which data are not available, it nevertheless indicates that urban populations in the poorer countries of the world usually have at least 20% higher rates of access to safe drinking water than do rural populations. Notable exceptions to this generalisation are Bangladesh, where 89% of the rural population as against 39% of the urban population have access to safe water, and Burkina Faso and Zimbabwe, where the corresponding figures are 72%:44%, and 80%:31% respectively.

The provision of nearby supplies of safe water also has important gender implications, since it is almost always women in the poorer countries of the world who collect and use water (Seager and Olson, 1986; Momsen and Townsend, 1987). If water can be provided near the household, this saves women from having to make long and arduous journeys to collect it, and if it is free from parasites, such as those causing schistosomiasis, then women's health can also be dramatically improved.

Further reading

UNEP/UNICEF (United Nations Environment Programme/United Nations Children's Fund) (1990), *The State of the Environment 1990: Children and the Environment*, New York: UNEP/UNICEF.

UNICEF (United Nations Children's Fund) (1992), *The State of the World's Children*, New York: Oxford University Press for UNICEF.

WHO (World Health Organisation) (1990), *International Water and Sanitation Decade 1981–1990: Decade Assessment*, Geneva: WHO.

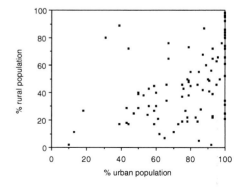

Figure 3.10b Percentages of urban and rural populations with access to safe water, 1988–1990

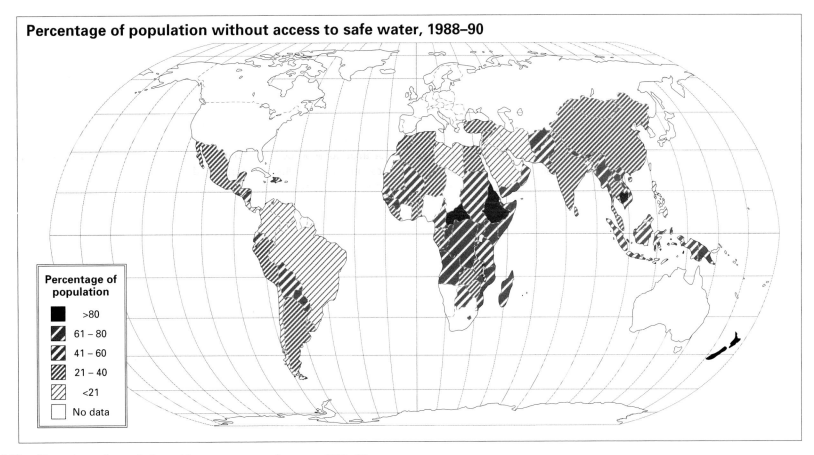

Figure 3.10a Percentage of population without access to safe water, 1988–90

3.11 NUTRITION
Elizabeth Dowler and Josephine Vespa

Assessment of a population's food and nutrition situation is based on two types of indicators: *intake* indicators which show the adequacy of nutrients or energy for survival or normal working life; and *outcome* indicators of body size, such as obesity or poor child growth, or clinical deficiency, such as anaemia or avitaminosis A. Both indicators have methodological and conceptual limitations. Moreover, enumerating the world's hungry is difficult and confusing because of disagreement over how to estimate intakes, calculate energy requirements, and define an adequate diet (Payne, 1990). Notwithstanding, recent FAO calculations suggest fewer people were underfed in 1989 than in 1975 (800 million rather than 1000 million). Part of this apparent fall is due to changed methodologies; some may be because of genuine improvement in national circumstances, particularly in China, and the Near East/north Africa (ACC/SCN, 1992).

The most widely available information used to estimate national and global food intake is the total *dietary energy supply* (DES) (Figure 3.11a). Energy intake is a marker of food adequacy, since it is the primary survival requirement. Although widely used, DES is not a reliable measure of intake, since DES data are usually obtained from national food balance sheets, which provide aggregate supply figures of food available for human consumption, rather than actual food intake. Through systematic error, DES tends to overestimate consumption in developed/industrialised countries and underestimate it in lesser developed/subsistence economies (Dowler and Seo, 1985). In addition, DES does not reflect seasonal or geographic variations within a

country, nor people's ability to purchase or otherwise obtain food. Its use for food security analysis is therefore limited (Maxwell, 1990). Sources of disaggregated food data include national household expenditure surveys, which give more accurate accounts of household food supply, and consumption (food intake) surveys, which measure what households or individuals are eating. These techniques, particularly the latter, are carried out irregularly because they are demanding and costly.

Despite its limitations, DES is widely used to monitor global trends in food availability, which have improved overall (FAO/WHO, 1992a). DES also identifies regions with severe food deficits, and where the situation is worsening: parts of Africa where drought is persistent, and parts of Asia where population growth is outstripping food availability (FAO/WHO, 1992a).

The most commonly used nutritional outcome measures are the *weights and heights of young children*, which are compared to those of a well nourished population as recommended by WHO. Median and centile values in this population are used as reference points: young children are

classified as 'at risk of malnutrition' if their weights or heights fall below specific cut-off points (Table 3.11). The cut-off points broadly delineate increasing mortality risks, particularly in younger children (Payne, 1990). Child growth status is also used to represent conditions of the household or population.

Regional figures of 'at risk' children vary according to the measurement and cut-off used. The prevalence of underweight children is a common indicator (Figure 3.11b); globally it fell from 42% in 1975 to 34% in 1990 (ACC/SCN, 1992). Trends have remained static or have deteriorated in sub-Saharan Africa. Child growth data can be disaggregated by time, location and household socio-economic characteristics. Figure 3.11c shows illustrative data from Sudan (Teklu *et al.*, 1991).

Growth data should be interpreted cautiously (Payne, 1990). Growth and body size are influenced by episodes of infection as well as by poor diet. Smaller body size may represent an adaptive strategy within a particular environment and, as such, not be viewed as necessarily negative, particularly in Asia (Martorell, 1985; Beaton,

Table 3.11 Three anthropometric indices providing different information about growth, all of which are sometimes used synonymously with 'malnutrition'

Anthropometric Indicator	Basis of Measurement	Characteristic
Wasting: * less than 80% reference	Weight/height or length	Indicates current or recent episodes
Stunting: * less than 90% reference	Height/length for age	Indicates cumulative effect of past episodes
Underweight: * less than 80% reference less than 60% reference	Weight for age	Composite measure of stunting and wasting

* −2SD (or Z scores) of reference median also used as cut-off
Source: author

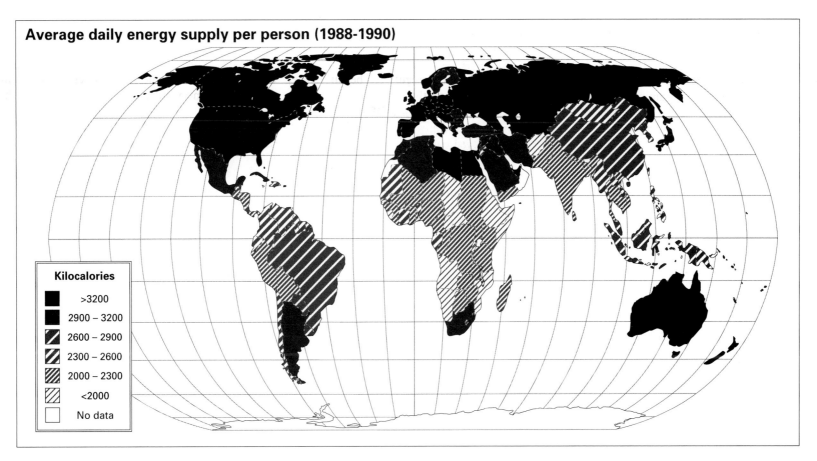

Figure 3.11a Average daily energy supply per person (1988–90)

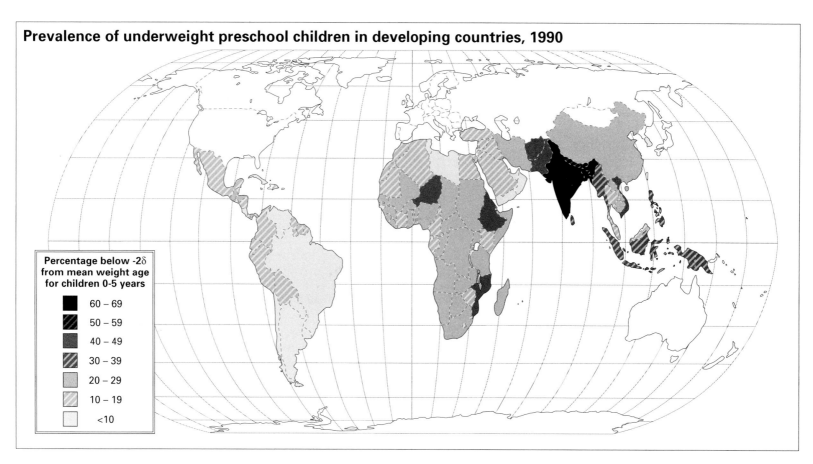

Figure 3.11b   Prevalence of underweight pre-school children in developing countries, 1990

1989; Pelletier, 1991). Reference standards are based on growth of children in industrialised populations who are not necessarily healthy; standards should not be prescriptive. Some argue that data on adults are more indicative of household survival capability; few national data are available (ACC/SCN, 1992). Other outcome indicators include prevalence of xerophthalmia (eye drying and eventual destruction caused primarily by vitamin A deficiency) (Figure 3.11d) (ACC/SCN, 1992).

Further reading

Beaton, G., Kelly, A., Kevany, J., Martorell, R. and Mason, J. (1990), *Appropriate Uses of Anthropometric Indices in Children*, Geneva: Administrative Committee on Co-ordination, Sub-Committee on Nutrition, State-of-the-Art Series Nutrition Policy Discussion Paper 7.

Dreze, J. and Sen, A. (1989), *Hunger and Public Action*, Oxford, Clarendon Press, WIDER Studies in Development Economics.

FAO/WHO (Food and Agriculture Organisation/World Health Organisation) (1992), *Nutrition and Development: a Global Assessment*, Rome: FAO/WHO, International Conference on Nutrition.

Gray, A. (ed.) (1993), *World Health and Disease*, Buckingham: Open University Press, OU Health and Disease Series, 3.

Payne, P.R. (1990), Measuring malnutrition, *IDS Bulletin*, **21**(3): 14–30.

UNICEF (United Nations Children's Fund) (1992), *The State of the World's Children 1992*, Oxford: Oxford University Press for UNICEF.

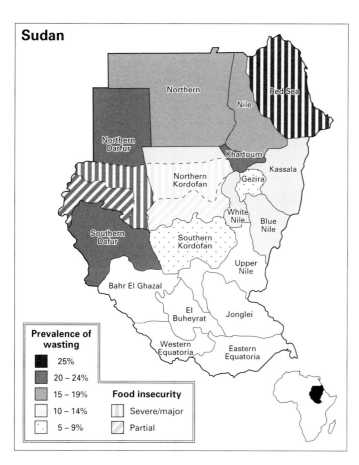

Figure 3.11c   Child growth data, Sudan

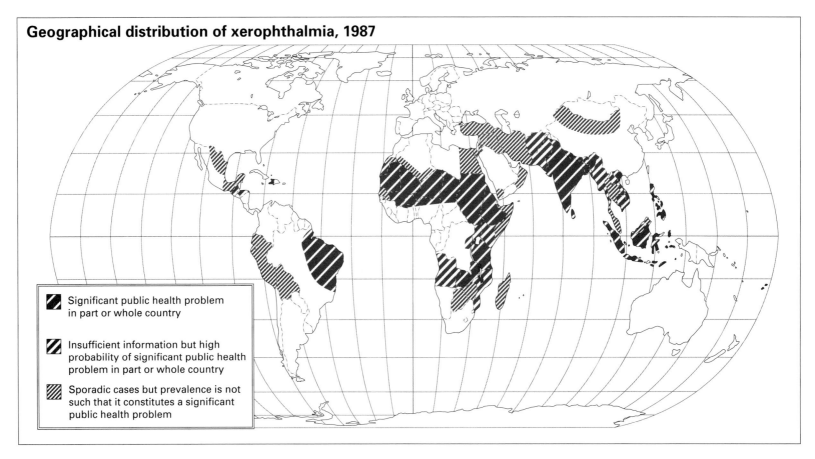

Figure 3.11d   Geographical distribution of xerophthalmia, 1987

3.12 POVERTY
Cecile Cutler and Dean Forbes

The poverty line can be defined as the 'income level below which a minimum nutritionally adequate diet plus essential non-food requirements are not affordable' (UNDP, *Human Development Report*, 1991: 195). Therefore, the poverty line will differ according to the income needs and expectations of the residents of any particular country. It is difficult to calculate as it is influenced by the costs within and outside any one country, and also by the expectations of individuals. Despite the problems in finding adequate information upon which to base a measure of poverty, it is a useful tool to help identify countries and regions of need.

Figure 3.12a shows the proportion of the rural population in the world who are living beneath the poverty line. The rural population was chosen because it is larger than the urban in the majority of developing countries. Africa and south Asia reveal a particularly high concentration of the countries with the largest proportions of their population in poverty.

Table 3.12, by contrast, illustrates the actual numbers living in poverty in particular countries. India has far more people living under the poverty line than any other country, followed by Bangladesh, China and Indonesia. However, India does not have the highest proportion of its population in poverty. Among the countries for which data are available, that dubious honour falls to Bangladesh, where 86% of the population were considered below the poverty line.

For most countries it is clear that rural poverty is of greater magnitude than urban poverty (Figure 3.12b). In other words, more of the rural than the urban population are in poverty.

Table 3.12 Total population below the poverty line, 1977–86

Rank	Country	Number (millions)
1	India	394
2	Bangladesh	94
3	China	87
4	Indonesia	68
5	Philippines	35
6	Pakistan	34
7	Ethiopia	29

Source: United Nations Development Programme, *Human Development Report* (1990, 132–133)

However, there are a number of countries for which the opposite is true, and still another group for which the levels of poverty are similar in both urban and rural areas. For instance, 32% of Pakistan's urban population, and 29% of the rural population, are below the poverty line.

In general, though, the low income countries have the largest proportions of their populations living in poverty, and the upper middle income economies the least. Rising incomes do not, of course, guarantee a reduction in poverty, but there is generally a clear association between the two.

Further reading

Cardoso, E. and Helwege, A. (1992), Below the line: poverty in Latin America, *World Development*, **20**(1): 19–38.

Green, R.H. (1991), Reduction of Absolute Poverty: a Priority Structural Adjustment, Institute of Development Studies, Discussion Paper 287.

Kabeer, N. (1991), Gender dimensions of rural poverty: analysis from Bangladesh, *Journal of Peasant Studies*, **18**(2): 241–262.

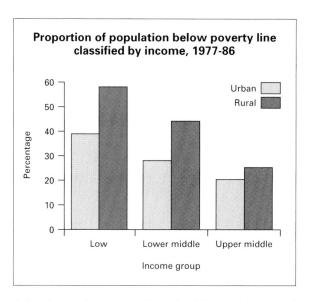

Figure 3.12b Proportion of population below the poverty line, classified by income and urban/rural status, 1977–86

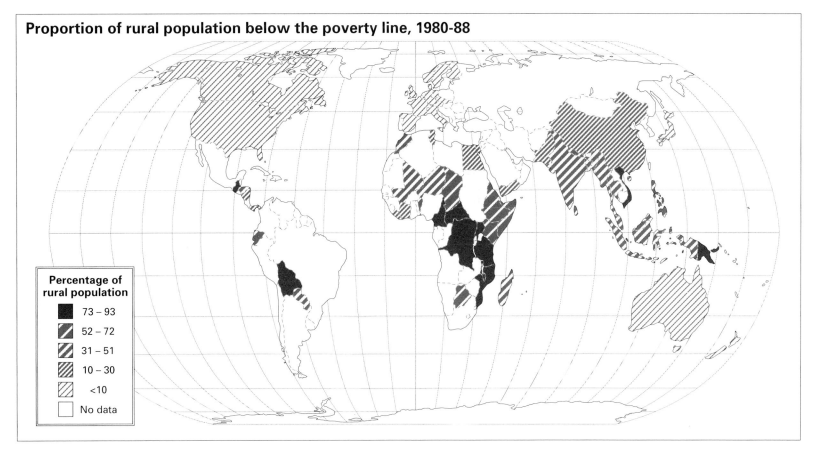

Figure 3.12a Proportion of rural population below the poverty line, 1980–88

3.13 CLASS AND INCOME DISTRIBUTION
Cecile Cutler and Dean Forbes

Class structure is commonly considered an important characteristic of developing countries. Yet it is a notoriously elusive empirical category (is it a social class, or an economic class?) and even more difficult to represent on a map. Instead we can examine some surrogate measures of class, of which income distribution is one.

The distribution of income within a society gives some indication of the wealth of particular groups within that society. What share of household income do the poor get, and what share the rich? One fairly typical measure of income distribution is the share of household income which accrues to the bottom 20% of households, compared to the measure of the control over resources at the top of the scale. By implication, it reveals something of the economic power of the wealthy, and the lack of economic power of those at the bottom of the ladder.

It is, of course, particularly difficult to collect accurate income distribution data. As a result, data are not available for most of the low-income economies, though there generally is rather more for the higher-income economies.

Nevertheless, a number of interesting patterns reveal themselves in the countries for which reasonably accurate data are available. Figure 3.13a shows the share of income controlled by the richest 20% of households. Across all countries this varies from about one third to about one half. Brazil, where the top 20% accrue 62% of income and Botswana, where the comparable figure is 59%, are at the extremes. The rich in these countries account for an exceptionally large share of overall income. Interestingly, there is not much of

Table 3.13 Ratio of income of top 20% of households to bottom 20%, 1980–87

Country	Ratio of highest 20% to lowest 20%
Greatest disparity	
Brazil	26.1
Botswana	23.6
Costa Rica	16.5
Colombia	13.3
Peru	11.8
Least disparity	
Pakistan	5.8
India	5.1
Indonesia	4.7
Bangladesh	4.2
Morocco	4.0
Developed countries	
Australia	9.6
USA	8.9
United Kingdom	6.8
Japan	4.3

Source: United Nations Development Programme, *Human Development Report* (1991: 152–153, 186)

a link between the overall wealth of the country and the share of income going to the top 10%.

Figure 3.13b and Table 3.13 look at the income going to the bottom 20% of households in major geographic regions. Latin America stands out sharply for the relative impoverishment of its poor. Interestingly, there are few striking differences between the remaining areas. It may be a surprise to note that the bottom 20% in developed countries have, on average, no greater share of income than in Africa or east and south-east Asia, and a smaller share than in eastern Europe or south Asia. Expanding the income pie does not, it would seem, also mean giving the poorest 20% a proportionately larger slice.

Further reading

Crone, D.K. (1993), States, elites and social welfare in Southeast Asia, *World Development*, **21**(1): 55–66.

Martin, M.F. (1990), Bias and inequity in rural incomes in post-reform China, *Journal of Peasant Studies*, **17**(2): 273–287.

Prior, F.L. (1990), Changes in income distribution in poor agricultural nations: Malawi and Madagascar, *Economic Development and Cultural Change*, **39**(1): 23–45.

Sofer, M. (1993), Uneven regional development and internal labour migration in Fiji, *World Development*, **21**(2): 301–310.

World Development (1991), Special issue – adjustment with growth and equity, *World Development*, **19**(11).

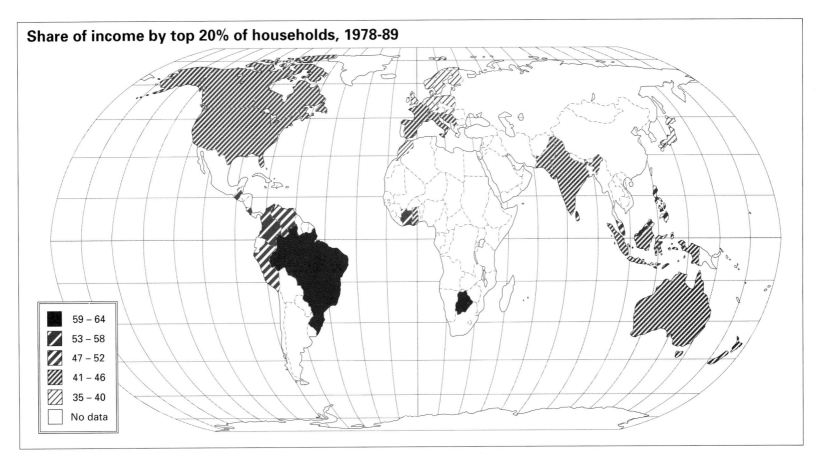

Figure 3.13a Share of income by top 20% of households, various years, 1978–89

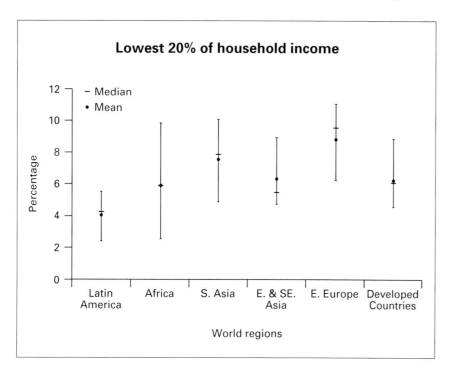

Figure 3.13b Share of income by bottom 20% of households, by world region, 1978–89

3.14 CLASS AND INCOME DISTRIBUTION IN INDONESIA
Cecile Cutler and Dean Forbes

Income distribution in Indonesia provides some clues to the distribution of economic classes within a developing country. This is not to say that Indonesia is 'typical', but that some of the characteristics which apply to Indonesia are also applicable to some other developing countries.

Jakarta is Indonesia's largest city with a population in 1990 of 8.2 million. Located at the western end of the main island of Java, it is the capital of the country, and is a major economic centre. Very few households in Jakarta had incomes beneath Rp 15 000 (approximately US$11) per month, whereas it had the largest share in Indonesia of households earning more than Rp 40 000 per month (Figure 3.14). High income earners in the surrounding province of West Java are second in importance to Jakarta.

This reflects the fact that the middle class are concentrated in Jakarta, and to a lesser extent in the regions surrounding Jakarta. This is also manifest in patterns of consumption within the city. New large shopping malls have sprouted up throughout the city, many concentrating on quality clothes and accessories, electrical goods and the like. The massive freeways and tollways that dissect the city are constantly choked by private automobiles.

The very high income earners are also disproportionately concentrated in Jakarta. In the most prestigious shopping malls, such as Plaza Indonesia in the business and commercial centre of the city, boutiques specialising in designer clothes from Europe and Japan crowd the first and second floors, while the car parks are loaded

with more than their fair share of new Mercedes Benz and BMW cars.

Growing in tandem with this concentration of the economically better-off, Jakarta has consolidated its central political and administrative role within Indonesia. Although the government has taken steps to promote regional development, and devolve power to provinces and districts, the concentration of the middle and ruling classes in Jakarta means its reputation as the centre of power in Indonesia is growing.

East and Central Java exhibit another distinctive pattern (Figure 3.14). More than one fifth of the population in these two provinces has an income of less than Rp 15 000, many times greater than anywhere outside Java. As Table 3.14 makes clear, as late as 1987 42.6% of the population below the poverty line lived in rural Java, whereas only 6.1% of the country's poor lived in urban Java. In other words, in examining the distribution of classes in Indonesia we need to take note of at least two aspects of geographic distribution: between the different islands, and between urban and rural areas.

The outer islands of Indonesia have a similar separation between the urban and rural areas. Figure 3.14 shows that throughout the outer islands income distribution is more evenly shared than on Java, with very small proportions earning under Rp 15 000 or over Rp 40 000 per month. However, Table 3.14 makes clear the fact that nearly half the poor in Indonesia lived in the rural areas of the outer islands, compared to 5.1% in the urban areas.

Further reading

Booth, A. (1992), Income distribution and poverty, in: Booth, A. (ed.), *The Oil Boom and After: Indonesian Economic Policy and Performance in the Soeharto Era*, Singapore: Oxford University Press, 323–362.
Hill, H. (1992), Regional development in a boom and bust petroleum economy: Indonesia since 1970, *Economic Development and Cultural Change*, **40**(2): 351–379.
Huppi, M. and Ravallion, M. (1991), The sectoral structure of poverty during an adjustment period: evidence for Indonesia in the mid-1980s, *World Development*, **19**(12): 1653–1678.
Sicular, D.T. (1991), Pockets of peasants in Indonesian cities: the case of scavengers, *World Development*, **19**(2–3): 137–162.

Table 3.14 The distribution of the urban and rural poor in Indonesia, 1969/70–1987

| | Java | | | Outer Islands | | |
	Number in poverty (millions)	Distribution (%) Poor	Total	Number in poverty (millions)	Distribution (%) Poor	Total
Urban						
1969/70	5.4	12.1	11.3	2.5	5.6	5.6
1987	1.5	6.1	19.7	1.3	5.1	8.2
Rural						
1969/70	26.6	59.6	53.0	10.1	22.7	30.1
1987	10.7	42.6	40.7	11.6	46.2	31.4

Source: Booth (1992: 347)

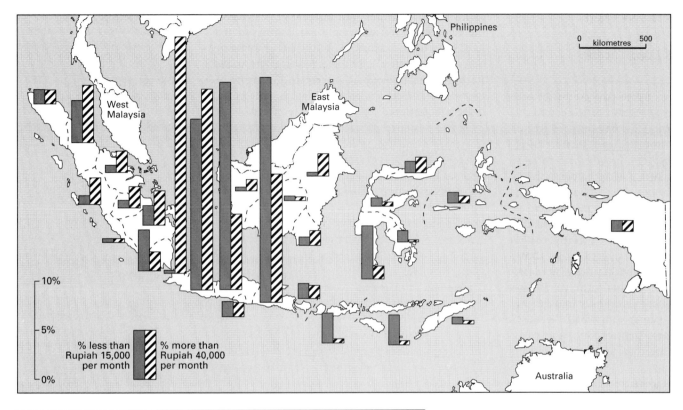

Figure 3.14 Household income distribution in Indonesia

3.15 EMPLOYMENT AND UNEMPLOYMENT
Cecile Cutler and Dean Forbes

Unemployment statistics in western countries are vital measures of the performance of the economy and the general well-being of the society. Fluctuations upwards or downwards send shock waves through the community.

However, there are two major problems with using measures of unemployment in developing countries. First, accurate statistics on unemployment only exist for a small handful of countries, and many are impossible to interpret. How could sense be made of World Bank figures which show 50% unemployment in Niger, and the level in Ghana as 0.6%? Second, the real problem is not so much unemployment as it is underemployment, that is, a measure of people who work (because they have to, or starve), but who do not have enough work, or income, to provide them with a decent standard of living.

Therefore we have to turn to other characteristics of the labour force such as poverty (Section 3.12) and the various measures of participation. Figure 3.15a illustrates the proportion of women in the age range of 15–64 who are in the labour force. In Islamic countries a very small proportion of the women work, only 4.2% in Bangladesh, 7.5% in Pakistan, and 24.2% in Indonesia. By comparison, in the remaining socialist countries the figure is much higher. In China 53.1% of women are in employment, and in Vietnam the proportion is 45%.

Participation rates for the total labour force, and for women in particular, exhibit a U-shape when categorised by country levels of income (Figure 3.15b). Labour force participation rates are highest in the poorest and most wealthy countries, though for quite different reasons. In the poorest countries people work because they have to in order to survive. In the richer countries they work because it is linked to lifestyle issues. Participation rates, particularly for women, are lowest in the lower middle and upper middle income countries.

Further reading

Beneria, L. (1992), Accounting for women's work: the progress of two decades, *World Development*, **20**(11): 1547–1560.

Kennedy, E. and Peters, P. (1992), Household food security and child nutrition: the interaction of income and gender of household head, *World Development*, **20**(8): 1077–1086.

Papps, I. (1992), Women, work and well-being in the Middle East: an outline of the relevant literature, *The Journal of Development Studies*, **28**(4): 595–615.

United Nations (1987), *Women's Economic Participation in Asia and the Pacific*, Bangkok: ESCAP.

United Nations (1991), *The World's Women 1970–1990. Trends and Statistics*, New York: United Nations.

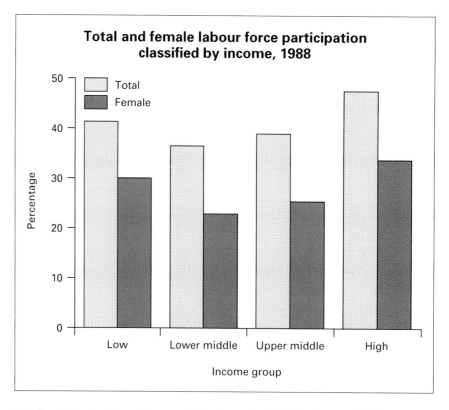

Figure 3.15b Total and female labour force participation, classified by income, 1988

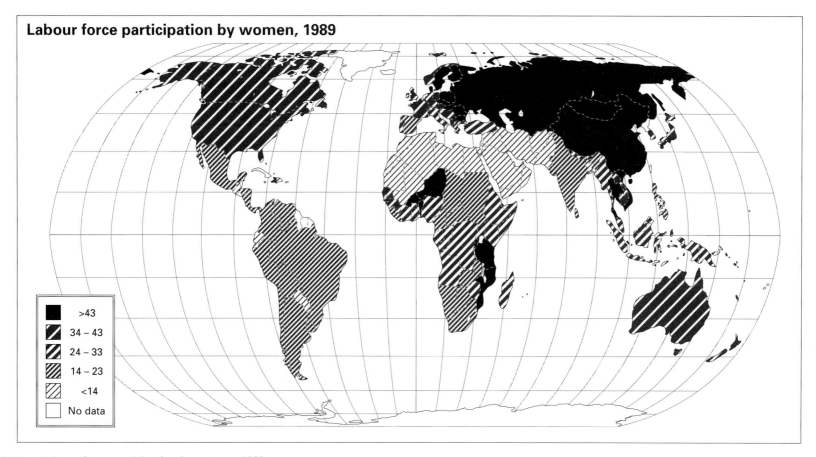

Figure 3.15a Labour force participation by women, 1989

3.16 TENANCY
John Briggs

Figure 3.16 shows that there are three broad types of tenancy arrangement, although under each of these general headings a myriad of variations exists. Private sector arrangements are where ownership rests with individuals, although different societies may have varying levels of legal controls over the ways in which the owner may use the land. The private sector can be usefully split into three sub-sectors. Owner-occupation is typical of the 'family farm' of North America and the European Union, and it is increasingly becoming more common in many parts of Africa and South America. Privately-rented land may entail a farmer requiring more land to increase potential levels of commercial output. In circumstances of land shortage, however, the landowner is likely to be in a more powerful bargaining position, and it is in circumstances such as these that rural poverty becomes more prevalent. An increasingly important sub-type is where a qualified manager operates the farm, but paid a salary not necessarily related directly to the output of the farm. In India, Africa and, to a lesser extent, South America, this may be a common arrangement where commercial commodity crop production dominates (such as tea, coffee, rubber or sisal). Frequently, these farms (or estates, or plantations) are owned by transnational corporations. In parts of the European Union, large finance houses saw land as a form of investment during the 1980s, and many farms were bought as an investment with farm managers being put in place.

Under communal arrangements, usufructuary land rights are still a common feature in many parts of Africa, South America and Asia, but have declined in importance over the last few decades.

Typically, land is owned by the community, and hence land speculation by individuals is not possible. Land is allocated by community leaders, who may be elected to oversee this process, or perhaps have become leaders through age, perceived wisdom or through family ties. Land can then be used by the family to whom it is allocated, usually in perpetuity, as long as the land is in active use. The product of the land belongs to the producers. Although a workable system where there exists a strong community (or tribal) base, the system breaks down under conditions of rapid population growth or agricultural commercialisation. This arrangement offers no collateral for investment by commercial banks, as the user cannot show that he/she has ownership rights. Some observers have suggested that usufructuary rights are a major obstacle to agricultural transformation.

State farms are similar to privately-operated farms, in the sense of being run by managers, with no direct stake in the farm itself, other than meeting production targets set by the state. The major difference is that ownership is held by the state, and hence such land has no commercial value *per se*. Between state and communal tenancy types lie collectives and co-operatives, depending on local circumstances. In the Soviet Union of the 1930s, for example, collectives were more part of the state sector than of the communal sector, whereas in Tanzania of the 1970s they would be better placed closer to the communal sector, although the state may have a key role in stimulating them in the first place, and, indeed, in maintaining their momentum in the future.

This typology is necessarily simplified, and in reality tenancy arrangements are much more complex, with an almost infinite number of individual arrangements. Even in the Soviet Union, state farms existed alongside collective farms and privately-owned farm-plots for decades. During the 1980s and 1990s, with the collapse of the Soviet Union, it is clear that there has been a move to embrace market principles more widely, and this has been reflected in the changing nature of tenancy arrangements. At a world-scale, state involvement has generally been reduced, such that China appears to be the only major country still maintaining the principles of state tenancy arrangements on any widespread scale.

Further reading

Grigg, D. (1984), *An Introduction to Agricultural Geography*, London: Hutchinson.
Ilbery, B.W. (1985), *Agricultural Geography: a Social and Economic Analysis*, Oxford: Oxford University Press.
Robinson, G.M. (1990), *Conflict and Change in the Countryside*, London: Belhaven Press.

T Y P E S	PRIVATE -------------------- COMMUNAL -------------- STATE Owner - occupation Usufructuary State farms Private - rented Collectives Farm - management Co-operatives	
E X A M P L E S	European Union Tropical Africa China North America Parts of South America	

Figure 3.16   Tenancy types

3.17 RESIDENTIAL TENURE: COLOMBIA

Alan Gilbert

Residential tenure varies greatly between countries across the globe. The proportion of households who own their own home varies from 90% in Bangladesh to 30% in Switzerland; from 74% in Eire to 37% in West Germany. Many factors influence the level of owner-occupation but one of the most significant is the proportion of the population living in rural areas. The higher the rural population, the higher the proportion of owner-occupation. The explanation is simple: more countryfolk own land on which they or their predecessors have built a home. In urban areas, by contrast, land tends to be scarcer and property more expensive. As a consequence, there are more tenants. In Sweden, two-thirds of urban dwellers rent a home but only one in ten country folk. In Colombia, whereas 31% of urban households are tenants, less than 7% of households in the countryside rent a home.

National wealth also influences the level of home ownership but in a very inconsistent way. Some affluent countries such as Switzerland contain mainly tenants, others such as Norway and Sweden mainly owner-occupiers. At the poorer end of the income spectrum, there is less variation because most very poor countries have a predominance of country folk; hence most own.

An extremely important factor influencing residential tenure in most developed countries is government policy. If the government builds many council houses and rents them to the population, the proportion of tenants will be high. If

Figure 3.17 Colombia: housing tenure for major cities, 1985

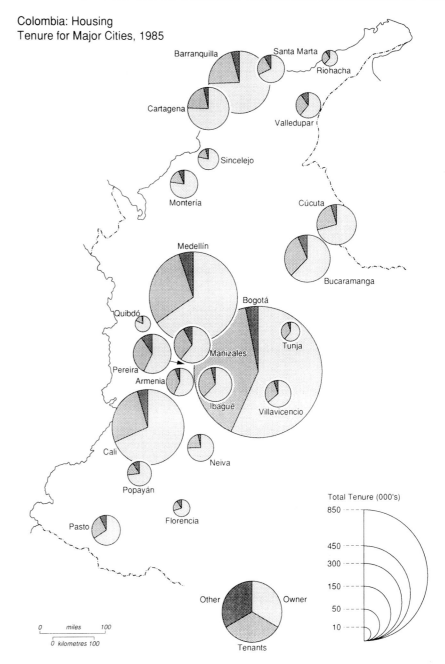

Colombia: Housing
Tenure for Major Cities, 1985

the government encourages families to buy their own property and provides tax relief on mortgage payments, many more families will become owner-occupiers. The effect of government policy has been clearly shown in Britain since 1979 where the proportion of home-owners rose from 56% in 1981 to 63% in 1986. Government sales of council houses to tenants and encouragement for owner-occupation have had a profound effect on residential tenure.

But there are also significant differences between cities within the same country. Figure 3.17 shows the differences in residential tenure between the cities of Colombia. Colombia is a middle-income economy where two-thirds of the population live in towns and cities. Some of the cities are quite large: Bogotá the capital has well over 4 million inhabitants, greater Medellín has more than 2 million and Cali and Barranquilla well over one million each. Home-ownership varies quite considerably between Colombia's cities. In Quibdó and Montería, two small cities in the northwest of the country, for example, four out of five households own their own home. By contrast in Bogotá, Armenia and Pereira less than three in five own their homes. The difference is reflected in the numbers of tenants. In Quibdó and Montería, one in five households are tenants; in Bogotá, two out of five rent their home.

Why are there such differences? The main reason is linked to the cost of owner-occupation. In a country such as Colombia, where many poor families build their own homes, the key constraint on owner-occupation is the ability to acquire a plot of land. In Quibdó and Montería land around the city can usually be acquired through land invasions. By contrast, in Bogotá and Manizales where peripheral land has a high agricultural value, invasions are strongly discouraged and poor people have to buy plots of land. Although the land lacks services and planning permission, it is seldom cheap and it takes quite a lot of saving to marshal the resources with which to buy a plot. Hence, many families are forced to rent a home in Bogotá, whereas they could obtain a free plot and live in a shack in Montería.

Further reading

Booth, A. (1989), *Raising the Roof on Housing Myths*, London: Shelter.

Gilbert, A.G. and Varley, A. (1991), *Landlord and Tenant: Housing the Poor in Urban Mexico*, London: Routledge.

Harloe, M. (1985), *Private Rented Housing in the US and Europe*, London: Croom Helm.

3.18 PERCEPTIONS OF RESIDENTIAL DESIRABILITY: A CARIBBEAN EXAMPLE

Robert B. Potter

In a book which has received much attention, Gould and White (1974) noted that in Nigeria, Ghana and Tanzania, trained personnel – doctors, lawyers and teachers – were attracted to the principal towns and cities, the very areas where, in terms of overall need, they were least required. The authors argued that these *perceptions* of national space, or *mental maps* show a strong *urban bias*, which can only be overcome by means of establishing marked wage differentials between rural and urban areas.

In identifying these facets, the authors were pointing to a perennial trend in the socio-economic landscape. Settlement patterns (Figure 3.18a: a) reflect individual and group *space preferences* (Figure 3.18a: b), that is broad areas of consensus perceptions which generally and persistently favour urban areas. Migration patterns, especially overall volumes of movement (Figure 3.18a: c), are strongly predicated on such perceptions of residential desirability. It is the role of planning and policy to modify such realities (Figure 3.18a: d).

Examples of space preferences are shown in Figure 3.18b: A, in relation to Trinidad and Tobago in the Caribbean. The four maps show average levels of residential desirability for the twenty-one areas making up the country, as perceived by Trinidadians interviewed in four locations. It is clear from the maps that, first and foremost, residents of Port of Spain, San Fernando, Sangre Grande and Mayaro-Guayaguayare all like their home areas. But there is a second underlying trend, and that is the persistently high evaluation of the main urban areas.

The latter aspect is best illustrated in Figure 3.18b: B, where positive residuals, that is areas which are liked more than might be expected on the basis of their distance from the point of survey, are shown. In all four of the maps it is the major urban areas that are associated with such positive residuals. Thus, the extended east-to-west linear urban corridor which makes up the Port of Spain capital region is clearly highlighted in each of the maps with the single exception of that relating to the residents of San Fernando, the second largest settlement. San Fernando in turn appears in all the maps with the single exception of that pertaining to Sangre Grande.

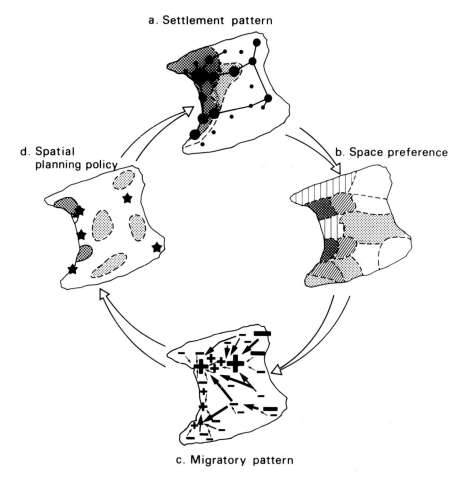

Figure 3.18a The interrelations between settlements, space preferences, migration paths and policy space

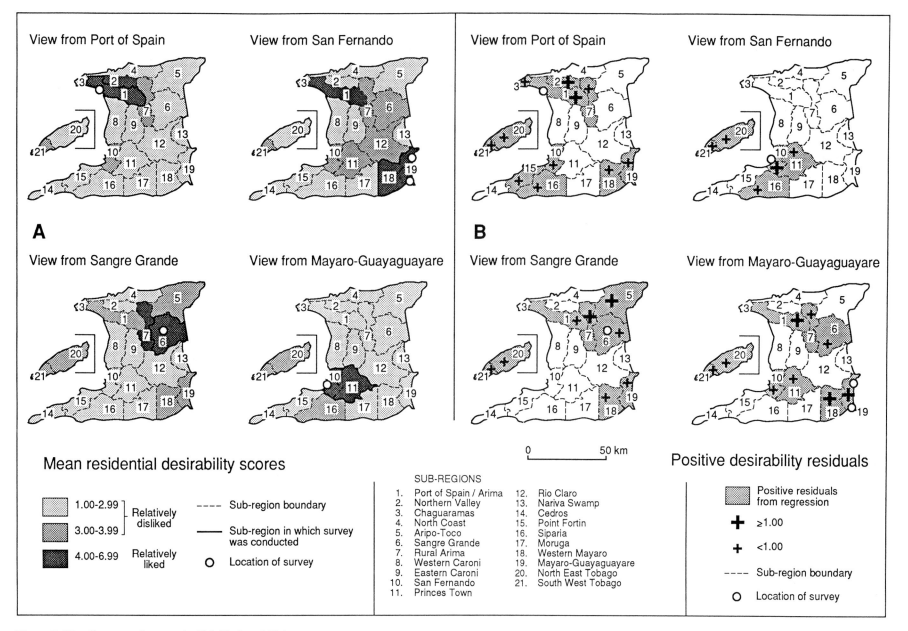

Figure 3.18b   Space preferences in Trinidad and Tobago

Such residential desirability surfaces and the mental maps that are associated with them clearly reflect many of the major problems of development which are faced within Third World nations. Programmes of agropolitan development linked to the idea of providing basic needs, together with integrated rural development projects, are centrally concerned not only with improving rural conditions, but also with reducing rural-urban bias and changing general perceptions of agriculture as the means of earning a living. A number of studies have referred to the existence of *myth maps* (Gould, 1969; Jones, 1978; Potter, 1985), which prescribe the areas of a nation which are persistently over- and under-perceived when looked at in terms of either objective or subjective indicators of social and economic conditions. For example, Jones (1978) showed how in the context of Venezuela, the rural south-east (eastern Llanos and eastern interior) was strongly under-valued in relation to a composite socio-economic index. In contrast, the cities of the central Andean cordillera and those serving as growth centres on resource frontiers in the west were consistently over-perceived. It is a vital task of development planning to endeavour to modify such persistent misperceptions. Research undertaken elsewhere in the Third World has shown, for example, that the relatively simple expedient of providing details of provincial job availability to those living in villages can substantially reduce migratory flows to the capital (Lightfoot and Fuller, 1983).

Further reading

Gould, P.R. and White, R. (1974), *Mental Maps*, Harmondsworth: Penguin.

Potter, R.B. (1985), *Urbanisation and Planning in the Third World: Spatial Perceptions and Public Participation*, London: Croom Helm; New York: St Martin's Press.

3.19 FARMERS' PERCEPTIONS OF AGRARIAN CHANGE
John Briggs

Smallholder farmers in Less Developed Countries (LDCs) generally have a well-developed knowledge of the environmental opportunities and constraints affecting agricultural production. This indigenous knowledge has evolved over generations, and is passed down from mother to daughter, or father to son. Of particular concern are generally issues of water availability and soil fertility and management, and knowledge of these at the micro-level is crucial to farmers' maintenance of output at levels high enough to support household consumption. Among pastoral communities, environmental knowledge, and hence how pastoralists perceive their environments, is equally crucial. Figure 3.19 demonstrates how Ababda and Bishari pastoralists in the Nubian desert of south-eastern Egypt make use of fragile environmental resources distributed over an extensive geographic space. Close to the shore of Lake Nasser, some cultivation takes place, but this area is more important as a reliable supplier of feed and water for livestock. The desert areas to the east provide winter grazing, especially for sheep, following sporadic rainfall at this time of year. This relieves pressure on the lakeshore grazing for two to three months each year. The desert areas also provide limited amounts of *acacia* wood, ideal for charcoal production and central to household income. A range of medicinal plants is also collected in various areas, reflecting differences in micro-environmental conditions. The whole system is in reasonable equilibrium, although pressures do occur, primarily when water is in even scarcer supply.

In terms of perceptions of agrarian change, one of the key tensions is invariably played out between farmers and planners. All too frequently, these tensions occur because of the differing objectives, priorities and perceptions of the two groups. They may be exacerbated by further circumstances such as the rural base of farmers and the urban base of planners; or by the household food needs of farmers and the cash crop needs of planners. The differing perceptions of these two groups may provide a clue as to why agricultural planning in many LDCs over the last two to three decades has not been outstandingly successful, nor produced a significant or sustainable agricultural revolution throughout much of the South.

All too often 'experts' with 'scientific' solutions have generated change in rural areas in conflict with the needs, priorities and perceptions of the farmers affected. An example of the Gummuiya scheme in central Sudan shows that the planners expected that farmers on the new 8000-acre irrigation scheme would grow sorghum and a variety of vegetables, such as okra, onions and tomatoes. This was based on the planners' understanding and perception of the existing Gummuiya agricultural system. In reality, the response of the farmers was to grow little sorghum and virtually no vegetables. Instead, the overwhelming proportion of the irrigated land was planted with fodder crops (lucerne and *abusabayn*, a variety of sorghum harvested early for the green fodder value of the stalks), a thoroughly rational response by Gummuiya farmers because of the central importance of livestock, especially cattle, to the security of the household economy. The planners, on the other hand, were mistaken in their perception of overgrazing being a problem in the area. This occurred because their survey was undertaken at the end of the dry season, when the area does indeed take on a degraded appearance. Four weeks after the first rains, even if only limited, the area is transformed.

Perceptions are based on knowledge, and the problem for many rural inhabitants in LDCs is that this knowledge, and the perceptions based on it, may be substantially different between farmers and planners. It is these differences which need to be reduced before meaningful and sustainable agricultural development can be achieved.

Further reading

Briggs, J. (1978), Farmers' responses to planned agricultural development in the Sudan, *Transactions of the Institute of British Geographers*, **3**: 464–475.

Chambers, R. (1983), *Rural Development: Putting the Last First*, London: Longman.

Harrison, P. (1987), *The Greening of Africa*, London: Paladin.

Timberlake, L. (1985), *Africa in Crisis: the Causes, Cures of Environmental Bankruptcy*, London: Earthscan.

Perception of natural resources and their use, Nubian Desert, south-eastern Egypt.

Differing perceptions, Gummuiya district, central Sudan.

Farmers' perceptions

- household security
- central importance of cattle
- no desire / incentive to produce cash vegetables

Planners' perceptions

- need to produce cash vegetables for urban market of Khartoum
- cattle discouraged because of grazing pressures

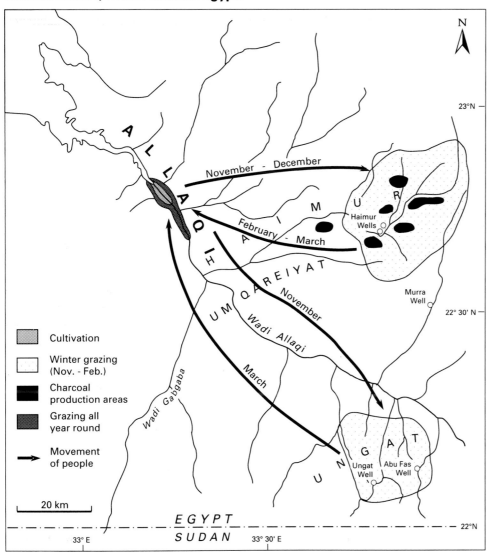

Figure 3.19 Perception of natural resources and their use, Nubian Desert, south-eastern Egypt

3.20 SOCIAL INFLUENCES ON THE ADOPTION OF NEW RICE TECHNOLOGY IN ASIA: SEARCHING FOR MEANING
Jonathan Rigg

Few issues in agricultural development have received so much attention as the factors that influence the adoption of new rice technology – the technology of the so-called 'Green Revolution'. Variations in the proportion of riceland planted to Modern Varieties (MVs) vary across Asia from a low of 2% in Laos, to over 75% in the cases of Indonesia, Malaysia, China, the Philippines and Sri Lanka (Figure 3.20a). Much of the attention has focused on economic variables. However, there are also a number of 'social' variables that may play a role in limiting adoption. The problem is that these are usually far harder to measure; they are disguised or 'hidden', and sometimes culturally sensitive. Such variables include levels of education, the role of women in agriculture, caste variations, local traditions of harvesting, and the role of patron-client ties. It is important to appreciate that such variables operate at different scales, just as levels of adoption vary according to the level of analysis (Table 3.20).

In areas where women play a subordinate role, female-headed households may find it difficult to gain access to new technology. They may be excluded from male dominated credit and marketing co-operatives, ignored in the provision of irrigation, and find it difficult to supervise wage labour. All, or one, of these can combine to limit the adoption of new technologies. It has been noted that 'women's' crops are rarely MVs, and in areas where women tend to be farmers – primarily Africa – MVs have had only a very limited impact. Where they have spread in Africa, the crop invariably becomes 'co-opted' by men (Lipton and Longhurst, 1989).

Although 'big' farmers are often rich farmers, bigness also means greater influence: the ability, for example, to sell crops at the best price, to get preferential access to new technology when it is scarce, and to secure cheap credit (Rigg, 1989). Clearly, economic and 'political' power feed off one another, but it is often the network of contacts and influence upon which big farmers can draw, rather than wealth *per se*, which is crucial.

The problem with attempting to evaluate such social variables, is that they may merely be proxies for other variables. Corbridge (1984), for example, notes that in Bihar, India, those districts populated by tribal groups exhibit a significantly reduced degree of adoption of new rice technology (Figure 3.20b). But as he points out, 'this has little to do with any cultural backwardness or with any lack of an entrepreneurial spirit amongst the tribals of the Jharkhand ... [it] simply reflects the constraints imposed by the region's geology' (Corbridge, 1984: 87). The tribal districts that comprise the Jharkhand region simply overlap with the highland areas least suited to irrigation and the application of the new technology.

It has sometimes been claimed that the power of 'tradition' can constrain technological change. The *bawon* (literally, 'share') system of harvesting in Java where every villager has the right to engage in the harvest, and therefore the right to the production, has often been presented as a stronghold of tradition. The system is seen to have retarded technical change. As Alexander and Alexander (1982: 614) say, this evokes 'a society in which tradition has acquired hegemony over economics'. But recent work has shown that many Javanese farmers have abandoned the *bawon* system and embraced the new rice technology.

Clearly, social variables can play a role in

Table 3.20 Social influences, scale and the adoption of new rice technology

Level	Intra-village	Inter-village/district	Inter-provincial	International
Example (adoption rate of MVs in parentheses)	Pooranur, Tamil Nadu (20%)	North Subang (100%) South Subang (14%) Subang district, Java	Punjab (100%) Madhya Pradesh (0%) Orissa (33%)	Laos (2%) Philippines (89%)
Source	(Bradnock, 1984)	(Hayami & Kikuchi, 1981)	(Barker *et al.*, 1985)	(IRRI, 1994)
Hypothetical social influences	patron-client ties, education	traditional structures caste	ethnicity	'culture'

Note: The levels of adoption at village, provincial and national level are taken from real studies; the social factors that might bear upon levels of adoption are hypothetical
Source: Bradnock (1984), Hayami and Kikuchi (1981), and Baker *et al.* (1985)

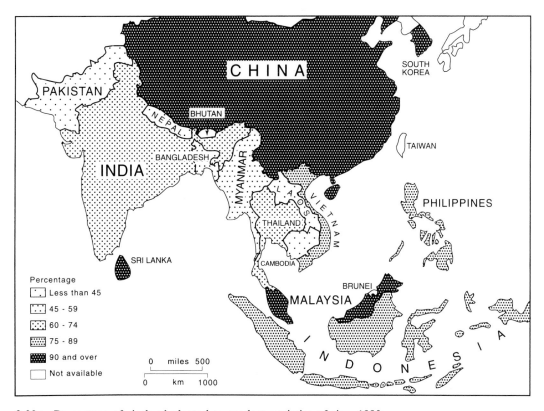

Figure 3.20a Percentage of riceland planted to modern varieties of rice, 1990

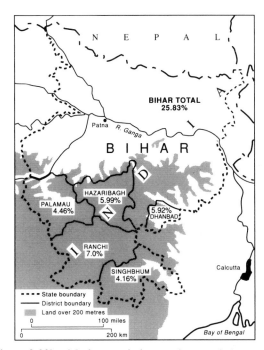

Figure 3.20b Modern varieties, geology and the Tribal peoples of Bihar, India

promoting or inhibiting the spread of the Green Revolution. But, it is important to realise that the revolution is on-going and dynamic. The caste, gender or educational constraints of one decade may have disappeared by the next. Similarly, one person's tradition-bound peasant is another's poor and exploited farmer. There are multiple factors inhibiting and encouraging technological change and it would be foolish to search for single determinants.

Further reading

Bayliss-Smith, T. and Wanmali, S. (eds) (1984), *Understanding Green Revolutions: Agrarian Change and Development Planning in South Asia*, Cambridge: Cambridge University Press.

Lipton, M. and Longhurst, R. (1989), *New Seeds and Poor People*, London: Unwin Hyman.

Rigg, J. (1989), The new rice technology and agrarian change: guilt by association?, *Progress in Human Geography*, **13**(3): 374–399.

3.21 LITERACY
Bill Gould

Literacy is a commonly cited measure of social development, included as one component of the United Nations Development Programme's (UNDP's) Index of Human Development, with the assumption that the more literate is a national population, the more exposed it has been to social and economic improvement and the more people will be able to benefit culturally as well as economically. Yet literacy is so subject to major problems of measurement and interpretation that international comparisons can be difficult. Both the World Bank and UNDP use one of the standard definitions of literacy: 'population over the age of fifteen who can, with understanding, both read and write a short simple statement on their everyday life'. Such a definition is clearly vague and subject to a wide range of nationally variable interpretations.

UNDP has estimated that there were about one billion illiterates in the world in 1990, a figure that has fallen as a proportion of the population aged over 15 years. The global pattern (Figure 3.21a) bears a strong relationship with levels of development in very general terms. In most High Income countries adult literacy rates are above 95%, but in six of the poorest countries, all in Africa (Somalia, Sierra Leone, Djibouti, Guinea, Benin and Burkina Faso), they were less than 20% in 1985. The World Bank estimates that while the 1985 literacy rate for its Low Income category of countries as a whole was 49%, it was much the same level for its Lower Middle Income category (74%) as for its Upper Middle Income category (76%).

However, there are important variations associated with national, cultural and political differences. Africa, the poorest continent, has many countries in the least literate categories, but some countries (Ethiopia, Madagascar, Zaire, Zambia and Kenya) have literacy rates that are much higher than their per capita GNPs would imply. In Asia there is a large contrast between the two population giants. China has a literacy rate of 68%, whereas India has a rate of only 44%. The political impetus for literacy (in school and in adult programmes) has been great in China since 1950, but India has not, despite massive expenditures on education, moved to a literate majority. Its performance is nearer that of its Muslim neighbours, Pakistan (30%) and Bangladesh (32%), and is in great contrast to Sri Lanka (87%) where social programmes have been given prominence in development priorities. Latin American and Caribbean countries almost all have literacy rates in excess of 65%, the clear exception being Haiti.

Literacy levels in the countries of north Africa and the Middle East are consistently lower than income alone would otherwise suggest. Saudi Arabia, the United Arab Emirates, Kuwait and Bahrain have rates of between 60% and 70%, levels that are very different from countries with similar very high incomes. Iran (48%), Iraq (52%) and Libya (56%) have levels that are among the lowest of Upper Middle Income countries, and Egypt (44%), Morocco (42%) and Algeria (49%) are among the lowest in the Lower Middle Income group. Many of the countries with the lowest literacy levels are both poor and predominantly Muslim, notably in the Sahel belt of Africa. It is partly a reflection of the cultural bias implied by definitions of literacy that the people of The Book, who learn to recite the Koran as an integral feature of their religious life, display low measured levels of literacy.

The particular problem of literacy and illiteracy in Muslim societies is further emphasised in differentiation by gender. In almost all countries male literacy rates are above those of women, but the extent of the difference varies. Gender differences are generally larger where overall literacy levels are lower. In Latin America, for example, female literacy rates are within 10 percentage points of male rates in almost all countries. In Sub-Saharan Africa, Asia and Middle East/north Africa, however, there is a much wider range (Figure 3.21b). In Africa, Lesotho has a higher female rate than male rate, but in Sudan and Burkina Faso female rates are less than one-third of the male rates. The modal group of countries has female rates at about half the male rate. This is also the modal group for the countries of Middle East/north Africa, all much richer, for which male:female rates are available. In Asia the male:female literacy gap is much less, with female rates mostly 10–20% below male rates. Nepal, where the female literacy rate is less than half the male rate, is the major exception. Literacy varies with culture as well as with income.

Further reading

UNDP (United Nations Development Programme) (1991), *Human Development Report, 1991*, Oxford: Oxford University Press.

Wagner, P.A. (1990), Literacy assessment in the Third World: an overview and proposed schema for survey use, *Comparative Education Review*, **34**(1): 112–138.

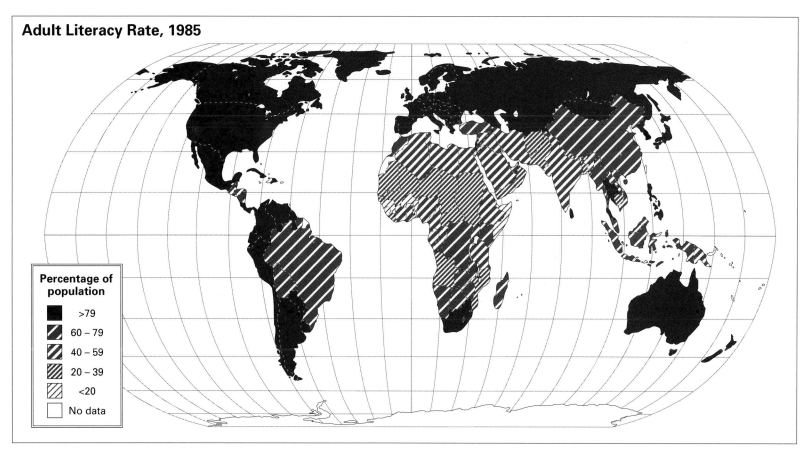

Figure 3.21a Adult literacy rate, 1985

SUB-SAHARAN AFRICA (N = 37)

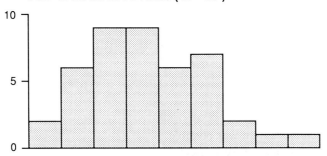

MIDDLE EAST / NORTH AFRICA (N = 19)

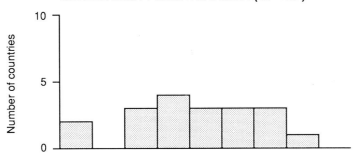

ASIA (N = 13)

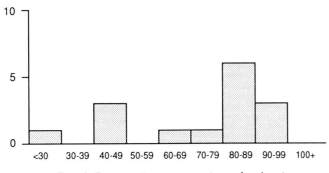

Female literacy rate as a percentage of male rate

Figure 3.21b   Female literacy rate as a percentage of male rate in sub-Saharan Africa, Middle East/north Africa and Asia

3.22 SCHOOL ENROLMENTS
Bill Gould

Formal education through learning by young people in schools has become characteristic of all countries, largely adopting the European model of secular education to ensure, at base, levels of literacy and numeracy that seem to be a necessary condition of development. In colonial countries the demand for education in the earlier part of the 20th century and before was suppressed by a lack of educational opportunities, especially at secondary and higher levels. However, with independence there was not only a great increase in demand for schooling (education being declared by UNESCO to be a basic human right), but newly independent governments ascribed a high economic priority to schooling, allocating a rising proportion of GNP and government expenditure to education. According to UNDP, in 1960 in all Developing Countries, 2.2% of GNP went to education. By 1986 that proportion was 3.7%, consuming over 25% of government expenditure in some countries. Enrolments expanded at all levels, satisfying both the political demand for that basic human right and the economic demand for a more educated population.

Largest expansions were at primary school level. Since many Third World countries in the last four decades have sought to achieve regional targets for universal primary education (upe) set by UNESCO, at this basic level the gap between rich and poor countries seemed to be closing. Indeed, gross enrolment rates (number of children in school as a proportion of the notional age group) in many Third World countries now considerably exceed 100% as a result of enrolment of over-age and even under-age children. Figure 3.22a: (a) identifies, for total and female gross enrolment rates, the extent of increase at primary school level between 1965 and 1988 for major income groups of countries. Largest increases, for both boys and girls, were in Sub-Saharan Africa and east Asia, but OECD countries, having achieved near universal rates by 1960, remained at that high level. There were, however, substantial increases in resources allocated in these countries to primary education such that quality of education was improving much more than was possible in poor countries, where resources were sufficient only for quantitative expansion. Quality of the schooling experience, as indicated by availability of learning materials and adequate buildings, was probably declining in many Third World countries. By the late 1980s in many of the poorest debt-affected countries even enrolment rates were falling.

The enrolment trend has been very different at secondary school level. Figure 3.22b shows the global pattern of secondary enrolment in 1988. Sub-Saharan Africa has lowest enrolment rates, with less than 18% enrolled overall. Asian countries have rates mostly in excess of 40%. Enrolments in the Middle East/north Africa region are higher than in Latin America and Asia, and they are generally in excess of 90% in the OECD countries. Figure 3.22a: (b) shows how at this level there were massive increases in OECD countries, between 1965 and 1988, from a weighted mean of 63% to 95% of the age-group in secondary school. There were also substantial expansions in the regions of the Third World, in proportional terms much larger, but from a much lower base. In this period the global gap in secondary school enrolments did not narrow.

Further reading

Gould, W.T.S. (1993), *People and Education in the Third World*, Harlow: Longman.

Najafizadeh, M. and Mennerick, L.A. (1988), World-wide educational expansion from 1950 to 1980: the failure of the expansion of schooling in Developing Countries, *The Journal of Developing Areas*. **22**(2): 333–358.

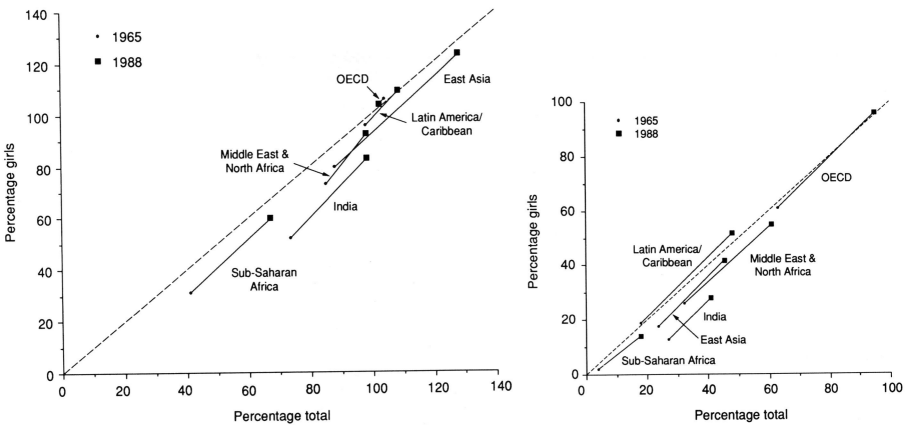

Figure 3.22a   Total and girls' enrolment ratios, (a) primary, 1965–88   (b) secondary levels, 1965–88

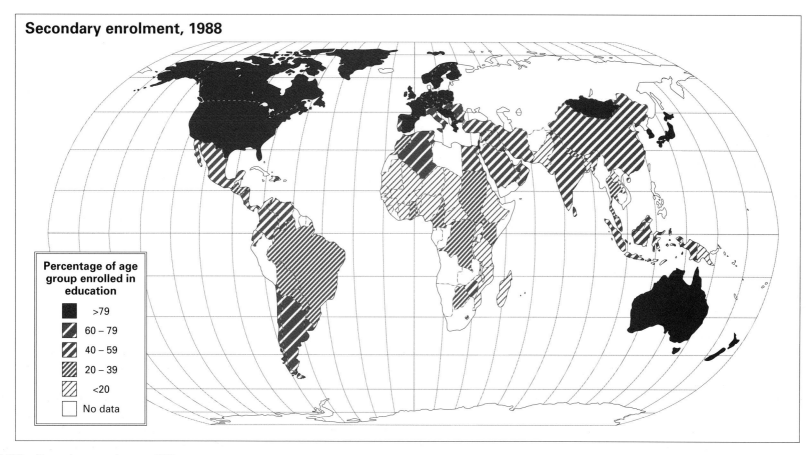

Figure 3.22b   Secondary enrolment, 1988

3.23 HIGHER EDUCATION
Bill Gould

Higher (or 'tertiary' or 'third-level') education is even more scarce and more variable between and within countries than primary or secondary education. For governments, provision of universities and other higher education institutions is extremely expensive. In Africa, typical costs per student place in this sector are more than 50 times the cost per place in primary school, and ten times the cost per place in secondary school (World Bank, 1988: 76), and unit costs are much higher than per capita GNP. In Asia and Latin America they are more similar to GNP (Table 3.23a). By comparison, in industrial countries higher education unit costs are only double those for primary school. However, the expense can be justified in economic terms, for higher education allows the formation of skilled manpower necessary for any country, and the level and type of provision have tended to be guided by manpower planning considerations. In addition, places in higher education are greatly prized since salaries of those with degree or equivalent qualifications tend in relative terms to be very high in Third World countries. The high cost of public provision and the substantial returns to individuals have created great pressures at this level for reducing public cost by reducing subsidies and raising fees and other user costs, even more in Developing Countries than in the rich countries.

Global comparison of enrolments at this level needs to be made with considerable qualification due to wide differences in 'quality' or what is counted as higher education, and in the range of institutions included. Zimbabwe and Bolivia, for example, two countries with similar levels of per capita GNP and similar levels on the UNDP Human Development Index, had 3.7% and 16.6% of the appropriate age group enrolled in higher education, 1986–88. Such a large difference is due largely to much more 'on-the-job' training in Zimbabwe and some technical training institutions being in 'secondary' school in Zimbabwe and 'higher' level in Bolivia. Nevertheless, global comparison of recorded enrolments reveals a pattern of very large differences between rich and poor countries. About 40% of children in OECD countries (over 60% in USA and Canada) progress to higher education; for many African countries that proportion is less than 1% (Figure 3.23). For Developing Countries as a whole it was 6.5% for the period 1986–88 (UNDP, *Human Development Report*, 1991: 147). There has however been substantial expansion in recent years in all groups of countries, including OECD countries where enrolment rates doubled between 1965 and 1988 (Table 3.23b). Among Developing Countries the Newly Industrialised Countries of Asia in particular experienced sharp increases in enrolments in this period, South Korea rising from 6% to 37% and Thailand from 2% to 16%. Ability to make such large investments in higher education is in part a cause, in part an effect of economic success.

Yet there is no necessary link between provision of higher education and economic success. Planning the creation of skilled manpower after 15–18 years in the education system requires a long gestation period. Expansion plans for manpower targets in any given year need to be laid perhaps 20 years earlier, and in a world of rapid technological and political change the possibilities of gross mismatch between manpower targets and the ability of economies adequately to absorb the manpower are very large. In the more economically successful Asian countries, including the oil-producers, there are often shortages of highly skilled manpower, despite the substantial expansion in higher education. In Africa, by contrast, higher education expansion has often been based on over-optimistic economic targets set in the 1960s and 1970s, and there is an increasing problem of graduate unemployment, which at one level leads to a demoralised and under-employed group, at another level fuels the Brain Drain (*see* Section 4.22).

Table 3.23a Unit costs of public education as percentage of per capita GNP

	Primary	Secondary	Higher
Sub-Saharan Africa	15	62	800
East Asia	11	20	118
South Asia	8	18	119
Latin America	9	26	88
All Developing Countries	14	41	370
Industrial Countries	22	24	49

Source: World Bank (1988: 75)

Table 3.23b Percentage of age group enrolled in Higher Education, 1965 and 1988

	1965	1988
Sub-Saharan Africa	<1	2
East Asia	1	5
South Asia	4	n.a.
Europe, Middle East, North Africa	8	14
Latin America and Caribbean	4	17
OECD	21	41

Source: World Bank, *World Development Report* (1991: 261)

Further reading

UNDP (United Nations Development Programme) (1991), *Human Development Report*, New York: United Nations Development Programme.
World Bank (1988), *Education in Sub-Saharan Africa. Policies for Adjustment, Revitalization and Expansion*, Washington D.C.: The World Bank.

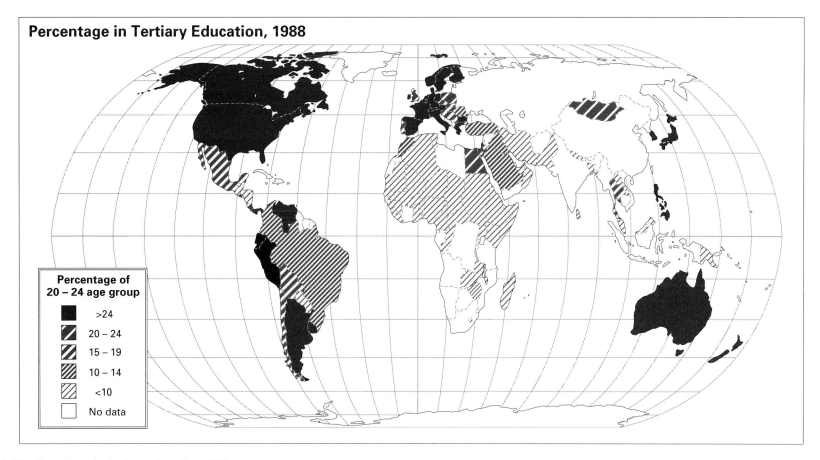

Figure 3.23 Percentage in tertiary education, 1988

3.24 RURAL SETTLEMENT AND SOCIETY: SOUTHERN ANDEAN PERU
Sarah A. Radcliffe

Figure 3.24 of an area of Cuzco department, in the southern Peruvian Andes, shows a settlement pattern with a cluster of small towns and three co-operatives in the Vilcanota river valley at 3200 m, and more dispersed settlements of peasant communities (*comunidades campesinas*) at 3500 m and above. The contemporary settlement pattern owes much to pre- and early-Hispanic social organisation. Pre-Colombian Inka development reflected a highly centralised imperial structure, through which populations and resources were moved over thousands of kilometres, while the Vilcanota river by Pisaq was canalised to control water flow onto irrigated fields. Before the Spanish Conquest of Peru in 1532/3, settlement patterns were dispersed, at times with kinship groups clustered in compounds, or *ayllus*, which controlled land and its usage. Under Spanish Viceroy Toledo, Andean settlement patterns were changed in 1570–75 when indigenous populations were concentrated into towns, *reducciones*. By moving amerindians to lower, more accessible areas, colonial authorities eased administration and Catholic conversion; Taray (Figure 3.24) was founded as the Oma y Taray *reducción* (Cook, 1982). Built on a grid pattern with a central *plaza*, a church and official buildings, *reducciones* housed amerindians and excluded Spaniards and *mestizos* (mixed bloods). However, within a few years, they experienced a decline in indigenous populations, decimated by disease and onerous labour tributes, while *mestizos* grabbed land and houses (Gade and Escobar, 1982). Dispersion quickened after independence as amerindians moved to higher altitudes to be close to fields and to avoid Spaniards, and since 1920 peasant communities can register independent control over land. For example, Ccaccaccollo registered as an 'indigenous community' with inalienable land rights in 1927 (Radcliffe, 1986, 1990a).

Ironically, today ex-*reducciones* such as Taray (population 418 in 1981), Coya (950) and Lamay (930) are generally *mestizo* towns, while indigenous peasants reside in high-altitude communities, and agrarian co-operatives (now largely parcelised) formed in the 1969 Agrarian Reform. Interactions between peasant villagers and residents in the valley towns are frequent. Sunday markets in Pisaq (population 1400), also frequented by foreign tourists, provide opportunities for exchange of highland and lowland products, such as fruit for grains. Peasants purchase plastic goods, alcohol and clothing in Cuzco. Urban *mestizos* occasionally visit villages hoping to buy livestock and crops at favourable prices. Ties of godparenthood, formalised at baptisms and weddings, link *mestizos* as patrons with peasants eager to gain access to urban services and contacts. Registrations of births, marriages and deaths take place in Taray, where the district mayor's office is located. Peasant church weddings and baptisms, although not required in law, take place in Taray's colonial church with godparents, other *mestizos* and villagers as guests. Law is maintained by peasant appointees of local policemen based in Pisaq, while NGOs work in communities attempting to generate agricultural development (Lehmann, 1982).

Facilities are relatively meagre, with no piped water or electricity in most communities. Houses are mostly one-storey adobe buildings roofed with grass, tiles or corrugated iron. Other buildings include chapels, visited by the Pisaq priest four times annually, and primary schools constructed by villagers. Male and female villagers hold inheritable usufruct rights to small plots of land scattered in varying ecological levels. Continuing a historical strategy for multiple activities in a 'vertical ecology' (Murra, 1956; Lehmann, 1982), families co-ordinate kin's labour in work-exchange parties to produce varied crops and livestock. Grazing takes place in high *puna* grasslands, in areas fallowed between crops of Andean tubers and barley; maize and beans are grown in irrigated lowlands. Cash is also necessary, gained by sale of produce (barley to breweries in Cuzco; onions; potatoes), and by migration to rural and urban labour markets.

While state authorities intervened to protect peasant control over land against *mestizo* attempts to appropriate it, attitudes to the nation are ambivalent (Radcliffe, 1990a). While acknowledging state legal protection, peasants recognise that resources are not invested in rural services. Standards of living in the Pisaq-Taray region are among the lowest in Peru, with widespread malnutrition, infant mortality and low life expectancy. Underfunded medical posts exist in Pisaq and Taray, although indigenous health specialists are most frequently consulted. Most communities now have a primary school attended daily by urban teachers, while secondary schools are found in Pisaq and Calca, and further education is found in Cuzco (population 181 000) (van den Berghe and Primov, 1977). In addition, syncretic beliefs find little sympathy among Hispanic urban decision-makers. Quechua-speakers' beliefs about an animate landscape, the deity *Pachamama*, inform behaviour such as *coca*-chewing (Allen, 1988), marking of boundaries (Radcliffe, 1990a) and pilgrimages (Sallnow, 1987).

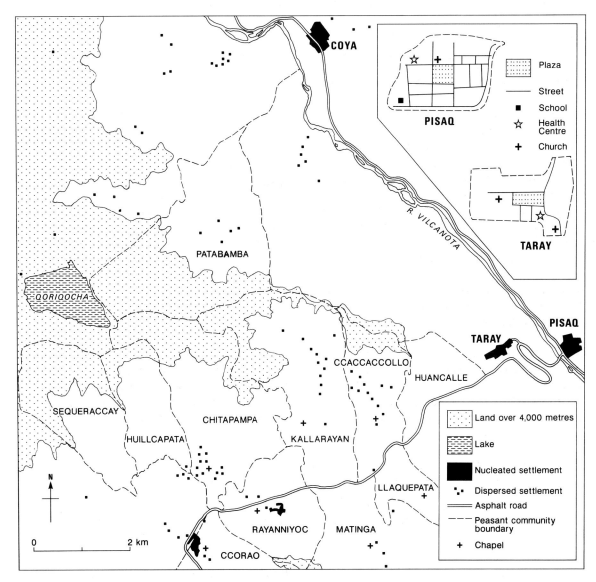

Figure 3.24 Rural settlement in part of Cuzco Department, Peru

Further reading

Gade, D. and Escobar, M. (1982), Village settlement and the colonial legacy in Southern Peru, *Geographical Review*, **72**(4): 430–449.

Lehmann, D. (ed.) (1982), *Ecology and Exchange in the Andes*, Cambridge: Cambridge University Press.

Radcliffe, S.A. (1990a), Marking the boundaries between the community, the state and history, *Journal of Latin American Studies*, **22**(3): 575–594.

Van den Berghe, P. and Primov, G. (1977), *Inequality in the Peruvian Andes: Class and Ethnicity in Cuzco*, Columbia: University of Missouri Press.

3.25 ETHNIC PLURALITY AND DEVELOPMENT
David Drakakis-Smith

Population movement across frontiers has been a constant feature of world history. Whether escaping from invasions or persecution, searching for new economic opportunities or, more infamously, seeking 'lebensraum', people have migrated over short and long distances into the territory of other ethnic groups. As a consequence, ethnic plurality was an identifiable feature of development long before the colonial era wrought large-scale changes on the ethnic and political map of the world. It was common, for example, to find several quarters within pre-colonial trading cities in south-east Asia where Arab, Chinese, Indian and Malay communities would live beside one another.

Initially, when the Europeans arrived, they were for a long period just another trading community, albeit one with considerably more military potential than the others. However, once the nature of colonialism changed from a mercantile or trading basis to one in which territorial acquisition became paramount, so the nature of ethnic interaction changed.

Although, in general, European settlement in colonial territories was relatively limited, there were colonies, such as Algeria, French Indo-China or the Dutch East Indies where more extensive settlement occurred. Here, even more than in other colonies, space was restructured to give the politically dominant power the best sites, whether for economic or social activities. More important, however, in the ethnic context was the way in which new ethnic groups were brought into the colonies in order to meet the labour demands of expanded colonialism.

In many cases these demands were in less populated rural areas and indentured or contract labour was imported in order to make possible new commercial activities in mining or agriculture. Often the expatriate employers drew from other parts of their colonial empire, so that, for example, Indians appeared in British East Africa and south-east Asia, Vietnamese in French Pacific territories. In addition, European powers encouraged regional expatriate groups to assume control of small-scale urban commerce, thus providing a social, economic and political buffer between the colonisers and indigenous populations. In this way, the Chinese penetrated most of urban south-east Asia and the Pacific, whilst Indian or Parsee communities spread around east Africa, the Middle East and parts of south-east Asia.

The consequence of this voluntary and forced movement of population, before and during the colonial period, has been very complex ethnic plurality in some countries. Figure 3.25 shows the main ethnic groups in Myanmar (Burma), for example. To this already complicated picture, the British introduced a variety of commercially oriented ethnic groups. By 1931, although Indians numbered only 7% of the population, they occupied over one-third of mining jobs, 15% of the jobs in trade and industry, 27% of those in the service sector and 43% of transport and policy employment. In particular, Rangoon became an Indian city, contributing over half the population by 1901 whilst the native Burmese comprised less than one-third.

The development dilemmas posed by such ethnic plurality, following independence, can be clearly seen in Malaysia where economic and political activity had taken on a clear ethnic dimension (Table 3.25). On independence, the indigenous Malays found themselves in political power but with little economic influence in their own country. Immigrant Chinese and Indian families dominated large and small-scale commerce and industry in urban and rural areas, as both owners and workers. Following the intercommunal riots of 1969, Malaysian economic development policy has been dominated by the desire of the government to restore some economic balance to national development, with the result that most investment programmes have been biased toward the Malay community.

Ethnic plurality has continued to intensify in the post-independence period throughout the Third World. Improved communications now mean that international labour migration is

Table 3.25 Malaysia: employment and ethnicity

| | % Labour composition 1930 | | | % Labour composition (1970) 1980 | | | |
	Estates	Mines	Padi	Primary	Secondary	*	Tertiary
Malays	3	1	97	(68)66	39	(38)	47
Chinese	23	92	1	(19)20	51	(51)	42
Indians	74	7	2	(12)13	9	(10)	11

Source: Mehmet (1986)
* Secondary and Tertiary employment combined

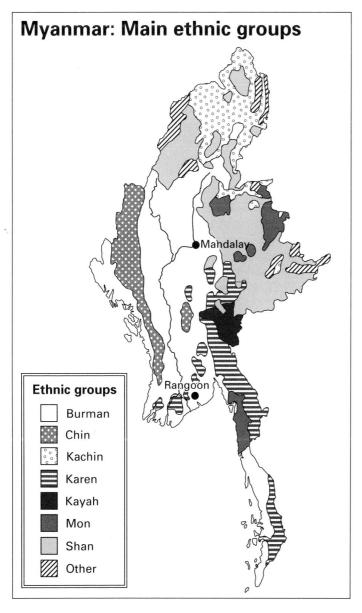

Figure 3.25 Myanmar: main ethnic groups

extensive, often across lengthy distances (*see* Section 4.23). Whilst many immigrant workers are absorbed with few problems, cultural and social contrasts often lead to tension and conflict at times of economic or political difficulties. The recent Gulf war revealed the cost in human suffering only too well.

Further reading

Drakakis-Smith, D. and Williams, S.W. (eds) (1983), *Internal Colonialism: Essays Around a Theme*, Edinburgh: Department of Geography, University of Edinburgh on behalf of the Developing Areas Research Group of the Institute of British Geographers, Monograph 3.

Parnwell, M. (1993), *Population Movements in the Third World*, London: Routledge.

Stavenhagen, R. (1986), Ethnodevelopment: a neglected dimension in development thinking, in: Anthorpe, R. and Krahl, A. (eds), *Development Studies: Critique and Renewal*, Leiden: E.J. Brill, 21–39.

3.26 THE SPREAD OF HIV IN OWAMBO, NAMIBIA
Douglas Webb

The spread of the Human Immuno-deficiency Virus (HIV), the generally assumed causative agent of Acquired Immune Deficiency Syndrome (AIDS) in the developing world, has attracted the attention of a wide range of scholars from various disciplines during the 1980s and 1990s. Motivations for the study of this particular condition relate to its relative infancy as a research topic, and the great potential which AIDS has in adversely affecting all development processes. In the social sciences, research to date has focused on two major themes: the social epidemiology of HIV/AIDS, and the socio-economic impact of AIDS. Much doubt still lingers as to the severity of the epidemic in the African context, and studies produced now must attempt to dispel the myths and confirm the urgent need for further research on the socio-economics of AIDS as well as impact alleviation strategies. Spatially, studies have tended to be quite rigid, unwilling to diverge from the micro-macro distinction, so making the application of research findings problematic at a wider scale, and in widely differing contexts. Integration of local and national perspectives in the understanding of the social epidemiology of HIV, for example, provides the framework for an analysis of the determinants of HIV spread, and the nature of their interaction within a given context.

The interaction of macro-structures, such as trade systems, with local structures, including transport networks, is demonstrated by the emerging pattern of the spread of HIV in Owambo, north Namiba (Figure 3.26). The data for this are derived from blood donations at the mobile clinic, based at Oshakati State Hospital.

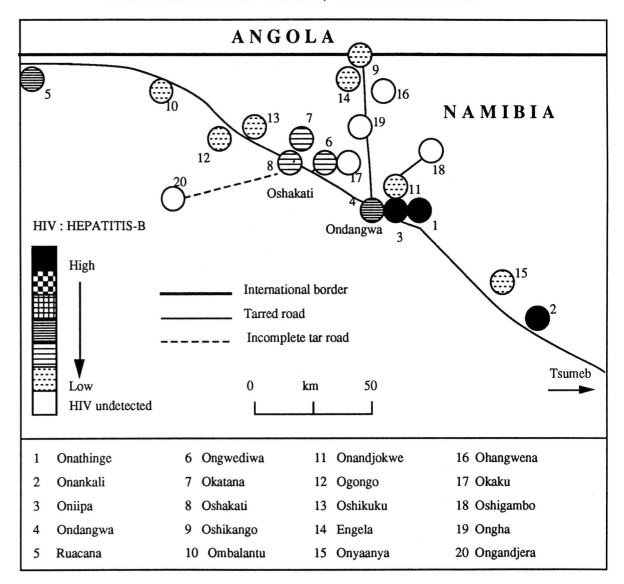

THE SPREAD OF HIV IN OWAMBO, NORTHERN NAMIBIA

1	Onathinge	6	Ongwediwa	11	Onandjokwe	16	Ohangwena
2	Onankali	7	Okatana	12	Ogongo	17	Okaku
3	Oniipa	8	Oshakati	13	Oshikuku	18	Oshigambo
4	Ondangwa	9	Oshikango	14	Engela	19	Ongha
5	Ruacana	10	Ombalantu	15	Onyaanya	20	Ongandjera

Figure 3.26 The spread of HIV in Owambo, northern Namibia

All blood is routinely tested for HIV, hepatitis-B and syphilis. Because of these tests, 12.5% of the blood donated on average has to be discarded. Hepatitis-B prevalence at February 1993 stood at 7.9%, syphilis at 2.3%, HIV-I at 2.8%. High HIV:Hepatitis-B ratios are evident, and the relationship of HIV prevalence with the main road is demonstrated. Factors related to traffic flow, though, are twofold: the origin of the traffic, and the propensity of the traffic to stop at a given location. HIV is still undetected in the settlements of Ongandjera, Okaku and Oshigambo which are relatively isolated from the main roads. Ongha and Ohangwena, despite being on the main Ondangwa-border road with an associated high traffic density, have a low HIV prevalence, as trucks from Angola or from the south tend to stop at Ondangwa or Oshikango at the border post, where there is also a small trading centre with a market. Ongha and Ohangwena are thus bypassed by most of the road traffic.

HIV:Hepatitis-B ratios are highest on the trunk road south of Ondangwa, the stretch of road with the greatest direct interaction with traffic from the major labour centres such as Windhoek and Walvis Bay to the south. This road is characterised by a series of small linear service settlements consisting of *cuca* shops (bars), garages, small shops and markets. The high ratio at Ruacana can be explained by the presence of a large military base, where 8.3% of a sample of military personnel were HIV-positive. The large scale introduction of HIV into Owambo can be traced back to the massive repatriation programme of 1989–90, when over 30 000 exiles and military personnel re-entered Owambo, following Namibian independence. The sexual networking of soldiers today is crucial in the spread of the virus, as 17.2% of a sample (n = 127) of Owambo military personnel are HIV-positive.

The HIV/AIDS epidemic is still in its early stages in Owambo, but analysis of such larger scale processes, operating at a local level, can give valuable insights into the present and future movement of the virus, allowing AIDS prevention programmes to respond accordingly.

Further reading

Barnett, T. and Blaikie, P. (1992), *AIDS in Africa: its Present and Future Impact*, London: Belhaven.

Cross, S. and Whiteside, A. (1993), *Facing up to AIDS: the Socio-Economic Impact in Southern Africa*, London: Macmillan.

Mann, J., Tarantola, D.J.M. and Netter, T.W. (eds) (1992), *AIDS in the World*, London: Harvard University Press.

Packard, R.M. and Epstein, P. (1991), Epidemiologists, social scientists, and the structure of medical research on AIDS in Africa, *Social Science and Medicine*, **33**(7): 771–794.

Panos Institute (1992), *The Hidden Costs of AIDS: the Challenge of HIV to Development*, London: Panos.

4 Production and Exchange: the Economic Structure of Development

TIM UNWIN

This chapter examines the global economy in terms of production and exchange at a range of scales from the international to the local. It begins with a survey of agricultural production and trade, focusing not only on basic crop production systems and staple foods, but also on issues such as international agribusiness, food security, and the range of environmental and social factors influencing agricultural production at the local scale, with examples being drawn from eastern Africa and Thailand. One measure of economic development that is often adopted is the structure of employment, with high percentages of the working population involved in agriculture being seen as indicative of low levels of economic development. The analysis of the global pattern of employment in Section 4.8 thus provides a useful link between the preceding discussion of agriculture, and the subsequent examination of industrial production and trade. The global organisation of manufacturing industry is described in Section 4.9, and this is followed by a more detailed analysis of the most dynamic component of the global manufacturing economy, namely Pacific Asia. One important local expression of industrial development has been the creation of company towns, and Section 4.11 therefore provides a case

study of the development of such settlements in Brazil.

The various parts of the global economy are connected together by numerous different transport links, and the next five sections combine an analysis of particular types of transport and trade routes with an account of some of the commodities carried. Section 4.12 thus examines the location of iron ore, bauxite and phosphate production, and the seaborne transport of such ores to processing plants, many of which are in the industrialised states of northern Europe, north America and Japan. This is followed by a description of road and rail networks, international shipping, and the markedly uneven expansion of air transport that has occurred in the last thirty years.

The relationship between urban growth and economic change is explored in the next two sections. Section 4.17 thus examines issues such as urban bias, the validity of such concepts as the rank-size rule, and the global expression of urban primacy, whereas Section 4.18 focuses on the practical problem of providing housing of sufficient quality for the rapidly growing populations of urban communities in poor states.

Increasingly, financial institutions and banks are playing a dominant role in the global

economy, not only through their provision of loans but also through the recycling of the profits of international capitalism, and their influence on indebtedness in many of the poorest countries of the world. The activities of the World Bank, the growing debt crisis, and the role of offshore banking are therefore analysed in Sections 4.19–4.21. These are followed by three sections examining the economic conditions giving rise to labour migration and the influences of remittances, at both the global scale and also through a local case study in southern Peru.

The final sections of the chapter address the very different subjects of mass communications, the exploitation of wildlife and international development aid. Television and radio have now become the most important forms of mass communication throughout the world, and yet there remain very different levels of access to the information that they provide. Wildlife exploitation often provides a source of both food and considerable foreign earnings for poor countries, and the tensions between local populations and the demands of conservation interests are highlighted in the context of the African savannas in Section 4.27. Finally, the economic significance of international aid is examined in Section 4.28, which draws attention to the need for donors and recipients to pay increasing attention to the close targetting of such intervention to the communities and sectors of the economy which will benefit most from it.

4.1 CROP PRODUCTION SYSTEMS
John Briggs

There have been a number of attempts to classify and map agricultural systems at a variety of scales. One of the best known is that by Whittlesey (1936) which produces a classification of 13 agricultural regions at the world scale. These agricultural regions were based on five sets of criteria: crop and livestock associations; the processing and disposal of farm produce; the intensity of land-use; the methods and degree of mechanisation; and the types and associations of buildings and other agricultural structures. More recent attempts at world-scale classifications include work by Helburn (1957), Tarrant (1974) and Grigg (1974).

The classification system adopted for Figure 4.1 is based on dominant enterprise and output. Six major types are proposed, with a seventh being areas where there is limited or no agricultural activity. The seven categories are:

(1) *Commercial crop production* – crops produced almost exclusively for the market, with little or no direct consumption within the household.
(2) *Predominantly commercial crop production* – although crops are grown primarily for the market, some part of the crop(s) may be retained for direct consumption within the household.
(3) *Predominantly subsistence crop production* – the fundamental production aim is to produce food crops for household consumption, although surpluses may be sold.
(4) *Mixed farming (crop/livestock mix)* – both crop production and the keeping of livestock form the basis of an interdependent agricultural system.

(5) *Commercial livestock production* – the production of livestock products for the market.
(6) *Predominantly subsistence livestock production* – livestock fulfil either social/cultural needs in the society or food needs, but may also be sold on an irregular basis.
(7) *Limited or no agricultural activity.*

Figure 4.1 shows a generalised pattern, and hence there is some loss of detail, a perennial problem when mapping at the world scale. The map is intended to provide a generalised pattern of world agriculture, as the basis for further study and research questions. By the fact of its scale, it cannot provide the necessary detail at the sub-national or regional level. This is one of the key criticisms levelled at the mapping of agricultural systems at this scale. Nevertheless, some clear geographic patterns emerge. Commercial crop production, where it is the sole agricultural enterprise, exists in only relatively small areas of the world's surface, primarily in the mid-west of the USA, the Prairies of Canada, and parts of South America and Australia. Much of South America, Africa and Asia is dominated by crop production systems, but where only a proportion of the crop is sold commercially. Whether these systems lie within Group 2 or Group 3 depends very much on the basic aim of farmers. There are few truly subsistence farmers today – most produce at least some output for the market, if only to generate cash for items such as household goods, clothes, school fees and so on. However, it would be true to say that most farmers in Less Developed Countries have the overriding aim of producing for household consumption as the main priority. Mixed farming is dominant throughout much of Europe, although there is considerable spatial variation within Europe, as well as a trend to

greater specialisation. Livestock production systems can be divided into two. Predominantly subsistence livestock production is located mainly in the drier areas of the tropics and sub-tropics, and especially in the desert-lands of Africa and Asia. It would, however, be misleading to suggest that livestock are never sold. Like Group 3 farmers, the priority is to secure household food requirements first and foremost, and this drives needs for sales of livestock. Commercial livestock production tends to be found in the more economically advanced countries.

Further reading

Grigg, D. (1974), *The Agricultural Systems of the World*, Cambridge: Cambridge University Press.
Helburn, N. (1957), The bases for a classification of world agriculture, *Professional Geographer*, **9**: 2–7.
Tarrant, J. (1974), *Agricultural Geography*, Newton Abbot: David and Charles.
Whittlesey, D. (1936), Major agricultural regions of the earth, *Annals of the Association of American Geographers*, **26**: 199–240.

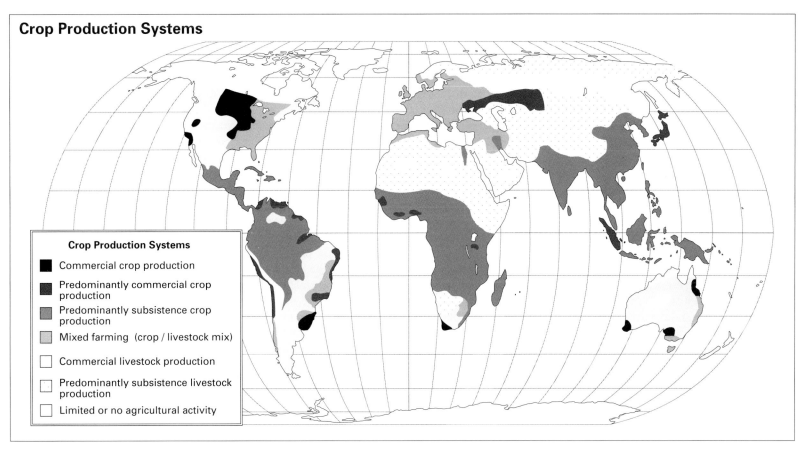

Figure 4.1 Crop production systems

4.2 STAPLE FOOD CROPS
John Briggs

The classification used in Figure 4.2 reflects the fact that very few, if any, societies rely exclusively on one staple food crop only, although it is equally clear that one or two staples dominate most people's diets. In parts of eastern and southern Africa, for example, it is common for 80% of the energy intake into the diet to be derived from maize. Rice in south and east Asia assumes a similar importance.

Rather than map the major staple food types, it was therefore decided to map the major staple food groups. Within the cereals group are included major staple crops such as rice, maize and wheat, which between them constitute the major staples for the majority of the world's population. Indeed, the map shows that either the 'predominantly cereals' group or the 'cereals/root crop mix' group are found widely throughout North and South America, Africa, Europe and much of Asia. Other cereal crops are locally important; for example, barley is common in temperate areas, grown as either animal feed or as a raw material for the brewing industry, whilst sorghum and millet are well-adapted to growth in drier environments.

Root crops include potatoes and cassava as important staples, but also include lesser crops such as sweet potatoes. Very few societies are predominantly dependent on root crops alone, and hence these are frequently found in conjunction with either cereal crops or tree crops. This clearly has the advantage of providing dietary variety. Although potatoes and most varieties of cassava are indigenous to Latin America, their geographic distribution is worldwide. Potatoes, however, do not grow successfully in hot con-ditions, nor where there are water availability difficulties. Cassava, on the other hand, can do well under such conditions, and hence the two crops rarely compete for the same space. The cereals/root mix is a major staple in much of North America, tropical Africa, western Europe and the states of the former Soviet Union.

Tree crops, similarly, rarely provide the sole staple, except in a few relatively small areas, such as central Africa. The main tree staple is plantains, or cooking bananas. These are different from sweet (or eating bananas) in that they are hard when harvested and require boiling to make them edible. Tree crops have their widest geographic extent when in combination with root-crops. They are particularly important in parts of south-east Asia, although rice may also be important. The forested areas of tropical central and west Africa and of South America are the main geographic regions of tree and tree/root crop mix.

The current trend appears to be for cereals to be increasing in importance as a world staple, and in particular, for wheat products to become relatively more important within the cereals group. Indeed, there is a trend for urban consumers in many Less Developed Countries to perceive wheat-flour as being more 'modern' than maize-flour. This has led to an increase in wheat imports by countries which can ill-afford to use scarce foreign exchange in this manner, whilst at the same time witnessing a decline in locally-produced maize output.

Further reading

Pierce, J.T. (1990), *The Food Resource*, London: Longman.

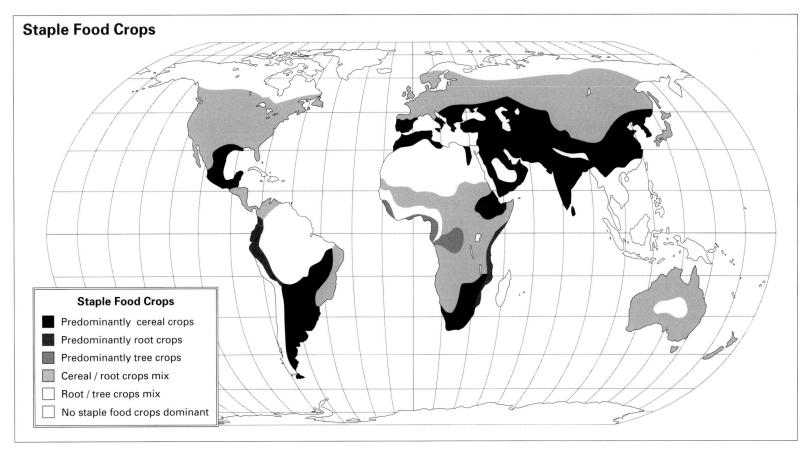

Staple Food Crops

Staple Food Crops

- Predominantly cereal crops
- Predominantly root crops
- Predominantly tree crops
- Cereal / root crops mix
- Root / tree crops mix
- No staple food crops dominant

Figure 4.2 Staple food crops

4.3 AGRIBUSINESS IN THE 1990s
David Preston

An important and widespread change in the methods of farming which has affected rural people throughout the world is the application of modern business methods to both the processes of growing crops and managing production. On the one hand this is nothing new since crops like wheat and sugar beet in the North and sugar cane and coffee in the South have long been associated with such styles of farming. What is new, in the past two decades, is the growing of crops needing special levels of care, and in particular the application of agrochemicals to control the environment in which the plants or livestock are growing, for export or for urban markets. A visit to any large supermarket in western Europe or North America and an inspection of the shelves of fruit and vegetables will reveal products from agribusinesses in the South. One such visit found asparagus from Thailand, mangetout peas from Zimbabwe, beans from Kenya and starfruit from Malaysia (Figure 4.3a). None of these products would have been found there fifteen years ago. They are produced not by peasant farmers, but by businessmen concentrating on high quality produce for export.

The globalisation of many sorts of production, from computers to jeans, is widely recognised. This includes many sorts of food including those which are perishable. Modern forms of transport and storage allow potatoes to be grown in Egypt and sold in western Europe, and strawberries to be grown in Mexico (or Tanzania) and sold in New York (or London). Other forces have promoted this style of production for faraway markets. The policies of the International Monetary Fund, World Bank and other sources of financial invest-ment in Developing Countries have encouraged many countries to increase exports at any cost. A consequence has been a mushrooming of what are known as Non-Traditional Exports, many of which are produced in rural areas. Such exports earn foreign currency which can then be used by national governments to pay the interest owed on foreign loans (*see* Section 4.19). The beneficiaries of this growth of export crops are not only the growers and the managers of national economies but also those who supply the agrochemicals, and those who transport and market the products.

The global pattern of agribusiness, in particular new agricultural export crops, is a function not so much of particular environmental advantages – a hot wet season during northern winters when fresh flowers, fruit and vegetables are in short supply – as the stimulus and facilities offered by national governments to growers, and the supplies of capital available for the necessary investment to get production started. A further factor may be abundant supplies of relatively cheap labour for those crops that are labour-intensive.

Figure 4.3b shows one particular agribusiness export commodity – fresh chickens. Chickens are one of the most efficient converters of vegetable foodstuff, in particular high protein food such as soyabeans, into meat for human consumption. A marketable chicken can be produced for sale in eight weeks, takes very little space and is highly valued in worldwide diets. As a consequence, some countries with national sources of capital have developed chicken production: Mexico capitalising on its proximity to the USA; Brazil using its role as a major soyabeans producer and with its own large city markets; and China, Thailand and Hong Kong with major urban markets and accustomed to intensive agricultural production.

Some types of agribusiness that are of increasing importance use little space. Factory-style livestock units housing 100 000 chickens or 1000 pigs can be located wherever investors have access to land, so long as there is access by vehicle to bring in foodstuff for the livestock and to take the produce to market. Factory farms may occur in unlikely places, in the mountains of southern Europe where a migrant investor owned some land, or near a fishing port with a fishmeal factory where high-protein meal and some otherwise discarded 'waste' was available. More likely locations are near to major urban markets such as the major cities.

Mexico is an exceptional case. Sharing a long frontier with the USA, with a climate warmer than that of Florida or California in winter, with excellent communications with the USA and a long history of cross-border investment, Mexico has become a sub-tropical extension of the US food production system. Strawberry production by US companies in Mexico was described in the 1970s. The varieties of fruit produced, the timing of harvest and the control of investment were all determined by the needs of the northern consumer market. Little produce was sold in Mexico. Now to strawberries can be added a range of other fruit, and vegetables and forage for livestock – from alfalfa to sorghum – as well as livestock themselves are produced in Mexico for US markets. This has developed to such an extent that the area of land sown to basic foodstuff for the Mexican population has decreased and Mexican food imports have greatly increased.

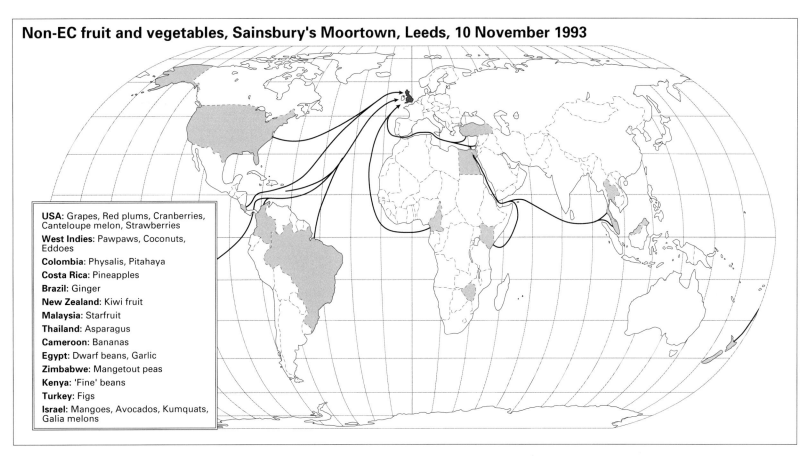

Non-EC fruit and vegetables, Sainsbury's Moortown, Leeds, 10 November 1993

USA: Grapes, Red plums, Cranberries, Canteloupe melon, Strawberries

West Indies: Pawpaws, Coconuts, Eddoes

Colombia: Physalis, Pitahaya

Costa Rica: Pineapples

Brazil: Ginger

New Zealand: Kiwi fruit

Malaysia: Starfruit

Thailand: Asparagus

Cameroon: Bananas

Egypt: Dwarf beans, Garlic

Zimbabwe: Mangetout peas

Kenya: 'Fine' beans

Turkey: Figs

Israel: Mangoes, Avocados, Kumquats, Galia melons

Figure 4.3a   Non-EC fruit and vegetables, Sainsbury's Moortown, Leeds, 10 November 1993

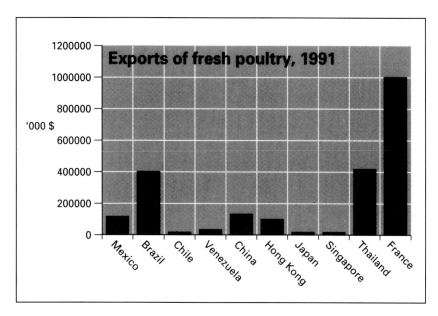

Figure 4.3b   Exports of fresh poultry, 1991

Further reading

Barham, B. *et al.* (1992), Nontraditional exports in Latin America, *Latin American Research Review*, **27**(2): 43–82.
Barkin, D. (1993), *Distorted Development. Mexican Agriculture in the World Economy*, Boulder: Westview, 2nd ed.
Burbach, R. and Flynn, P. (1980), *Agribusiness in the Americas*, New York: Monthly Review Press.

4.4 AGRARIAN PRODUCTION AT THE LOCAL SCALE
John Briggs

The examples of agrarian production in this section are based in eastern Africa, where a combination of environmental, economic and social conditions influences agricultural decision-making, choice of crops to be grown, and the allocation of labour and capital to agricultural activity. It is the case that where capital, and hence usually technology, is lacking, environmental factors can take on a relatively greater importance, and this is so in east Africa. It should be stressed, however, that this does not relegate economic and social factors to a position of irrelevance.

Figure 4.4a comprises a histogram of monthly rainfall totals for Nairobi and an agricultural calendar for six key agricultural activities. It is clear that the Nairobi region experiences two rainfall maxima in any twelve-month period, with the March to May rainy period being particularly marked. The period between June and early October is sufficiently dry that successful crop growth is extremely difficult and tenuous. The 'short rains' of November to December provide some respite for agriculture, but the rainfall is neither sufficiently plentiful nor sufficiently reliable for secure agricultural activity.

The calendar of agricultural activities, typical of farmers in central Kenya, is heavily influenced by the rainfall pattern, and hence water availability. Of all the activities, the most crucial is that of planting, in that its timing is vital. If seed is planted too early, it may fail to germinate because of lack of water. Alternatively, if planting is delayed, there may not be sufficient rainfall over the subsequent few weeks to produce a successful

harvest. Either way, this has very severe implications for household income, and, in the extreme, for household survival. Weeding is the least popular activity, and is frequently overlooked by many households. It is exacerbated by the fact that weeding takes place during the rainy season, and hence working conditions in the fields may not be at their most pleasant. Harvesting and processing are seen in a very positive light, largely because this is the stage of obtaining the final product.

Figure 4.4b demonstrates the nature of annual rainfall variability, based on the example of Baydhabo in southern Somalia. Based on records from 1922 until 1981 (although there are missing data for 1941–1950 and 1975–1977), there is a coefficient of variation of over 37%. Given that the mean annual rainfall is 580 mm, variations of this magnitude mean that cultivation is a potentially hazardous activity, especially in those years when rainfall is below average. However, there is no way that farmers can predict accurately a given

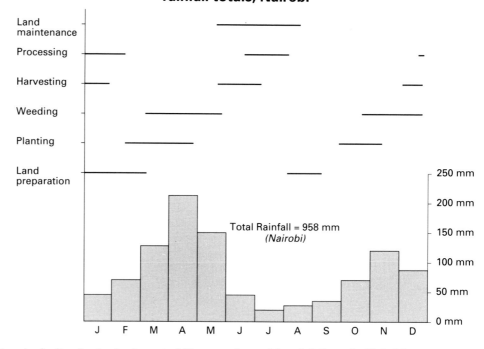

Figure 4.4a Agricultural calendar in central Kenya and monthly rainfall totals, Nairobi

year's rainfall and plant land accordingly, nor can they take decisions about labour or capital allocations with any certainty in advance.

Social and economic factors also influence agrarian production. In eastern Africa, a key issue revolves around the fact that much of the agricultural work is undertaken by women. However, farming is one of several crucial production tasks. Others include running the household, fetching water and firewood, and looking after the welfare of children. Hence, the land may not always receive the attention it merits, because of all these conflicting demands. Pressure may be exerted by the state to produce cash crops, at the expense of food crops, to generate foreign exchange. There may be transport problems which result in inputs such as seed or fertiliser not reaching farms in time for the start of the rainy season. After harvest, further transport difficulties may result in produce not reaching the market, a major disincentive for farmers to produce in subsequent seasons.

Further reading

Richards, P. (1985), *Indigenous Agricultural Revolution*, London: Hutchinson.
Mortimore, M. (1989), *Adapting to Drought: Farmers, Famines and Desertification in West Africa*, Cambridge: Cambridge University Press.

Annual rainfall totals for Baydhabo, Somalia.

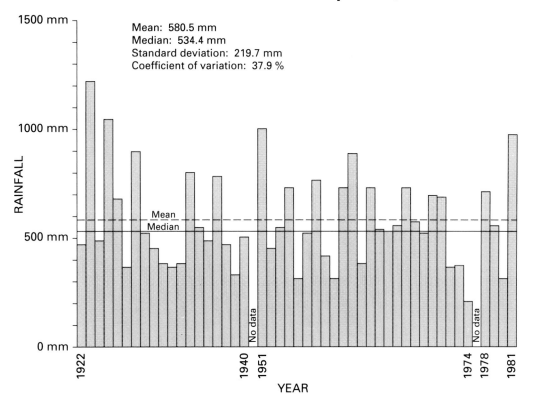

Mean: 580.5 mm
Median: 534.4 mm
Standard deviation: 219.7 mm
Coefficient of variation: 37.9 %

Figure 4.4b Annual rainfall totals for Baydhabo, Somalia

4.5 LAND OWNERSHIP, SECURITY OF OWNERSHIP AND FARM PRODUCTIVITY IN THAILAND

Jonathan Rigg

A key question in agricultural development is what effect differences in land ownership, and security of land ownership, have upon production. It has been generally observed that the closing of the land frontier in many developing countries, coupled with the commercialisation of life and livelihoods, has led to an increase in tenancy. Land has become concentrated in the hands of a relatively small number of wealthy and influential farmers, while the area of land which is tenanted rather than owner-occupied has proportionately risen. At the same time, it is also the case that many 'owner-occupiers' lack secure title to their land.

Thailand has been fortunate in being relatively land rich, and it has only been in the space of the last twenty years that the frontier in farmland expansion has closed. But today, farmers across the country are only too aware that their children will find it difficult, if not impossible, to clear new land for agriculture. There has been a corresponding shift in agricultural strategy from extensification, to intensification, requiring that farmers invest in new agricultural technology.

Many commentators feel that if farmers do not own their land, then they will be less willing – and less able – to invest scarce financial resources in land improvement and yield increasing technologies. They face the threat of eviction, and therefore the possibility that they might be denied the benefits of any investment. In the case of Thailand there is no doubt that tenancy is rising, in certain areas to disturbingly high levels (Figure 4.5a).

Overall, 12.7% of farmland is rented (Figure 4.5b). But in the more densely populated and commercialised regions, such as the Central Plains and the North, the figures are 26.2% and 17.3% respectively, while for certain provinces – like Ayutthaya and Pathum Thani in the Central Plains – the figure is over 50% (Figure 4.5a) (MOAC, 1990). But, at the macro level, there is no clear link between land ownership and productivity: in the Northeast, for example, not only is the rate of tenancy lowest, but also farm investment and – often – yields (Figure 4.5b). In this instance, the effects of tenancy are disguised by other factors – in particular the role of the environment.

But, it is not just a case of varying tenancy arrangements; even 'owner-occupiers' must feel assured that they have *secure* ownership before they invest in their land and crops. In Thailand, only 53% of cultivated land is documented or titled (Table 4.5) (Feder *et al.*, 1988). Without documentation, farmers are unable to use their land as collateral to borrow money from institutional lenders to buy inputs to raise crop yields and therefore, incomes (Figure 4.5c) (Kemp, 1981; Feder *et al.*, 1988). If they wish to borrow money they are forced to go to informal money lenders who often charge interest rates of 100% per year,

Table 4.5 Land documentation in Thailand

	million hectares	%
Land under cultivation	24.6	100
Documented land	13.1	53
Title deed (chanot, NS-4)	2.9	12
Certificate of use (NS-3, NS-3K)	10.2	42
Undocumented land	11.7	47
Private land (including NS-2, SK-1)	6.4	26
Public land, squatters	5.3	21

Source: Feder *et al.* (1988)

or more (Rigg, 1986). In Feder *et al.*'s (1988: 21) study of the effect of secure land ownership on farm productivity in Thailand, they conclude that 'The effect of land ownership security [on productivity] is substantial, since it represents a permanent productivity differential of 12 to 27 percent ...'.

Across the developing world, attempts to

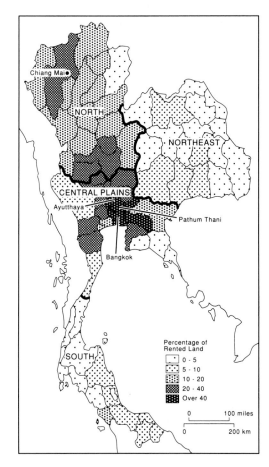

Figure 4.5a Thailand: rented land as a percentage of total farm land, 1988

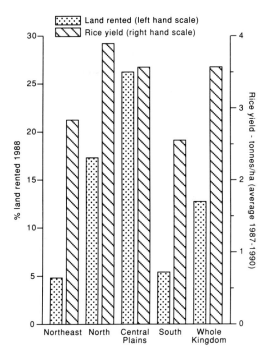

Figure 4.5b Thailand: rented land and rice yields, by region

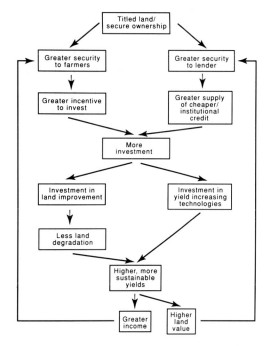

Figure 4.5c Security of land ownership and productivity

increase yields in the face of rising populations when the land resource is stagnant, or even declining, have been constrained by insecure land ownership. Farmers have had less incentive to invest in their crops and land, and have been denied access to cheap credit to finance productivity enhancing and land improving technologies. This has not only reduced output and depressed incomes, but has sometimes also increased land degradation fuelling rural-to-urban migration and contributing to farmer disenchantment.

Further reading

Feder, G. (1987), Land ownership security and farm productivity: evidence from Thailand, *Journal of Development Studies*, **24**(1): 16–30.

Feder, G., Onchan, T., Chalamwong, Y. and Hongladarom, C. (1988), *Land Policies and Farm Productivity in Thailand*, Baltimore: Johns Hopkins University Press.

Kemp, J. (1981), Legal and informal land tenure in Thailand, *Modern Asian Studies*, **15**(1): 1–23.

4.6 FOOD SECURITY
John Tarrant

Security of food supplies has been and remains a necessity for civilisation. A regular supply of food requires organisation of production, distribution and consumption and this organisation was one of the characteristics of the earliest civilisations.

Food security requires that there is enough food to allow all people to maintain at least a minimum standard of nutrition throughout the year (*see* Section 3.11). The adequacy of the overall level of production is the first requirement of food security. This production must be responsive to future demands as population grows and food demand becomes more sophisticated. In countries with low average incomes the income elasticity of demand for food is very high – a large proportion of any extra income will be spent on food. Thus, food production has to grow considerably faster than population to secure the supplies needed.

There is more than sufficient food produced to feed the world's population to a more than adequate level. Food security at a world level is of little practical importance, however, when there is such obvious juxtaposition of starvation and plenty in the world. Food supply and security is more than sufficient in the developed world, while insufficient and becoming worse in much of the developing world. Daily calorie supply in the low and middle income countries of Sub-Saharan Africa and south Asia is low and has changed little since the mid-1970s (Figure 4.6a).

In most countries of the developing world domestic food production is insufficient to meet local demands and imports are rising and often now represent a very high proportion of domestic production (Figure 4.6b). Low and middle income countries of south Asia have reduced their reliance

Table 4.6 World cereal production and year-end stocks

Year	Production (million tonnes)	Stocks (million tonnes)	Stocks as % production
1970	1213	136.1	11.2
1975	1366	177.8	13.0
1980	1565	249.5	15.9
1985	1843	336.5	18.3
1989	1865	295.2	15.8

Source: FAO, *Production Yearbooks* and *The State of Food and Agriculture* (various years)

on both imports and food aid, while in Sub-Saharan Africa imports and aid have both risen substantially (Figure 4.6c), despite which daily calorie supplies have fallen.

There is no shortage of food in the world, nor are world stocks of grain worryingly low, having more than kept pace with the level of world production (Table 4.6). Food insecurity at national or personal levels results from a lack of money to purchase food. Thus food consumption

will not be sufficient, nor will food security be achieved, until poverty is reduced. The consumption side of food security remains much more important than the production side. India exports grains nearly every year but this self-sufficiency cannot be equated with food security while perhaps 20% of the population are able to eat less than 80% of their daily calorific requirements.

Further reading

Anderson, J.R. and Hazell, P.B.R. (1989), *Variability in Grain Yields*, Baltimore: Johns Hopkins University Press.

Hollist, W.L. and Tullis, F.L. (eds) (1987), *Pursuing Food Security: Strategies and Obstacles in Asia, Africa, Latin America and the Middle East*, Boulder: Lynne Rienner.

Huddleston, B. (1990), FAO's overall approach and methodology for formulating national food security programmes in developing countries, *IDS Bulletin*, **21**(3): 72–80.

Maxwell, S. (1990), Food security for developing countries: issues and options, *IDS Bulletin*, **21**(3): 2–13.

Mellor, J.W. (1988), Global food balances and food security, *World Development*, **16**(9): 997–1011.

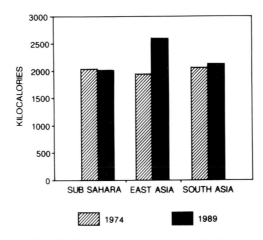

Figure 4.6a Daily per capita calorie supply for middle and low income countries, 1974 and 1989

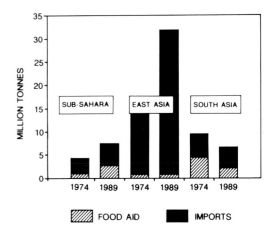

Figure 4.6c Cereal imports and cereal food aid for middle and low income countries, 1974 and 1989

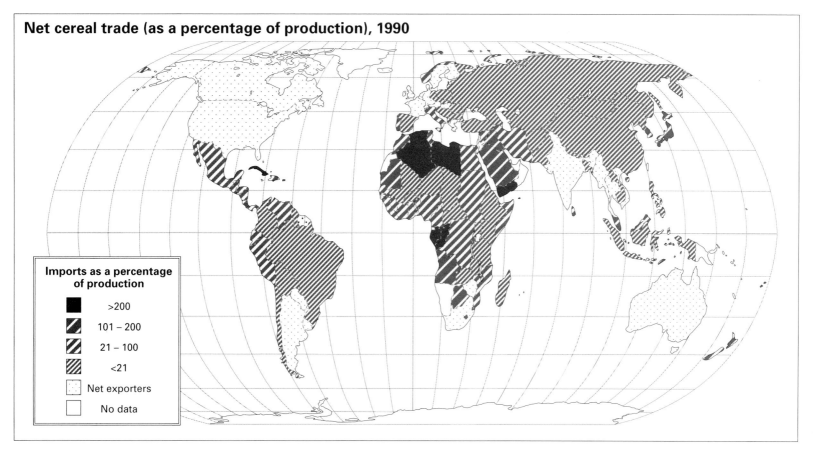

Figure 4.6b   Cereal imports as a proportion of cereal production

4.7 INTERNATIONAL TRADE IN AGRICULTURAL COMMODITIES
John Tarrant

Agricultural trade makes up 8.64% of all world trade by value. An important share of this agricultural trade is of cereals (Table 4.7a). There are considerable variations in the importance of agricultural trade between countries and between regions (Table 4.7b).

Agricultural trade is a result of a mismatch between supply and demand. This mismatch is itself a result of the productivity and specialisation of the agricultural production and the purchasing power of the market. About half the world's agricultural trade takes place within Europe, where populations and incomes are generally high, producing a large and well differentiated market. Agricultural specialisation is also marked and, as much national production is based on comparative advantage, there is extensive reliance on trade.

World cereal trade has grown very rapidly over the last 30 years with a polarisation between the developed and the developing worlds (Figure 4.7a). The dominance of North America as a net exporter has developed since the 1960s (Table 4.7c). In contrast Europe has a smaller net export position from a large trading volume, and the countries of the former Soviet Union account for 13% of world imports (Figure 4.7b). All regions of the developing world are net importers, despite substantial exports from some countries in Latin America and in the Far East.

Wheat accounts for just under half of all traded grains with over 107 million tonnes exported each year. Most of these exports come from just five exporting regions which divide the import needs of the rest of the world between them (Figure 4.7c). In two of the exporting regions the surpluses of

wheat, which produce this trade, are a result of policies to maintain high prices (in the EC) and other government devices to support farmers (in the USA). The surpluses generated by such policies are disposed of through exports, a substantial proportion of which are at subsidised prices or even free, through the mechanism of food aid.

Further reading

Morgan, D. (1979), *Merchants of Grain*, London: Weidenfeld and Nicolson.
OECD (Organisation for Economic Co-operation and Development) (1990), *National Policies and Agricultural Trade*, Paris: Organisation for Economic Co-operation and Development.
OECD (Organisation for Economic Co-operation and Development) (1991), *Agricultural Policies, Markets and Trade: Monitoring and Outlook*, Paris: Organisation for Economic Co-operation and Development.
Tarrant, J.R. (1985), A review of international food trade, *Progress in Human Geography*, **9**(2): 235–254.

Table 4.7a Agricultural trade, 1989

Product group	Exports ($\times 10^9$)
Cereals	36.2
Meat and meat products	35.7
Dairy products	20.0
Coffee, tea, and cocoa	17.5
Sugar	13.6
Fruits	13.4
Fibres and rubber	12.9
Vegetable oils	10.1

Source: Food and Agricultural Organisation of the United Nations, *Trade Yearbook*, 1990

Table 4.7b Importance of agricultural trade

Region	Share of trade which is agricultural (% by value)
Latin America	25.15
Oceania	15.74
Africa	14.90
North America	10.46
Europe	9.39
Far East	8.15
Near East	4.87
USSR	0.73

Source: Food and Agricultural Organisation of the United Nations, *Trade Yearbook*, 1990

Table 4.7c World net grain trade (positive numbers denote exports)

Region	1934–38	1960	1970	1980	1990
			(millions of tonnes)		
North America	+5	+39	+54	+133	+113
Latin America	+9	0	+4	−15	−10
Western Europe	−24	−25	−22	−11	+27
Eastern Europe and USSR	+5	0	−2	−56	−33
Africa	+1	−2	−4	−18	−25
Asia	+2	−17	−37	−64	−83
Oceania	+3	+6	+8	+19	+14

Source: L.R. Brown (1975); FAO, *Production Yearbooks* (various years)

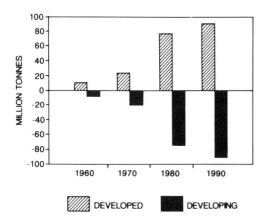

Figure 4.7a   Growth of world cereal trade, 1960–90

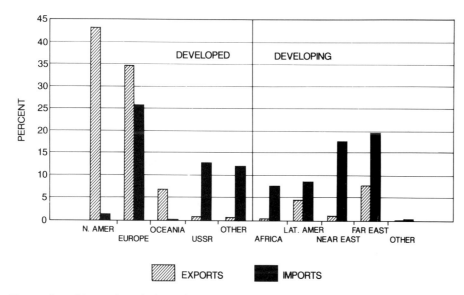

Figure 4.7b   Share of world cereal trade by region, 1989

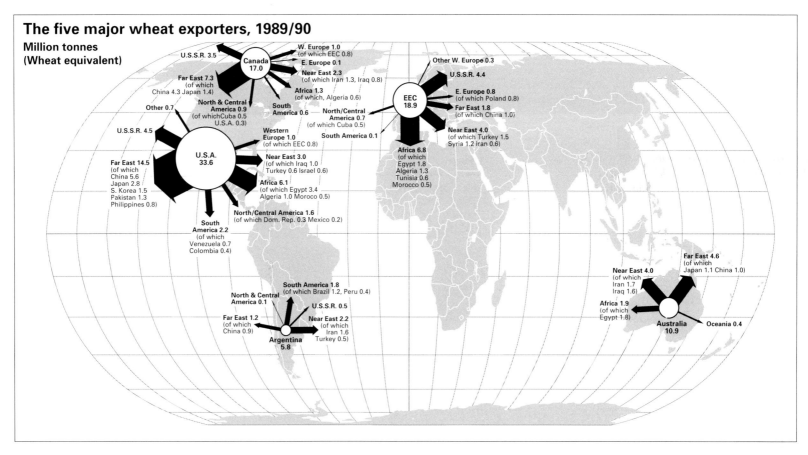

Figure 4.7c   The five major wheat exporters, 1989–1990

4.8 THE GLOBAL PATTERN OF EMPLOYMENT
Chris Dixon

Official labour statistics provide a very broad indication of the global pattern of employment (Figure 4.8). There are, however, not only major shortcomings in the data for many countries but also serious flaws in the definitions used (ILO, 1990). Terms such as 'work', 'working-population', 'labour force', 'economic activity' and 'employment' are firmly rooted in the context of advanced capitalist economies, and their application elsewhere frequently seriously distorts the depiction of the labour situation. In general, official statistics only refer to formally structured waged work, thus the so-called 'informal' sector and much female labour are largely excluded. The refinement of statistical collection frequently means little more than the stricter application of the international definitions and thus increased under-reporting and distortion. This almost certainly accounts for the reported decline in female participation in agriculture in many parts of Sub-Saharan Africa (Seager and Olson, 1986: 108).

At the global scale there is a general relationship between the structure of employment and the level of economic development (Table 4.8a). More detailed examination reveals some marked variations. Thailand, for example, one of the more developed of the middle range of Third World countries, has 66% of the labour force in agriculture. Similarly, Japan has a much higher proportion of its labour force in agriculture (12%) compared to the USA (2%), Canada (5%) and Europe (ranging from 2% in the UK to 8% in France). These differences are not simply explained. They stem from a complex of historical experience, agricultural systems, and government

Table 4.8a   The structure of employment and level of development

Level of development	Agriculture†		Industry		Services	
	1965	1989–91	1965	1989–91	1965	1989–91
High	28	16	32	33	40	51
Medium	73	61	11	16	16	23
Low	74	63	10	11	16	26
All less-developed	72	61	11	14	17	25
Industrial	22	7	30	26	42	67
World	57	48	19	17	24	35

† includes forestry and fishing
Source: United Nations Development Programme, *Human Development Report* (1993)

policy, exaggerated in some cases by the method of statistical reporting.

Since the industrial revolution there has been a long-term shift in the patterns of economic activity and employment from agriculture to manufacturing to services. Amongst members of the Organisation for Economic Cooperation and Development (OECD), employment in the manufacturing sector declined from 35% to 30% of total employment between 1960 and 1990, while agricultural employment fell from 22% to 8% and service employment rose from 43% to 62%.

As the relative importance of the manufacturing sector has declined, so the composition of its employment has changed, with sharp declines in textiles and metals being offset by the growth of electronics, telecommunications and biotechnology. These growth areas are far less labour intensive than the areas they have replaced. Capital has been increasingly substituted for labour: between 1975 and 1990 labour productivity increased by over 250%. Thus, since the early 1970s almost every industrial economy has been faced with structural unemployment. Within the members of the OECD the official rate of

unemployment rose from *c.* 3% during the early 1960s to *c.* 7% in the early 1990s.

It has become apparent that economic growth is no longer accompanied by a similar expansion of employment. In the USA between 1950 and 1990 manufacturing output increased by 300% while employment rose by only 30%. This has also been the experience of Third World countries with the expansion of manufacturing sectors having a much greater influence on national income and export earnings than on employment (Table 4.8b). With the limited exception of the Newly Industrialising Countries (NICs), manufacturing has

Table 4.8b   Percentage contribution of manufacturing 1990

World Bank income class	Employment	Gross Domestic Product	Export Earnings
low	10	27	54
lower middle	16	23	50
upper middle	31	25	68

Source: World Bank, *World Development Report* (1992)

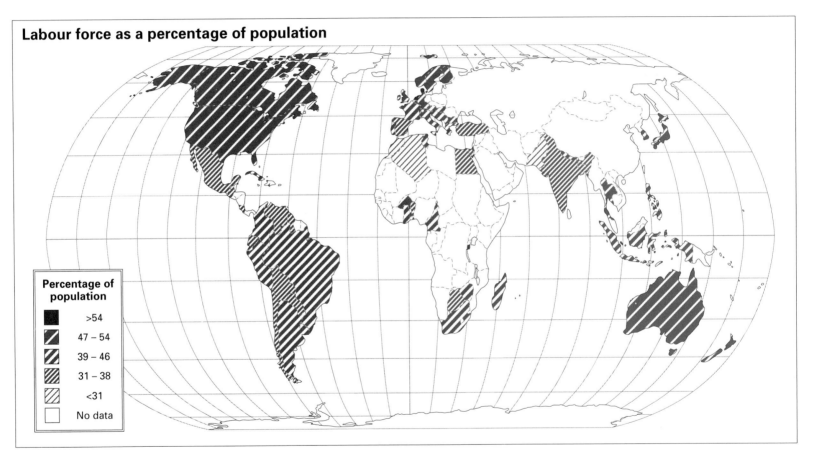

Figure 4.8   Labour force as a percentage of population

failed to generate sufficient employment to absorb a significant proportion of the annual increment to the labour force.

While for most of the global economy the problem is increasingly one of insufficient manufacturing employment, a small number of economies are beginning to experience labour shortages. This is most striking in Singapore where the government has chosen to encourage larger families rather than to allow a major influx of foreign labour. Other less-developed countries in Pacific Asia have expressed fears that they will face similar problems early in the 21st century. Although most have substantial labour surpluses they all face serious shortages of skilled labour. Hence the increasing concern with training programmes.

Further reading

ILO (International Labour Office) (1992), *World Labour Report*, Geneva: International Labour Office.

Renner, R. (1992), Creating sustainable employment in industrial countries, in: Brown, L.R. (ed.), *State of the World*, London: Earthscan, 138–154.

Seager, J. and Olson, A. (1986), *Women in the World*, London: Pan.

United Nations Development Programme (UNDP, 1993), *Human Development Report*, New York: Oxford University Press, 30–51.

4.9 THE GLOBAL ORGANISATION OF INDUSTRY
Tim Unwin

The location of industrial activity at a global or regional scale is in part influenced by the varied distribution of mineral resources (*see* Sections 2.3 and 4.12). However, traditional location theory, derived largely from the work of Weber (1929) and Hotelling (1929), cannot satisfactorily explain the complex pattern of global manufacturing industry illustrated in Figure 4.9 (Massey, 1973). Economic 'development' is widely interpreted as involving the transformation of a country's economy from one dominated by agriculture, both in terms of labour and contribution to Gross Domestic Product (GDP), to one dominated by the service sector. Thus World Bank (1992b) figures indicate that in 1965 the average distribution of GDP in low-income economies was 41% from agriculture, 26% from industry and 32% from services, in contrast to high-income countries where it was 5% from agriculture, 43% from industry and 54% from services. Such empirical observations, though, do not explain the reasons for the spatial distribution of industrial activity in different areas of the world, and to do this it is essential to examine the complex and changing organisation of global capitalism. In particular, it is important to see industrial location as reflecting the ways in which differences between places are exploited by international capital in order to maximise profits (Massey, 1984). Above all, decreasing costs of transport, an increase in raw material sources, and reorganisation of production, have meant that labour factors, including costs, productivity levels, unionisation rates, skills, and patterns of social reproduction, have become increasingly important in determining the location of manufacturing activity (Walker and Storper, 1983). These have generally all been associated with an increasing internationalisation of production, in which multinational corporations seek to exploit the specific international division of labour that has emerged in recent years.

Manufacturing is widely seen as being the most dynamic element of the industrial sector, since the location of primary industrial activities, such as mining, is largely determined by the distribution of mineral resources. However, the term 'manufacturing' covers a wide variety of processes from the making of textiles to the production of computers, and similar levels of manufacturing activity frequently indicate very different economic structures. At a global scale, developing countries, as defined by the United Nations Industrial Development Organisation (1992), contributed only about 15% of total value added in manufacturing in 1990. Figure 4.9 illustrates that sub-Saharan Africa generally has the lowest percentages of GDP contributed by manufacturing, followed by south Asia and northern Africa, with south America, Europe and parts of eastern Asia having generally much higher levels. Nevertheless, these generalisations hide fundamental differences in economic structure. For example, in 1990 Denmark and India both had 19% of their GDP contributed by manufacturing, but in Denmark agriculture contributed only 5% in contrast to the 31% of GDP contributed by agriculture in India (World Bank, 1992b). Among the countries for which World Bank (1992b) figures are available, two states stood out in 1990 as having particularly high shares of GDP contributed by manufacturing: Zambia (43%) and China (*c.* 38%). Significantly, these are both classified by the World Bank as low-income economies. Beneath them, a group of Pacific Asian and south American states, namely Uruguay, Singapore, Japan and Korea also had high rates of manufacturing, ranging from 28% to 31%. Pacific Asia is currently the most rapidly growing component of the global manufacturing sector, and its key role is examined in more detail in Section 4.10. However, as the Pacific Asian economies experience rising production costs and they attempt to attract investment into higher value and service activities, it is likely that over the next two decades a new group of countries in southern Africa, south America and eastern Europe may well come to prominence as major manufacturing areas.

Further reading

Corbridge, S. (1993), *World Economy*, New York: Oxford University Press.

Forbes, D. (1984), *The Geography of Underdevelopment*, London: Croom Helm.

Smith, N. (1989), Uneven development and location theory: towards a synthesis, in: Peet, R. and Thrift, N. (eds), *New Models in Geography: the Political-Economy Perspective, Volume 1*, London: Unwin Hyman, 142–163.

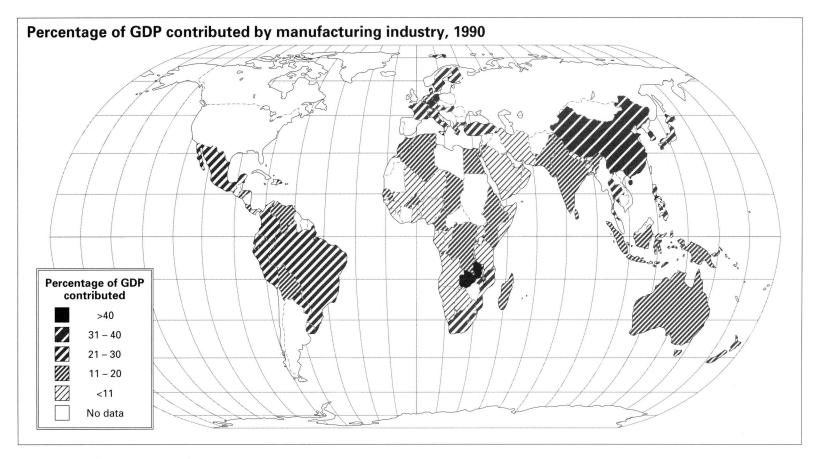

Figure 4.9 Percentage of GDP contributed by manufacturing industry, 1990

4.10 MANUFACTURING IN PACIFIC ASIA
Chris Dixon

The Pacific Asian region is emerging as by far the most dynamic component of the global manufacturing economy. While industrial output within the region remains dominated by Japan the rapid development of manufacturing sectors in the other Asian economies has produced a remarkably complex and interlocking pattern of production. Japanese economists frequently liken the regional industrial structure to a flight of geese, with Japan leading, followed by the Asian Newly Industrialising Countries (NICs) (Hong Kong, Singapore, South Korea and Taiwan), the ASEAN Four (Indonesia, Malaysia, the Philippines and Thailand), and those centrally planned economies which are endeavouring to re-engage with the global economy, notably China and Vietnam.

During the late 1960s the Asian NICs were uniquely placed to develop labour-intensive manufacturing, as Japan vacated such areas in the wake of rising costs — particularly for labour — and the appreciation of the Yen. In addition these countries proved attractive locations for European and North American based transnational corporations and investors seeking low-cost locations for their manufacturing operations. Since the early 1960s, the Asian NICs have experienced exceptionally rapid rates of growth of GDP, manufacturing output and exports (Table 4.10).

From the late 1970s the Asian NICs began to lose their comparative advantage in labour intensive manufacturing production. Rising costs, particularly of labour, concern over pollution and shortages of industrial land caused domestic and transnational investors to look for lower cost, less pollution conscious locations. Since the early 1980s much labour intensive production has therefore been relocated into the ASEAN Four, particularly Malaysia and Thailand, and the Asian NICs have moved into more skill and capital intensive production. In the case of Singapore this was encouraged as a matter of deliberate policy. From 1979 the Singapore government embarked on its so-called 'Second Industrial Revolution'. Between 1979 and 1981 wage rises of between 54 and 58% were recommended. This was coupled with industrial training programmes, infrastructure improvement and a range of tax concessions and incentives, all of which were aimed at promoting the production of higher value-added products. In the words of the Director of the Economic Development Board: 'We decided ... that making transistor radios was not a job for us. Nor do we want workers in the rag trade. We want technical services' (cited in Smith *et al.*, 1985: 87).

Much of Singapore's labour intensive manufacturing sector has been relocated in the neighbouring Malaysian state of Johore and the islands of the Indonesian Riau group. These low cost locations adjacent to the advanced facilities of Singapore have also proved attractive for international investors, particularly from east Asia. These developments are forming an 'inner triangle of growth' in south-east Asia (Figure 4.10).

The relocation of labour intensive manufacturing processes from the Asian NICs into the low labour cost ASEAN economies is creating a marked Regional Division of Labour within the Pacific Asian region. However, the further development of this pattern is by no means assured. In Thailand, a major recipient of East Asian investment between 1987 and 1992, rising costs, shortages of skilled labour, lack of infrastructure, congestion and political uncertainty are diverting investment elsewhere, notably into the Guangdong province of China and Vietnam. Indeed, Thai investors themselves are showing increasing interest in the raw materials, and cheap labour of the former Indo-Chinese states and Myanmar.

Table 4.10 Growth of the Asian NICs, annual average percentage rates

	GDP		Manufacturing		Exports	
	1965–80	1980–90	1965–80	1980–90	1965–80	1980–90
Hong Kong	8.6	7.1	na	15.0	9.1	6.2
Singapore	10.0	6.4	13.2	6.6	12.4	7.4
South Korea	9.9	9.7	18.7	12.7	27.2	12.2
Taiwan	7.5	9.8	14.6	8.7	26.6	9.1
OECD	3.7	3.1	3.1	3.3	7.2	4.1
World	4.0	3.2	8.3	3.0	2.5	−1.4

Source: World Bank *World Development Report* (various issues); *Industry of Free China*, Taipei: Executive Yuan, various issues

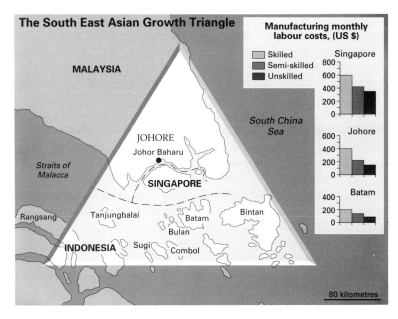

Figure 4.10   The South-east Asia growth triangle

Further reading

Ariff, M. and Hill, H. (1985), *Export-Oriented Industrialisation: the ASEAN Experience*, London: Allen & Unwin.

Dixon, C. and Drakakis-Smith, D. (eds) (1993), *Economic and Social Development in Pacific Asia*, London: Routledge.

Henderson, J. (1989), *The Globalisation of High Technology Production*, London: Routledge.

Perry, M. (1991), The Singapore growth triangle: state, capital and labour at a new frontier in the world economy, *Singapore Journal of Tropical Geography*, **12**: 25–46.

4.11 COMPANY TOWNS: THE BRAZILIAN EXPERIENCE

John Dickenson

The need to provide accommodation at new sites of economic activity has long been integral to the development process, from pithead villages, industrial and philanthropic settlements (Pullman, Port Sunlight) to socialist planning in eastern Europe (Nova Huta, Dunaujvaros). Single enterprise communities continue to be established in the Third World, most commonly where resource endowments requiring substantial capital investment occur in environments lacking established settlement. Such 'company towns' are particularly associated with agribusiness, lumbering, mining, and industries dependent on bulky raw materials or cheap energy. Their precise form varies from temporary camps exploiting ephemeral resources such as timber, or at project construction sites; tracts of company-built workers' housing grafted onto existing settlements; to complete 'new towns' set into existing urban networks or at the resource frontier.

In Brazil the earliest 'company towns' were associated with 19th century mines and water-powered textile mills (Figure 4.11a). In Minas Gerais the little cotton town of Biribiri was laid out at a remote waterfall in the Serra do Espinhaço, consisting of the mill, church, store, schoolhouse and a neat square of 40 houses. The British-owned St John del Rey gold-mining company, established in 1834, built a town for its workers at Nova Lima where, until the 1950s, there was social segregation between British managers and foremen, and Brazilian labourers. Railway building fostered the construction of company housing adjacent to railyards and workshops, as at Divinópolis.

The steel industry has created several company towns where plant size, coupled with raw material requirements, compelled companies to build steel mills and substantial settlements at green field sites. The iron ores of Minas Gerais generated steel towns in the Doce Valley, at Monlevade (1935), Acesita (1944) and Ipatinga (1956). Brazil's classic company town is Volta Redonda, established at a green field site in the Paraíba valley in 1941, to service the country's first coke-fired steelworks. The Cia. Siderúrgica Nacional initially built 2000 houses, adding a further 2000 by 1952. It also provided churches, hotels, cinemas, sports facilities, hospitals, primary and secondary schools and a technical school to train employees. The town is socially zoned, with workers' housing near the plant, and more substantial properties for technicians and managers on the hillsides. Population grew from 200 in 1941 to over 30 000 in 1954 and 180 000 by 1980. In addition, the company built small settlements at its iron and coal mines (Casa de Pedra, Lauro Muller, etc.).

Other company towns have been associated with manganese (Serra do Navio), paper (Harmonia), oil refining (Mataripe and Paulínia),

Figure 4.11a The location of company towns in Brazil

and hydroelectric projects (Paulo Afonso and Itaipú). In Amazonia there have been abortive plantation settlements at Fordlândia, Belterra and Jari.

The domination of these settlements by a single enterprise influences their economy, population and townscape. The company provides employment, controls rents, zones land, and supplies essential utilities, social services, recreational facilities, and sometimes retail provision. Populations have grown rapidly, and tend to be immigrant, youthful and relatively affluent; employment opportunity is male-dominated. Town plans are simple, uniform in layout and date, with standardised housing which varies only in size and site with employee status.

Brazil's most recent company town is at the iron mine of Carajás (Figure 4.11b). Its sponsor, the Cia.Vale do Rio Doce, had built earlier towns at its mines in Minas Gerais and port of Tubarão (Espírito Santo). Carajás was established in 1980, for a planned workforce of 2000 to be housed in single men's flats and family houses, with the company providing essential services. The townsite is screened from the mine, and includes leisure areas and protected forest reserves. Though carefully planned, Carajás demonstrates some of the difficulties engendered by company towns, being located in an ecologically sensitive area, offering very little employment for women, and attracting spontaneous migrants to unplanned adjacent settlements.

Further reading

Goodland, R. (1985), Brazil's environmental progress in Amazonian development, in: Hemming, J. (ed.), *Change in the Amazon Basin*, Manchester: Manchester University Press, volume 1, 5–35.
Long, R.G. (1948), Volta Redonda: symbol of maturity in industrial progress in Brazil, *Economic Geography*, **24**: 149–154.
Mills-Tettey, R. (1986), New Bussa: the township and resettlement scheme, *Third World Planning Review*, **8**: 31–50.
Porteus, J.D. (1973), The company state: a Chilean case study, *Canadian Geographer*, **17**: 113–126.

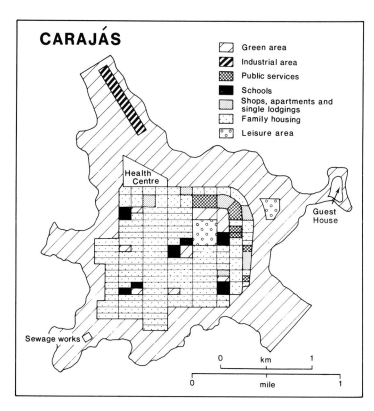

Figure 4.11b Layout of the company mining town of Carajás, Pará

4.12 THE INTERNATIONAL TRADE IN INDUSTRIAL COMMODITIES
David Hilling

The separation of supplies of industrial raw materials and the location of the demand for them has led to substantial trade between Less Developed Countries (LDCs) and the main industrial states of the world. The varying nuances of this trade are well illustrated by the examples of iron ore, bauxite and phosphate rock. In origin iron and later steel production was very much based on local fuels and ore, as in Britain, Germany and the USA, but with time ores were moved to the coalfields for processing, with for example the transport of Swedish and Spanish ore to Britain. After 1950 there was rapid growth in world demand for steel and this was met by expansion in already industrialised countries (Europe, Japan, North America) and the emergence of new capacity in countries such as Brazil, India and Korea. Traditional sources of ore were inadequate in quantity or quality and there was an increasing geographical separation of steel production and ore sources. The large deposits of easily worked, high grade ore were found in Canada, Australia and South Africa but there was a growing dependence on ores from LDCs (Brazil, Chile, Venezuela, India, Liberia and Mauritania) and iron ore has now become the most important dry-bulk commodity of seaborne trade (Figure 4.12a, Table 4.12a).

Over 56% of world steel production is in the hands of the 20 largest companies, headed by Nippon Steel, US Steel, British Steel and Bethlehem Steel (USA). There has been increasing demand for ore from a declining number of major steel producers who have sought to control their supplies of ore by vertically integrating the mining with their own activities. The scale of the new mining operations, as in Carajás, Brazil, involves massive investment and the internationalisation of the industry is a result.

In the depression of the 1980s capacity has proved excessive and smaller, more expensive mining operations, often independent producers, have been forced out of business (Marampa, Sierra Leone; Bomi Hills, Liberia) and a number of planned developments (Wologisi, Liberia; Mekambo, Gabon) have not materialised.

Bauxite ore is the main source of aluminium hydroxide, Al_2O_3, and the raw material for aluminium production. The ore is usually found close to the surface (80–90% is worked by open cast methods) and is a weathered, aluminium-rich residual from which other constituents have been leached out. While small reserves are found in temperate latitudes, for example in Greece and Yugoslavia, the most important reserves are in the tropics (Table 4.12b). World production of bauxite increased from 27.8 million tonnes in 1961 to 94.8 million in 1987, with Australia (36.2 million), Guinea (16.3 million), Brazil (8.8 million) and Jamaica (7.7 million) as the leading producers. At source the bauxite may be crushed, washed and dried, is sometimes converted to alumina, but rarely converted into aluminium. This is an electrolytic process dependent on large amounts of cheap electricity. Australia apart, there is a polarisation of advanced economies as producers of aluminium, and LDCs as producers of bauxite (Figure 4.12b).

Table 4.12a Iron ore production and consumption, 1988 (million tonnes)

Ore producers		Ore exporters		Ore consumers	
USSR (former)	249.7	Brazil	105.3	USSR	206.6
China	154.4	Australia	98.3	China	164.8
Brazil	145.0	USSR	43.1	Japan	123.7
Australia	99.5	India	32.3	USA	71.3
USA	56.4	Canada	30.5	Germany	45.2
India	49.5	Sweden	17.7	Brazil	39.7
Canada	40.7	Liberia	13.6	France	24.9
South Africa	24.7	Venezuela	12.3	Benelux	20.8
Sweden	20.3	South Africa	11.1	South Korea	20.6
Venezuela	18.2	Mauritania	10.0	UK	18.1

Source: *The Economist* (1990)

Table 4.12b World bauxite reserves (million metric tonnes)

Guinea	5600
Australia	4440
Brazil	2250
Jamaica	2000
India	1000
Indonesia	750
Guyana	700
Cameroon	680
Greece	600
Surinam	575
Ghana	450
Yugoslavia	350

Source: Patterson (1986)

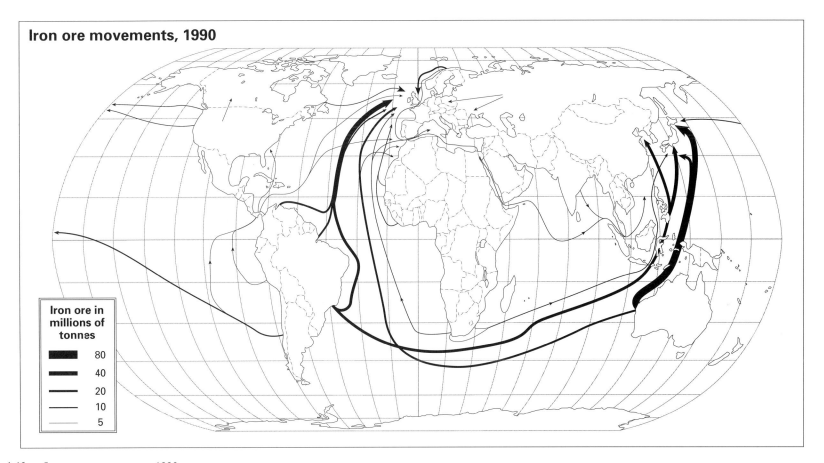

Figure 4.12a Iron ore movements, 1990

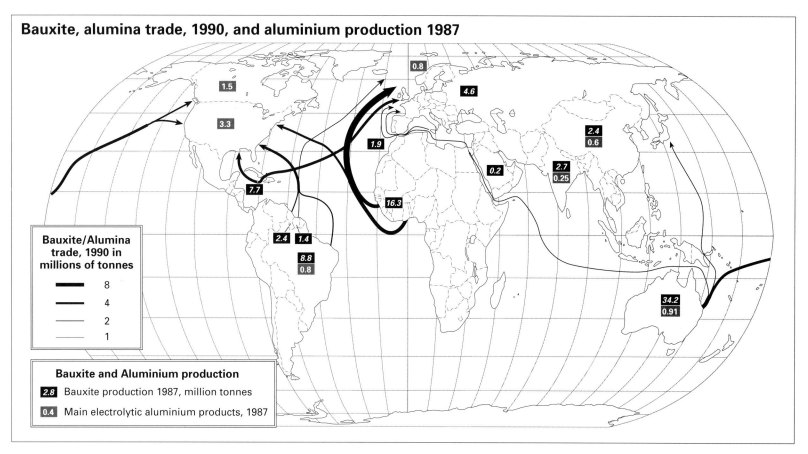

Figure 4.12b Bauxite, alumina trade, 1990 and aluminium production, 1987

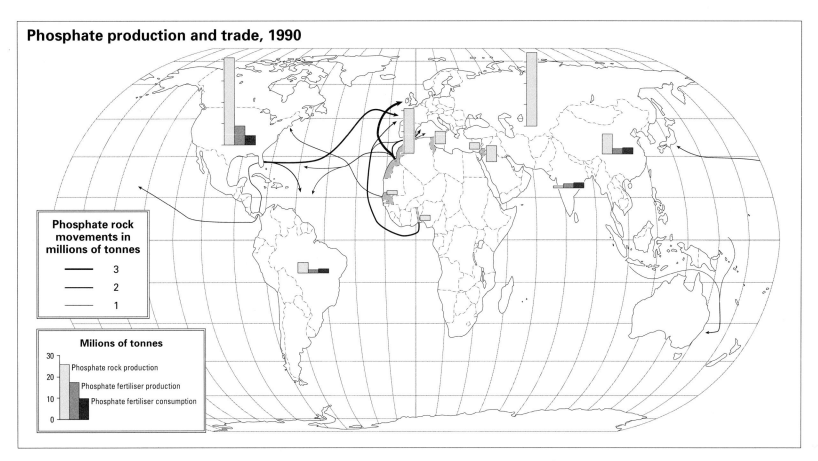

Figure 4.12c Phosphate production and trade, 1990

Historically, the industry has been dominated by the six 'majors' (Alcoa, Alcan, Reynolds, Kaiser, Pechiney, Alusuisse) with patented processes, heavy capital requirements and high levels of technology and quality control as barriers to entry. An example of a LDC caught up in this transnational web is Ghana, which exports raw bauxite from Takoradi in the west of the country, although its own aluminium smelter (Kaiser – 90%; Reynolds – 10%) uses alumina from a Kaiser plant in Louisiana produced from Jamaican bauxite and imported through the eastern port of Tema. Plans for Kaiser to use Ghana's bauxite have come to nothing – all they require is the cheap HEP.

Most projects involve the majors often in joint enterprises and in countries with favourable factors (Brazil, Venezuela and Australia). New aluminium producers have increased the amount of 'untied' metal on the market and reduced to some extent the influence of the majors.

Phosphate rock, or phosphorite, has a high concentration, sometimes as much as 30%, of phosphorous pentoxide, P_2O_5, either in nodules or compact masses, and is the primary raw material of most world production of phosphate fertiliser. It is the favoured commercial ore because it releases the phosphate easily and ground phosphate rock is the cheapest form of fertiliser and greatly in demand in developed and less developed countries alike. A country such as India embarking on a 'Green Revolution' will increase demand.

The uptake of phosphate by the plant is slow but greatly enhanced by the use of superphosphate produced by a method patented in 1842 and involving the addition of sulphuric acid to phosphate. To some extent phosphates have been superseded by more complex fertiliser compounds but world production of phosphate rock still amounts to 144 million tonnes (1987) with the United States, the former Soviet Union and China as the main producers (Figure 4.12c). The leading exporters are Morocco, USA, Jordan, Israel, Senegal, Togo and Christmas and Naura Islands in the south-west Pacific. Seaborne movements amounted to 41.4 million tonnes in 1990, the fifth largest dry bulk commodity in world trade, with north-west Europe, the Mediterranean and the Americas as main importing regions.

Further reading

Bradbury, J. (1982), Some geographical implications of the restructuring of the iron ore industry, 1950–1980, *Tijdschrift voor Economische en Sociale Geografie*, **73**(5): 295–306.

The Economist (1990), *The Economist Book of Vital World Statistics: a Complete Guide to the World in Figures*, London: Hutchinson.

Economist Intelligence Unit (1990), *World Commodity Outlook, 1991 – Industrial Raw Materials*, London: Economist Intelligence Unit.

OECD (Organisation for Economic Co-operation and Development) (annual), *Maritime Transport*, Paris: OECD.

Patterson, S. (1986), *World Bauxite Resources*, Washington DC: United States Geological Survey, Professional Paper No.1076.

4.13 TRANSPORT SYSTEMS: ROAD NETWORKS
Brian Turton

Road, rail and maritime transport have played an essential part in economic development, the relative significance of each mode varying both in time and in space. Railways made a major contribution to the industrialisation process during the 19th and early 20th centuries but modern motor transport, with its flexibility and adaptability, has now captured the majority share of freight and passenger traffic in most European states and in Anglo-America. Many independent states in Africa, south-east Asia and South America were also dependent upon railways in their early phases of colonial development but road transport is now dominant (Leinbach, 1975).

The density and quality of road systems (Figure 4.13a), and the amount of motor traffic which they carry, vary considerably throughout the world and most states still devote the greater parts of their transport investment budgets to programmes of road improvement and new building (Ezeife, 1984). Data relating to road quality in individual states are not always comparable but the broad classifications into primary and secondary, and sealed and unsealed roads do enable a broad comparison of facilities at the global scale to be made (Figure 4.13b). Road densities in individual states, expressed in kilometres per 100 square kilometres, vary from over 200 to less than 20. The most complex networks are found in the states of the European Union but in much of Africa, South America and Australia only very rudimentary systems exist. The proportion of a national network which has a sealed all-weather surface reflects both climatic conditions and traffic volumes, and in Europe many states have at least 90% of their roads sealed. In Africa and South America, where traffic flows are much lighter, few states have more than 20% of their networks constructed to all-weather standards and a large proportion of the roads are surfaced with gravel or laterite.

The rapid expansion of motor road transport since 1950 exposed the deficiencies of many conventional roads, and the resultant congestion was relieved by the construction of new routes specifically designed for high speed traffic. These motorways are largely confined to western Europe and Anglo-America, where they link major cities and also provide improved access within larger towns and cities (Starkie, 1982). Less extensive motorway systems have also been built in some of the larger cities of the southern hemisphere.

Since independence many of the developing countries in Africa and south-east Asia have made investment in roads the leading priority in their overall transport budgets. Agricultural areas and mining centres developed by European colonialists were usually provided with good-quality road links to railheads or commercial centres, whereas the land occupied by subsistence farmers was invariably served by unsurfaced tracks with only a limited length of gravel roads capable of taking wheeled vehicles. Current investment is often concentrated upon programmes for the upgrading of rural road networks and, where appropriate, the improvement of inter-urban routes to accommodate modern high-capacity trucks. The former projects are usually part of comprehensive plans for rural development, enabling farmers to travel to markets for commercial crops and the population in general to secure improved access to schools, clinics and minor service centres (Figure 4.13c) (Airey, 1985; Smith, J.A., 1989).

Many large scale road projects are associated with the formation of international economic blocs and are designed to facilitate increased trade by road between member states. The European Community now has the world's most complex network of motorways and these routes often account for over 10% of the principal road length within individual countries (Figure 4.13d). In contrast, the road systems of nations in the Economic Community of West African States still require massive investment to bring them up to the planned standard (Figure 4.13e) (Omiunu, 1987).

Although there are current attempts to increase the attractions of railways for freight and passenger traffic it is unlikely that the dominant position occupied by the world's road networks within the global transport system will be displaced.

Further reading

Addus, A.A. (1989), Road transportation in Africa, *Transportation Quarterly*, **43**(3): 421–433.

Barwell, I., Edmonds, G.A., Howe, J.D. and Veen, J. de (1985), *Rural Transport in Developing Countries*, London: Intermediate Technology Publications.

Hoyle, B.S. (1988), *Transport and Development in Tropical Africa*, London: John Murray.

Hoyle, B.S. and Knowles, R.D. (1992), *Modern Transport Geography*, London: Belhaven.

Owen, W. (1987), *Transportation and World Development*, London: Hutchinson.

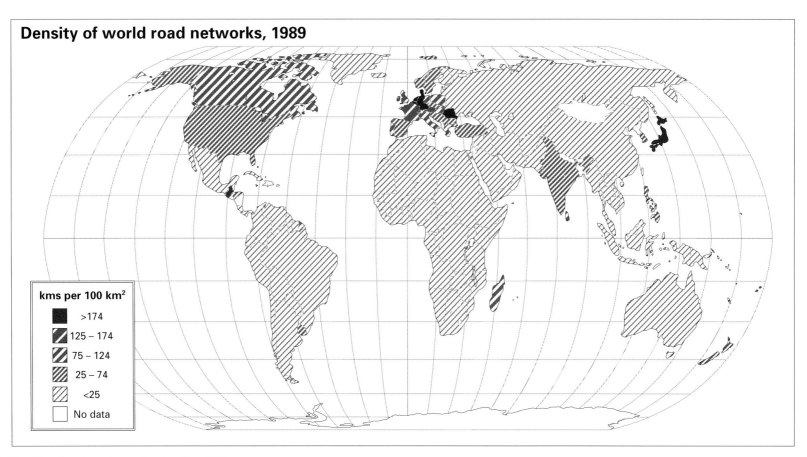

Figure 4.13a   Density of world road networks, 1989

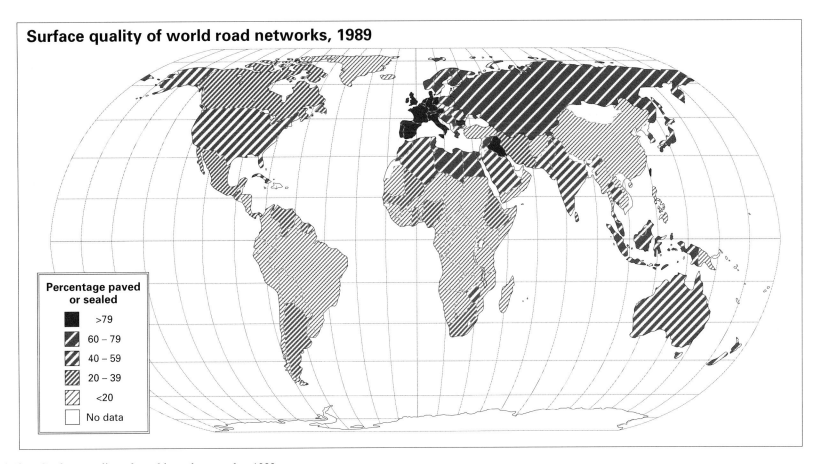

Figure 4.13b   Surface quality of world road networks, 1989

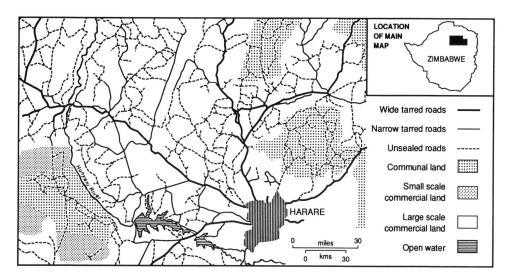

Figure 4.13c Roads in commercial farming and communal farming areas in Mashonaland, Zimbabwe

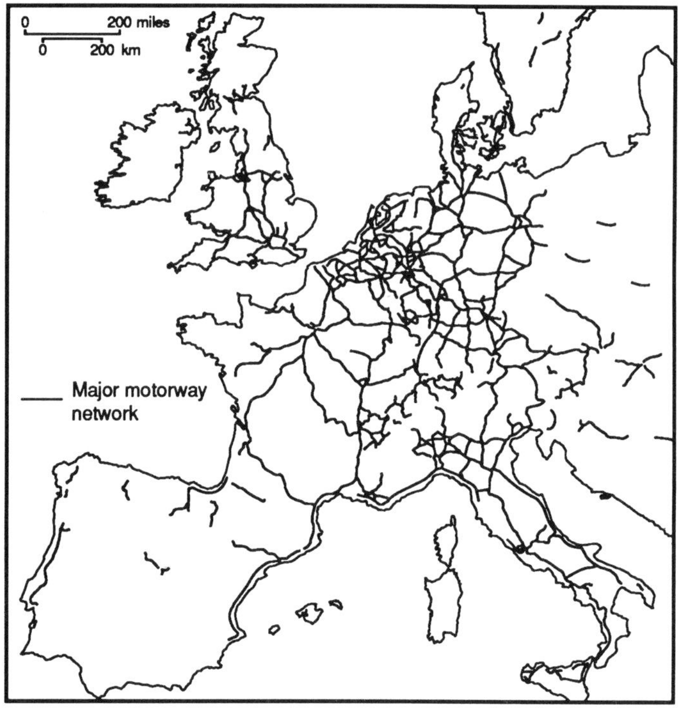

Figure 4.13d The motorway network in Europe, 1991

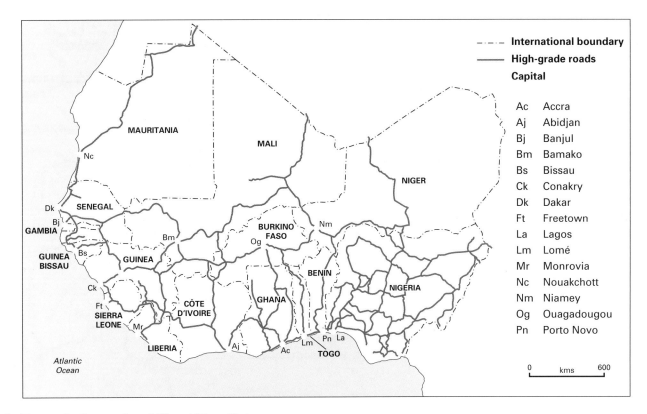

Figure 4.13e Roads in the Economic Community of West African States

4.14 REGIONAL RAIL NETWORKS
David Simon

As in other parts of the Third World, the railway system of southern Africa presents both opportunities for, and constraints on, regional development. Apart from extensions and a few latecomers, most notably the Tazara, the main lines of rail were constructed during the late 19th and early 20th centuries as essential instruments of British, German and Portuguese colonial policy. As such, the location and baseload traffics of these lines reflected the principal objectives of exporting raw materials, especially minerals (most notably diamonds, gold, copper, coal, iron ore and chrome) and importing manufactured and capital goods via the most direct route between the nearest port and main points of production and consumption.

While the railways may be a necessary condition for development, they are not sufficient in themselves, as has often been implied in the literature and by agencies like the World Bank, which subscribe essentially to modernisation theory. Moreover, the advent of the railways was not wholly beneficial or neutral in its effects. Their construction and financing were often highly political issues, while the British imperial fiat that the colonial administration in Nyasaland Protectorate (now Malawi) should guarantee the construction costs of the Trans-Zambezia Railway, for example, was largely responsible for that territory's subsequent poverty and underdevelopment. Economic dependency on foreign financial institutions and on politically hostile neighbours has also

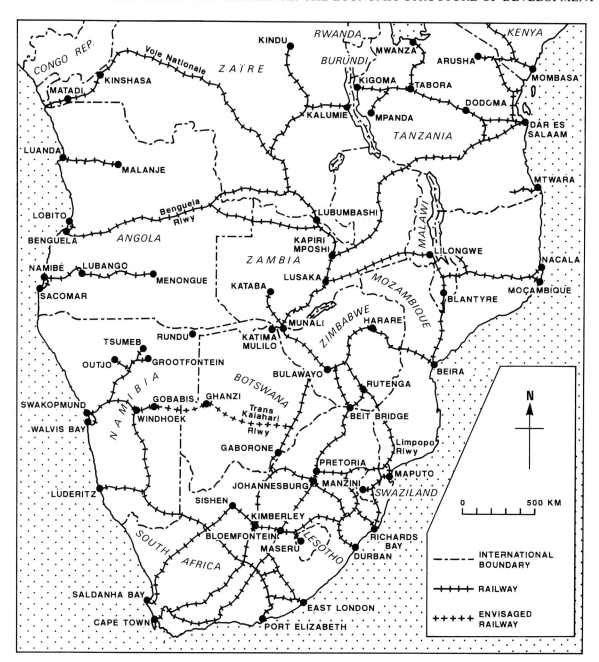

Figure 4.14 The rail network in southern and central Africa

been an enduring problem in the region right up to the present. Moreover, the siting of railways and the structure of tariffs were used to promote white settler agriculture and to undermine the African peasantry with whom they increasingly came to compete. Transport riders and others associated with earlier modes of long distance transport were driven out of business, while the recruitment hinterlands for migrant labour were greatly extended (Pirie, 1982, 1993).

South Africa possesses by far the most extensive and efficient railway and port system (Figure 4.14), which has traditionally served as an important conduit for regional traffic. Ever since the 1960s, when decolonisation of the region began and South Africa faced increasing ostracism over apartheid, the railways have formed a principal arena of conflict on account of their fundamental economic importance. Botswana, Lesotho, Malawi, Swaziland, Zambia and Zimbabwe, the region's six landlocked states, are most vulnerable. Poor management, inadequate maintenance and investment, foreign exchange shortages, war and deliberate sabotage have reduced the reliability and efficiency of non-South African routes to the sea, both old and new. Even the Tazara Railway, completed only in 1975 to provide Zambia with a safe alternative port at Dar es Salaam, has suffered the same fate, rendering Zambia and Tanzania unable to repay the Chinese construction loan (Mwase, 1987). The Benguela line from the Copperbelt to the Angolan port of Lobito has been closed since 1976 on account of that country's brutal war. During the 1980s, South African-sponsored destabilisation of its neighbours, designed to enhance their dependence on its facilities, included railway sabotage, most persistently by Renamo rebels along the routes through Mozambique linking Zimbabwe, Malawi (and South Africa) to the ports of Maputo, Beira and

Nacala. For all these reasons, some 90% of investment undertaken by the Southern African Development Co-ordination Conference (SADCC), formed in 1980 to promote co-operation and reduce members' reliance on South Africa (see Section 5.2), has been allocated to the rehabilitation of regional railways, ports and operating systems, especially in Mozambique. Meanwhile, the choice between ideology and pragmatism for these states has been hard.

Just as this programme neared completion, the regional political situation changed dramatically. Namibian independence in 1990, the 1991 Angolan peace agreement, and the dismantling of apartheid in South Africa hold out the hope of 'peace dividends' such as a reopened Benguela Railway and a new era of regional co-operation, even though the Angolan war was resumed with venom in late 1992. It might seem, therefore, that there is now an unparalleled opportunity to reduce the 60–70% of SADCC external trade which still passes through South Africa. On the other hand, a post-apartheid South Africa will be no less economically dominant and the competitiveness of its railways and ports is likely to persist for the time being. Hence, the basic regional features of inequality and dependence will remain, and SADCC members are already increasing their own trade with South Africa significantly. In 1992, SADCC was reconstituted as the Southern African Development Community (SADC) so as to respond better to changing circumstances (see Section 5.2).

Further reading

Foreign and Commonwealth Office (1989), *Transport Routes of the Frontline States, Malawi and Zaire*, London: Africa Section, Research Department, Foreign and Commonwealth Office.

Kennedy, T.L. (1988), *Transport in Southern Africa*, Johannesburg: South African Institute of International Affairs.

Mwase, N. (1987), Zambia, the TAZARA and the alternative outlets to the sea, *Transport Reviews*, **7**(3): 191–206.

Pirie, G.H. (1982), The decivilizing rails; railways and underdevelopment in southern Africa, *Tijdschrift voor Economische en Sociale Geografie*, **73**(4): 221–228.

Pirie, G.H. (1993), Slaughter by steam: railway subjugation of ox wagon transport in the eastern Cape and Transkei, 1886–1910, *International Journal of African Historical Studies*, **26**(2): 319–343.

Reichardt, M. and Duncan, D. (1990), Rail transport and the political economy of southern Africa, 1965–1980, *Africa Insight*, **20**(2): 100–110.

Simon, D. (1991), Namibia in southern Africa: the regional implications of independence, *Tijdschrift voor Economische en Sociale Geografie*, **82**(5): 377–387.

4.15 INTERNATIONAL SHIPPING
David Hilling

Between 1965 and 1989 world seaborne trade increased from 1640 million to 3940 million metric tonnes with dry cargo rising from 780 to 2212 million and oil and oil products from 860 to 1728 million tonnes. In 1989, oil and oil products and the five main dry bulk cargoes (iron ore, coal, grain, bauxite/alumina and phosphate) (*see* Section 4.12) accounted for 63% of the tonnage carried and trends in these main trades tend to determine the overall demand for shipping and, in relation to supply of tonnage, the freight rates.

The carrying capacity (deadweight tonnage – dwt) of the world fleet rose from 376 million in 1971 to 667 million in 1990 (Figure 4.15a) with oil tankers accounting for 39% and bulk carriers and general cargo vessels for 36% and 26% respectively of the tonnage. Rapidly rising demand for oil in the 1960s and early 1970s led to great ordering of tankers and increased vessel size (the largest over 500 000 dwt) to derive economies of scale on long hauls from the Middle East to Japan, and north Europe by way of the Cape of Good Hope. Successive oil crises resulted in reduced demand for oil and tanker tonnage – many Ultra Large Crude Carriers (ULCCs – of over 300 000 dwt) were laid up and more recently scrapped.

In contrast, fluctuating but generally growing demand for iron ore and coal has combined with long hauls from newer producing areas (coal – Australia, South Africa, Colombia and Indonesia; iron ore – Australia and Brazil) to traditional markets in Japan and Europe to stimulate expansion of dry bulk carrier tonnage, although recent recession has slowed down this growth. The overall capacity of general cargo tonnage has been relatively static since 1975 although a smaller number of large container and roll-on/roll-off vessels have replaced a larger number of small vessels.

A distinction has to be made between the nationality of a ship's owner and the flag under which they choose to register their ships and the once close relationship between the two is now a thing of the past. The first 'open registry' (i.e. not restricted to vessels owned by nationals of that country) or flag of convenience (FOC) as they are sometimes known, was Panama which dates from 1925, but like all other flags it has now been eclipsed by Liberia (1947). These countries saw

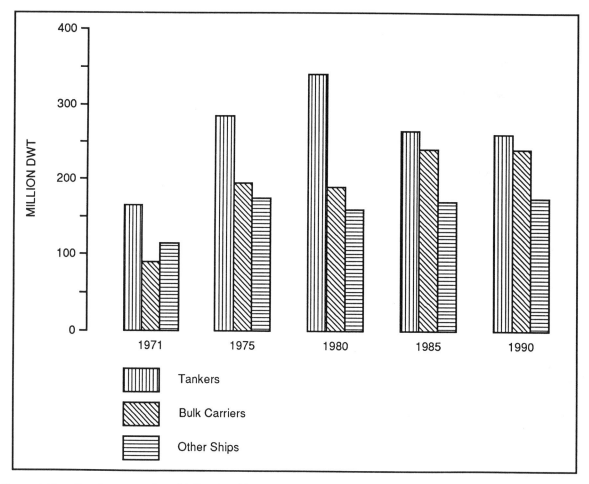

Figure 4.15a Development of world fleet by ship type, 1971–90

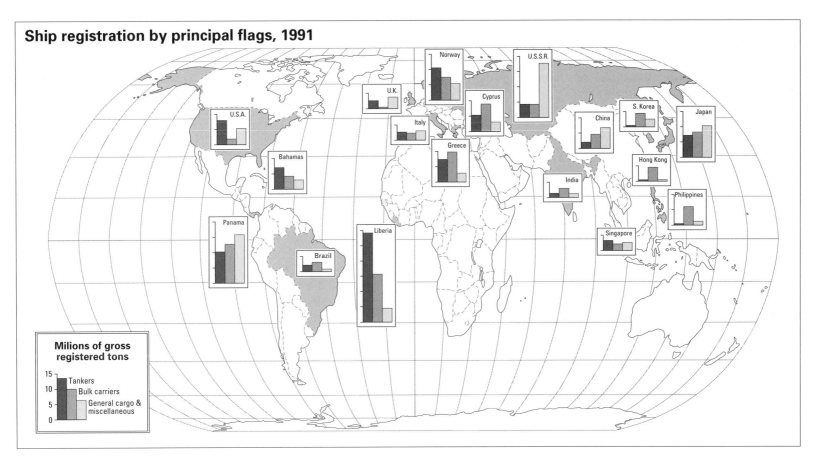

Figure 4.15b Ship registration by principal flags, 1991

that there was income to be derived from providing ship registry services and ship owners saw such open registries as a way of avoiding possibly onerous restrictions of their own flags and also as a way of reducing costs – registration fees were lower, there was little or no taxation on shipping income, low-cost crews could be employed, and access was easier and regulations less rigid.

A number of other Third World countries have created open registries (Cyprus, Bahamas, St Vincent and Vanuatu) and such registries have been gaining tonnage while traditional flags such as Norway and the United Kingdom have been

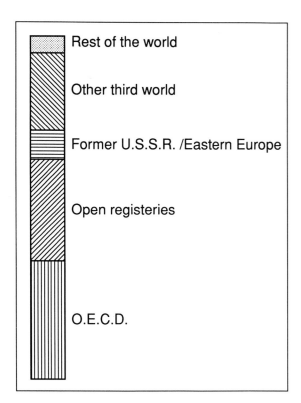

Figure 4.15c Ship registration by economic grouping

declining. While some of the tonnage registered under FOCs is old and sub-standard, it is also the case that much recent tanker and bulk carrier tonnage owned in the USA or Europe is registered in Liberia or the Bahamas – 28% of the world tanker fleet is under these two flags. Panama has attracted more older tonnage especially general cargo carriers (Figure 4.15b). A number of European, especially German, owners have transferred modern short-sea ships to the Cyprus flag. A recent trend of growing importance is that of second or international registries created by Norway, Denmark, Germany and France under which tax exemptions for national seamen or freedom to employ non-nationals as crew helps to reduce costs.

Third World countries have been making great efforts to expand their shipping industries – merely to provide a flag for tonnage owned elsewhere is not really enough. Shipping owned in Third World countries amounted to 21.3% of the world fleet in 1990 (Figure 4.15c) – far less than the proportion of world trade generated by such countries (e.g. about 90% of oil, and 35% of dry bulk). To encourage Third World countries an UNCTAD Convention on Liner Conferences (conferences were the traditional organisations of shipping companies employed in general cargo trades) stipulates that in the trade between any two countries, 40% should be carried by one partner, 40% by the other and the remaining 20% to be available to third parties. Many Third World countries have established shipping lines (e.g. Ghana, Nigeria and India), and a number, especially in Latin America, have adopted protectionist policies which have come in for considerable criticism. In general, the 40-40-20 balance is not easily achieved and there has been resistance to the idea that it be extended to the liquid and bulk trades. If the Third World countries are still

under-represented in shipping in general they have made negligible impact in container shipping in which 60% of the capacity is provided by the ships of just four countries (USA, UK, Japan and Germany).

To cut costs, many ship owners in high cost countries have reduced or even eliminated officer training and globally there is a growing dependence on seafarers from Third World countries. About two-thirds of all those employed are now from such countries, with Philippines, India and Korea as the principal suppliers.

Further reading

Bremen Institute of Shipping Economics (1992), *Shipping Statistics*, Bremen: University of Bremen.

Fairplay Publications (annual), *World Shipping Statistics*, Coulsdon: Fairplay.

Gardiner, R. (1992), *The Shipping Revolution*, London: Conway Maritime.

Gold, E. (1981), *Maritime Transport*, Lexington: D.C. Heath.

Kendall, L.C. (1986), *The Business of Shipping*, Maryland: Centreville, Cornell Maritime.

OECD (Organisation for Economic Co-operation and Development) (annual), *Maritime Transport*, Paris: OECD.

4.16 AIR TRANSPORT
David Hilling

Since the end of World War II, air transport has undergone rapid technological change in terms of propulsion (piston, turbo-jet, turbo-propeller, bypass jet) and aircraft size (32-seat DC3 to 490-seat B747) with associated increases in range, speed and capacity and significant reductions in real unit cost in comparison with other modes.

While often seen as technically the most sophisticated form of transport, air transport can paradoxically be the pioneer mode. Where distances are great (Brazil), the terrain difficult (Andean countries), countries large (Zaire) or fragmented (Indonesia, Philippines), and surface transport either poorly developed or absent, air transport may provide the only means of effecting resource surveys and providing the initial access on which the development of such resources is dependent. In Mauritania and Liberia, air transport was used in mineral surveys and the establishment of base camps for the construction of mining facilities and rail export routes.

During the 1960s and 1970s, the growth of air transport averaged 12% and 15% a year for passengers and freight respectively, but with rather slower growth in the 1980s (Figure 4.16a). Projected growth for 1990 to 2010 is 6.5% a year for passengers and 8.5% for freight, with international traffic growing faster than domestic. There is a demonstrable positive relationship between the overall use of air transport and levels of development and, in particular, variables such as income, urbanisation, industrialisation, education and leisure time. While business travel has increased, a spectacular growth in tourist travel has been stimulated by the lower real cost of air transport. Some 80% of the passengers through

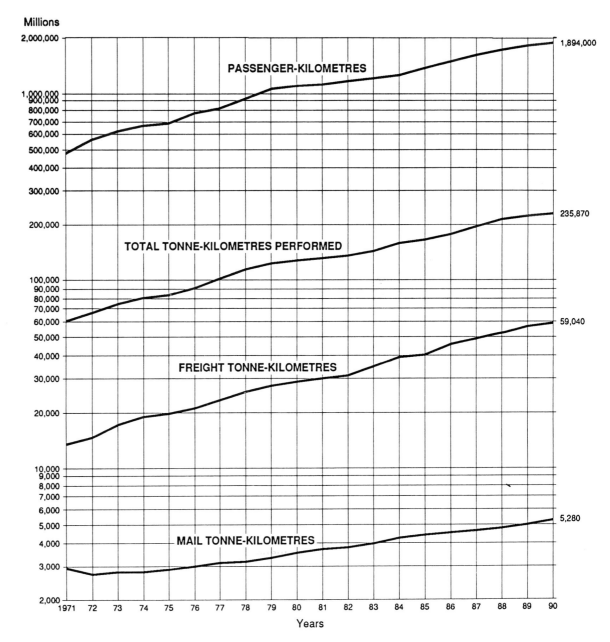

Figure 4.16a Growth of air transport, 1971–90

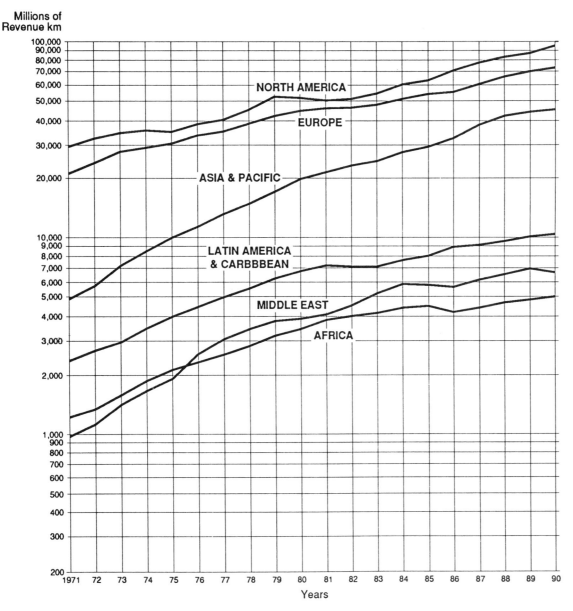

Figure 4.16b   Regional contrasts in development of air transport

London's airports are tourists, and package holiday arrangements in association with air transport have allowed many remoter areas to develop significant tourist industries. Developing areas such as Caribbean islands, The Gambia, east Africa, Seychelles, Indonesia and Thailand have become heavily dependent on air transport based tourism, and areas less remote to tourist markets such as the Mediterranean have likewise experienced rapid growth.

In the early days of air transport, airlines were heavily dependent on revenue from mail contracts to support passenger carrying services. More recently, especially with the considerable surplus 'belly' capacity of wide configuration aircraft, the air cargo market has developed largely as a function of growth in passenger travel. A Boeing 747 has 18 tonnes cargo capacity after passengers and luggage have been accommodated. From providing an emergency and high premium freight service (once described as for 'Rembrandts and race horses'), air transport now provides for a growing range of routine cargo movements – the frequency, speed, reduced packaging and time-saving all lower the real cost of air transport and allow producers to penetrate markets that would not otherwise be open to them: Kenyan and Colombian cut flowers to Britain, Côte d'Ivoire lobsters to France, shark fins from The Gambia to Hong Kong. Fruit provides Thailand with its fastest growing export and it is shipped almost entirely by air.

The expansion and utilisation of air transport has been markedly uneven (Figures 4.16b and 4.16c) and globally there is a particularly sharp contrast between the advanced, industrial economies and the developing world. North America has always had a leading role in terms of aircraft production and utilisation, and in 1990 accounted for 38.5% of global scheduled services and over

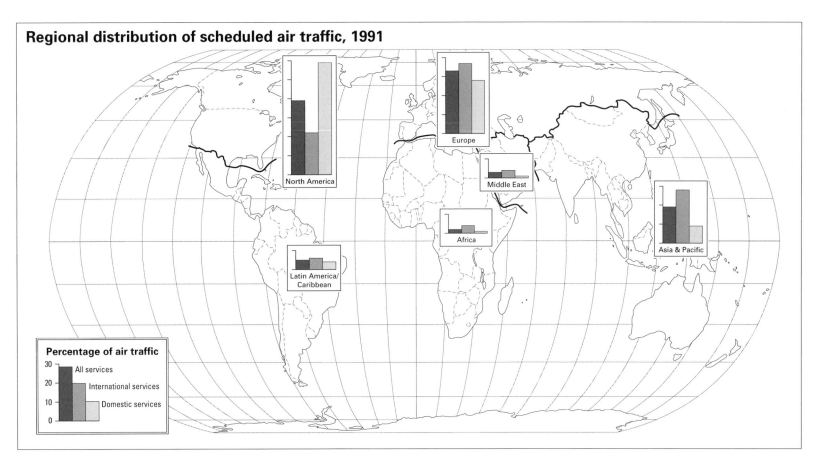

Figure 4.16c   Regional distribution of scheduled air traffic, 1991

58% of all domestic traffic. Adding Europe's 32% of all services and 35% of international traffic shows the overwhelming dominance of these developed regions. Africa is undoubtedly the lagging region, having been overtaken in 1975/6 after the oil price crisis by the Middle East. Most spectacular growth has been in the Asia and Pacific region which now accounts for 20% of all services and 28% of international services, and where the air transport market is projected to grow at 11.6% a year making it the largest single market after the American domestic market which is showing only sluggish growth. Growth in Asia is largely accounted for by the Pacific rim countries such as Japan and the Newly Industrialising Countries such as Korea, Taiwan, Hong Kong and Singapore.

While the Less Developed Countries in general have not made a great impact on global air transport, Brazil appears 12th (1989) in the world ranking in terms of passengers, and Brazil, China, India, Mexico and Indonesia all appear in the top ten for domestic air traffic. In terms of the number of airports, Brazil, Mexico, Bolivia, Paraguay, Colombia, Indonesia and Zimbabwe all feature on the top ten list by virtue of large numbers of airfields serving private mining, forestry and agricultural enterprises.

Further reading

Cole, Viscount (1989), General aviation – the developing world's indispensable transport, in: Heraty, M. (ed.), *Developing World Transport*, London: Grosvenor Press International, 325–327.

Doganis, R. (1985), *Flying Off Course*, London: Allen & Unwin.

Gidwitz, B. (1980), *The Politics of International Air Transport*, Lexington: D.C. Heath.

International Civil Aviation Organisation (monthly, annual statistics), *International Civil Aviation Organisation Journal*.

Naveau, J. (1989), *International Air Transport in a Changing World*, London: Nijhoff.

Taneja, N.K. (1989), *Introduction to Civil Aviation*, Lexington: D.C. Heath.

4.17 URBAN SETTLEMENT HIERARCHIES
Alan Gilbert

Many governments are concerned that the form of urban development in their country is distorted. Normally their concern relates either to the presumption that urbanisation is occurring too rapidly, *urban bias*, or to a belief that the largest city in a country is too dominant in the urban hierarchy, urban primacy.

Urban bias is a complaint frequently expressed in the countryside; rural folk regret that their children are leaving for work in the cities and feel that their taxes are being mis-spent by urban bureaucrats. Many feel that urban bias is inequitable, for most of the poor live in the countryside. But urban bias may also be inefficient; too many resources are being spent in the urban areas that could be devoted more productively in developing agriculture. In practice, it is extremely difficult to demonstrate the case in support of urban bias, although there is no doubt that in some countries it certainly exists.

Distortions in the urban settlement system are often described as *urban primacy*. One way of measuring the degree of primacy is to compare the size of the first city with that of the second. If the first city is more than twice as large, the urban system might be considered to be primate. A better way is to consider the population of the first city compared to the combined population of the next three cities. If we assume that the concept of the *rank-size rule* provides a logical basis for establishing the most desirable urban pattern, then the largest city should be twice as large as the second city, three times as large as the third and four times as large as the fourth. This means that if the population of the largest city relative to the next three exceeds a ratio of 12:13, it is primate. [If the largest city has a population of 12 units, the second should have 6 units, the third 4 units and the fourth 3 units; hence, 12 to $6 + 4 + 3 = 13$.]

The difficulty with this approach is that many writers increasingly question the wisdom of the rank-size rule. In addition, the measure is insensitive to the level of urbanisation in a country. What is more significant? If most of a country's population live in a single city or if the largest city has three times or more inhabitants than the second city? For this reason, Figure 4.17 measures primacy in a different way. It records the proportion of the total population of the country living in the largest city. The advantage of using this measure is that it clearly reveals which primate cities genuinely dominate their countries.

As Figure 4.17 shows, there are a number of countries around the world where one city contains a high proportion of the national population. There is no obvious pattern. The countries with more than 25% of their population living in the largest city include both rich countries, such as Austria and New Zealand, and poor countries, such as Mongolia, Peru and the Congo. Physically small countries are more likely to have dominant cities, but some large nations such as Argentina also share this feature. By region, Africa and the Indian sub-continent have relatively few dominant cities, largely because of their low levels of urban development, whereas a considerable number of Latin American countries do. Among the latter there are several examples of particularly dominant cities: one in two Uruguayans live in Montevideo, one in three Argentinians live in Buenos Aires, and one in three Chileans live in Santiago.

Further reading

Gilbert, A.G. and Gugler, J. (1982), *Cities, Poverty and Development: Urbanization in the Third World*, Oxford: Oxford University Press.

Lipton, M. (1977), *Why Poor People Stay Poor: a Study of Urban Bias in World Development*, London: Temple Smith.

Richardson, H. (1989), The big, bad city: mega-city myth, *Third World Planning Review*, **11**: 355–372.

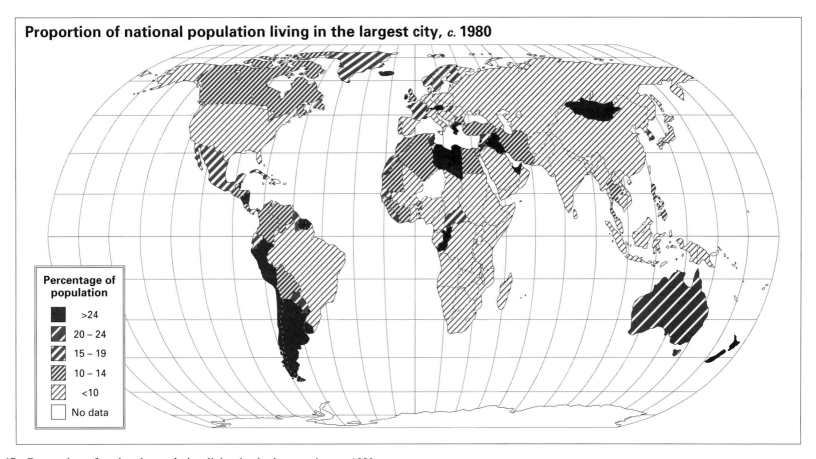

Figure 4.17 Proportion of national population living in the largest city, *c.* 1980

4.18 HOUSING UPGRADING
Robert B. Potter

It is generally accepted that at least one-fifth, and perhaps over one-half of Third World citizens live in housing which might by conventional yardsticks be described as substandard. Many dwellings have been constructed by means of individual or extended community *self-help*. Self-help may be defined as a situation where the owners of a dwelling control the building process themselves. Viewed frequently in the past as the cause of the overall housing problem rather than as a symptom of it, self-help housing areas have often been cleared by governments when it has suited them to do so. On the other hand, there is plenty of evidence suggesting that such areas, whether they are inhabited illegally (*squatter areas*), or merely poorly constructed (*shanty towns*), have been tolerated where the state has seen advantage in so doing, for example, in times of economic boom and labour shortage.

Opinion has now undergone a sea-level change so that self-help is frequently encouraged by local officials, as well as the principal international aid agencies such as the World Bank and the United States Agency for International Development (USAID). Hence, as shown in Figure 4.18a, *spontaneous self-help* has given rise to *aided self-help*. Frequently, such dwellings are capable of great improvement. However, usually they have been constructed without an overall plan for the neighbourhood. As a result, net residential densities are high and infrastructural provision relating to pathways, access, drainage and sanitation is poor.

The approach which is increasingly preferred is that of upgrading. This represents the simplest and most effective form of *aided self-help* (ASH). It has many advantages, including preserving the existing economic, community and housing systems of the low-income groups involved (Martin, 1983). The alternative is the relocation of all residents, with the attendant upheavals, including long journeys to work. As such, the approach conforms with the philosophies expounded in the 1960s by the architects John Turner (1967) and William Mangin (1967).

An example of upgrading is shown in Figure 4.18b. This has been adapted from the work of Alan Turner (1980), and is based on an actual site in Manila in the Philippines. The houses in the area are mainly built of wood and other materials, making it quite possible for a group of people to move them. At the outset, the areas had no water supply, no paved paths and no sewerage system, although some houses did have pit latrines.

There are a number of components to any upgrading scheme. The first involves the realignment and relocation of certain of the existing structures. Figure 4.18b: (A) shows the original house spots, including the dwellings which are to be repositioned on lots and those which are to be demolished. Such *reblocking*, as it is referred to, reduces residential densities and allows paths to be introduced, as shown by the shaded areas in Figure 4.18b: (B). Secondly, basic services have to be introduced. In the example, a number of water points in the form of standpipes and toilet blocks are being provided. Small spaces have been opened up between the houses here and there, and trees have been planted. The final site development plan is shown in Figure 4.18b: (C). Lots may be provided to residents on a freehold or a leasehold basis.

Upgrading goes hand in hand with other housing schemes, not least because it involves the relocation of the families whose houses are demolished in order to rationalise the site plan. Sometimes as many as 30% of all the original structures are affected in this way. Thus, upgrading schemes generally go together with *site and service schemes* (where land and basic facilities are provided on greenfield sites), and *core housing schemes* (where the beginnings of a dwelling – usually the sanitary unit – are provided for self-builders). Interesting case studies of upgrading are afforded by the Tondo Foreshore Development Project in the Philippines (*see* Laquain, 1983; Skinner and Rodell, 1983), and on a small scale by the island of Barbados (Potter, 1986). Such examples serve to stress the flexibility and diversity which are inherent in such projects, involving not only the size of plots, and the extent of relocation and reblocking, but also the level of infrastructural provision.

Further reading

Payne, G.K. (ed.) (1984), *Low-Income Housing in the Developing World: the Roles of Sites and Services and Settlement Upgrading*, Chichester: Wiley.

Skinner, R.J. and Rodell, M.J. (eds) (1983), *People, Poverty and Shelter: Problems of Housing in the Third World*, London: Methuen.

Turner, A. (ed.) (1980), *The Cities of the Poor: Settlement Planning in Developing Countries*, London: Croom Helm.

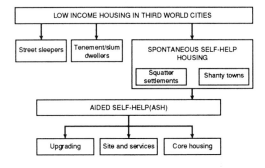

Figure 4.18a Low-income housing in Third World cities

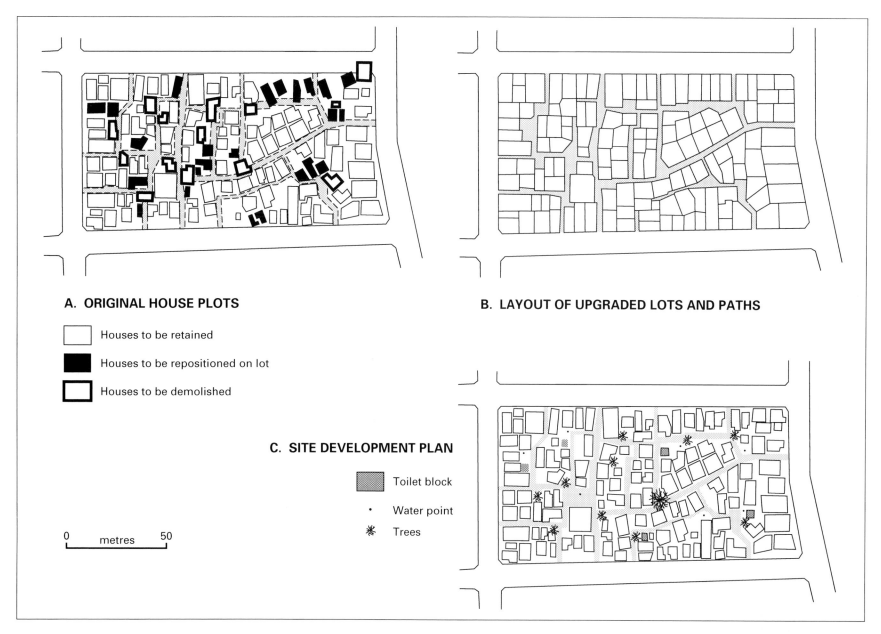

A. ORIGINAL HOUSE PLOTS

Houses to be retained

Houses to be repositioned on lot

Houses to be demolished

B. LAYOUT OF UPGRADED LOTS AND PATHS

C. SITE DEVELOPMENT PLAN

Toilet block

Water point

Trees

0   metres   50

Figure 4.18b   Housing upgrading

4.19 THE WORLD BANK
Bill Gould

The World Bank is the world's largest development agency. It comprises a group of institutions, notably the International Bank for Reconstruction and Development (IBRD), founded in 1945 along with its sister global institution the International Monetary Fund (IMF), the International Development Association (IDA), founded in 1960, and the International Finance Corporation (IFC). It is a bank 'owned' by its member states, 45 in 1945 and 155 by 1991. A common objective of the World Bank Group is 'to help raise standards of living in developing countries by channelling financial resources to them from developed countries' (World Bank, 1991 annual report). The Group raises capital backed by commitments of its member governments and lends to governments on the basis of criteria established within the World Bank. Voting power in the institution is according to the proportion of that capital commitment. In 1991, as in 1976, the voting power of the 'G7' countries, the seven richest countries in the world, was over 50% of the total. Only six Third World countries had over 1% of voting power in 1991 (Table 4.19a). The President of the World Bank has always been a US citizen, and the location of its headquarters two blocks from the White House in Washington and across the street from the IMF headquarters is symbolic of the power and priorities of the Group.

In principle its lending is directly to governments, though IFC lends to the private sector. IBRD lending, about two-thirds of the total, is at rates rather below (normally about 1%) commercial rates. The more developed countries in the Europe, Middle East and North Africa Region of the Bank (including countries such as Algeria,

Table 4.19a   IBRD voting power, 1976 and 1991, selected countries: percentage of total votes in Executive Council

Developed countries	1976	1991	Third World countries	1976	1991
Canada	3.36	3.11	Argentina	1.39	0.86
France	4.54	6.02	Brazil	1.21	1.39
Germany	4.83	6.28	China	2.70	3.03
Italy	3.05	3.88	India	3.32	3.32
Japan	3.64	8.13	Indonesia	0.85	1.07
UK	9.13	6.02	Iran	0.33	1.15
USA	22.60	17.89	Saudi Arabia	0.48	2.18
G7 countries	51.15	51.42			

Source: World Bank, *Annual Reports* (1976, 1991)

Table 4.19b   IBRD and IDA loans, 1945–76, 1982 and 1991, by region (US$ millions)

	1945–76		1982		1991	
	loan	%	loan	%	loan	%
IBRD						
Sub-Saharan Africa	3593.5	12.1	961.7	9.3	662.9	4.0
Asia†	7840.0	26.5	4087.1	39.6	4583.0	28.0
Europe, Middle East, North Africa†	7970.9	26.9	2317.6	22.4	6079.1	37.1
Latin America and Caribbean	10 182.0	34.4	2962.9	28.7	5067.2	30.9
TOTAL	29 586.4	100.0	10 329.3	100.0	16 392.2	100.0
IDA						
Sub-Suharan Africa	2243.0	22.2	839.8	31.3	2731.3	43.4
Asia†	6539.7	65.0	1760.8	65.5	2907.9	46.2
Europe, Middle East North Africa†	926.5	9.1	61.5	2.2	484.6	7.7
Latin America and Caribbean	360.9	3.5	25.0	0.9	169.4	2.7
TOTAL	10 090.1	100.0	2687.1	100.0	6293.2	100.0

† The boundaries of these statistical regions changed between 1982 and 1991. For the earlier years Pakistan was in 'Asia', for 1991 it was in 'Europe, Middle East and North Africa'.
Source: World Bank, *Annual Reports* (1976, 1982, 1991)

Iran and Turkey and in the last few years joined by east European countries) and its Latin America and Caribbean Region (Mexico is the largest borrower) together borrow nearly 70% of IBRD loans (Table 4.19b). IDA lending is even more strongly concessionary at very low rates of interest, and is only to the poorest countries. In 1991, 40 countries, mostly in Africa and Asia, with a per capita GNP of less than $580 were eligible. While many of the poorest countries borrow on IBRD terms,

90% of IDA loans are to Africa and Asia. In the earliest years of IDA, India and Pakistan dominated its lending portfolio, but Sub-Saharan Africa has now increased its use of this support for it remains the poorest region, and only a few countries outside Asia and Africa are eligible.

The geographical distribution of lending is also reflected in the sectoral allocations of the two major loan types (Figure 4.19). Agriculture and

Rural Development has been and remains the dominant sector for both IDA and IBRD loans, and in the past these have been matched by investments in the energy sector and in basic infrastructure (transportation, urban development and sewerage). However, in recent years there has been a substantial shift to investment in human resources – education, population, health and nutrition programmes – reflecting the priority needs in this sector in Africa and Asia.

The role of the World Bank in the study as well as the practice of development has also been very substantial. This has been most obvious in the annual *World Development Report*, sometimes with general discussion of development, sometimes with theme issues such as *Population and Economic Development* (1984) and *Poverty* (1990), and always with an invaluable up-to-date and wide-ranging statistical appendix. The World Bank classification of countries is widely used (as in this Atlas). Its many publications are built on the vast data base collected as a result of the lending programme, and on the research programme that underpins the policies and methodologies developed to identify needs for and to evaluate implementation of the loans. World Bank research in all aspects of development is extensively reported in its own publications and has been a prominent component of material in major journals, such as *World Development*. It also forms the basis for regular policy papers in particular sectors, as on urban development (World Bank, 1991), or for particular regions, such as Africa (World Bank, 1989b).

Since the World Bank is a leader in both the theory and practice of development, it has been able to set much of the global agenda in Development Studies. In the late 1970s and early 1980s, for example, it was at the forefront of the 'basic needs' equity strategy in development, with its

WORLD BANK LENDING BY TYPE AND SECTOR, 1980, 1984, 1988, 1991

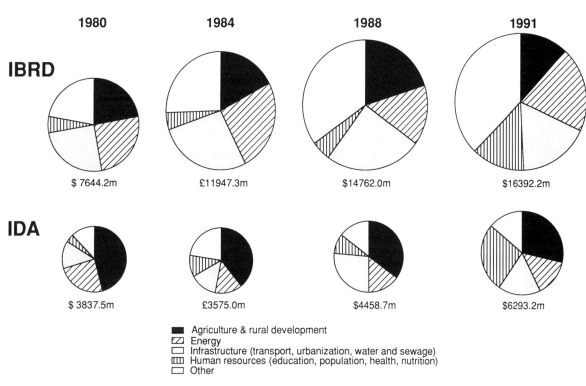

■ Agriculture & rural development
▨ Energy
▢ Infrastructure (transport, urbanization, water and sewage)
▥ Human resources (education, population, health, nutrition)
▢ Other

Figure 4.19 World Bank lending by type and sector, 1980, 1984, 1988, 1991

lending programmes and priorities disproportionately targeted to the rural poor. In the 1990s,
however, its lending strategies are very different,
now strongly associated with Structural Adjustment policies, with a priority for ensuring macro-
economic efficiency as a pre-condition for
increases in individual incomes and improvements
in the quality of life. The range of lending strategies and their effectiveness have been a source of
major debates in Development Studies.

Further reading

Mosley, P., Toye, P. and Harrigan, J. (1991), *Aid and
    Power. The World Bank and Policy-based Lending*,
    London: Routledge.
World Bank (annual since 1946), *Annual Report*,
    Washington D.C.: The World Bank.
World Bank (annual since 1978), *World Development
    Report*, New York: Oxford University Press for The
    World Bank.

4.20 INTERNATIONAL DEBT
Alan Gilbert

Many countries around the world have long suffered from a deficit in their balance of payments. They have imported more than they have exported and they have, therefore, gone into debt. The number of countries in this situation, however, increased dramatically during the 1970s. The essential reason lay in the decision of the world's major oil exporters in 1973 to cut oil production, thereby raising world oil prices fourfold. This posed a major problem, for most oil importers and countries such as Brazil, Egypt and Korea went heavily into debt. At first, this caused little difficulty because cheap credit was readily available. Credit was easy because the oil exporters of the Middle East had so much money that they put their surplus revenue into the banks of Britain, Switzerland and the United States. These banks, anxious to lend the money to maintain their profits, sought out customers among the highly indebted oil importers of the Third World. The banks also found customers among certain oil exporters, such as Mexico and Venezuela, which were trying to diversify and modernise their economies as quickly as possible.

Unfortunately for these debtors, world interest rates rose dramatically in 1979. The world's largest debtor, the United States, increased interest rates in order to attract funds to cover its huge balance-of-payments and Federal Government deficits. Changing monetary policies in other developed countries also led to a rise in interest rates. Those Third World countries which had borrowed funds from the commercial banks on a short-term basis saw their debt-service ratios rise dramatically. Their efforts to increase exports were damaged by a worldwide recession. As a result, annual interest payments relative to export earnings rose spectacularly. In 1974, Latin America spent 9% of its export earnings on interest payments; by 1983, the worst year of the 'debt crisis', the ratio had risen to 41%.

The largest debtors (Table 4.20) were the newly industrialising countries. Such countries were forced to devalue their currencies, cut back on imports and reduce their government expenditure. This brought about severe adjustment problems, particularly for the poor who found that rapid price inflation was undermining the value of their earnings. Some countries, such as Korea, adjusted very successfully and no longer face a serious debt situation. As Figure 4.20 shows, however, some countries, generally those which failed to increase their export earnings, never recovered. Many of these countries are in eastern Europe but by far the worst affected are in Africa. There, a combination of war, climatic change, poor government and population pressure has led to economic decline in numerous countries. Today, debt as a proportion of gross domestic product (GDP) has risen to a spectacular level; 436% in Mozambique and 350% in Zaire. Elsewhere, a few other countries find themselves in equally miserable circumstances: the debt/GDP ratio is 522% in Guyana and 407% in Nicaragua. These countries simply cannot pay their debts.

Recently, some efforts have been made to forgive the debts of the poorest countries. Deals have also been struck with some of the largest debtors, such as Mexico. But the debt crisis still continues to bring a great deal of pain to poor countries as they seek to restructure their economies and pay most of the interest accruing on their debts.

Further reading

George, S. (1988), *A Fate Worse than Debt*, Harmondsworth: Penguin.

Gilbert, A.G. (1992), *An Unequal World*, Walton-on-Thames: Thomas Nelson.

United Nations (1990), *Debt: a Crisis for Development*, New York: United Nations.

Table 4.20 The world's largest debtors in 1988

Country	Total foreign debt (US$ billion)	Debt as % GDP
Brazil	114.6	32.3
Mexico	101.6	55.3
Argentina	58.9	69.5
India	57.5	21.3
Indonesia	52.6	63.6
Egypt	50.0	182.6
South Korea	43.2	27.0
China	42.1	12.6
USSR	40.9	10.5
Turkey	39.6	56.1
Poland	39.2	56.1
Venezuela	34.7	54.4
Nigeria	30.7	100.5

Source: *The Economist* (1988) *The Economist Book of Vital World Statistics: a Complete Guide to the World in Figures*

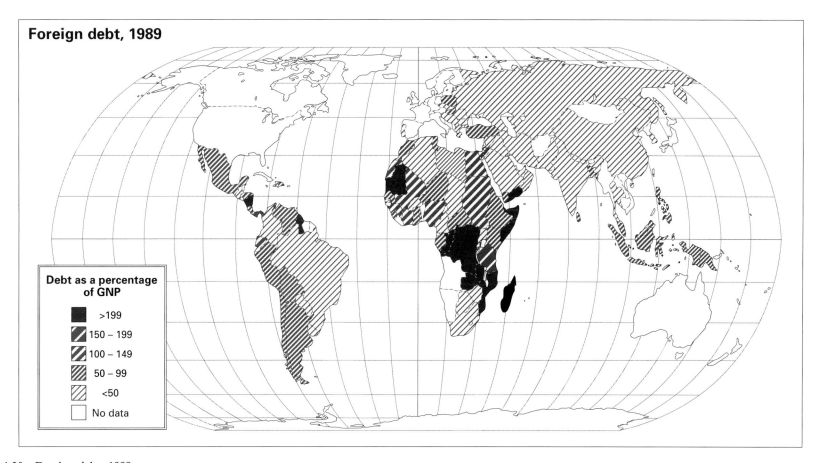

Figure 4.20   Foreign debt, 1989

4.21 GLOBAL FINANCE: OFFSHORE BANKING AND CAPITAL FLIGHT
Gareth A. Jones

There would appear to have been an incontrovertible transition toward a global banking system in the past 25 years, producing a 'single world market for money and credit supply' which is increasingly unrestrained by the friction of time and place (Harvey, 1989: 161). But, to what extent is there a global market in stateless money and how far is there a global banking network to facilitate it? Evidence of the global reach of banking is sketchy. Indeed, the vice-chairman of Citibank, one of the most vulnerable US banks during the debt crisis, has hinted quite strongly that what saved the system in 1982 was the absence of global banking which prevented the chain reaction of debtor default-bank failure (*The Economist*, 12th September 1992). In addition, a survey by *The Banker* found that while 40 of the largest banks have 25% of the group business outside their home country, only five have more than 50% of their assets outside their home country (*The Banker*, 1992).

In support of the global finance argument is the growing financial interdependence between developed and developing countries as attested to by the system survival strategies of the Baker, Bradley and Brady plans. Until 1980, the growing role of developing countries in global finance produced almost 30 years of uninterrupted net capital inflow. The onset of Casino Capitalism at a global level was triggered by the stricter financial regulation in the US during the 1960s which provoked a 20–50% per annum expansion in the Eurodollar market as US multinationals sought to acquire capital offshore. Then, following the oil shocks of 1970–73, the banking network received an injection of OPEC surpluses, as well as funds from Japan which was emerging as a net supplier of capital. The resulting growth in global money supply was an important motivation for the lending to developing countries: albeit in the form of 'stupid bankers [who] made stupid loans to stupid countries' (Payer, 1985: 18). The 1980s, however, witnessed a net capital transfer from developing countries due to a combination of debt payments, a drying up of new lending and diminished Foreign Direct Investment, plus capital flight (Corbridge and Agnew, 1991). Finally, the US government became a net importer of capital in order to fund the US$ 1 trillion federal deficit (Corbridge and Agnew, 1991).

These influences, however, have not acted independently. Rather, those countries which experienced the highest levels of capital flight were also the largest debtors (India is the exception). In order to explain this relationship, one must look at the role of the offshore bank network which became the principal conduit for capital flight, partly encouraged by the US to lure capital from the developing world to cover domestic deficits (Naylor, 1987). Offshore banks offer a number of unique services. For the client, the protection offered by fee based services to 'high net worth individuals' allows access to secondary forms of investment at minimal risk through a process known as 'round tripping'. This works by using funds placed in a dollar-denominated offshore account to support a loan to the sender of the original funds. The loan is then used to embark upon risky domestic investments and allow further quantities of capital to be exported under the guise of interest on the loan. In all, an estimated US$ 198 billion was transferred out of the leading 18 developing economies between 1976 and 1985. The preferred destination is US real estate, often on mortgage terms with the flight capital offered as collateral. In all, it is estimated that the value of US real estate held by nationals from developing countries is US$ 210 billion.

Figure 4.21 presents the geography of the global financial system. First order financial centres include New York and London, Frankfurt, Paris, Tokyo and Sydney. Others (not shown) such as Toronto, Madrid and Zurich (included here as an offshore centre), and the emerging financial centres in developing countries such as Mexico City, Rio de Janeiro, Bombay and Seoul have yet to acquire supranational status. The latter, however, have recently developed stock markets worth US$ 719 billion. The 43 offshore banking centres identified include the Bahamas, Panama, Vanuatu and Cook Islands, Bahrain and Beirut, as well as the better known Hong Kong, Singapore and Cayman Islands, and 'developed' centres such as Switzerland, Luxembourg, Liechtenstein, Malta and Cyprus (Blum, 1981). Moreover, following the 'Big Bang' deregulation of the 1980s, first order centres have developed what are essentially offshore facilities (Roberts, 1994).

The geography of offshore banking is related to a number of factors. First, banks have sought to establish offshore functions in time zones which allow transactions with major financial centres and, simultaneously, with source regions – notably in the 1980s, developing countries suffering from capital flight. Thus, Panama and the Caribbean have become channels for funds from Latin American countries, Beirut serves north Africa and the Middle East (Naylor, 1987). Second, geopolitical reasons have dictated location. Offshore financial centres, by their nature, are highly deregulated and attractive to so-called 'hot money' flows. In order to preserve financial credibility, therefore, banks have had to maintain

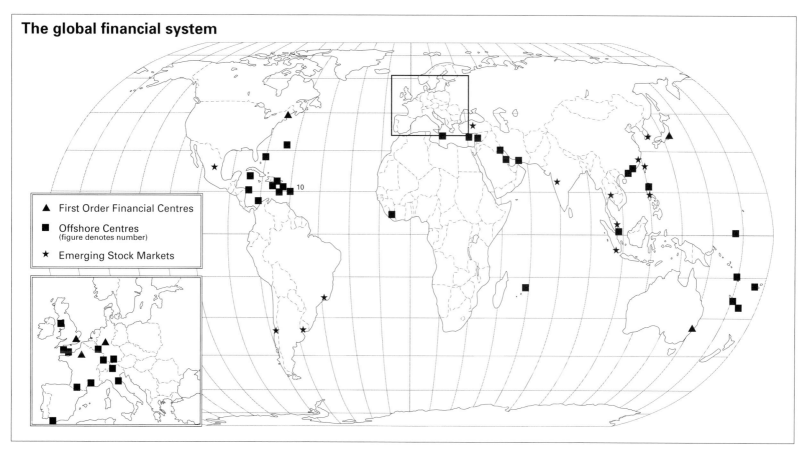

Figure 4.21 The global financial system

a degree of supervision over offshore functions. The lack of interest in the local market is highlighted by Roberts (1994) who notes that, on paper, there are 546 banks in the Cayman Islands, but only 69 with formal offices and only six offering clearing bank facilities for local residents. Finally, the offshore centres are competitive among themselves. Thus the Cayman Islands compete with the Bahamas and Panama, while Cyprus competes with Beirut, Malta and Turkey. Indeed, one might propose that while the movement of money is fairly global, although there remains considerable time-space friction in making transfers from developing to developed countries, the banking network is rather more regional than the received wisdom suggests.

Further reading

Corbridge, S., Martin, R. and Thrift, N. (eds) (1994), *Money, Power and Space*, Oxford: Basil Blackwell.
Fryer, D.W. (1987), The political geography of international lending by private banks, *Transactions of the Institute of British Geographers*, **12**: 413–432.
Thrift, N. (1990), The geography of international economic disorder, in: Johnston, R.J. and Taylor, P.J. (eds), *A World in Crisis: Geographical Perspectives*, Oxford: Basil Blackwell, 16–78.

4.22 THE BRAIN DRAIN
Bill Gould

The 'Brain Drain' is widely used to describe the international migration of skilled professional workers from poor countries to rich. It was first applied in the years after World War II to the migration of European scientists to North America, and is still widely used in that context. However, it is now more commonly associated with migrations from Third World countries to North America, particularly to the USA, and to a lesser extent to Europe. The Brain Drain is typically viewed to be one important symptom and exacerbating cause of the widening gulf in economic conditions and quality of life between rich and poor countries.

Highly educated and highly skilled workers are in short supply in poor countries, where their potential contribution to the development effort should be immense. Their emigration to work in richer countries constitutes not only a loss, a drain from the country of origin that has borne the high costs of specialist training, but also a gain in the human resources available to the country of destination. The extent of the migration has been exacerbated by studentship and training programmes that have offered the most able students the opportunity to study abroad, and many have remained abroad and have found a job at the end of their period of study. In the poor source country, doctors, engineers, scientists and university teachers have considerable social prestige, but they are poorly paid by international standards, and their professional skills are usually hampered by shortage of equipment (e.g. in hospitals and laboratories) and poor career opportunities. Since at destination, on the other hand, personal and professional opportunities are so much greater,

the demand for migration among professionals and their families tends to be high.

Much more important, however, for the increasing number of 'brain drain' migrants from Third World countries since the 1960s had been the shift in European, North American and Australasian countries to policies for immigration based on economic criteria rather than national or ethnic criteria. Skilled professional workers were in relatively short supply in these rapidly expanding economies in the 1960s, 1970s and 1980s, and changed immigration rules permitted the shortfalls to be filled by migrants whose occupations and qualifications were in short supply. They came disproportionately from Third World countries. In the USA in the 1980s about 80% of immigrants in the professional category ('Social Scientists, Natural Scientists, Engineers and Physicians') were from 18 Third World countries for which data are separately available (Figure 4.22) (MacPhee and Hassan, 1990). These are mostly large population countries, with a bias to Latin America and South Asia in the earlier decades, but with major migrations from East Asia from the 1970s. Absolute numbers are relatively small (less than 12 000 out of over 500 000 migrants from these 18 countries in 1987), but they are of immense economic significance for the USA and for the countries of origin. However, brain drain migrants from most Third World countries cannot be separately identified from US data. Their numbers are small for the USA, but may constitute a significant proportion of the human resources of small countries.

In particular, there are no separate data for any African country, though with the serious and continuing economic difficulties of most African states, brain drain migrations have become very prevalent. For example, it is estimated that over 10 000 Nigerian professionals are employed in the

USA (World Bank, 1992a). The United Nations Commission on Trade and Development estimates that 30% of the continent's stock of skilled professionals now reside abroad, and this can be as high as two-thirds as in the case of Sudan, most of whom are working in the Gulf states. The extent of the migration is most severe from those countries, such as Sudan, Ghana and Uganda, that have experienced major economic declines in recent years, but have maintained an output of graduates from local universities that the local economies cannot absorb. While many Ghanaian and Ugandan professionals are working elsewhere in Africa (Gould, 1988), many are in Europe and North America.

Brain drain migrants, particularly to the richest countries, tend to become permanent rather than temporary migrants. They tend to be better integrated, culturally as well as economically, into the destination society than are less highly educated migrants, and are less likely to send remittances to their home country, even though their earnings are generally far higher. Schemes to redirect the flow of benefit back to the countries of origin have been developed to sponsor permanent resettlement, often with financial incentives, or through temporary consultancy assignments in the country of origin, as in the UN Transfer of Knowledge through Expatriate Nationals (TOKTEN) programme (Logan, 1990).

Further reading

Gould, W.T.S. (1993), *People and Education in the Third World*, Harlow: Longman.

MacPhee, C.R. and Hassan, M.K. (1990), Socio-economic determinants of Third World professional immigration to the United States: 1972–87, *World Development*, **18**(8): 1111–1118.

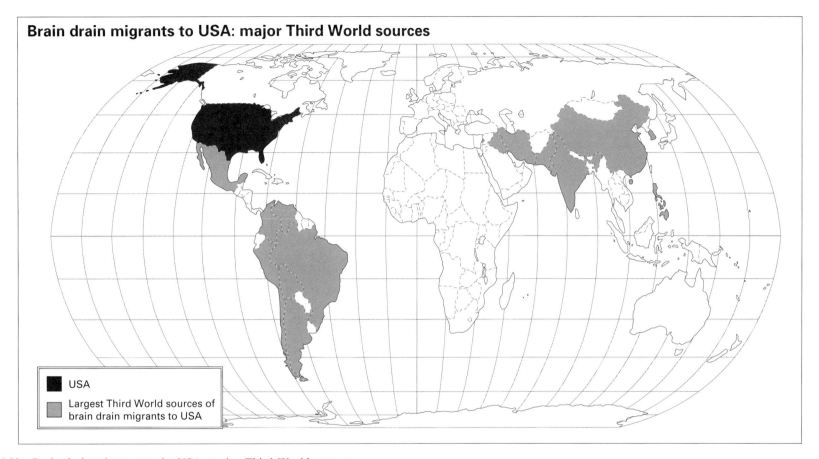

Figure 4.22   Brain drain migrants to the USA: major Third World sources

4.23 INTERNATIONAL MIGRATION AND REMITTANCES
Allan M. Findlay and Juliette Brown

International labour migration flows in the 1980s focused on a small number of destination regions. The most significant in terms of volume were the Middle East oil states, but other significant labour flows moved towards the USA, Canada and South Africa. There is much dispute about the numbers of persons involved with different estimates being produced by sending and receiving nations, and with some confusion arising because of failure to distinguish between labour migrants and their dependants. In 1990 an estimated 20 million persons were international labour migrants. Some major zones of immigration in the 1960s and early 1970s such as western Europe (with a stock of over six million labour migrants at the peak in the mid 1970s), closed their doors to further labour migration in the late 1970s and 1980s (Salt, 1989). Other countries such as the USA and Canada continued to permit immigration, but adopted immigration policies which increasingly favoured the entry of skilled and business migrants. The 1980s witnessed significant switches in the sources from which migrants were being drawn. In the Arab oil states, Arab immigrant stocks declined in proportional terms, being displaced by cheaper labour from countries such as Pakistan, India and Bangladesh. North America witnessed new waves of immigration from the other side of the Pacific as well as pressure from Hispanics entering from the south both legally and illegally.

One way of gauging the significance of international migration is to measure the volume of remittances sent to and from countries by migrants (Keely and Tran, 1989). Figure 4.23a shows that in the late 1980s the main countries to 'benefit' from remittances were those located close to the major labour markets of western Europe, the Middle East and the USA. The capital-rich, labour-poor Arab oil states drew their labour from a particularly large number of countries across southern and eastern Asia as well as from other parts of the Arab world.

Figure 4.23b ranks the top six countries in the world in terms of their dependence on remittances relative to earnings from exports. It is evident that by this measure the Islamic countries were far more dependent on remittances than other countries. In Yemen throughout the 1980s remittances were worth about five times the value of earnings from the export of goods and services, and all top six countries received the equivalent of at least three quarters of their export earnings from remittances. For some countries, such as the two Yemens and Jordan, remittances were valued at well over a quarter of their Gross Domestic Products in the early 1980s and even by the end of the decade were still recording values in excess of 10% of their GDP (Table 4.23).

In these economic circumstances international migration became a significant element in moulding the development course of these countries. The withdrawal of labour through the migration process resulted in wage levels rising steeply in Jordan and Yemen. It has been estimated that a 500% rise in Yemeni rural wages took place over a five year period. Children and women were drawn into the labour force to fill jobs left vacant by the withdrawal of emigrant labour and replacement immigration also occurred from other countries. The increase in wage levels stimulated changes in agricultural production including a switch to higher value crops. In the towns and cities, migrant remittances fuelled a construction boom and contributed to the physical expansion of the urban area (Findlay, 1985). International migration also acted as a vector for the transfer of ideas and innovations, while the use of a significant proportion of remittances to buy imported consumer goods led to a substantial increase in the volume of imports to these countries.

Table 4.23 The world's most migrant dependent states

	Remittances relative to value of exports*		Remittances relative to value of GDP		
	1980–85	1986–89	1984	1987	1989
Yemen Arab Republic°	4.8	6.4	0.23	0.24	nd
PDR Yemen†	3.9	nd	nd	nd	nd
Jordan	3.4	2.1	0.21	0.13	0.10
Bangladesh	1.5	0.9	0.04	0.06	0.05
Pakistan	1.0	1.0	0.11	0.11	0.08
Egypt	0.7	0.3	0.21	0.08	0.04

*Exports are defined as goods and services
°Export data only available for 1986–7. Thus the main downturn in remittance income is not apparent for the YAR in this data set
†Data only available for exports of goods
Source: derived from International Monetary Fund (1991) *International Financial Statistics Yearbook 1990*

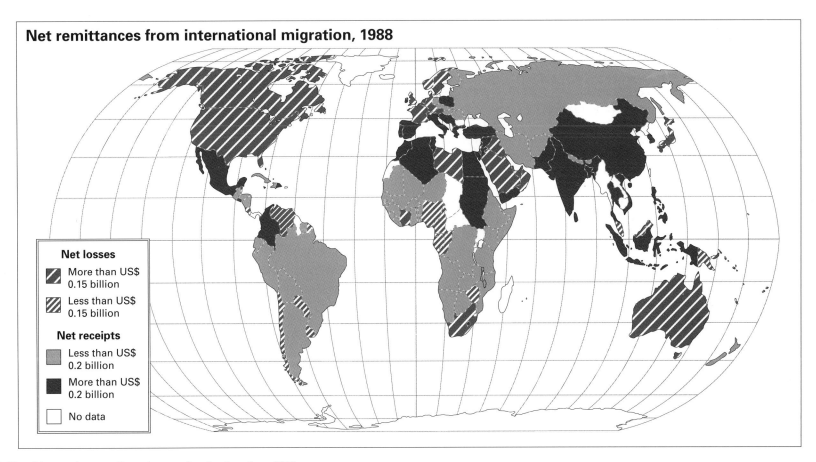

Figure 4.23a   Net remittances from international migration, 1988

During the 1980s labour market conditions in the main countries of immigration changed. In the oil states the stagnation of oil revenues in the early 1980s was followed by a crash in revenues in 1985–86. This led initially to a fear in labour-sending countries of a massive return migration of workers. In practice no mass exodus resulted (Findlay, 1987). Instead the oil states forced down migrant wages and continued the process of switching to cheaper migrant labour sources. The result of these changes is evident in the downward trend in the ratio of remittances to exports shown in Figure 4.23b over the decade. Even in cases such as Yemen, where the ratio bucked the trend, the absolute value of remittances fell rapidly from US$ 1084 million in 1983 to US$ 242 million in 1989. Countries, such as Morocco and Turkey, whose migrants were working mainly in Europe, experienced no decline in their remittance income, but no new opportunities emerged for further emigration from these countries to work legally in the EC.

In the Middle East, the Iraqi invasion of Kuwait brought to an end the migration era described by Figures 4.23a and 4.23b. Hundreds of thousands of Egyptians were expelled from Iraq. Saudi Arabia sent home an estimated 800 000 Yemeni migrants, and large numbers of Palestinians were sent back to Jordan by Kuwait. Some of the vacancies in the Saudi labour market were taken up by Egyptians, but like all the oil states Saudi Arabia began more vigorously to seek to reduce its dependence on immigrant labour.

Further reading

Findlay, A. (1985), Migrants' dreams and planners' nightmares, *Cities*, **2**: 331–339.

Findlay, A. (1987), *The Role of International Labour Migration in the Transformation of an Economy*, Geneva: International Labour Office, International Migration for Employment Working Paper No.35.

Keely, C. and Tran, B. (1989), Remittances from labour migration, *International Migration Review*, **87**: 500–525.

Salt, J. (1989), A comparative overview of international trends and types, 1950–80, *International Migration Review*, **87**: 431–456.

Ratio of remittances to exports for the six countries of the world most dependent on remittances

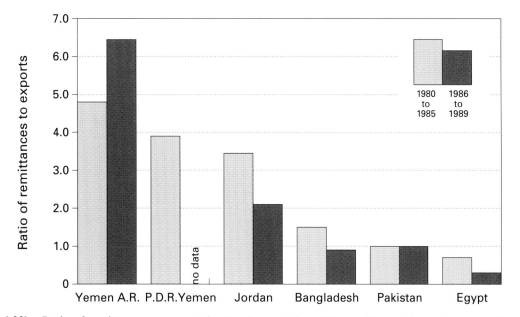

Figure 4.23b   Ratio of remittances to exports for the six countries of the world most dependent on remittances

4.24   LOCAL MIGRATION: SOUTHERN PERU
Sarah A. Radcliffe

The Andean Sierra region of Peru provides the majority of rural-urban migrants in that country, many of them peasant smallholders, dependent on vulnerable high altitude agriculture and livestock herding for survival. Nearly three million smallholders are grouped in peasant communities while others are scattered between larger *hacienda* estates. *Minifundio* farms produce around 3% of Gross National Product and receive less than 4% of national income, yet comprise a sixth of the population (Gonzales, 1984: 17). Forced by poverty and lack of local resources, peasants from Sierran and other rural areas have flocked to cities during the past 50 years; Peru is now majority urban.

Figure 4.24 demonstrates a case study region of outmigration from one Andean peasant community of smallholder agriculture, Kallarayan. In this Andean region, 90% of village peasants own under five hectares of land (Radcliffe, 1990b: 233). Kallarayan is one such village, where 500 inhabitants combine a range of tasks, inside and outside the community, to gain a livelihood. Due to an increasingly insecure agricultural base, migration involves up to 14% of villagers at any one time. With gender ideologies and sexual divisions of labour which organise livelihood strategies as well as gendered labour markets (Radcliffe, 1986, 1990b, 1992), female and male migration patterns are distinct. Men tend to combine short-term circulatory migration moves into Cuzco town and to semi-tropical commercial farms on eastern Andean slopes, with local agricultural labour. By contrast, women undertake longer-term and permanent moves into cities, and to a lesser extent to tropical 'valley' estates. Work undertaken at these

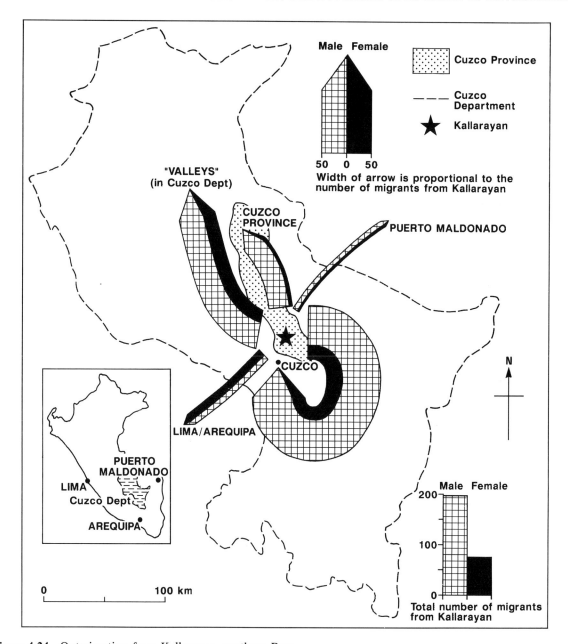

Figure 4.24   Outmigration from Kallarayan, southern Peru

destinations is usually gender-differentiated. While both men and women undertake contract work in tropical fruit and coffee estates for three months on average, women tend to work in cooking as well as harvesting, whereas men spend more time in the fields. Local migration in the immediate region ('province' in Figure 4.24), includes moves by men to harvest white maize in the Vilcanota valley during early summer, and domestic service work by young women in district capitals. In the city of Cuzco, a regional market centre and tourist attraction, young peasant female migrants work as domestic servants in middle class and elite homes. Once they leave this employment on marriage or childbearing, they tend to move into marketing agricultural produce, or informal street vending. By contrast, the range of jobs open to men is much wider, including carpentry, portering, mechanics, tailoring and construction. On average, men migrate into Cuzco for under a month during slack periods of the agricultural cycle. Both men and women migrate to cities to undertake secondary education, unavailable in the village. The capital city Lima, located in the developed coastal area (Slater, 1989), is another attractive destination for highland migrants, including those from Kallarayan. Lima grew from 0.64 million to 4.7 million largely due to immigration between 1940 and 1981. Due to distance, cost of travel and lack of education, peasant job opportunities in Lima depend on networks of kin and co-villagers who provide accommodation and information for newly-arrived migrants. Kallarayan migrants rely upon these networks to find work in factories and tailoring (men), and domestic service (women). Migration to Puerto Maldonado is linked to the expansion of informal gold-panning opportunities, undertaken largely by men, although young women may migrate there as cooks.

With the military-guerrilla war in Peru since 1980, the number of refugees escaping violence in the central Andean departments has risen dramatically. At the centre of conflicts, the town of Ayacucho has seen a ten-fold increase in population as rural refugees flee remote areas (Gamini, 1992). Refugees, largely women and children, have also arrived in Lima where they face difficulties in gaining employment. The context for migration has also been changed as a result of legislation which aims to redistribute population around the national territory (Anon., 1985: 789). Passed in 1985, the National Population Policy Law aims to encourage migration to secondary cities and frontier zones, and promote rural development, although the implications of this law, especially in light of recent political upheavals, remain to be seen (*see also* Section 3.24).

Further reading

Butterworth, D. and Chance, J. (1981), *Latin American Urbanization*, Cambridge: Cambridge University Press.

Green, D. (1991), *Faces of Latin America*, London: Latin America Bureau.

Orlansky, D. and Dubrovsky, S. (1978), *The Effects of Rural-Urban Migration on Women's Role and Status in Latin America*, Paris: UNESCO.

Preston, D. (1987), Population mobility and the creation of new landscapes, in: Preston, D. (ed.), *Latin American Development: Geographical Perspectives*, London: Longman, 229–259.

Radcliffe, S. (1990b), Between hearth and labor markets: the recruitment of peasant women in the Andes, *International Migration Review*, **24**(2): 229–249.

Radcliffe, S. (1992), Mountains, maidens and migration: gender and mobility in Peru, in: Chant, S. (ed.), *Gender and Migration in Developing Countries*, London: Belhaven, 30–48.

4.25 COMMUNICATIONS: TV AND RADIO
Cecile Cutler and Dean Forbes

Radio and TV have become the most important forms of mass communication throughout the world, edging out the print media in the geographical reach of their impact. The growth and spread of satellite broadcasting has given additional impetus to TV, the footprints of which increasingly extend beyond national boundaries, even penetrating remote rural areas in several countries. The number of TVs per 1000 inhabitants provides a useful measure of access to TV broadcasts. Several patterns in the geographical distribution of TVs emerge from Figure 4.25a.

There is a clear link between the number of TVs (and radios) per 1000 inhabitants and per capita incomes (Figure 4.25b). In low income countries there are, on average, 11.5 TV sets and 123 radios per 1000 inhabitants, compared to 219 and 387 respectively in upper middle income countries. In other words, TVs and radios are considered highly desirable consumer goods and are acquired if, and when, household incomes improve.

Some anomalies within this pattern are of interest. Several of the Pacific Island states, including American Samoa (238) and Guam (714), and Caribbean countries such as Bermuda (904) and the US Virgin Islands (568) have more TVs per capita than might be expected. The influence of American culture and incomes in both sets of island states goes some way to explaining this. Latin American countries including Argentina (217), Brazil (194) and Chile (184) have higher than average numbers of TVs. So too do a number of the Gulf states, including Oman (740), Bahrain (400) and Saudi Arabia (269).

While radios are cheaper, and therefore more ubiquitous than TVs, there are still significant disparities between countries. In the United States there were 2120 radios per 1000 inhabitants in 1988, compared to 20 in Tanzania. In other words, in Tanzania a radio is shared by, on average, 50 people; in the United States every inhabitant has, on average, over two radios each.

Further reading

Hills, J. (1990), The telecommunications rich and poor, *Third World Quarterly*, **12**(2): 71–90.
Schneider, C. and Wallis, B. (eds) (1988), *Global Television*, New York: Wedge Press.

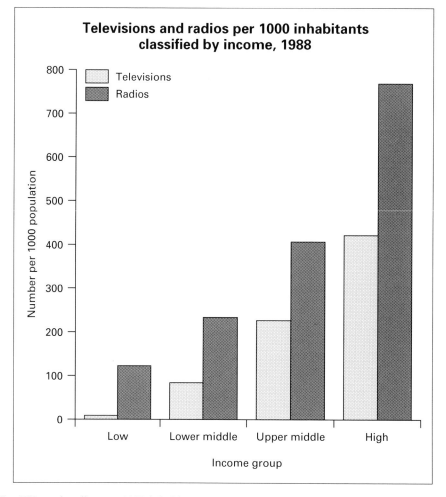

Figure 4.25b TVs and radios per 1000 inhabitants, classified by income, 1988

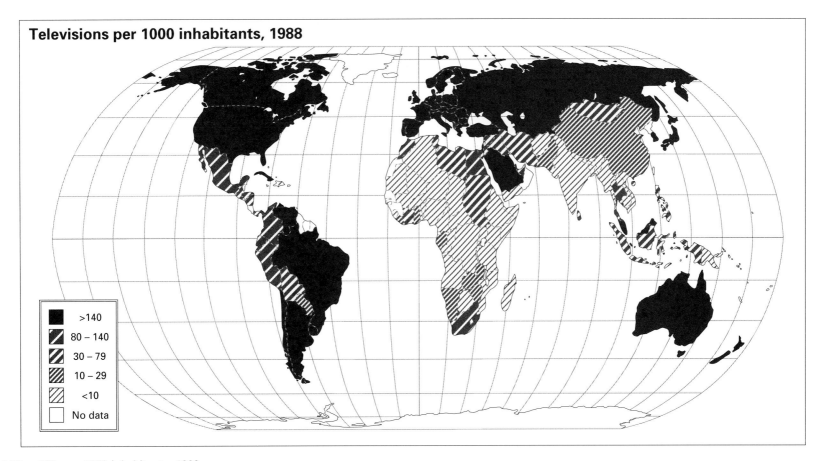

Figure 4.25a   TVs per 1000 inhabitants, 1988

4.26 WILDLIFE EXPLOITATION
Peter Vujakovic

The exploitation of wild animals is an important element of the economy of developing areas. Wild food resources, while only a small proportion of total world food production, ranging between 0.5% and 1.7% (Eltringham, 1984), form an essential element in the diet and cash income of many communities.

Protein intake is often supplemented by resort to hunting and fishing. About half of the nations of sub-Saharan Africa obtain 40% or more of their per capita protein intake from wild sources, while in the case of the Congo and of Ghana, this rises to over 75% (Prescott-Allen and Prescott-Allen, 1982). Worldwide, fish and seafood provide the bulk of protein intake. Freshwater fisheries are of major importance, especially in Asia, where the annual catch is greater than that for the rest of the world put together. 'Game' meat is locally important, especially in Africa; for example, game provides at least 25% of the per capita animal protein in Zaire and Rwanda (Prescott-Allen and Prescott-Allen, 1982). The utilisation of small animals (rodents, reptiles, amphibians, invertebrates) is also a significant source of food; they are often numerous (even in areas of high human population density), have high reproductive rates, and are rarely covered by game laws (Vos, 1977).

Wild meat and fish also provide an important source of foreign earnings for developing nations. The exploitation of marine fisheries is particularly significant (Figure 4.26); at least three nations (Peru, Panama and Senegal) earn over 10% of their total export income from this source (Prescott-Allen and Prescott-Allen, 1982). Marine fisheries are particularly important to small island

nations with limited land resources. Such nations have benefited from the establishment of 200 nautical mile Exclusive Economic Zones (EEZs) (*see* Section 5.13). For example, Tuvalu benefits from a land to sea ratio of 1 to 30 214 (Tsemenyi, 1988). EEZs have allowed them to control exploitation over relatively large areas of sea, to derive revenue from licensing foreign fleets and to support local processing of fish products. Exploitation of molluscs and crustaceans is also significant; much of the world production goes to high-value markets such as Japan and the United States. For example, the top five world shrimp producers are all developing nations, of which Ecuador (ranked second after China) relies on this product for about 20% of its total export earnings (Webb-Vidal, 1992). Shrimp farms are stocked almost exclusively from the wild.

Other major economic uses of wildlife include the trade in live animals (pet trade, zoological collections, and biomedical research) and in non-meat products (skins, furs, ivory). The demand for show birds, principally from western Europe with 84% of the world trade (Eltringham, 1992), and for aquaria specimens, has created an international trade in which millions of wild animals are exported by tropical countries every year, many species of which are now regarded as endangered. Non-meat products include the trade in furs and skins. While much of this trade is now regulated by international agreements, there is still over-exploitation. Even where exports have been officially banned for conservation purposes, as in the case of reptile skins from India, products still find their way on to the world market (Eltringham, 1992).

Wildlife based tourism is estimated to be a growing market for developing economies. Dixon and Sherman (1990) estimate that special interest tourism (linked to wildlife and adventure) is

growing at 10–15% per annum, in contrast to 8% for traditional mass tourist activities. Wildlife tourism is significant in being a non-consumptive use of wild resources, although it must be sensitively managed to ensure sustainability (Barnes *et al.*, 1992). Hunting remains a significant aspect of wildlife tourism in some African countries, while recreational fishing is a growth area in many tropical locations.

Further reading

Furtado, J.I., Morgan, W.B., Pfafflin, J.R. and Ruddle, K. (eds) (1992), *Tropical Resources: Ecology and Development*, Philadelphia: Harwood Academic.

Prescott-Allen, R. and Prescott-Allen, C. (1982), *What's Wildlife Worth?*, London: Earthscan.

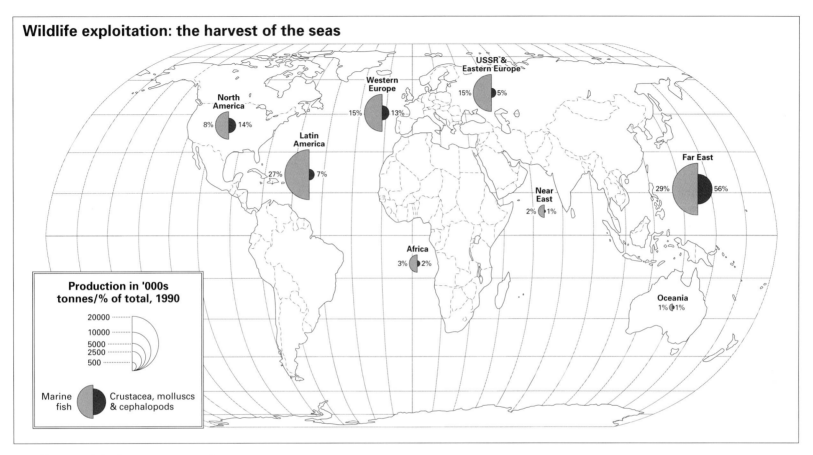

Figure 4.26 Wildlife exploitation: the harvest of the seas

4.27 WILDLIFE EXPLOITATION IN THE AFRICAN SAVANNAS
Peter Vujakovic

The savanna ecosystems of sub-Saharan Africa present a number of dilemmas for sustainable exploitation of wildlife resources. Conflicts often exist between local economic interests and national conservation objectives. The predominant official response to the protection of wildlife has been to take control of large areas as national parks or game reserves. This approach has been criticised as rooted in elitist western approaches to resource management and as inimical to the interests of local communities (Barbier, 1992). However, alternative community-based programmes of wildlife management are being developed in response to these problems.

The savanna fauna of Africa has historically provided an important source of subsistence. Today the contribution of 'game meat' to per capita animal protein supply varies greatly between countries; for example, 2.6% in Kenya, compared with 15.8% in Botswana (with some populations involved in extensive cattle production taking as much as 80% from wild sources) (Prescott-Allen and Prescott-Allen, 1982). Muir (1989) notes that even where legal restrictions on subsistence hunting occur, poaching may provide substantial input to the local economy, as in the Angwa communal lands of the Zambezi Valley (Zimbabwe), where 74% of subsistence income is still derived from 'game'.

Conflicts between local populations and conservation interests have increased as communities lose access to wildlife resources, and as protected species damage crops and compete with domestic stock. 'Buffer zones' are being developed by several countries in an attempt to mitigate these conflicts. These zones are areas of low-intensity land-use surrounding parks and reserves, which are managed for community-based wildlife exploitation (du Toit, 1985). Zimbabwe created Project CAMPFIRE in 1984, to involve residents of communal lands in management of wildlife resources and to provide them with immediate and identifiable benefits (Barbier, 1992). Botswana is planning to set aside some 21% of its total land area as Wildlife Management Areas (WMAs) which are intended for community-based wildlife utilisation (Carter, 1982) and to act as 'wildlife corridors' between the national parks and game reserves (Figure 4.27). Exploitation of wildlife is seen as providing benefits for both the local populations and for conservation interests; local populations will hopefully come to regard wildlife as worth protecting as an economic asset. However, 'buffer zones' remain susceptible to encroachment and subsequent degradation by other land use, and this is particularly a problem in areas with a strong social tradition of cattle production (Vujakovic, 1987).

Commercial wildlife utilisation (culling and ranching) has long been suggested as a solution to the sustainable use of savanna ecosystems. The ecological advantages of native species over introduced livestock have been extensively argued (Eltringham, 1984). However, practical problems of culling, such as the unpredictability of wild herd movements and problems of hygienic processing, have militated against large scale economic development (Eltringham, 1992). The most economically effective form of wildlife exploitation appears to be where wildlife is tolerated and exploited in conjunction with domestic animals on ranches (Luxmoore and Swanson, 1992).

Wildlife tourism provides a non-consumptive alternative to meat production. It is a means of developing a 'high value-added industry' while conserving wildlife; for example, a study of the tourism value of elephants to Kenya estimated their 'viewing value' at US$ 25 million per year in the late 1980s, which compared with US$ 35–45 million for total yearly exports of ivory from the whole of Africa during the same period (Brown and Henry, 1989; cited in Barnes *et al.*, 1992). Recreational hunting, while consumptive, may have a part to play in sustainable economic development if integrated with conservation culling practices and community-based wildlife management. For example, wildlife tourism contributes some US$ 10 million per year to the GNP of Botswana, of which 27% is contributed by safari hunting (Barnes *et al.*, 1992).

Further reading

Eltringham, S.K. (1984), *Wildlife Resources and Economic Development*, Chichester: Wiley.

Swanson, T.M. and Barbier, E.B. (eds) (1992), *Economics for the Wilds: Wildlife, Wildlands, Diversity and Development*, London: Earthscan.

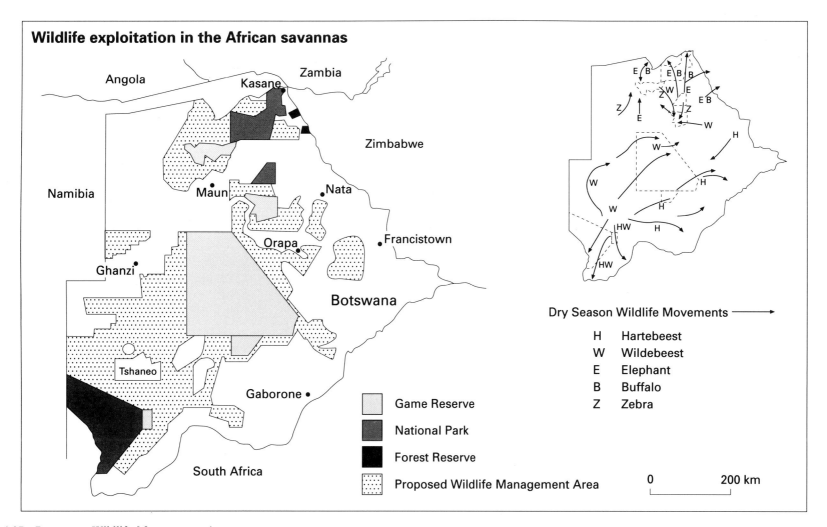

Figure 4.27 Botswana: Wildlife Management Areas

4.28 INTERNATIONAL DEVELOPMENT AID

Steve Wyn Williams

According to the World Bank (1990: 129), official aid 'comprises grants and loans (with at least a 25% grant element) from official sources that have promotion of economic development and welfare as their main objective'. Prior to the geopolitical changes in 1989 three main groups of donor countries could be identified:

(1) Development Assistance Committee (DAC) of the OECD consisting of eighteen developed industrialised countries. In the late 1980s this group accounted for approximately 80% of official aid;

(2) Organisation of the Petroleum Exporting Countries (OPEC) accounting for 9% (the bulk being accounted for by the Arab donors); and

(3) Centrally Planned Economies accounting for approximately 10%, dominated by the USSR and focused on a handful of client states.

Assessing the contribution of individual countries depends on the data being used. In absolute terms from the late 1970s through the 1980s, the USA was the largest donor, although in the late 1980s and early 1990s Japan has become a close second. However, in terms of percentage of GNP the USA is near the bottom of the list (0.21% in 1990). In contrast, small economies such as Norway and the Netherlands have consistently exceeded the UN's 0.7% of GNP guideline.

Official aid (Figure 4.28) is disbursed in two ways. Bilateral, or government to government aid, accounts for the largest proportion of official aid. However, this is frequently criticised for placing political, strategic and commercial reasons ahead of humanitarian concerns, and in terms of per capita aid receipts the largest do not always go to the poorest countries. Approximately two-thirds of DAC aid is tied. This involves recipients being required to buy goods and services from the donor country which can adversely affect the real value of aid. As ex-President Nixon of the United States is reputed to have said, the purpose of American aid is not to help other nations but to help America. Multilateral aid (accounting for approximately 20% of official aid) is aid channelled through the Development Banks and the functional agencies of the UN. The most important of the Development Banks is the World Bank insofar as its policies can and do influence the policies of other development agencies, as evidenced by the recent emphasis on poverty reduction and environmental concerns. The concessional arm of the World Bank is the International Development Agency (IDA) with 90% of its loans going to the poorest countries. In general the multilateral agencies pay more attention to development criteria but are also perceived as technocratic and insensitive to the needs of the Third World.

Broadly speaking development finance is disbursed for two main purposes. First, it is provided as general budgetary support to countries with balance of payment difficulties. During the 1980s these became known as structural adjustment programmes. While these funds are disbursed fairly rapidly, the conditions attached to such loans can cause significant problems for the recipients. These include the need to cut internal demand and public expenditure, boost exports and open borders to foreign capital resulting in increased social and spatial inequalities and pressures on the environment. The second purpose is to finance development projects in specific sectors. Project aid, however, still tends to be focused on large scale projects, such as dams, power stations, railways and telecommunications.

Projects with a specifically poverty focus represent only a small proportion of the total.

For low-income countries aid represents nearly 70% of net external finance, and for many of these countries it is more important than exports in terms of foreign exchange. Consequently, while many countries have benefitted, some of the poorest countries have been trapped in a cycle of aid dependency, whereby aid is used to maintain the present low quality of life rather than improving it. To some extent this reflects the dominant philosophy of aid policies, which all too frequently have been characterised by a top-down approach. Recently, however, aid agencies have recognised the value of participatory approaches involving Non-Governmental Organisations and Community Based Organisations which it is suggested will result in more appropriate, effective and closely targetted interventions.

Further reading

Bauer, P. (1984), *Reality and Rhetoric*, London: Weidenfeld and Nicolson.

Griffin, K. (1991), Foreign aid after the Cold War, *Development and Change,* **22**: 645–685.

Hancock, G. (1989), *Lords of Poverty*, London: Macmillan.

Hayter, T. (1989), *Exploited Earth: Britain's Aid and the Environment*, London: Earthscan.

World Bank (1990), *World Development Report*, New York: Oxford University Press.

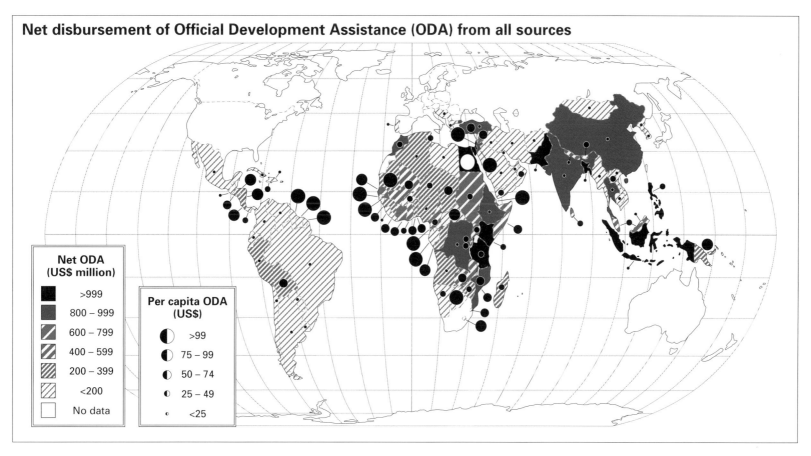

Figure 4.28   Net disbursement of Official Development Assistance (ODA) from all sources

5 States, Wars and Elections: the Political Structure of Development

TIM UNWIN

The disintegration of the former Soviet Union at the end of the 1980s and in the early 1990s has not led to the new era of peace that many at first predicted. In contrast, the collapse of one of the great political powers of the 20th century has heralded a period of marked instability and political reorganisation, not only among its immediate satellites, but also in many other parts of the world. The invasion of Kuwait by Iraq, the subsequent Gulf War, the bloody disintegration of the former Yugoslavia, and the involvement of United Nations forces in violent 'peace keeping' missions in states such as Somalia, all provide vivid reminders of the ever-present reality of warfare and armed conflict throughout the world. Indeed, for a large percentage of the poorest people of the world, the most important daily reality is quite simply how to avoid the bombs, mines, bullets and shellfire that are a part of their lives.

This chapter explores the structures and processes influencing the distribution of power in different parts of the world. It begins with a survey of patterns of political allegiance at a global scale and then in the regional context of southern Africa. These sections are followed by an examination of political instability and warfare,

looking at the widely differing types of stability and instability that exist at a global scale, the significance of the global arms trade, and the ways in which internal violence within states operates through the institution of capital punishment. Section 5.7 then surveys the social revolutions of the 20th century, paying particular attention to the revolutionary movements that have been active in Mozambique over the last twenty years, and Section 5.8 assesses some of the main economic influences of the political reorganisation of the former Soviet Union.

Political violence and instability usually result in large movements of people, either seeking voluntarily to escape the zone of oppression, or as a result of forced population displacements. The next two sections examine different aspects of such mass movement, through a survey of the distribution and influences of refugees throughout the world, and a focused case study of resettlement schemes for nomads in Somalia during the 1970s.

Political regimes vary enormously in character, from multiple party systems to military dictatorships. During the 20th century, many national constitutions have sought to legitimise their status through the use of party systems, which permit

political opposition as a potential alternative government. However, party systems themselves vary greatly in character, as illustrated in Section 5.11. Voting behaviour within democracies also varies appreciably, and some of the factors influencing this variability are examined in Section 5.12, which provides an overview of recent voting behaviour in India, widely referred to as the world's largest democracy.

Boundary determination is an important part of the political process, and need not always be a cause for military confrontation. The increasing significance of oceanic resources, particularly hydrocarbons and fisheries, during the second half of the 20th century, for example, generated the need for international agreement, and some of the processes associated with the resultant 1982 United Nations Convention on the Law of the Sea, are therefore examined in Section 5.13. This is followed by two case studies, of the Gulf and the Spratly Islands, which indicate the great complexity of maritime boundary delimitation.

The chapter concludes with two further analyses of the complexity of political processes. The first illustrates the way in which tribal affiliations, political processes and development are inextricably intertwined through an examination of

Kenya's recent elections. The second focuses on the legacy of apartheid in South Africa, and argues that future development policy in the state needs to redress the imbalances within and between regions caused by the former regime.

5.1 PATTERNS OF POLITICAL ALLEGIANCE
James Sidaway

Events of the past few years have decisively shifted many global patterns of political allegiance. The collapse of the bipolar Cold War between Soviet-led and United States-led alliances has resulted in a much more fluid and complex pattern of political allegiance. Some observers have therefore utilised the notion of a 'geopolitical transition' to refer to the reorientations since 1989, which they compare with those of 1945–46, when the Cold War system began to coalesce. Taylor (1993a), for example, sees such transitions as characterised by simultaneous changes in the overreaching global patterns of political allegiance and rapid reorientation in 'geopolitical codes', that is to say the geopolitical assumptions of individual foreign policy elites. A map of the broad patterns of political allegiance prior to the revolutionary events of 1989 (*see* Section 5.7) would have revealed a bipolar East-West division, with a number of neutral states, and others, such as China, antagonistic towards both blocs. However, constructing a map to represent contemporary patterns is more difficult. A more 'flexible geometry' replaces the apparently stable inter-bloc competition that characterised the Cold War. As the first major post-Cold War conflict, the 1991 Gulf War is revealing of one such 'geometry'. As Figure 5.1a indicates, almost all states approved UN resolution 678, authorising the use of force against Iraq. However, the official stance of governments was contested by populations in large parts of the Arab and Islamic worlds, and many states experienced popular protests against the war.

In the post Gulf War Middle East, and in other regions of the world that continue to be characterised by conflict, such as the Balkans and the Horn of Africa, new and sometimes dauntingly complex local and regional maps of political allegiance have emerged, reinforcing the notion that the post-Cold War, or 'New World Order' is more unstable and unpredictable than that of the Cold War. Whilst transatlantic and trans-Pacific military alliances remain in place (through NATO and the US-Japan accord respectively), increasing tensions in the realm of trade and geo-economic competition suggest other emergent patterns of political allegiance. In particular, commentators throughout the world are positing the emergence of three broad geo-economic blocs: East Asia (centred on Japan and including the Association of South East Asian Nations, and increasingly incorporating China), Europe (the European Union, centred on Germany) and the Americas (centred on the USA and the North American Free Trade Area, which includes Mexico and Canada) (*see* Figure 5.1b). All this is complicated by rapid economic change and the simultaneous existence of dynamism and crisis tendencies in the world capitalist economy. In particular, the extremely rapid growth of the 'Pacific rim' economies is feeding into this, adding to the complexity and uncertainty as core and periphery continue to shift. In such a dynamic framework, future patterns of global political allegiance are uncertain and open; they will emerge out of the complex dialectics of geo-economics and geopolitical competition. However, whilst the trajectory of the former Soviet Union continues to be characterised by considerable uncertainty, a return to the bipolar Cold War confrontation seems very unlikely.

Further reading

Chomsky, N. (1991), *Deterring Democracy*, London: Verso.

Goldgeier, J.M. and McFaul, M. (1992), A tale of two worlds: core and periphery in the post-cold war era, *International Organisation*, **46**(2): 467–491.

Nijman, J. (1992), The political geography of the post cold war world, *The Professional Geographer*, **44**: 1–3.

Smith, G. (1993), Ends, geopolitics and transitions, in: Johnston, R.J. (ed.), *The Challenge for Geography. A Changing World: a Changing Discipline*, Oxford: Blackwell, 76–99.

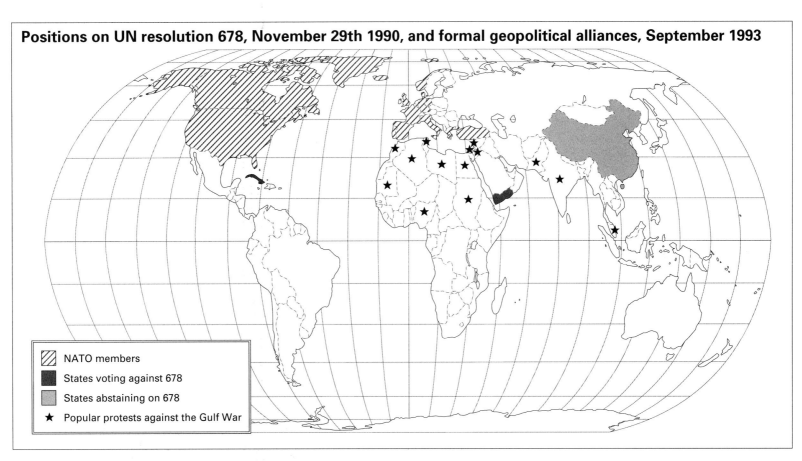

Figure 5.1a Positions on UN resolution 678, November 29th 1990, and formal geopolitical alliances, September 1993

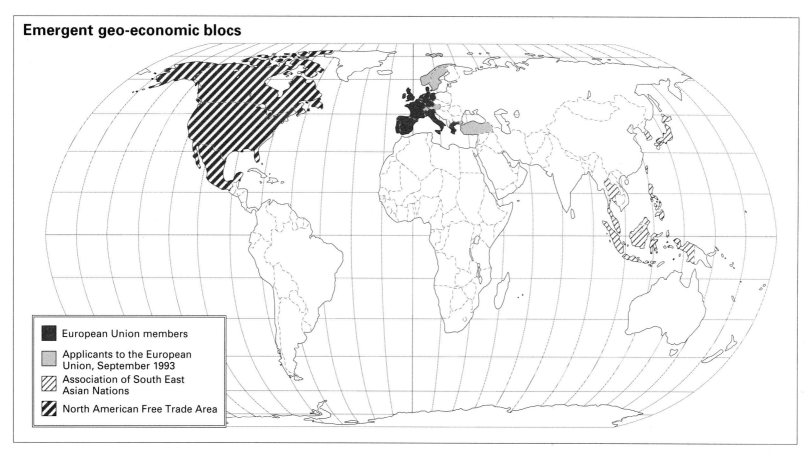

Figure 5.1b Emergent geo-economic blocs

5.2 INTERNATIONAL POLITICAL GROUPINGS: THE REGIONAL SCALE

David Simon

Groups of countries within particular continental or geographical regions have increasingly sought to promote co-operation and strengthen their mutual bargaining power with the rest of the world through formal institutional structures. Such initiatives have mushroomed in the period since World War II as a reflection of the changing international political economy brought about by the Cold War and decolonisation of the Third World in particular. The plethora of regional groupings is extremely diverse in terms of objectives, number and range of members, structure and mode of operation.

The earliest such groupings were established in parts of the north and had overtly political and military objectives, as with the North Atlantic Treaty Organisation (NATO) and the Warsaw Pact. However, the need to underpin and reinforce political allegiances through economic co-operation soon gave rise to economic counterparts embracing most, if not all, of the same countries, as was the case with the European Community (EC) and the Council for Mutual Economic Assistance (CMEA). The latter was subsequently enlarged to include loyal state socialist countries in the Third World, such as Cuba and Vietnam. The USA was also instrumental in forging strategic regional groupings around the world in order to bind it to neighbouring states or to allies in the north and south alike, most notably the Organisation of American States (OAS), the Association of South East Asian Nations (ASEAN) and the Australia-New Zealand-US Pact (ANZUS).

The era of decolonisation spawned several distinct types of international organisation. A few of these are global, such as the Commonwealth and the Communauté Française – which bind Britain and France to their respective former colonies and have both political and economic dimensions – and the Non-Aligned Movement (NAM), an essentially political forum. Other political fora embrace entire continents, for example the Organisation of African Unity (OAU). By far the majority, though, are subcontinental in scope and geared primarily to economic co-operation, as with the Caribbean Economic Community (CARICOM) and Economic Community of West African States (ECOWAS). In practice, though, economic and political objectives are often interwoven. The record of such organisations, particularly the earlier generation, has generally been extremely modest at best. A number failed completely and, like the East African Community (EAC), were disbanded.

To the extent that generalisation is possible among such diverse organisations, failure or the lack of progress can usually be attributed to some combination of the following reasons, several of which represent formidable obstacles to success:

(1) Overambitious or diverse objectives, goals and targets.
(2) Unnecessarily complex institutional structures and large bureaucracies, often beyond what member states can support in terms of financial subventions or skilled personnel.
(3) Inadequate real political commitment by member states, particularly in terms of the need to balance narrow self-interest with the wider collective interest.
(4) Closely related to the previous point is an imbalance between the costs and benefits of membership to the various constituent countries. The principal beneficiaries have often been the largest or economically most sophisticated members, which have thus hosted the organisation's headquarters and attracted a disproportionate share of new public and private investment. These countries have consequently been the strongest advocates of regional organisations, whereas smaller, weaker members have commonly felt increasingly marginalised or even exploited over time.
(5) Inadequate economic complementarities between member states. Particularly in the Third World, where many national economies are extremely narrowly based and export oriented, countries within a given sub-region often produce the same or similar primary commodities. Not only is the potential for trade among them therefore very limited but they are actually direct competitors for a share of the world market in bananas (Caribbean, Latin America), sugar (Caribbean, Latin America, Indian Ocean rim), coffee (Brazil, west and east Africa), cocoa (west Africa), tea (Indian subcontinent, east Africa), palm oil and rubber (south-east Asia, west Africa, Amazon Basin), diamonds, copper and other base metals (southern and central Africa), bauxite (Caribbean) or whatever. Even where complementarities do exist, as with respect to oil outside the Middle East, the potential for trade may be limited because non-producing members are unlikely to have the resources to pay, or other commodities to trade.
(6) Transport and communications problems resulting from the outward orientation of individual countries' infrastructure. This reflects the colonial imperative of exporting to, and importing from, the metropolitan power rather than developing the colonial economy and intra-regional trade. The improvement of links between member states has therefore

been high on the agenda of most regional organisations.

These issues are all evident to some extent in the three very different contemporary regional organisations in southern Africa. Their contrasting histories, memberships, objectives, organisational structures and modes of operation reflect not only the difficulties of regional co-operation but also the entrenched political and economic conflicts which have been focused even more sharply than elsewhere by apartheid in South Africa, the country with the continent's most sophisticated economy. International condemnation of that policy and attempts until 1990 to isolate South Africa highlighted the extent of regional economic integration and asymmetrical interdependence. Curiously but perhaps understandably, only Lesotho and Swaziland, the two smallest and weakest states in the region, belonged to all three groupings until they were joined by independent Namibia.

The Southern African Customs Union (SACU)
This, the oldest organisation by some seventy years, was established by Britain at the time of the creation of the Union of South Africa in 1910, in order to safeguard the trade requirements of Bechuanaland, Basutoland and Swaziland, the three small and weak High Commission Territories neighbouring the new state. This was also designed to provide a platform for their eventual absorption within a greater South Africa, something which never came about, principally on account of the introduction of apartheid but also growing nationalist sentiment in the territories.

The basic present treaty dates from 1969, having been renegotiated after the three territories gained independence from Britain as Botswana, Lesotho and Swaziland respectively (the BLS states). SACU is an extremely asymmetrical union, biased heavily in South Africa's favour. The secretariat is located in Pretoria and staffed and run exclusively by South Africa. The other members do not even have direct access to the records and data, or the right to demand this. Furthermore, the revenue-sharing formula according to which total receipts are divided among the members, was weighted against the small members. Following protests, this was amended in 1975, and although South Africa now claims that they are in a favourable position, there is still some dissatisfaction among the BLS states and Namibia, which joined SACU in its own right following its independence in 1990. South Africa also forced the admission of its four so-called 'independent' bantustans in the late 1970s, but they have never been recognised by the other states (Figure 5.2a).

The major source of conflict since 1990 has been a clause in the treaty specifying that new industries within the SACU area must supply at least 60% of local demand in order to qualify for tariff exemption. This clearly discriminates against the smaller members, and may be waived or amended. Obviously South Africa has been able to use its strength through SACU and other means to exert considerable leverage over the other members. The BLS countries have actively considered leaving SACU at several junctures since their independence, but have ultimately remained because of their very high dependence on trade with and through South Africa. Consequently, also, their respective shares of the revenue pool provide major sources of state revenue and foreign exchange. Speculation (since the end of 1992) suggests that SACU will soon be disbanded in view of a post-apartheid South Africa's likely membership of SADC and the PTA.

The Southern African Development Co-ordination Conference (SADCC) and Southern African Development Community (SADC)
Established in 1979/80 as a direct response to the sharpening conflicts in the region, the SADCC embraced the five Frontline States (Angola, Botswana, Zambia, Mozambique and Tanzania) already active in opposing South Africa and the four other states with a need and desire to join, namely Lesotho, Malawi, Swaziland and newly independent Zimbabwe. Namibia was welcomed as the tenth member in 1990 (Figure 5.2a). SADCC had four related objectives, namely:

(1) the reduction of economic dependence of its members (principally but not exclusively) on South Africa;
(2) the promotion of genuine and equitable regional integration;
(3) the mobilisation of resources for the promotion of national, interstate and regional policies; and
(4) concerted action to secure international co-operation within the framework of a strategy for economic liberation.

It was thus specifically not a customs union or common market, and also sought to learn from the mistakes and shortcomings of other regional organisations by seeking consensus, ensuring mutual benefit and by minimising the central bureaucracy. It operated on a decentralised basis with only a very small secretariat (well under fifty staff) based in Gaborone, the Botswanan capital. Each member state was responsible for one or more appropriate portfolios which were handled by its own civil servants. The Southern African Transport and Communications Commission in Maputo is the only dedicated organisation, a reflection of the centrality of transport initiatives to the region. The SADCC also tried to avoid

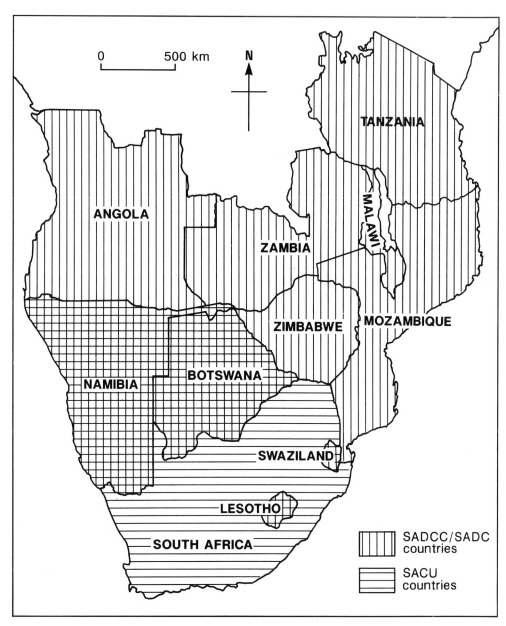

Figure 5.2a Membership of the SACU and SADCC/SADC

conflicts of interest and competition over resources with individual members by mobilising additional donor funds by promoting strategic regional programmes benefiting several members directly. Although supposedly therefore complementary to bilateral aid, some donor funds were inevitably diverted to multilateral SADCC initiatives.

SADCC's principal initial objective was to ensure the availability of transport networks bypassing South Africa (*see* Section 4.14) so as to reduce regional dependence on transit through and trade with it. Consequently, rehabilitation of transport links, especially railways and highways, absorbed over 90% of SADCC investment during the 1980s. Only once these schemes neared completion towards the end of the decade, did other sectors gain more attention.

Notwithstanding real problems, the SADCC's relative success reflected its degree of realism and prudence, its modest objectives, the willingness of donors to commit funds and expertise as an anti-apartheid gesture and to enhance their own trade with member states, and the undoubted costs to SADCC of South African destabilisation during the 1980s. Even so, the aid actually committed consistently lagged substantially behind pledges made. On the negative side, intra-SADCC trade barely increased in relative terms, and still accounted for only 5% of total regional trade in the early 1990s. Namibia's membership and the end of active destabilisation greatly enhanced SADCC's potential to promote development as opposed to reconstruction, but South Africa's envisaged future membership necessitated a fundamental re-think of the organisation's aims, *modus operandi* and relationship with the PTA (*see below*).

Hence, in August 1992, SADCC was transformed into the Southern African Development

Community (SADC) which, while adhering to the same basic principles and many similar objectives, is explicitly designed to establish common political values, systems and institutions. Prominent in this respect is a customs union, seen as the key to promoting greater interaction and integration than was achievable under the SADCC, especially in view of the limited extent of trade to date, and providing a framework appropriate to South Africa's membership. Despite this broader agenda, the question of managing SADC's relations with South Africa will inevitably remain problematic.

The Preferential Trade Area for Eastern and Southern Africa (PTA) Although long under discussion, the PTA was formed only in 1981, in the spirit of the OAU's Lagos Plan of Action which was designed to promote intra-regional trade, currency unions and common markets in different parts of the continent. This, in turn, reflected the realisation that, with persistently depressed world commodity prices, the onset of the debt crisis and falling real levels of aid, individual African countries, some of them among the poorest in the world, would never be able to achieve development alone.

In some ways, the PTA is the least coherent of the three organisations being profiled. Headquartered in Lusaka, membership has grown progressively to the point where it now groups 20 countries (19 of them full members) from Lesotho in the south to Sudan in the north (Figure 5.2b). Botswana is now the only SADC member not also in the PTA. The problems of diversity and conflicting interests are exacerbated by the number of members, the vast distance over which they stretch, their non-contiguity, and an ambiguous

Figure 5.2b Membership of the PTA

relationship with SADC. Zambia has consistently favoured the PTA, while Botswana and Zimbabwe, the two wealthiest SADC members, backed the latter. However, Zimbabwe and Namibia have recently joined the PTA with enthusiasm.

The PTA's achievements have been modest in terms of trade promotion and tariff barrier reduction. Although by the end of 1989, 73% of intra-PTA trade was taking place through the PTA clearing house, the underlying problem, as with the SADC, is the paucity of intra-regional trade in relation to members' total trade. Once again, the organisation's principal advocates are the members which stand to benefit most, especially Zambia, Kenya and latterly also Zimbabwe. This reflects their economic structures and relative power. More positively, the PTA introduced a common currency, the Unit of Account of PTA (UAPTA) in 1988, and PTA travellers' cheques. Although both still something of a novelty, their use has begun to grow. By the end of 1989, 59% of intra-PTA trade was still in national currencies.

While the end of apartheid has removed, at least superficially, part of the SADC's *raison d'être*, donors like the EC now appear to favour the PTA as the best vehicle for future progress on account of its specific trade focus and allegedly greater pragmatism. Ultimately and despite their different objectives, some form of merger may arise, particularly once South Africa is officially welcomed back into the African fold. This may also herald the demise of SACU, which has aims for its members in common with the PTA. Whatever the outcome, South Africa's economic dominance will be a very mixed blessing once it is fully integrated with the region.

Further reading

Blumenfeld, J. (1991), *Economic Interdependence in Southern Africa: from Conflict to Co-operation?*, London: Pinter.

Cobbe, J.H. (1980), Integration among unequals: the Southern African Customs Union and development, *World Development*, **8**(4): 329–336.

Development Dialogue (1987), The Maseru seminar on 'Another development for SADCC countries': an agenda for action, *Development Dialogue*, **1987**(1): 74–111.

Guma, X.P. (1987), The revised Southern African Customs Union Agreement: an appraisal, *South African Journal of Economics*, **58**(1): 63–73.

Hardy, C. (1987), The prospects for growth and structural change in southern Africa, *Development Dialogue*, **1987**(2): 33–58.

Kumar, U. (1990), Southern African Customs Union and BLS-countries (Botswana, Lesotho and Swaziland), *Journal of World Trade*, **24**(3): 31–53.

Lancaster, C. (1992), The Lagos Three: economic regionalism in sub–Saharan Africa, in: Harbeson, J.W. and Rothchild, D. (eds), *Africa in World Politics*, Boulder: Westview, 249–267.

Maasdorp, G. (1992), Economic co-operation in Southern Africa: prospects for regional integration, *Conflict Studies* **253**.

SADCC (Southern African Development Co-ordination Conference) (annual), *Progress Report*, Luanda: SADCC.

5.3 POLITICAL STABILITY
Peter J. Taylor

Political stability can be defined in many ways. Every change of government can be viewed as an instance of instability. But if that change is a constitutional one, as occurs when the opposition wins an election, then the alternation of government will actually strengthen the political system by confirming both its formal and popular legitimacy. Hence such 'smooth' changes of government should not be viewed as political instability. A political system is unstable when there are persistent unconstitutional threats to the government, that is to say it is the state itself that is challenged. The limiting case is where no government can rule and stability can only be maintained through outside agency, as the UN attempted in Somalia in 1993.

Political stability can be assessed only over some period of time. The period since 1945 will be used in the typology that follows, except for the many states that achieved independence in the post-World War II period where the assessment is wholly post-independence. In all cases the emphasis is on how the state arrived at its current political order or disorder.

Civilian stability These are countries where political stability has been achieved through civil society dominating the state. Here the coercive arm of the state, the armed forces as the ultimate guarantor of order, is firmly under civilian control. This includes both the pluralist political systems of the 'North', and many states in the 'South' that are less pluralist but where the army stays out of politics.

Military stability In many poorer countries the armed forces are the strongest element of the state apparatus and 'men in uniforms' have been able to form strong governments. This political stability is created through coercion of civil society.

Communist stability This is an attempt to merge state and civil society through the agency of the Communist Party. The political stability of such 'People's Democracies' depends on the 'People's Army' as the coercive arm of the state.

Traditional stability There remain a few states where political stability is based upon allegiance to a traditional sovereign.

Although traditional stability has been overturned throughout our period, in the last few years there has been a major decline in political order based on both military power and Communist Parties. In both cases the change has been towards civilian stability based on political pluralism but it is too soon to say whether the basis of a new stability has been firmly established. Both movements have been largely regional in nature:

Communist stability and transition The stability of Eastern European states based upon the Communist Party has been destroyed and civil society is trying to cope without a state-imposed political order.

Military stability and transition In the 1960s and 1970s many Latin American states had repressive military regimes that lost power in the 1980s, leaving civil society to try and reconstruct a less coercive stability.

The military as a coercive force do not guarantee political stability. In poorer countries the military can act more like state-destroyers than state-builders:

Multiple coup instability In many countries the political elites fight for control of the state through a continual sequence of coups, both successful and unsuccessful. In such situations the military, as the means to power, become a source of severe political instability.

Civil war instability Where the legitimacy of the government is challenged by an alternative government that cannot be eliminated from the state territory, political instability is chronic as two militaries destroy the country.

State breakdown instability In a few countries political stability has totally collapsed because there is no government at all, just armed factions imposing their 'gun law'.

These nine types of political stability are sometimes difficult to determine in particular cases – when does civil war become total state breakdown for instance? It is all a matter of interpretation in the light of past practices and the current situation, and this is what is recorded in Figure 5.3.

Further reading

Johnston, R.J. (1989), The individual and the world-economy, in: Johnston, R.J. and Taylor, P.J. (eds), *World in Crisis*, Oxford: Blackwell, 200–228.

Johnston, R.J., O'Loughlin, J. and Taylor, P.J. (1987), The geography of violence and premature death, in: Vayrynen, R. (ed.), *The Quest for Peace*, London: Sage, 241–295.

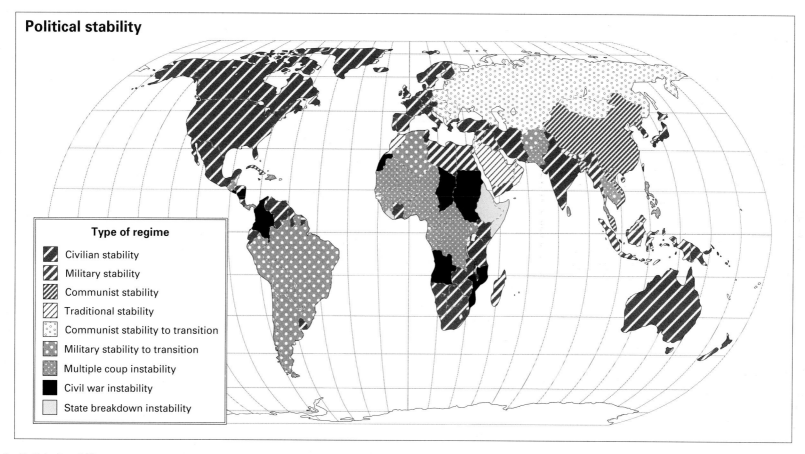

Figure 5.3 Political stability

5.4 WARFARE
Steve Wyn Williams

Warfare has always occupied an ambiguous position in geopolitical discourse. On the one hand it undoubtedly leads to terrible suffering and loss of life and has serious impacts on socio-economic development; on the other, it is seen as a basic institution performing important functions for the ordering and maintenance of the international system. Indeed, since Thucydides' account of the Peloponnesian War between Sparta and Athens over twenty-five centuries ago no consensus on the causes of war has emerged.

Examining the changing character of warfare, however, is a less hazardous task; and, in charting the changes in its history and geography, 1945 can be used as an appropriate watershed. Before 1945 the increasing globalisation and destructiveness of warfare was reflected in the lethality of weapons, size of armies (and casualties), and the number of states involved. However, in the post-1945 period the most striking trend has been the increasingly localised nature of the majority of conflicts, and the marked spatial contrast which this has demonstrated (Figure 5.4). Thus, as a result of a stable system of alliances and clearly defined spheres of influence, until 1989 Europe experienced the longest period of peace in its history. In contrast, during the same period the developing world experienced 130 or so significant conflicts. From the 1950s up to the early 1970s, the most frequent conflicts were anti-colonial in nature, whereby violence was used to secure a more rapid transition to independence. Decolonisation, however, often produced a new range of problems and conflicts, many of which were based on territorial disputes (for example, India versus Pakistan and Algeria versus Morocco). According to SIPRI (1991,

1992), the remaining post-1945 conflicts can be subdivided into three categories, and these are indicated in Figure 5.4 for 1990–91:

(1) *Inter-state conflicts.* During the post-1945 period these have been relatively rare phenomena, and for the period 1990–91 the only conflict in this category was the Gulf War.
(2) *Internal conflicts.* These have been the most frequent category of conflicts, involving disputes over control of government by an armed opposition (recent examples include Ethiopia, Somalia and Iraq). Many have been ideological in nature and until recently involved not infrequent intervention by external powers, reflecting Cold War alignments (as in Vietnam and Afghanistan).
(3) *State-formation conflicts.* These involve non-government opposition forces aiming at secession or the gaining of autonomy to change the constitutional status of territory and can occur whenever state boundaries and the sense of racial, ethnic or religious identity do not coincide (with recent examples including Sri Lanka and Indonesia).

While the post-Cold War world and the emerging 'New World Order' have established new parameters for the pursuit of international peace and security, local conflicts are likely to be recurrent features of the geopolitical landscape. In this context, the necessity for an effective United Nations to provide a forum for the resolution of such conflicts is of pressing importance. There have been significant efforts in terms of preventive diplomacy, peace-making and peace building, but the manifest impotence and incompetence of the United Nations in Bosnia and Somalia respectively suggest that rhetoric and resolutions are no substitute for firm and decisive action.

Further reading

Brogan, P. (1992), *World Conflicts*, London: Bloomsbury.
Geeraerts, G. (1991), Basic research on war: theoretical need and practical relevance, *Bulletin of Peace Proposals*, **22**(3): 346–552.
Heldt, B. (1992), *States in Armed Conflict 1990, 1991*, Uppsala: Department of Peace and Conflict Resolution, Uppsala University.
Luard, E. (1988), *The Blunted Sword: the Erosion of Military Power in Modern World Politics*, London: Tauris.
SIPRI (Stockholm International Peace Research Institute) (1991, 1992), *SIPRI Yearbook: Armaments and Disarmament*, Oxford: Oxford University Press.

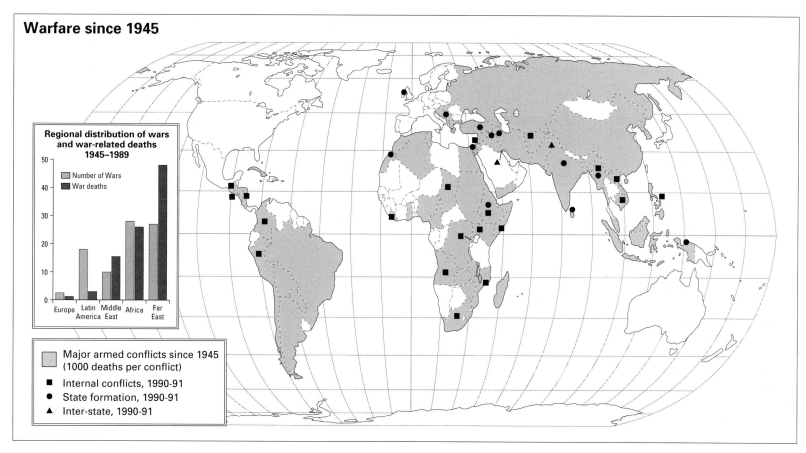

Warfare since 1945

Regional distribution of wars
and war-related deaths
1945–1989

Number of Wars
War deaths

Europe   Latin   Middle   Africa   Far
         America   East   East

Major armed conflicts since 1945
(1000 deaths per conflict)

■ Internal conflicts, 1990-91
● State formation, 1990-91
▲ Inter-state, 1990-91

Figure 5.4 Warfare since 1945

5.5 THE INTERNATIONAL ARMS TRADE

Steve Wyn Williams

Since the end of World War II the international arms trade has been a major feature of the world military order, reflecting both strategic and economic imperatives. Initially, weapons were directed by the USA and USSR to their friends and allies in Europe and selected states in the Third World. However, from the mid-1960s, and accelerating in the 1970s, the Third World increasingly became the principal focus for the 'arms bazaar' with commercial and strategic issues being closely entwined. In this context two major influences can be identified. First, the four-fold rise in oil prices in 1973/74 resulted in the petrodollars flowing to the Middle East being recycled through the arms market, the most notable example being the build-up in Iran in which the principal suppliers were the USA, UK and France. Secondly, the so-called 'Nixon Doctrine' urged the USA's allies (such as Israel) to stand on their own feet – but with the support of massive arms transfers. On the Soviet side arms transfers were clearly an important instrument of foreign policy, but were increasingly seen as a good income earner.

The peak of the arms trade was reached in the early-mid 1980s (largely as a consequence of the Iran-Iraq war). Thereafter, arms sales in general, and to the Third World in particular, followed a downward trend. The reason for this decline was due to a number of factors including mounting debt problems, falling oil prices and few conflicts rather than any arms transfer restraint. Further decline was evident during 1990–91, with a major factor being the break-up of the USSR and the severing of arms transfer relations with former allies and clients. Thus, the total value of arms delivered in 1991 was US$22.1 billion compared with US$45.9 billion in 1987. The Iraq-Kuwait war led to a partial revitalisation of the arms trade in the Middle East, but the Israel-Palestine peace accords could well be a moderating influence on this. The relative decline in importance of the Middle East contrasts with increased imports to Asia which now occupies the number one position. India in particular has recorded high levels of arms imports in recent years, while a ready market for Russia's overstocked arsenal has been found in south-east Asia.

In terms of supply the arms trade has been, and will continue to be, dominated by a handful of exporters. Nevertheless, the number of so-called second-tier producing states (including several in the Third World) has increased in recent years (Figure 5.5). This proliferation of suppliers has made the need for multilateral controls on exports all the more necessary.

Undoubtedly, the effect of the arms trade on the Third World has been negative. While it is not possible to argue that an increase of weapons will automatically lead to an increased risk of war, the ready availability of modern armaments does make it easier for states to choose the military rather than the diplomatic option to resolve local disputes. Furthermore, even if such weapons are never used millions of people are harmed indirectly as a result of the opportunity costs incurred. Thus, less money is available for basic needs such as health and education, while an increasing proportion of limited supplies of wealth, skills and resources is devoted to the servicing of weapons rather than people (CAAT, 1990).

Further reading

Brzoska, M. and Ohlson, T. (1987), *Arms Transfers to the Third World 1971–85*, Oxford: Oxford University Press.

CAAT (Campaign Against Arms Trade) (1990), *Death on Delivery: the Impact of the Arms Trade on the Third World*, London: Campaign Against Arms Trade.

Catrina, C. (1988), *Arms Transfers and Dependence*, London: Taylor and Francis.

SIPRI (Stockholm International Peace Research Institute) (annual), *World Armaments and Disarmament Yearbook*, Oxford: Oxford University Press.

US Arms Control and Disarmament Agency (1991), *World Military Expenditure and Arms Transfers*, Washington DC: US Government Printing Office.

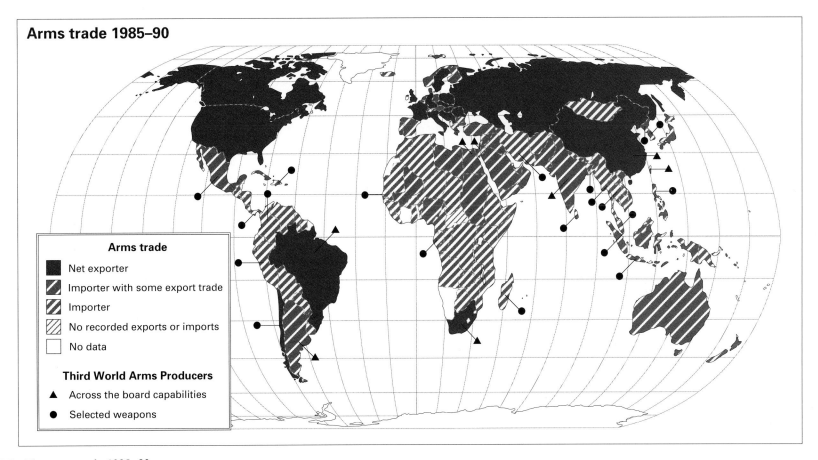

Figure 5.5 The arms trade 1985–90

5.6 'WHEN THE STATE KILLS': THE GEOGRAPHY OF THE DEATH PENALTY
David Simon

Capital punishment has sometimes been dubbed legally sanctioned murder by governments. Indeed, Amnesty International's (1989a) comprehensive report on capital punishment is titled *When the State Kills*. Few debates have been as long-running or as emotive as that surrounding the continued application of the death penalty. In many parts of the world, its continued existence on the statute book and its routine application, at least for certain categories of crime, are regarded as 'a necessary deterrent', 'right', 'natural justice' or are even defended on biblical or koranic grounds.

Debate has centred at two levels, the morals and ethics of taking a life in retribution for criminal deeds, and the humaneness or otherwise of different forms of execution. The diversity of opinion on both issues is well illustrated by the United States of America, where the key decisions rest at state rather than federal level. Many states retain the death penalty, although some have not carried out executions for a number of years. The favoured form of execution also varies, ranging from hanging to the electric chair, gas chamber and injection with a lethal dose of drugs. In other countries, strangulation, the firing squad and stonings may also be used. In certain countries, executions are routinely carried out in public to maximise the supposed deterrent effect and intimidate opponents of the regime. Sometimes, too, political executions are disguised by means of spurious criminal convictions.

There is now a substantial body of evidence from different countries that the death penalty does not act as an effective deterrent to murder. The majority of homicides are crimes of passion, where premeditation – and hence the possibility of deterrence – does not exist. Others are committed by mentally disturbed people, who are not subject to the death penalty in the law of many countries on grounds of diminished responsibility. Even in Malaysia, which has a mandatory death penalty for drug trafficking, an offence defined in law as possession of more than arbitrary quantities of specified narcotics, a top police officer has apparently admitted that there was no evidence of deterrence. While emotionally appealing in some quarters, retention of the death penalty for certain categories of offence, most commonly treason, murder by terrorists, drug-related killings and those of children and police officers, is open to the same doubts regarding effectiveness. This also creates anomalies by implying that society places a higher value on some people's lives than on others. In all cases it remains a cruel, inhuman and degrading form of punishment. Moreover, there is also the not-uncommon problem of miscarriages of justice. Upon discovery, a jailed prisoner can be pardoned and freed, but there can be no appeal or release from the grave.

Internationally, there have been many moves, both within the United Nations and other fora, to restrict and abolish the death penalty. The UN issues quinquennial reports on capital punishment, and Amnesty International, the world-renowned human rights organisation which is itself committed to the abolition of the death penalty, publishes periodic reports and up-to-date fact sheets. The earliest abolitionists were Venezuela (1863), San Marino (1865) and Costa Rica (1877). Progress has been slow and although a total of 44 countries had abolished this ultimate punishment entirely by the end of 1991, they remain in a small but growing minority (Figure 5.6a). The best year to date has been 1990, when no fewer than seven countries, including Namibia at independence, took this step.

An additional 16 countries have abolished the death penalty for ordinary crimes only (the exceptions being crimes under military law or under conditions of war) (Figure 5.6a). A third group comprises 21 countries and territories regarded as abolitionist *de facto*, in that no executions have been carried out there for at least the last ten years (Figure 5.6b). However, an overall majority of the world's countries and territories still retain and use capital punishment for ordinary crimes. Most of the 106 states in this group (Figure 5.6b), which includes those of the former Soviet Union, have carried out executions within the last decade, although some have since instituted moratoria. In 1991 alone, 2703 death sentences are known to have been passed in 62 countries, and 2086 executions carried out in 32 countries, although the true totals were undoubtedly higher. The number of known executions was higher than in any year since 1981 apart from the 2229 recorded in 1989. Nevertheless, 89% of the total were accounted for by just two countries, China (1084) and Iran (775). South Africa, formerly a frequent user of capital punishment, instituted a moratorium in 1990, although two executions did take place in its nominally 'independent' bantustan of Venda in 1991.

Although not dealt with here, extra-judicial killings, both by repressive governments or elements in their security forces and by non-governmental entities such as guerrilla movements, are common in some countries and territories. They are often brutally and summarily carried out, and remain extremely difficult to document.

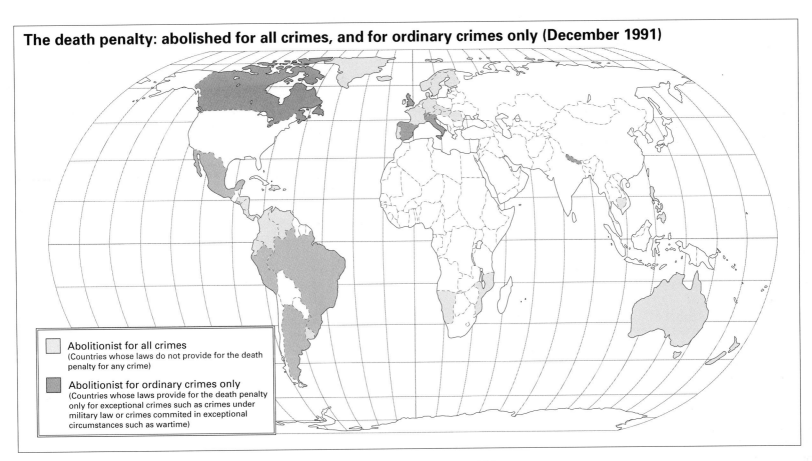

The death penalty: abolished for all crimes, and for ordinary crimes only (December 1991)

☐ Abolitionist for all crimes
(Countries whose laws do not provide for the death penalty for any crime)

■ Abolitionist for ordinary crimes only
(Countries whose laws provide for the death penalty only for exceptional crimes such as crimes under military law or crimes commited in exceptional circumstances such as wartime)

Figure 5.6a   The death penalty: abolished for all crimes, and for ordinary crimes only (December 1991)

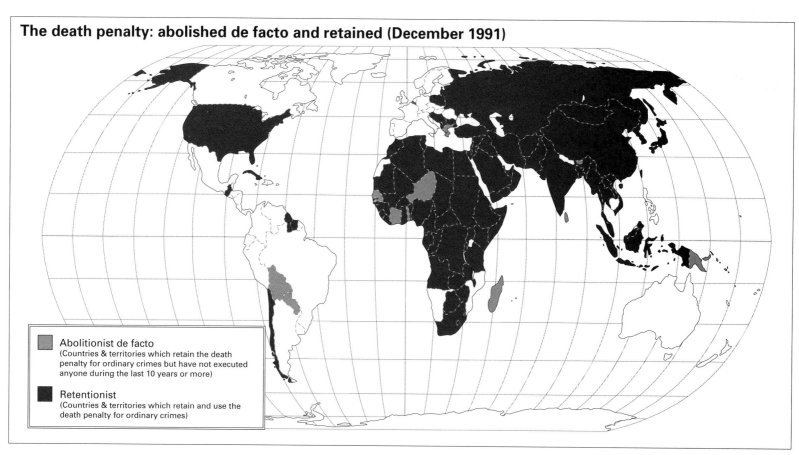

Figure 5.6b   The death penalty: abolished de facto and retained (December 1991)

Further reading

Amnesty International (1987), *USA: the Death Penalty*,
London: Amnesty International.

Amnesty International (1989a), *When the State Kills*,
London: Amnesty International.

Amnesty International (1989b), *Jamaica: the Death
Penalty*, London: Amnesty International.

Amnesty International (1989c), *Religions and the Death
Penalty*, London: Amnesty International.

Amnesty International (1989d), *Death Penalty: Facts
and Figures*, London: Amnesty International.

Amnesty International (1991a), *Amnesty International
Report 1991*, London: Amnesty International.

5.7 REVOLUTION
James Sidaway

Revolution is notoriously difficult to define. In part this is because revolutions are complex events. However, it is also because rapid and sometimes violent political shifts may occur which still fall short of constituting a social revolution. The term 'revolution' has a broad remit; hence we speak of 'industrial revolution', 'informal revolution', and 'sexual revolution'. However, *social revolution* should be distinguished from other forms of political and social change. The author of a much acclaimed comparative study of revolution reminds us that 'social revolutions are rapid, basic transformations of a society's state and class structures ... [they] are set apart from other sorts of conflicts and transformative processes above all by the combination of two coincidences; the coincidence of societal structural change with class upheaval; and the coincidence of political with social transformation ... What is unique to social revolution is that basic changes in social structure and in political structure occur together in a mutually reinforcing fashion' (Skocpol, 1979: 4).

Such a definition goes some way to resolve the problem of differentiating social revolution from wider political instability. Whilst the history of modern revolution should be traced at least from the upheaval in France in 1789, social revolution became linked to socialist transformation after the victory of the Bolsheviks in the Russian revolution of 1917. After 1917, the Western world faced a state where capitalist rule had been overthrown and replaced by a society of a fundamentally different form. The original hope of those who made the Russian revolution, that of a society in which workers' democracy could be established, degenerated into a system based on the dictator-ship of the party leadership. Similar social systems were established in Mongolia from 1921 and following the Second World War throughout eastern Europe.

After 1945, what became known as the Third World experienced a number of waves of social revolution whereby regimes based on Bolshevik inspired principles came to power: China (1949), Korea (from 1945), Indochina (from 1945), Cuba (1961), Aden (1967). Not all of the revolutionary transformations of this era produced communist regimes. Hence the revolutions, in a number of cases initiated by an army *coup d'état*, in Bolivia (1952), Burma (1961 onwards), Egypt (1952), Syria (1963 onwards), Somalia (1969 onwards), Iraq (1958 onwards), and Libya (1969 onwards) produced radical nationalist (but not communist) regimes. During this time many other revolutionary insurgencies in the Third World were repressed; in the Philippines, Malaya and Indonesia. This process was accompanied elsewhere by the overthrow of radical nationalist regimes, such as that of Mosadeq in Iran in 1953, and of Arbenz in Guatemala in 1954.

However, these counter-revolutionary successes were followed by a wave of successful social revolutions in the 1970s. The US defeat in Indochina and the collapse of the remaining European colonial empire in Africa produced a crop of new left-wing regimes (*see* Figure 5.7a). There were also revolutionary successes in central Asia (Afghanistan), the Middle East (Iran), elsewhere in Africa (Ethiopia) and in the Americas (Nicaragua and Grenada). In one of these social revolutions (Iran), the ideology of religious populism was dominant. But in four others, communist parties played the leading role (Vietnam, Cambodia, Laos, Afghanistan) and in the rest, mixtures of radical nationalism and socialism combined with the prospect that they would adopt some affiliation to Marxism-Leninism.

Changed international circumstances in the 1980s and 1990s have meant that, to date, no new radical social revolutions in the Third World have taken place since 1980. Indeed, a growing doubt concerning the viability of the revolutionary model of development was accompanied by a vigorous US policy of supporting counter-revolution (known as the Reagan doctrine) and the end of decolonisation. Moreover, the 1980s culminated in a new wave of revolutions resulting in the collapse of the Communist systems in eastern Europe. By the early 1990s only Cuba, North Korea, Vietnam and China remained officially committed to Marxism-Leninism. The collective human action that makes revolutions had again demonstrated its capacity to surprise and transform.

Figures 5.7b and 5.7c provide estimates of the situation in Mozambique in 1974 and 1990, and illustrate that social revolution and counter-revolution are socio-spatial phenomena in that they take place in, and transform, space (*see* Sidaway and Simon, 1990). In 1974 the Mozambican revolutionary liberation movement of FRELIMO, then based in the north of the country, was fighting the Portuguese colonial regime (Figure 5.7b). Fifteen years after gaining independence FRELIMO was itself facing the rural insurgency of the rebel movement known as RENAMO. The result was that in large parts of Mozambique FRELIMO's rule became limited to urban centres and a set of transit corridors (Figure 5.7c) (*see* Sidaway, 1991, 1992).

Further reading

Halliday, F. (1986), *The Making of the Second Cold War*, London: Verso.

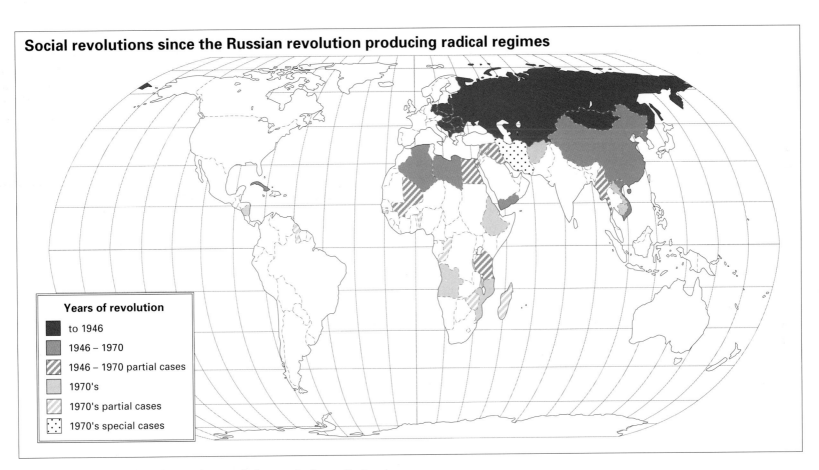

Figure 5.7a Social revolutions since the Russian revolution producing radical regimes

Kimmel, M.S. (1990), *Revolution, a Sociological Inter-*
pretation, Cambridge: Polity Press.
Post, K. and Wright, P. (1989), *Socialism and Under-*
development, London: Routledge.
Skocpol, T. (1979), *States and Social Revolutions*,
Cambridge: Cambridge University Press.
Third World Quarterly (1992), Special issue: rethinking
socialism, *Third World Quarterly*, **13**(1).
White, G. and Murray, R. (1983), *Revolutionary*
Socialist Development in the Third World, Brighton:
Wheatsheaf Books.

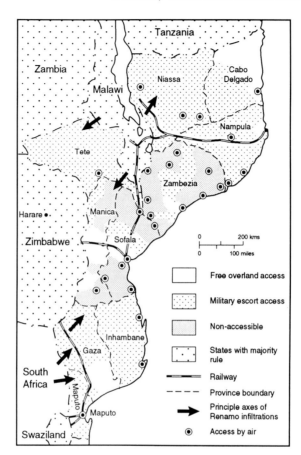

Figure 5.7c Geostrategic situation in Mozambique in
1990

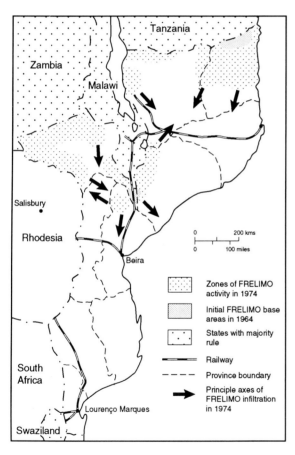

Figure 5.7b The extent of FRELIMO insurgency in
1974

5.8 POLITICAL AND ECONOMIC DEVELOPMENT IN THE POST-SOVIET REPUBLICS

Michael J. Bradshaw

In the past, in atlases such as this, the Soviet Union would have been treated as a single monolithic state. For those familiar with the economic development of the Soviet Union, this was a frustrating simplification. Despite the ideological commitment to the equalisation of living standards, throughout the Soviet period there remained substantial differences in the levels of economic development of the 15 Union Republics that comprised the Union of Soviet Socialist Republics (USSR). Now, in the post-Soviet era, it is these fifteen republics, often referred to as the Newly Independent States, that are the focus of this analysis.

Four months after the abortive August Coup, on 25 December 1991, the USSR ceased to exist as a 'geopolitical entity'. A few days earlier, on 21 December, 11 of the 15 republics of the Soviet Union had signed an agreement creating the Commonwealth of Independent States (CIS). The CIS represents a loose amalgam of Post-Soviet Republics; it has no central government of its own and agreements reached at CIS Summits must be ratified by the individual parliaments of the member states. At best the CIS provides a forum for the leaders of the member republics to discuss mutual problems. The constant fear of the other republics is that if the CIS were given more power it would simply become an instrument of Russian Imperialism. At the time of formation, the four republics that did not join were the three Baltic States: Latvia, Lithuania and Estonia, and the Republic of Georgia. For a while, to protest against perceived Russian support for Armenia,

the Republic of Azerbaijan left the CIS; however, it rejoined in September 1993. Following a prolonged civil war and economic collapse, in September 1993 the Republic of Georgia finally became a member of the CIS. Thus, in late 1993, the CIS comprised all the Post-Soviet Republics except the three Baltic States.

Two fundamental challenges face the Post-Soviet Republics: the creation of legitimate sovereign states; and the transition to a market-oriented economy. Already a number of these newly-independent states have been forced to defend their territorial integrity. In the Caucasus region, Armenia and Azerbaijan have engaged in military conflict over Nagorno-Karabakh; the Georgian Government has had to face separatist movements in South Ossetia and Abkhazia, and has lost control of the Abkhaz Republic. The very existence of the Republic of Moldova is threatened by those who wish to secede to rejoin Rumania and those, predominantly ethnic Russians, who wish to remain within an independent, though possibly smaller, state. Elsewhere conflict has resulted from power struggles between factions within the state apparatus. The most obvious case is the conflict between the Russian Parliament and the Russian Government. This was finally resolved in September 1993, in favour of President Yeltsin, by the use of force on the streets of Moscow. The Republic of Tajikistan is currently embroiled in an internal power struggle between tribal groups. For many of these states, the instability created by

Table 5.8a Socio-economic characteristics of the republics of the former Soviet Union 1989

	Natural increase (per 1000)	Infant mortality rates (per 1000)	Percent urban	Employment structure (%)†	
				Industry	Agriculture
Ex-USSR	7.6	22.7	66	39	19
Russia	3.9	17.8	74	43	13
Ukraine	1.7	13.0	67	41	19
Belarus	4.9	11.8	66	42	20
Uzbekistan	27.0	37.7	41	24	39
Kazakhstan	15.4	25.9	57	32	23
Georgia	8.1	19.6	56	31	25
Azerbaijan	20.0	26.2	54	26	32
Lithuania	4.8	10.7	68	42	18
Moldova	9.7	20.4	47	30	33
Latvia	2.4	11.1	71	41	16
Kyrgyzstan	23.2	32.2	38	28	33
Tajikistan	32.2	43.2	32	22	43
Armenia	15.6	20.4	68	42	18
Turkmenistan	27.3	54.7	45	21	42
Estonia	3.7	14.7	72	42	13

† Employment data are for 1990
Sources: data derived from: Goskomstat SSSR (1990), *Demograficheskiy ezhegodnik SSR 1990*, Moscow: Finansy i statistika; Goskomstat SSSR (1991a), *Narodnoye khozyaystvo SSSR v 1990g*, Moscow: Finansy i statistika; Goskomstat SSSR (1991b), *Soyuzniye respubliki: osnovnyye ekonomischeskiye i sotsial'nyye pokazateli*, Moscow: Informatsionno-izadetel'skiy tsentr Goskomstat SSSR.

political struggle, combined with a collapse in inter-republican trade, has resulted in economic ruin.

From a rudimentary analysis of the economic development of the Post-Soviet Republics, it is possible to identify three groupings (*see* Table 5.8a and Figure 5.8): a 'developed' core comprised of the Baltic States and the Slavic Republics, a semi-periphery comprised of Moldova, Georgia, Armenia and Kazakhstan, and a periphery containing Azerbaijan and the four central Asian republics. The results of this simple analysis, based on GNP and population growth, are confirmed by a more detailed analysis conducted by Cole (1991) using 21 measures of development. Cole produced an index of development on which the average score for the USSR equalled 100. The republics with the highest score, and thus the 'most developed' were Latvia 125, Estonia 121.2 and Lithuania 116.4; those with the lowest score,

and therefore the least developed, were Turkmenistan 69, Tajikistan 69.1, Uzbekistan 71.7 and Kyrgyzstan 73.7. Russia had a score of 108.3. Examination of the economies of the republics reveals that the core republics are highly urbanised industrial economies, while the central Asian republics are distinguished by lower levels of urbanisation and an agriculturally-oriented economy. The semi-peripheral republics are characterised by relatively high levels of urbanisation, with pockets of industrialisation amid an otherwise agrarian economy. Variations in demographic characteristics reflect both economic and cultural factors. The most obvious distinction is between the Islamic states of Azerbaijan and Central Asia, characterised by high birth rates, relatively low death rates and high levels of natural increase, on the one hand, and the Slavic Republics and the Baltic States on the other hand, characterised by low birth and death rates and

low, and now in some cases negative population growth. More recent data published by the World Bank (1993) suggest that the current political and economic crises across the former Soviet Union are suppressing population growth and that the gap between the richest and poorest republics is actually widening (Table 5.8b). The 1993 World Bank development indicators have classified the Post-Soviet Republics under two headings: Lithuania, Belarus, the Russian Federation, Latvia and Estonia are in the Upper Middle Income category; the rest are in the Lower Middle Income category. It is probably only a matter of time before some of the republics are categorised low income; the question remains which of them, if any, are likely to become high income countries?

Further reading

Bradshaw, M.J. (1993), *The Economic Effects of Soviet Dissolution*, London: Royal Institute of International Affairs.
Cole, J. (1991), *The USSR in the 1990s: Which Republic*?, Nottingham University, Department of Geography, Working Paper 9.
European Commission (1993), Reform issues in the former Soviet Union, *European Economy*, **79**.
McAuley, A. (1991), The economic consequences of Soviet disintegration, *Soviet Economy*, 7: 189–214.
World Bank (1993), *Statistical Handbook 1993: States of the Former USSR*, Washington DC: The World Bank, Studies of Economies in Transformation.

Table 5.8b Economic development of the post-Soviet republics in 1991

	Population growth 1990–91 %	Average growth of net material production 1990–91	Per capita net material product 1991 (current rubles)
Russia	0.1	− 14.3	6351
Ukraine	0.2	− 13.4	4314
Belarus	0.0	− 1.9	6133
Uzbekistan	1.9	− 3.7	2408
Kazakhstan	0.6	− 14.9	3997
Georgia	0.0	− 20.9	2719
Azerbaijan	0.1	− 1.9	2861
Lithuania	0.8	− 9.3	8680
Moldova	0.0	− 18.0	4300
Latvia	− 0.4	− 3.8	6505
Kyrgyzstan	1.3	− 4.3	3068
Tajikistan	2.1	n/a	1973
Armenia	2.1	− 11.6	3279
Estonia	− 0.3	n/a	6710

Source: World Bank (1993: 6–11)

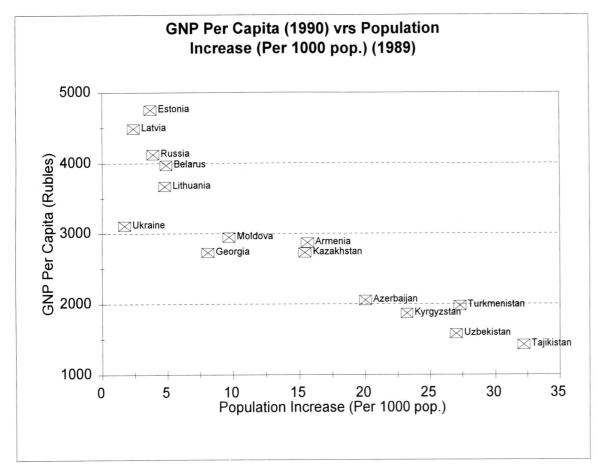

Figure 5.8 GNP per capita (1990) versus population increase (per 1000 pop.) (1989) in states of the former Soviet Union

5.9 REFUGEES
Richard Black

One of the most enduring political problems of recent years has been that of forced displacement of populations. At the end of 1990, the total number of officially-recognised refugees in the world stood at over 16 million. Meanwhile, another 3.3 million were estimated to be in 'refugee-like circumstances', remaining unrecognised by their host nation, whilst as many as 25 million were forcibly displaced within their own country.

In international law, refugees are defined by the 1951 Geneva Convention as people who are forced to leave their home country 'owing to a well founded fear of persecution for reasons of race, religion, nationality, or membership of a particular social group or political opinion'. However, both legal and practical definitions of refugees vary from country to country, and continent to continent. In most European countries, rules have been set up to process applications for asylum, in order to assess whether each individual applicant has left his or her home for the reasons defined under the Geneva Convention, or for economic reasons. In this sense, refugees are in a very precise legal category. Those rejected are either deported, or allowed to remain on humanitarian grounds, or in some cases via normal immigration channels. In contrast, few Third World countries seek individually to assess the motivations of refugees, instead recognising groups of refugees. In part, this reflects the differential nature of the refugee impact on 'developed' and Third World countries, with over 90% of the world's refugees being concentrated in the latter.

Refugee flows are not only concentrated in the Third World, but also represent a particular area of concern for the world's poorest countries (Figure 5.9). For example, in 1991 there were 23 countries in the world that hosted over 100 000 refugees. Of these, thirteen were low-income countries (defined as those with a level of GNP per capita of less than $500), and a further seven were lower-middle income countries. On their own, the thirteen low-income countries accounted for over half the world's refugees, excluding Palestinians in the Occupied Territories. Meanwhile, all except five of the 41 low-income countries of the world were in 1991 either significant receivers, or producers of refugees.

In certain countries, the scale of refugee movements is dramatic in demographic terms. In Malawi, for example, where GNP per capita stands at just US$ 180, one in ten of the population is a refugee; in Guinea, the figure is one in 13, whilst in tiny Djibouti, in the Horn of Africa, the figure reaches one in three, the highest concentration of refugees in any sovereign state in the world.

At such concentrations, refugees are clearly a major factor in development. They place potential strains on infrastructures, such as schools, hospitals and other welfare services, whilst especially in the emergency phase of their flight, they need food, clothing and shelter. Given the poverty of many receiving countries, this emergency assistance must usually come from the international community. Recent studies show, however, that this assistance is often far from adequate. Keen (1992), for example, documents a succession of cases in Africa and elsewhere where food rations have fallen short of the minimum level for sustenance recommended by the World Health Organisation (WHO) of 2000 KCal per person per day, or where in some cases food rations have not been provided at all. The result is that many refugee populations have suffered from a range of diseases and avoidable deaths caused by malnutrition.

Despite these problems, however, refugees can also represent an opportunity for receiving states. For example, they may bring resources with them, in the form of skills and assets. Ugandan refugees fleeing to southern Sudan in the early 1980s provide an example where the influx of people provided a market for products, and stimulated agricultural production in a region that was one of the poorest in sub-Saharan Africa. Within a few years of their arrival, refugee farmers were able to export food outside the region, notably during the famine that affected other parts of the Sudan in 1984/5.

Further reading

Black, R. (1991), Refugees and displaced persons: geographical perspectives and research direction, *Progress in Human Geography*, **15**(3): 281–298.

Black, R. and Robinson, V. (eds) (1993), *Geography and Refugees: Patterns and Processes of Change*, London: Belhaven Press.

Keen, D. (1992), *Refugees: Rationing the Right to Life: the Crisis in Emergency Relief*, London: Zed Press.

Leatherby, J. (1989), The millions forced to flee, *Geographical Magazine*, December: 14–19.

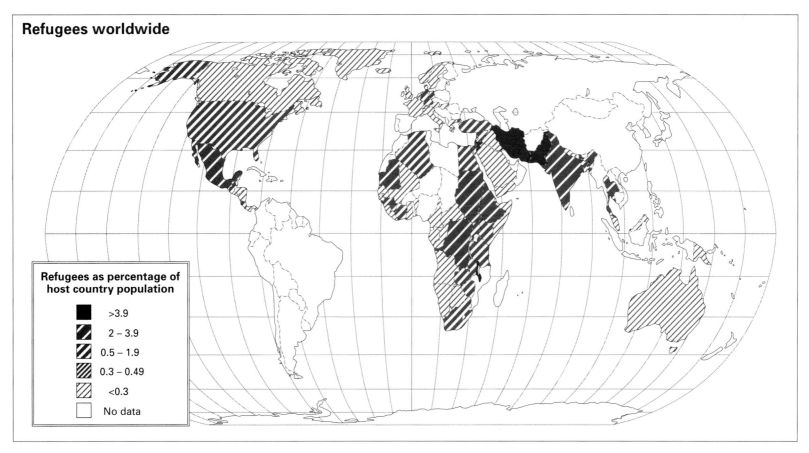

Figure 5.9 Refugees worldwide

5.10 RESETTLEMENT SCHEMES FOR NOMADS: THE CASE OF SOMALIA

Jörg Janzen

When looking at the ongoing sedentarisation process in the nomadic countries of the dry belt of the Old World, it is necessary to differentiate between two main types of sedentarisation:

(1) the more or less *voluntary resettlement* of an increasing part of the pastoral nomads, generally based on new infrastructural facilities and/or new extrapastoral economic possibilities; and

(2) more or less *enforced sedentarisation* of nomadic livestock keepers by governmental programmes.

Figure 5.10 illustrates such an enforced sedentarisation programme undertaken by the Somali Government.

Until now, the majority of the Somali government representatives have taken the view that the sedentarisation of the largest possible number of the Somali nomadic population is an important prerequisite for their integration into the economic and social development of the country. This view dates back to the Soviet influence on Somali development policy at the beginning of the 1970s (Janzen, 1984, 1986).

In 1974 a disastrous drought, the Dabadheer drought, was responsible for the economic ruin of approximately a quarter of a million nomads in the northern and central parts of Somalia. As a resumption of livestock keeping was at the time impossible for most of the nomads, Somalia's socialist government jumped at the chance of resettling a large proportion of the drought victims (Somali Democratic Republic, 1977). This was done with a considerable amount of force, hardly leaving any alternative for the impoverished nomadic families. Based on experiences in the Soviet Union when carrying out the enforced resettlement of nomads in its southern republics, the Somali government launched a spectacular programme for the sedentarisation of nomads. In 1975, nearly 120 000 nomads were settled in initially three agricultural and three fishery projects (Haakonson, 1979), far away from their traditional living space. In accordance with socialist aims, the projects were assigned the status of (production) co-operatives with a rigidly organised political and administrative structure (Labahn, 1982).

The nomads settled in this way were in fact hardly involved in decision making within the co-operatives. The main economic aim of the settlement projects was the creation of self-supporting economic units. However, these ambitious aims could not even partly be realised. On the contrary, the population had to be supplied with large amounts of food from the World Food Programme, well after the initial phases of the project and up to the second half of the 1980s. Consequently, a large number of nomads turned their backs on the settlement projects, even during their first few years. The main reason why many of the newly settled nomads deserted the projects was the complete change in lifestyle to that of a fisherman or farmer in an environment which was also totally different, not only physically, but also socially, economically and politically.

While women and children often remained in the settlements, so that they could continue to enjoy the free food rations as well as the education system and medical care, the majority of the men migrated to the capital Muqdisho or even to the Gulf States, and a small number returned to nomadic livestock keeping.

The course of the sedentarisation programme has shown that this type of project is doomed to failure if it is badly planned and does not satisfactorily take into consideration the specific needs of the former nomads. Thus, the example of the Somali settlement projects should act as a warning to those responsible elsewhere not to carry out this type of large-scale, state-controlled sedentarisation programmes in the future.

Three conclusions can be drawn from the experiences of the Somali government in trying to sedentarise the largest possible number of nomads. First, if the sedentarisation of the nomads was regarded initially by many experts as the only possible alternative for the integration of this population group into the modern development of the country, then it could be said that a change of opinion has taken place in the recent past, following new research results. This is not surprising, since the manifold negative socio-economic and ecological effects of sedentarisation have only become apparent during the last two decades. The rapid onset of the desertification process in the Sahel Zone is largely attributable to the greatly restricted mobility of numerous groups of livestock keepers.

Secondly, nearly all of the large and costly nomadic programmes, including the Somali example, carried out by national and international development institutions have proved to be more or less failures, because as a rule too little interest has been shown in the real needs of the nomads, while their special economic and ecological know-how and skills were either disregarded or paid too little attention to in the planning process.

Thirdly, as a transition to arable farming is either not possible, or is highly uneconomical and risky, for most of the nomads in the dry belt of the Old World due to climate, hydrology and lack of suitability of the soil, mobile livestock keeping represents the only alternative for an economically efficient use of the natural resources in large areas. In fact, with the exception of the two particularly favoured areas at the Jubba and Shabeelle rivers, this holds true for most of Somalia.

State-controlled sedentarisation of the majority of the nomadic population in large settlement projects must therefore be regarded as having been detrimental to the economic efficiency of Somalia. Evidence of this can be seen in the failure in the planned form of Somalia's nomadic resettlement projects, which could only be maintained with extensive help both from the state and abroad (Mohamed and Touati, 1991).

If representatives of the Somali government referred to the Soviet model, which presented the enforced sedentarisation in a very favourable light, then it must be emphasised that the Soviet Union of 60 years ago had a very different situation and background to that of a present-day, developing African country, such as Somalia. Further, it should not be forgotten that the enforced sedentarisation of nomads in the Soviet Union did not take place peacefully, and was only achieved at the cost of great sacrifice of human life and livestock, and the loss of cultural identity for the nomadic peoples concerned.

Further reading

Haakonson, J.M. (1979), *Survey of the Fishing Cooperatives for Resettled Nomads in Somalia*, Montreal: Report Prepared for the Somali Democratic

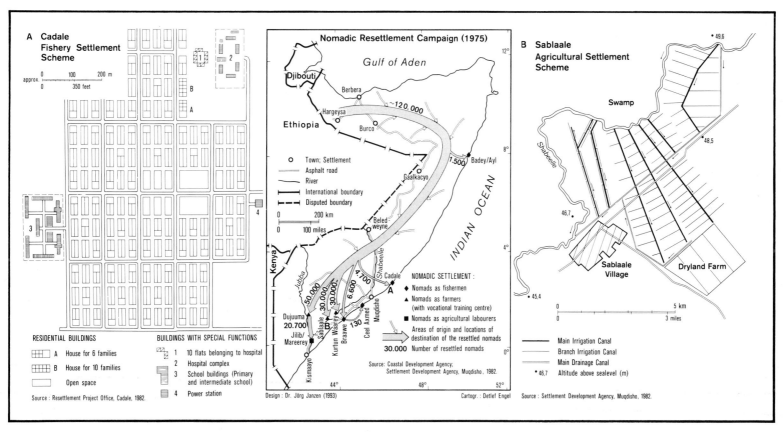

Figure 5.10 Resettlement schemes for nomads: the case of Somalia

Republic, Ministry of Fisheries by the Food and Agriculture Organisation of the United Nations.

Janzen, J. (1984), Nomadismus in Somalia, *Afrika-Spektrum*, **19**(2): 149–171.

Janzen, J. (1986), The process of nomadic sedentarisation – distinguishing features, problems and consequences for Somali development policy, in: Conze, P. and Labahn, T. (eds), *Agriculture in the Winds of Change*, Saarbrücken: EPI-Dokumentation 2, 73–91.

Labahn, T. (1982), Nomadenansiedlungen in Somalia, in: Scholz, F. and Janzen, J. (eds), *Nomadismus – Ein Entwicklungsproblem?*, Berlin: Abhandlungen des Geographisches Instituts – Anthropogeographie 33, 81–95.

Mohamed, A.F. and Touati, J. (1991), *Sedentarisierung von Nomaden – Chancen und Gefahren einer Entwicklungsstrategie am Beispiel Somalias*, Saarbrücken: Bielefeld Studies on the Sociology of Development, 48.

Scholz, F. (ed.) (1991), *Nomaden, Mobile Tierhaltung. Zur gegenwärtigen Lage von Nomaden und zu den Problemen und Chancen mobiler Tierhaltung*, Berlin: Das Arabische Buch.

Scholz, F. (ed.) (1992), *Nomadismus/Bibliographie*, Berlin: Das Arabische Buch.

Somali Democratic Republic (1977), *Objectives and Policy of the Resettlement*, Mogadishu: Settlement Development Agency (SDA).

5.11 PARTY SYSTEMS
Peter J. Taylor

Invented in Western Europe and North America in the 19th century, political party systems have come to have a crucial legitimising role throughout the world in the 20th century. Political parties have become the vehicles for transmitting the concerns of civil society to the state through elected party government.

The key to the emergence of party systems was the acceptance of a political opposition as an alternative government. This legitimated a divided polity which could be organised by parties as representing, literally, 'part' of civil society. But parties are not divisive if they constitute a party system. By expressing divisions within the civil society and giving them a voice in the polity, parties are fundamental integrative forces in modern states. It is no wonder that they exist in some form or other in nearly all states in the late 20th century.

In the regions where they were invented – the 'North' in recent parlance – political party systems are integral to the existence of liberal democratic states. Competition for government by multiple parties is at the heart of liberal democracy. Parties represent economic class interests and cultural positions within civil society so that governments are legitimated as reflecting public opinion. In the ideal case there is not only political competition but also more than one party with a realistic chance of regularly entering government. In countries that use a proportional representation electoral system, such government pluralism is largely guaranteed. In constituency-based majority systems – 'first-past-the-post' as it is commonly called – government pluralism is not guaranteed but has occurred in several countries, if we take a long view, since 1945. These party systems are *Multiple Party, Multiple Party Government Systems*.

In some countries, despite having multiple parties, there has been in reality one party that is widely viewed as the party of government. This can take several forms. In Mexico the Authentic Revolutionary Party has enjoyed continual control of the national government since 1945 despite electoral challenges by opposition parties. In India the Congress Party has ruled since independence in 1947 with just two minor interludes where in both cases opposition parties collapsed in government. In Japan the Liberal Democratic Party ruled continuously from 1955 to 1993. These party systems are *Multiple Party, One Party Government Systems*. In all such systems, civil society legitimates political domination and the possibility of political change is ever-present.

In contrast, in *One Party Systems* all opposition parties are eliminated so that elections to legitimate government are between candidates of the same party. The notion of a one party system is, etymologically, a contradiction in terms but it makes sense theoretically as the party expressing the concerns of a unified revolutionary society where party fuses state and civil society. Communist states have been the most common example of using one party systems but they are found elsewhere, as for instance with the Ba'ath party in Iraq.

With the demise of Communist states in Eastern Europe, there have been attempts to produce multiple party systems. There is a problem. The use of parties as the link between state and civil society cannot be simply legislated. Parties build up support based on particular interests over long periods of time so that they have core bodies of support in society. In the former Communist countries, past dominance of civil society by the state means that competitive parties are new and have had no time to generate long term loyalties. Hence although many commentators optimistically dubbed the first plural elections in these countries 'foundation elections', implying a movement towards liberal democracy, this is by no means inevitable. The confusion of the elections with large numbers of parties and former communists usually faring better than expected are signs that these party systems remain a special category: *Post-Communist Multiple Party Systems*.

In many poor countries there are what can be termed *Intermittent Party Systems*. Here the strongest arm of the state is the army and they have regularly intervened to replace elected governments. Even when elections are held they have an implicit veto over the result – the military declared Nigeria's 1993 election void for instance. When formally in government the army may ban political parties as too divisive for the country's good. Such *No Party Systems* are also found in traditional regimes where the sovereign does not recognise the concept of a loyal opposition.

Allocating countries to one of these five party system categories as shown in Figure 5.11 is sometimes quite difficult. For example, when does an intermittent system become a multiple party system? To argue that the military veto over election results still exists in several Latin American countries, or that it has been dispatched to history, is a matter of interpretation that will only be tested in the future.

Further reading

Taylor, P.J. (1986), An exploration into world-systems analysis of political parties, *Political Geography Quarterly*, **5** (supplement): 5–20.
Taylor, P.J. (1990), Extending the world of electoral geography, in: Johnston, R.J., Shelley, F.M. and Taylor, P.J. (eds), *Developments in Electoral Geography*, London: Routledge.

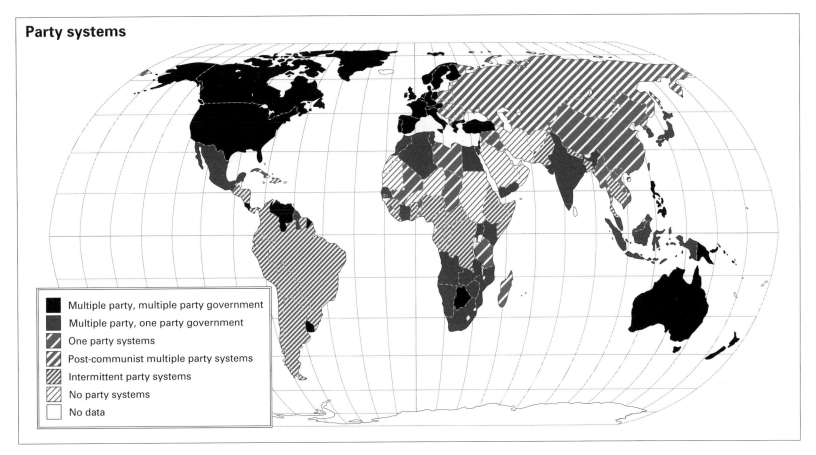

Figure 5.11 Party systems

5.12 ELECTIONS AND VOTING BEHAVIOUR IN INDIA
Robert W. Bradnock

India, with over 520 million electors in 1991 and widely referred to as the world's largest democracy, is one of the few former colonial countries to have experienced almost unbroken democratic government since Independence in 1947. With the exception of the State of Emergency imposed by Mrs Gandhi between 1975 and 1977, all Indian governments have been formed as the result of direct elections to the Lok Sabha, or lower House of Parliament, established on the British model, and today comprising 552 members elected by the first-past-the-post electoral system in single member constituencies. Unlike Britain, however, 233 of the 245 members of the Rajya Sabha, or upper House, are elected by members of the State Legislatures using a system of proportional representation, the remaining 12, normally leading figures in literature, art or social service, being nominated by the President. India's electoral geography is further complicated by the fact that under its federal constitution elections take place to Legislative Assemblies (Vidhan Sabha) in the 25 states which make up the Union. It often happens that the state governments are formed by different parties from that governing at the Centre.

The first General Election, held on the basis of universal adult suffrage, was in 1951–52, with subsequent elections in 1957, 1962, 1967 and 1971. The electoral process was interrupted by the Emergency in 1975, but resumed with the Election of 1977, followed by 1980, 1984, 1989, when the voting age was lowered from 21 to 18, and 1991. Superficially the Congress Party appears to have dominated India's electoral politics for much of the period since Independence. Yet both at national and state levels patterns of electoral support have been complex, with a wide variety of regional parties competing with both communal parties such as the Bharatiya Janata Party (BJP), a Hindu Party, or the Muslim League, and with secular parties such as the Communist Party of India (Marxist), the CPI(M). Furthermore, even when the Congress Party commanded massive majorities in the Lok Sabha it has rarely won more than 45% of the popular vote, its success reflecting the extent to which opposition parties were split as much as its own strength.

The three maps in Figure 5.12 illustrate the range of contrasting electoral fortunes of the parties contesting Lok Sabha elections in three elections, which represent two extremes of support for the Congress, and the 1991 elections, which produced a Congress Government without an absolute majority in the Lok Sabha. They illustrate striking regional contrasts, and the frequently major swings in electoral support which India has experienced.

The 1977 election took place in the wake of Mrs Gandhi's emergency. The Congress became highly unpopular across much of northern India, often referred to as the 'Hindi Belt' or as the 'cow belt', a reflection of the region's role as the heartland of traditional Hinduism. However, the failure of the Congress resulted in large measure from the merging of a wide range of Opposition Parties under the single flag of the Janata (or 'People's') Party. It is striking that the Congress retained its hold on much of south India, with the exception of the south-easternmost state of Tamil Nadu, where the two regional parties, the Dravida Munnetra Kahagam (DMK) and its factional rival the All India Anna DMK, had the field largely to themselves.

By the 1980 election the Janata Party had split, leaving the field open for the Congress to return to power. The 1984 election saw Congress support soar in the wake of Mrs Gandhi's assassination, and represented a complete reversal of its overwhelming defeat in northern India some seven years previously. However, it lost ground in parts of the south, notably Andhra Pradesh, where it was routed by the Telugu Desam, another regional party. In 1989 the Congress lost power to a group of parties of widely differing ideologies fighting together as the National Front. This too broke up, and in much of India the 1991 elections, in the course of which Rajiv Gandhi was assassinated, became a contest between the Congress and the BJP, which fought on a platform of Hindu nationalism. The BJP made particularly striking inroads in parts of the north and north-west, illustrating the continuance of major regional contrasts in political support for the major parties, and the volatility of the Indian electorate as a whole.

Further reading

Basham, A.L. (ed.) (1975), *A Cultural History of India*, Delhi: Oxford University Press.

Farmer, B.H. (1993), *An Introduction to South Asia*, London: Routledge, 2nd ed.

Robinson, F. (ed.) (1989), *The Cambridge Encyclopaedia of India, Pakistan, Bangladesh, Sri Lanka, Nepal, Bhutan and the Maldives*, Cambridge: Cambridge University Press.

Schwartzberg, J.E. (1993), *An Historical Atlas of South Asia*, Chicago: Chicago University Press, 2nd ed.

Sopher, D.E. (1975), The geographic patterning of culture in India, in: Sopher, D.E. (ed.), *The Discovery of India*, Boulder: Westview Press, 289–326.

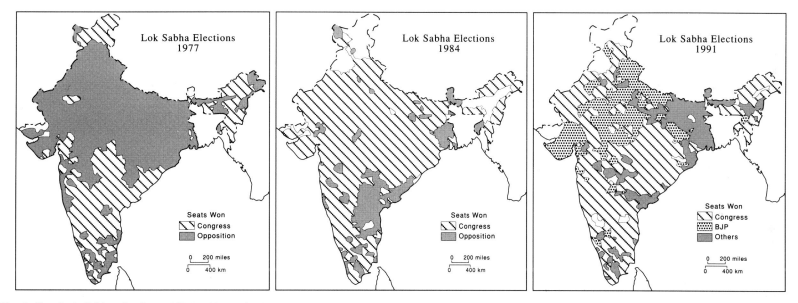

Figure 5.12 Indian Lok Sabha elections, 1977, 1984 and 1991

5.13 THE EXCLUSIVE ECONOMIC ZONE
Gerald Blake

From the 1950s coastal states took an increasing interest in ocean resources, especially oil and gas in the continental shelf, and fisheries in adjacent seas (Couper, 1983). States generally exercised three types of offshore sovereignty: territorial sea, continental shelf, and exclusive fishing zones. The territorial sea allows the state absolute sovereignty over the seabed, the waters above, and the airspace, although ships of other states have the right of innocent passage in territorial seas. Coastal states also enjoyed the right to exploit the resources of their continental shelves. Unfortunately the limits of territorial waters and continental shelves were never satisfactorily defined in the UN Conventions on the Law of the Sea in 1958 and 1962. Thus, national maritime claims began to escalate to distances up to 200 nautical miles (nm) offshore (1 nm = 1.156 statute miles). In 1973 a fresh round of UN law of the sea conferences began with the aim of drafting an international agreement to define the rights and obligations of coastal states and the limits of offshore jurisdictions. It took until 1982 for a Convention on the Law of the Sea to be hammered out, providing a widely accepted framework for an offshore regime (United Nations, 1983). In general the provisions of the Convention are favourable to developing countries.

Two articles in the 1982 UN Convention are pivotal: first, territorial waters are restricted to a standard 12 nm, and secondly states have the right to claim a 200 nm exclusive economic zone (EEZ). Within the EEZ the coastal state has exclusive rights to all resources including hydrocarbons and fish, and the right to control scientific research.

Permanent installations may be located within the EEZ in connection with resources exploitation. EEZ rights do not extend to the control of airspace or navigation, but there are fears that coastal states will be tempted to restrict shipping within their EEZs progressively. One of the achievements of the 1982 Convention is that it restricts national maritime claims. Beyond 200 nm the seabed is regarded as the 'common heritage of mankind' (United Nations, 1983: 42). Under Article 137 the resources of the deep seabed (called 'The Area') are to be managed by a UN organisation (known as 'The Authority'). The Authority may exploit resources directly, and also grant concessions to multinationals to do so. In all these activities the interests of developing countries are paramount. Earnings from the exploitation of resources from The Area, notably polymetallic nodules, are to be used primarily to benefit developing states. The Authority also undertakes to transfer technology to developing states to enable them to exploit The Area, and to regulate maritime mineral production to protect land producers. To date, seabed minerals remain uneconomic, but they could become commercially attractive in the future. Meanwhile, the EEZs of the world are much more important for resources, being responsible for over 90% of the world's fish catch, virtually all the oil and gas production, and a variety of other minerals such as tin (Glassner, 1992: 485). Some states, including several developing countries, have found themselves excluded from former fishing grounds by the introduction of the EEZ, while others have gained from the new regime. To be valid, states must formally declare their EEZ; so far about two thirds have done so (US Department of State, 1990).

Figure 5.13 shows the EEZ at world scale. The map is not large enough to include maritime boundaries between coastal states, of which there are estimated to be potentially 420 (US Department of State, 1990: 3), one third of which have been formally agreed (Charney and Alexander, 1993). Approximately 30% of the oceans fall within the EEZ (Smith, R.W., 1986: 3), about one tenth of which is territorial sea. Several large states with long coastlines have inherited substantial areas of EEZ. A few, with continental shelves extending beyond 200 nm are entitled to a share of continental shelf resources up to a maximum distance of 350 nm. Landlocked states are entitled to a share of the fishing resources of the nearest EEZ if it can be shown that a surplus exists in these waters, although this right would be difficult to implement in practice. The map also indicates those states which had signed and ratified the 1982 UN Convention by 1992 (United Nations, 1992: 7–8). The Convention comes into force in November 1994, twelve months after its ratification by the 60th state. Some major states, including the United States, United Kingdom, and Germany have not yet signed, but may do so in due course.

Further reading

Couper, A. (ed.) (1983), *Times Atlas of the Oceans*, London: Times Books.
Prescott, J.R.V. (1985), *The Maritime Political Boundaries of the World*, London: Methuen.
Smith, R.W. (1986), *Exclusive Economic Zone Claims: Analysis and Primary Documents*, Dordrecht: Martinus Nijhoff.

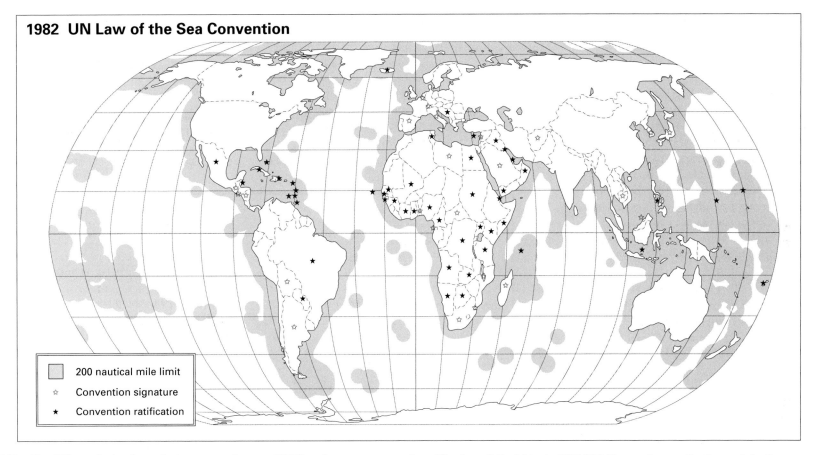

1982 UN Law of the Sea Convention

200 nautical mile limit
☆ Convention signature
★ Convention ratification

Figure 5.13 The 200 nautical mile exclusive economic zone (EEZ) and progress towards ratification of the historic 1982 UN Convention on the Law of the Sea

5.14 THE GULF
Gerald Blake

The Gulf (or Persian Gulf) graphically illustrates the complexities of maritime boundary delimitation (Figure 5.14). Large offshore oil and gas fields, often close inshore and in shallow water, provided powerful incentives for boundary delimitation. The process began with the Bahrain-Saudi Arabian boundary agreement in 1958. Eight further agreements were concluded by 1974, leaving seven major potential boundaries as yet undecided. If boundaries between the federal states of the United Arab Emirates, and those of the Iranian-occupied islands of Abu Musa are added, the number of undelimited boundaries increases considerably (Drysdale and Blake, 1985). Nevertheless the proportion of agreed boundaries is higher in the Gulf than in many parts of the world.

Three major problems complicated boundary agreements in the Gulf; the large number of coastal states (eight) in relation to the seabed to be divided (230 000 km^2); the presence of islands, some of which are disputed; and extensive oil and gas fields which are best managed undivided by international boundaries. The Gulf states have devised some ingenious solutions in reaching their agreements. For example, oilfields have been divided equally and profits shared (Abu Dhabi-Qatar), or revenues shared in an area of seabed formerly in dispute (Bahrain-Saudi Arabia). Similarly, islands have sometimes been treated as if mainland and given full effect (Bahrain-Saudi Arabia) or given partial effect (Iran-Saudi Arabia). Nevertheless several tricky disputes are unresolved, especially the Iraq-Kuwait boundary, which is likely to leave Iraq with very little seabed, and Bahrain-Qatar where the Huwar Islands are

hotly contested and may be settled by the International Court. Iran's partial occupation of Abu Musa island in 1971 is still a cause of resentment among Arabs, while Kuwait and Saudi Arabia contest two islands in the former Neutral Zone ('The Divided Zone') (El-Hakim, 1979). Technically and legally most boundary problems in the developing world are soluble: what may be lacking is the political will to reach agreement.

Further reading

Amin, S.H. (1981), *International and Legal Problems of the Gulf*, London: Menas Press.

Drysdale, A.D. and Blake, G.H. (1985), *The Middle East and North Africa: a Political Geography*, New York: Oxford University Press.

El-Hakim, A.A. (1979), *The Middle Eastern States and the Law of the Sea*, Manchester: Manchester University Press.

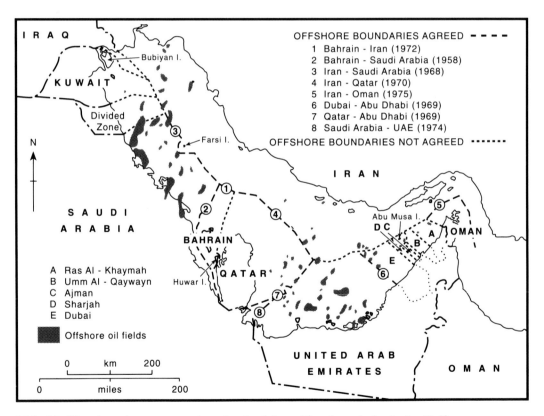

Figure 5.14 Maritime boundary agreements and potential maritime boundaries in the Gulf

5.15 THE SPRATLY ISLANDS
Gerald Blake

The Spratly Islands occupy a large area of the South China Sea covering several thousand square miles. There are hundreds of islands and reefs, most of which are low-lying, uninhabited and of little economic value. Since World War II interest in the islands has grown both because of their strategic importance in relation to shipping routes, and the likelihood of oil being found in the surrounding waters. There are five major claimants: China, Vietnam, Taiwan, Philippines and Malaysia, plus Brunei which claims two nearby islands. Over the years these contenders have pressed their claims with increasing vigour, particularly by establishing small military outposts sometimes within sight of each other. Vietnam occupies the greatest number (24), followed by Philippines (8) and China (6) which only began island occupation in 1988. China and Taiwan claim all the islands in the South China Sea, including the Paracels and Spratlys. Philippines claims most of the northern Spratly islands, Vietnam all the Spratly Islands, while Malaysia's claim is confined to certain southern Spratly islands close to the Malaysian coast (*see* Figure 5.15). Altogether this represents one of the world's largest, most dangerous, and intractable disputes over islands and their surrounding seas. China and Vietnam have already had one serious military encounter in the Spratlys. In 1974 China enforced its claims to the Paracels by driving Vietnamese forces off the islands, and there are fears that a military solution may also be sought in the Spratlys.

The difficulty of finding a negotiated solution to the Spratlys dispute lies in the nature of the claims, most of which are both difficult to estab-

lish and equally difficult to refute. China's claim (formally made in 1947) relies on long historic associations and sovereignty, and use of certain islands by Chinese fishermen. Taiwan's claims are essentially those of China. Vietnam's claim relies on the occupation and annexation of nine islands by the French in 1933, where they remained until ousted by the Japanese in 1939 (Thomas, 1990:

416). The Philippine claim appears to have been first articulated in 1956, with a large number of islands being formally annexed in 1978 based on arguments of proximity and history. Malaysia's claim, made in 1979, is to those islands and reefs which are located on Malaysia's continental shelf. Thus some of the southern Spratlys are claimed by all the main contenders. All kinds of ingenious

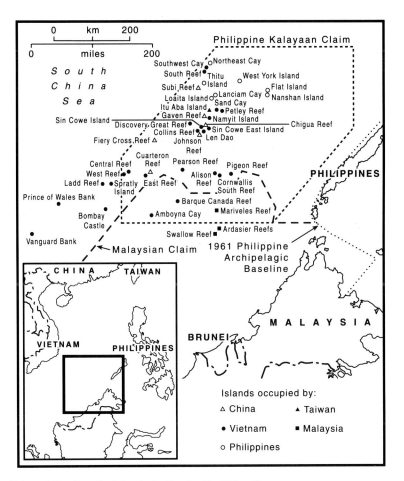

Figure 5.15 Geopolitics of the Spratly Islands in the South China Sea

solutions to the dispute have been proposed, including delimitarisation, condominium, internationalisation, and resource sharing, but little concrete progress is evident.

Further reading

Hill, R.D., Owen, N.G. and Roberts, E.G. (eds) (1991), *Fishing in Troubled Waters: Territorial Claims in the South China Sea*, Hong Kong: Centre of Asian Studies, University of Hong Kong.

Thomas, B.L. (1990), The Spratly Islands imbroglio: a tangled web of conflict, in: Grundy-Warr, C.E.R. (ed.), *International Boundaries and Boundary Conflict Resolution*, Durham: International Boundaries Research Unit, 413–428.

5.16 KENYA: THE POLITICS OF PLACE
Roddy Fox

The interplay of political, electoral and administrative processes in Kenya has ensured that where you live, your tribal affiliation and your rural area's development prospects are fundamentally interrelated. The link between politics, place and development comes from the strongly entrenched patron-client system since attempts to achieve development for a rural area have depended on your MP or other 'big man' being in a position of power. Ministers and other power brokers often seek the allocation of development programmes to their home areas to satisfy constituents' pressure and ensure their loyalty. Since the rural areas are clearly defined and perceived in tribal terms (tribe being in common usage in Kenya to distinguish ethnic groups), then tribalism becomes related to the development process.

In the colonial period land was apportioned by race. Thus the White Highlands (to use colonial terminology), Crown Land, Forest Reserves, National Parks and urban centres were white land whilst the Native Land Units and Reserves were black land. The two divisions received significantly different investments with white space the principal beneficiary. The black areas were further subdivided into tribal blocks with 'harmonious' groupings found together in the eight colonial Native Land Units. From west to east these were: the Kavirondo Native Land Unit, Nandi Native Land Unit, Lumbwa Native Land Unit, Kerio Native Land Unit, Masai Native Land Unit, Kikuyu Native Land Unit, Kamba Native Land Unit and Coast Native Land Unit. The tribal map of 1962 shows that the black areas were a mosaic of homogeneous zones where each tribe

dominated their space in percentages that usually exceeded 90% (Fox, 1991). The White Highlands and urban centres were more mixed but, again, there was usually one tribe dominating with percentages of from 50–74%.

Two processes were enacted in the period immediately preceding and following independence in 1963 which entrenched tribal distributions into the political and thence the development process. First, new boundaries were drawn up along tribal lines for the administrative districts of the country by a Regional Boundaries Commission (Forster-Sutton *et al.*, 1962). More than one tribe could be found in each of the administrative districts as long as their submissions to the Commission demonstrated that they wished to be together. Districts were further aggregated into Provinces where, again, there appeared to be compatibility. The 1992 constitutional amendments utilised the potential of this demarcation when coalitions were built across and within Provinces to win the multi-party Presidential election. Immediately following independence, the electoral significance of the administrative districts was that Senators were elected to represent each district in the short-lived upper chamber. Latterly, the administrative districts have become an important level for spatial planning. The District Focus policy has, in fact, ensured that development programmes must have tribal connotations.

Secondly, Kenya uses the first-past-the-post electoral system based upon electoral constituencies that were essentially drawn up along tribal and clan lines. Using a Geographic Information System, it is possible to overlay the 1962 tribal map and 1992 electoral constituencies. This procedure shows that only 23 of the 175 rural constituencies can be thought of as mixed in composition. Most of the 23 more mixed constituencies were in the former White Highlands, and they have

become more homogeneous since independence as resettlement schemes acted to extend tribal borders (Fox, 1991; Leo, 1984). The remaining 152 constituencies follow the tribal boundaries very closely.

The 1992 multi-party elections can be used to assess the electoral geography of Kenya and show where electoral support comes from, and thus where development programmes can be expected to flow to (Figures 5.16a and 5.16b). The politics of Kenya have been dominated by the ruling party, KANU (Kenya African National Union), since the 1960s when it was a coalition of Kikuyu and Luo. KADU (Kenya African Democratic Union) was the early opposition; a coalition of minor tribes such as the Kalenjin, Masai and Mijkenda. Ironically, KANU is currently dominated by President Moi's tribe, the Kalenjin, with many of his early KADU allies. It is pertinent that Arid and Semiarid lands have been stressed increasingly as the destination for development aid since President Moi came into power in 1978 (Adams, 1990), (Figure 5.16a) and this is the geographical area from which his 1992 support came.

Kenya's population is ethnically diverse. The 1979 census (Republic of Kenya, 1981) recorded 70% of the total population of 15 282 237 as belonging to the five major tribes: Kikuyu 3 200 967; Luhya 2 118 786; Luo 1 954 687; Kamba 1 723 734; and Kalenjin 1 651 939. The remaining 30% was split between a further 36 different tribes. Four of these tribes are non-Kenyan and three are non-African: Europeans, Asians and Arabs.

The parliamentary returns given in Table 5.16a show that KANU's support came overwhelmingly from the tribes of the Arid and Semiarid Districts. They were the Kalenjin group (the Nandi, Kipsigis, Elgeyo, Marakwet, Pokot, Sabaot, Tugen); the Eastern Nilotes (Masai, Samburu, Turkana,

Iteso); the Cushitic (Somali) and Eastern Cushitic tribes (Rendille, Boran, Gabbra, Sakuye, Orma); and certain Bantu tribes. The opposition parties gained almost all of their support from the tribes of the high agricultural potential areas and the urban centres. Thus support for the Democratic Party, FORD Asili and FORD Kenya came from the Kikuyu, Luo, Luhya, Kamba and Meru.

Only six tribes split their vote between KANU and the opposition parties: the Luhya, Kamba, Meru, Kisii, Samburu and Mbere. These tribes were geographically and numerically significant within the Provinces. The constitutional amendment referred to earlier said that the winner of the 1992 Presidential election had to have at least 25% of the vote in five of the eight Provinces and be in the arithmetic majority. The Luhya were thus very important in Western Province, Kamba, Meru and Mbere in Eastern Province, Kisii in Nyanza and Somali in North-Eastern Province.

Table 5.16b shows the very skewed voting patterns that arose in the presidential elections. President Moi was only strongly supported in three Provinces: Coast, North-Eastern and Rift Valley, but his support was sufficient among the Kamba of Eastern and Luhya of Western Province to give him the 25% necessary in five of the eight Provinces. If the FORD opposition party had remained united behind one leader it would have beaten President Moi nationally and taken five of the eight Provinces. Similarly, a Matiba/Kibaki Kikuyu coalition would have beaten President Moi. It can be appreciated, therefore, that place, tribe, politics, the electoral system and the constitution are enwrapped together in Kenya whether dealing with election of members of Parliament or the election of the President.

Table 5.16a 1992 Multi-party elections: tribal support (number of seats won) for political parties

Tribe	Kanu	Democratic Party	FORD Asili	FORD Kenya	Minor Parties
Kikuyu		12	18	1	
Kamba	12	4			
Meru	2	4		1	
Embu		1			
Tharaka		1			
Kisii	6	1		1	1
Luhya	8		7	6	
Luo				19	
Somali	8			1	1
Masai	6				
Samburu	2				
Turkana	3				
Iteso	1				
Rendille	2				
Boran	3				
Gabbra	1				
Orma	2				
Nandi	3				
Kipsigis	5				
Elgeyo	2				
Marakwet	3				
Pokot	4				
Sabaot	1				
Tugen	3				
Mijkenda	8				
Taita	3				
Bajun	1				
Kuria	1				
Mbere	1				1
Mixed: Kikuyu	6				
TOTAL	97	23	25	29	3

Source: author

Further reading

Adams, M.E. (1990), Slow progress with integrated rural development programmes in Kenya's Arid and Semiarid lands, *Land Degradation & Rehabilitation*, **2**: 285–299.

Forster-Sutton, S., Thornley, C.S. and Hyde-Clarke, M. (1962), *Report of the Regional Boundaries Commission*, London: HMSO (Cmnd 1899).

Fox, R.C. (1991), *Ethnic Distributions in Colonial and Postcolonial Kenya*, Pretoria: Human Sciences Research Council.

Leo, C. (1984), *Land and Class in Kenya*, Toronto: University of Toronto Press.

Republic of Kenya (1981), *Kenya Population Census 1979, Volume 1*, Nairobi: Central Bureau of Statistics.

Table 5.16b 1992 Multi-party elections: provincial voting (%) for main presidential candidates

Province	D.T. Moi (Kanu)	K. Matiba (FORD Asili)	M. Kibaki (DP)	O. Odinga (FORD Kenya)
Nairobi	16.1	44.1	18.6	20.2
Coast	64.1	11.4	7.6	16.1
North Eastern	78.1	10.1	4.5	7.1
Eastern	36.8	10.2	50.5	1.7
Central	2.1	60.1	36.1	1.0
Rift Valley	67.8	18.7	7.6	5.7
Western	40.9	36.3	3.6	17.9
Nyanza	14.4	3.3	6.4	76.7
NATIONAL	36.3	26.0	19.5	17.5

Source: author. Note: FORD = Forum for the Restoration of Democracy

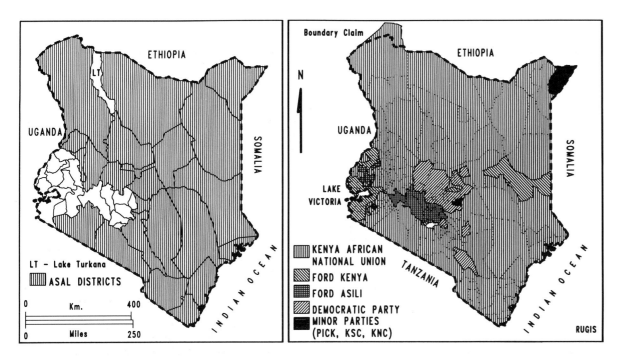

Figure 5.16a Kenya: Arid and Semiarid Administrative Districts

Figure 5.16b Kenya: Parliamentary returns (Rural Constituencies) Multi-Party Elections December 1992

5.17 SOUTH AFRICA: THE LEGACY OF APARTHEID
Roddy Fox

Figure 5.17a shows the political, administrative and development regions of South Africa as they were constituted before the Multi-Party Negotiating Forum sat in 1993 to draw up a new constitution and propose new regional boundaries. Apartheid, separate development, rigidly demarcated white space from black space; black space was further subdivided ethnically into the TBVC states, defined below, and self-governing territories shown in Figure 5.17a.

White South Africa was divided into four Provinces: Cape, Natal, Orange Free State, Transvaal. There were four quasi-independent black states (the TBVC states): Transkei, independent since 1976; Bophuthatswana since 1977; Venda since 1979; Ciskei since 1981. In addition to these were the self-governing territories that had a lesser degree of autonomy: Gazankulu, KaNgwane, KwaNdebele, KwaZulu, Lebowa, Qwaqwa. Generally speaking, the white areas contained the bulk of the natural resources although there were exceptions, such as the mineral (particularly platinum) deposits in Bophuthatswana and high potential agricultural land in Transkei and KwaZulu.

The nine development regions date from the Good Hope Conference of 1981. They aggregate together different black homelands with portions of the four Provinces. The development regions were used in the regional industrial decentralisation policy, which ensued following the Good Hope Conference, to allocate different levels of incentives to industrialists willing to locate or relocate in the peripheral areas of the regions. The most peripheral development regions, regions D,

E, G (Figure 5.17a) received the highest levels of incentives; within the regions themselves incentives were generally higher in the black homelands than in white South Africa. The spatial and organisational pattern resulting is clearly complex and is a reflection of the tortuous logic of apartheid that involved a constant dialectic between political/administrative separation and functional integration: between the locational, resource and infrastructural advantages of the white areas, and the political need to justify apartheid by attempting to foster development in the disadvantaged black periphery. The policies themselves have been assessed in detail by Fair (1982), Lemon (1976, 1987), Pickles (1988), Pickles and Weiner (1991), and Smith, D.M. (1982, 1985).

In the early 1980s Fair (1982) characterised South Africa's spatial system as:

(1) *The Core*, the major and minor metropoles in white South Africa;
(2) *The Inner Periphery*, the rest of white South Africa and the coloured and Asian areas;
(3) *The Outer Periphery*, the African homelands.

Figure 5.17b shows that these patterns were clearly discernible at the end of the 1980s on the three maps of regional contributions to Gross Geographical Product. In each case there were abrupt differences in economic performance, regardless of the economic sector concerned, between white and black space. Agricultural productivity was always lower in the black areas

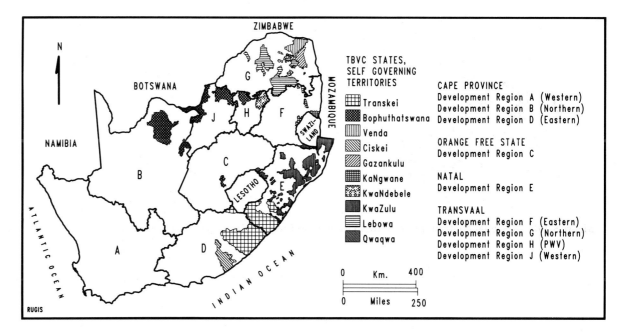

Figure 5.17a South Africa: political and administrative regions

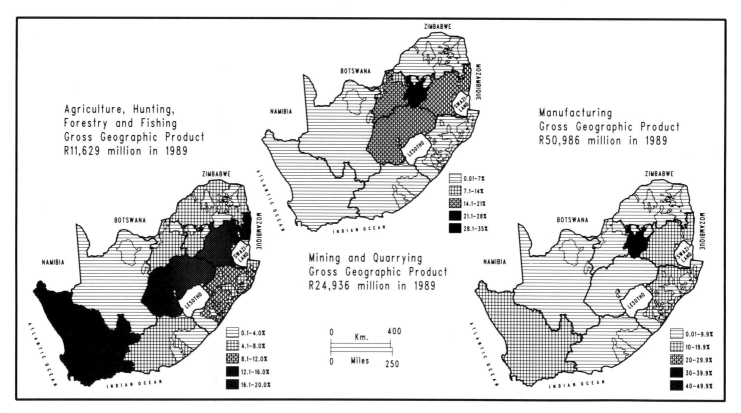

Figure 5.17b   Regional contribution to Gross Geographic Product, 1989: agriculture, hunting, forestry and fishing; mining and quarrying; and manufacturing.

of Development Regions C, D, E, F, G, H and J. Mining and Quarrying was different within Regions C, H and J; Manufacturing in Regions E, F and H. Clearly this is the reflection of the skewed allocation of these resources in the first place and then the distorted patterns of development that ensued under colonial, and later, apartheid rule.

Table 5.17 attempts to derive a composite development index for South Africa's development regions through calculating rankings from socio-economic indices. Each region is ranked from one (low score) to nine (high score) for each variable and the rankings added to get a composite index. The maximum that a region could score would be 63, a very high degree of development derived from scoring the maximum nine for every one of the seven indices, and the minimum would be seven.

A three tier geography appears from the aggregate rankings:

(1) The Core: Region H (PWV) ranked 57 and Region A (W. Cape) ranked 56.
(2) The Inner Periphery: Region F (E.Transvaal) 45, Region C (OFS) 36.5, Region J (W. Transvaal) 34.5, Region E (Natal) 31.5.
(3) The Outer Periphery: Region D (E. Cape) 20.5, Region B (N. Cape) 20, Region G (N. Transvaal) 12.

The regional scale used above is relevant to the perceptions employed in the current constitutional debates since both the African National Congress and the National Party (the two main players in the negotiating process) are proposing regions based on variations of the nine development regions. Future development policy and programmes will need to be framed to redress the imbalances both within, as seen in Figure 5.17b, and between, as seen in Table 5.17, the regions which are eventually delimited. The challenge is thus to overcome the striking spatial legacy of apartheid at these two different spatial scales.

Further reading

Fair, T.J.D. (1982), *South Africa: Spatial Frameworks for Development*, Cape Town: Juta.

Lemon, A. (1976), *Apartheid: a Geography of Separation*, Farnborough: Saxon House.

Lemon, A. (1987), *Apartheid in Transition*, Aldershot: Gower.

Pickles, J. (1988), Recent changes in regional policy in South Africa, *Geography*, **73**(3): 233–239.

Pickles, J. and Weiner, D. (1991), Rural and regional restructuring of Apartheid: ideology, development policy and the competition for space, *Antipode*, **23**(1): 2–32.

Smith, D.M. (ed.) (1982) *Living Under Apartheid: Aspects of Urbanization and Social Change in South Africa*, London: George Allen & Unwin.

Smith, D.M. (1985), *Apartheid in South Africa*, Cambridge: Cambridge University Press.

Table 5.17 Socio-economic indices, development regions 1989

Development Index	Development Region								
	A	B	C	D	E	F	G	H	J
Literacy rate (%)	81.3	59.0	70.2	65.5	68.4	65.2	61.2	78.8	67.5
Ranking	9	1	7	4	6	3	2	8	5
Unemployment rate (%)	9.6	14.5	11.1	25.0	18.7	8.7	16.7	13.6	14.7
Ranking	8	5	5	1	2	9	3	6	4
Dependency ratio	1.3	2.4	1.6	3.1	2.8	1.6	4.8	1.1	1.9
Ranking	8	4	6.5	2	3	6.5	1	9	5
Nominal GGP (Rm)	26 788	3947	12 939	14 644	30 505	19 366	6246	80 295	12 219
Ranking	7	1	4	5	8	6	2	9	3
Nominal GGP/capita (R)	7629	3585	4918	3116	3554	9835	1461	9424	6830
Ranking	7	4	5	2	3	9	1	8	6
Personal income/capita (R)	4343	1984	2184	1630	1737	2347	725	4558	2166
Ranking	8	4	6	2	3	7	1	9	5
Life expectancy	65.5	62.6	63.2	63.7	63.8	63.7	62.9	64.7	63.8
Ranking	9	1	3	4.5	6.5	4.5	2	8	6.5
Sum of ranks	56	20	36.5	20.5	31.5	45	12	57	34.5

Source: Erasmus, J. *et al.* (1991), *South Africa: An Inter-Regional Profile*, Midrand: Development Bank of Southern Africa

6 Images, Religion and Language: the Ideological Structure of Development

TIM UNWIN

Political, social and economic relationships are frequently legitimated through reference to particular ideologies. The final chapter of this atlas therefore explores a range of different ideological aspects of development, ranging from religion and language to the places that people imbue with specific status. It begins with two sections concerned with images of development. These illustrate how cartography can be used to propagate particular messages, as well as the way in which maps have been used as political graphics. Section 6.3 then addresses the issue of underdevelopment in the developed world, through an analysis of the exploitation of Australia's Aborigine population.

The next four sections explore linguistic and religious diversity at both global and regional scales, with the latter examples being drawn from the highly complex cultural environment of India. These reflect the great contrasts in belief systems and the diversity of languages that must be taken into consideration in the formulation of any development policies that are to be of lasting success. The role of non-government organisations in the provision of aid is then examined both at a global scale and then through the operation of a single charity, Christian Aid, again in the context of India. The reasons why people support such charities, most of which are based in the richer countries of the world, are complex, but reflect a range of ideological positions and belief systems. Frequently, though, the work of such charities is designed specifically to benefit the poor, and those for whom inter-government aid is often of less direct benefit.

The final sections of the atlas reflect three further very different aspects of the ideology of development. Section 6.10 thus explores the introduction of Ujamaa Villages in Tanzania in the late 1960s, as an expression of a particular ideology designed to create rural communities in which people could live and work together for the good of all. Section 6.11 examines the character of urban form resulting in South Africa from the imposition of apartheid ideology, and Section 6.12 surveys the processes giving rise to the recognition of World Heritage Sites, emphasising that such specification frequently derives from an elite definition of landscape and heritage.

6.1 PROPAGATION OF THE MESSAGE: PERSUASIVE CARTOGRAPHY

Peter Vujakovic

Maps are used by many nations as vehicles for propaganda and are to be found in numerous forms, from national atlases to postage stamps. National atlases are produced by governmental or public agencies as works of national significance. Parry (1987) estimates that some 64 were in print in 1986. Of 37 new national atlases published since 1979, 25 were from developing areas. The importance of national atlases to developing nations may have its roots in periods of colonisation, when European states used '... maps as an intellectual tool for legitimising territorial conquest ... and cultural imperialism' (Monmonier, 1991: 90). Atlases represent an important means by which governments disseminate information for education, and the management of natural resources and the economy, as well as acting as cultural ambassadors. However, they are also used to propagate and maintain specific ideologies of nationhood; often concealed behind the supposed neutrality and scientism of cartography. Cartographic 'silences' are often used to cloak subjects officially perceived as threatening or negative, as exemplified by the omission or downgrading of '... Black (African) settlements whether large or small, formal or informal ...' on South African maps (Stickler, 1990: 329).

The production of national atlases by developing countries is often affected by the paucity of statistical information. Where atlases have been published, they are generally in a single language and are often in the tongue of a former colonial power. Kent (1986) notes that a single language may be used to emphasise national unity and to diminish ethnic differences; however, this can also be seen as a mechanism for controlling access to information, and reinforcing the position of elites.

Persuasive cartography is frequently used to define national identity and territorial integrity. Newly independent states have often used maps on stamps and bank notes as a means of inculcating feelings of national pride and unity, while proclaiming their status to a large international audience. A classic example is the stamp issued by the small African republic of Rwanda to celebrate independence in 1962; Rwanda is shown in its approximate geographical location, but at about ten times its true size relative to the rest of Africa.

Territorial claims and defence of territory can be strengthened. Thus, the threat of Arab aggression is suggested by a cartogram (Figure 6.1) published by the Israeli Ministry of Foreign Affairs (1985), which purports to show the population of Israel and the Arab states, although no scale is used and the Arab population is exaggerated by almost 400%. The deception is disguised by diminishing some Arab populations in relation to Israel, while inflating others. Hence it could be claimed that a true comparison was not intended.

Territorial disputes are often fought through 'map wars'. Examples have included India and Pakistan's claims for Jammu and Kashmir, and a number of Latin American border conflicts (Monmonier, 1991). British, Argentinian and Chilean disputes over Antarctica and various South Atlantic islands, and their strategic resources, have involved long term propaganda wars. Atlases have been used to strengthen claims; for example, Chile does not record any

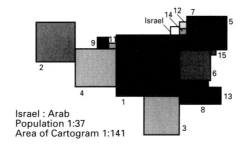

'Israel and the Arab States : Population'- redrawn from 'Facts About Israel' (not to scale)

Israel : Arab
Population 1:37
Area of Cartogram 1:141

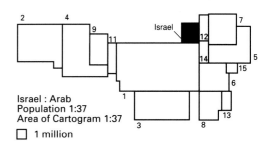

'Israel and the Arab States : Population'- drawn to a standard scale

Israel : Arab
Population 1:37
Area of Cartogram 1:37

☐ 1 million

Population 1985

1 Egypt	44, 670, 000	6 Saudi Arabia	9, 680, 000	11 Libya	3, 220, 000
2 Morocco	20, 650, 000	7 Syria	9, 600, 000	12 Lebanon	2, 740, 000
3 Sudan	18, 900, 000	8 Yemen	7, 160, 000	13 South Yemen	2, 090, 000
4 Algeria	18, 670, 000	9 Tunisia	6, 730, 000	14 Jordan	2, 420, 000
5 Iraq	12, 000, 000	10 Israel	4, 300, 000	15 U A E	1, 180, 000

Figure 6.1 Propaganda cartography: Israeli and Arab populations

Antarctic bases other than its own, while Argentina refers to other bases as *bases extranjeras* (foreign bases). Each state attempts to legitimise its claim by using its own names for geographical features. Hence, the peninsula named 'Graham Land' by Britain is shown in Argentinian atlases as 'Tierra de San Martin', and as 'Tierra de O'Higgins' by Chile. Since the 1930s these 'wars' have also been fought through the medium of postage stamps. Both Britain and Argentina have issued stamps showing the Falkland Islands/ Malvinas as their own; for example, Argentina issued a stamp in 1983 inscribed *1982-2-April-1983 First recovery of Malvinas, S.Georgia and S.Sandwich Is.* (Davis, 1985), with the clear message that it is only the first attempt at recovery.

Further reading

Monmonier, M. (1991), *How to Lie With Maps*, Chicago: University of Chicago Press.
Davis, B. (1985), Maps on postage stamps as propaganda, *The Cartographic Journal*, **22**: 125–130.

6.2 IMAGES OF DEVELOPMENT: MAPS AND POLITICAL GRAPHICS
Peter Vujakovic

Political graphics containing maps are a significant form of geographical propaganda. They influence our perception of developing nations in many ways; through the creation of stereotypes, to the subversion of dominant ideologies. However, as 'texts' they are 'unstable', dependent on the interpretation made of them by different readers (Duncan and Barnes, 1992). Political graphics take numerous forms, from posters to satirical cartoons. They are considered to be easily comprehended, which is seen as an advantage to propagandists who wish to influence or educate populations with low literacy levels. However, alternative 'readings' can undermine the intended message.

While persuasive or propaganda cartography often serves to legitimise goals of the state, maps in satirical graphics have frequently been used to subvert and to challenge official versions of 'reality'. For instance, Regan *et al.* (1988: 52–55) provide examples of the use of maps to satirise US obsession with left-wing takeovers in Latin America. The uses of maps in political graphics fall into several broad categories: identifying the arena of action, as surrogate or metaphor for the 'real world', and maps as nations personified, or as national icons (Vujakovic, 1990). Examples incorporating some of these aspects are shown in Figure 6.2a and Figure 6.2b.

The use of maps allows identification of people with the land. This has been particularly evident in graphics concerned with Africa, for example, Karakashev's poster *Let Not the Dawn of Liberty Fail!*, supporting African struggles for independence in the 1960s; this Soviet poster superimposes a black African face on the continent (above broken chains). A more recent example by the cartoonist Nasser (Egypt) simply shows Africa as a head demanding 'water!'.

Many instances exist of maps as metaphors for nations or peoples. One much used device, dating to the last century, shows a map being cut or torn apart to represent political separation or national conflict. A similar device is used by Vujakovic (UK) to lampoon Saddam Hussein's attempt to destroy Kuwait's national identity and incorporate it into Iraq as its '19th province' (Figure 6.2a) (Iraqi propaganda during the Gulf War included requisite changes to official maps of Iraq!).

Another potent use of maps is to satirise the relationship between nations of the developed and the developing worlds. Batellier (France) successfully subverts US iconography in a cartoon produced in 1975. He shows the stripes of the US flag as a series of parallel red carpets, while the blue field on which the stars are displayed is the map of America. Representatives of various developing nations are seen to be rolling up the red carpets, indicating that US interference is

Figure 6.2a Maps in political graphics: the Iraqi invasion of Kuwait

Figure 6.2b The European Community: the accession of Spain and Portugal

countries as backward or less developed is reinforced.

Further reading

Regan, C., Sinclair, S. and Turner, M. (1988), *Thin Black Lines: Political Cartoons and Development Education*, Birmingham: Development Education Centre.

unwelcome (one individual is clearly a Vietnamese soldier). Not all cartoons are sympathetic to developing areas. As political propaganda they are also used to attack developments which may appear as potentially harmful to the developed world, hence Garner's (USA) 1980 cartoon of an Arab (representing OPEC) literally 'milking the globe' of oil dollars (Regan *et al.*, 1988: 34).

The problem of the instability of such texts is indicated by an example from Europe (Figure 6.2b). An illustration (using anthropomorphised maps) to accompany European Commission (1986) material on Spanish and Portuguese entry to the Community appears to show the Iberian countries as inferior in status to the original ten. The Iberian states are represented as a diminutive, rounded figure gazing up, child-like, at a tall, refined individual created from the map of the other member states. The effect is one of condescension. It is very unlikely that such a 'message' was intentional, but the maintenance of a stereotype image of these southern European

6.3 UNDERDEVELOPMENT WITHIN THE DEVELOPED WORLD
David Drakakis-Smith

Underdevelopment within developed countries can take a variety of forms: sometimes spatial, with regional disparities; sometimes social, with class, gender or ethnic disparities in the development process. Moreover, the transfer of value implicit in the process of underdevelopment may accrue either to domestic or to international capital. Often a complex combination of the above occurs and the nature of underdevelopment can vary enormously.

Many developed countries contain cultural contrasts but not all of these have unequal access to power resulting in discriminatory development. With the regrowth of nationalistic movements in Europe many of the pre-industrial cultural groups are seeking to re-establish their national identity. This has most rapidly occurred in eastern Europe but in the European Community too there are discontented groups, such as the Basques or Walloons, agitating for greater independence.

But do these instances constitute examples of underdevelopment, where culture and geography fuse into regionally specific exploitation of one group by another? Some have argued (Drakakis-Smith and Williams, 1983) that real underdevelopment in developed countries needs also to contain that contrast in modes of production which allegedly characterises the underdevelopment process in the Third World. Such situations, where they exist, have been cited as examples of internal colonialism (Hechter, 1983). The best known examples relate probably to the exploitation of North American Native Peoples but there are others and the remainder of this section concentrates on one of these, namely the case of Australian Aborigines.

Australia's 250 000 Aborigines account for only about 1.5% of its total population and yet in large areas of the centre and the north they constitute a substantial proportion of the population (Figure 6.3). Although they had inhabited a harsh continent for some 40 000 years, living in a harmonious spiritual and physical balance with the environment, Australian Aborigines were denied any treaty by the invading British. The following 200 years saw a savage lack of concern for the welfare of Aborigines resulting in a decline of their numbers from an estimated 400 000 to less than 100 000 by 1901.

In spite of this situation Aborigines and their land have been crucial to the economy of central and north Australia and continue to retain this role today. Aboriginal land, taken without treaty, forms the basis of the pastoral industry of Tropical Australia, and Aboriginal labour, both male and female, has been indispensable to the development of this activity. As in South Africa this labour exploitation had a spatial context, Aborigines being reared and conserved on government and mission reserves and then recruited on labour contracts for distant properties.

In recent years, the situation seems to have improved drastically for Aborigines. From the late 1960s, for example, they received equal pay and eligibility for unemployment and pension benefits. The result was twofold: an increase in the number of Aboriginal redundancies and the creation of a large cash economy in Tropical Australia. The black cash economy is the basis for the survival of most white businesses in this part of Australia, underpinning urban economies by up to 70% (Ross and Drakakis-Smith, 1983). In addition, exploitation of Aboriginal collective consumption through the delivery of various welfare programmes and the use of the Aboriginal cultural tradition to attract tourists to the region both add up to massive and continuing exploitation of Aboriginal people in central and northern Australia. In short, their land, labour, culture and consumption underpins much of the local economy.

What do Aborigines receive in return? The response must be 'very little', for Aborigines constitute the most underprivileged group in Australia (Table 6.3). This exploitation can surely be said to constitute an example of internal colonialism; cultural underdevelopment in one of the world's most advanced economies. Although the situation is improving, it remains a little publicised but substantial blemish on the youthful face Australia presents to the world.

Further reading

Antipode (1984), Special issue: The Fourth World: a geography of indigenous struggles, *Antipode*, **16**(2).

Drakakis-Smith, D.W. (1984), Underdevelopment in the tropics: the case of North Australia, *Singapore Journal of Tropical Geography*, **5**(2): 125–139.

Howitt, R. (1990), A different Kimberley: Aboriginal marginalization and the Argyle diamond mine, *Geography*, **74**(3): 232–238.

Johnston, R.J. (1987), The minority problem in a multicultural world. *Geography Review*, September: 23–28.

Table 6.3 Selected ratios for Aboriginal/non-Aboriginal populations

Death rate from circulatory diseases	2:1
General mortality rate	3:1
Unemployment	4:1
Owning businesses	1:5
Reliant on state benefits	6:1
Formal educational qualifications (15 years and over)	1:15
Imprisonment	27:1

Source: Tickner (1991)

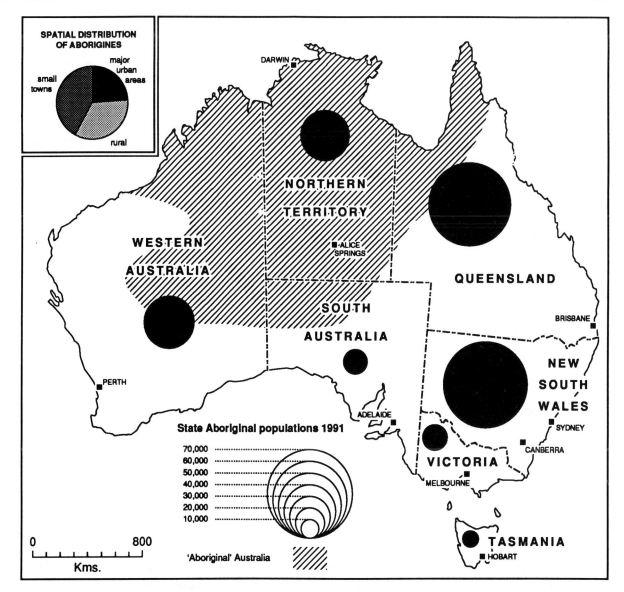

Figure 6.3 Aboriginal populations in Australia

6.4 GLOBAL LANGUAGE DIVERSITY
Colin Williams

Today, as ever, language is power: the power to communicate, to inform, to entertain, to control, to socialise, to unite, to separate, to privilege and to deny.

The essential feature of global language divisions is their unevenness and inequality. At least 6170 living languages, exclusive of dialects, have to be accommodated in only 185 or so sovereign states and territories. Because the modern bureaucratic-territorial state operates effectively in only a few standard languages, most of the languages of the world are not official state languages and thus do not appear in Figure 6.4. Although the sovereign state may be functionally multilingual (Cameroon, for example, contains over 170 living languages but only two official languages), interaction with its citizens is undertaken in only a few, and in most cases, in a single language, conferring additional power, status and influence on that official tongue.

Official status is a major determinant of the vitality of language maintenance and spread. Table 6.4 indicates the rank order of the seven major international languages. Geolinguists suggest that languages having an international status can be functional on a number of different levels and are international because: '(1) they are used in a number of countries as mother tongues by a substantial proportion of the population (basic role); (2) they are used widely in a number of countries as auxiliary languages in formal and semi-formal settings (subsidiary role); (3) they are used in a number of countries as the principal, second "foreign" language taught (restricted formal mode)' (McConnell, 1991: 81).

Mandarin is the world-dominant language in terms of its total number of speakers, but only English and French fulfil all three roles, and thus English is the true lingua franca of the modern world system. In comparison with the seven international languages listed in Table 6.4, Bengali, Russian and Hindi, though demographically strong, with 150 million, 160 million and 400 million respectively, are restricted in terms of the number of countries in which they are the mother tongue.

Language spread is of course closely associated with conquest, religious diffusion and colonialism. More than half of the states have either French, English or Spanish as an official language. Former imperial languages are now perceived as being ideologically neutral because of their communicative dynamism and their promise of accessibility to a wider world of ideas, commerce and leisure. But in addition to being complex and diverse, the world language situation is also unstable.

If, in the past, colonial politics and state-building have privileged 75 major state languages (fourteen in the former Soviet Union, the fourteen constitutional languages of India, 30 European, 40 Asian and 5 African), today demography strengthens regional link-languages such as Arabic in the 22 countries of the Arab league (172 million), Hindi and Urdu in the Indo-Pakistani complex (780 million), Malay-Indonesian (with 166 million speakers) and Swahili in the six East African states (130 million) (Breton, 1991: 129).

As with many other elements of the development process, data on spoken, read and written languages are notoriously unreliable or unavailable. In part this is due to the familiar difficulty of enumerating a state's population in many parts of the world, but it is also often a deliberate ploy of state language policy. Communicative competence is far more than a functional requirement of the modern state; it can also be a symbol and instrument of nation-state building where degrees

Table 6.4 Global languages ranked in importance

International languages	Basic role		Subsidiary role		Restricted formal role	
	Number of countries	Population (millions)	Number of countries	Population (millions)	Number of countries	Population (millions) 1970s/1980s
Chinese (Mandarin)*	2	670	2	18.2	—	—
English	9	299.7	69	147.9	69	65.1/118.5
Spanish	21	250.9	2	0.4	—	—
Portuguese	2	141.4	6	1.1	—	—
Arabic	21	134.4	3	3.4	—	—
German	7	86.1	0	0	—	—
French	5	60.3	38	38.5	38	14.7/36.3

Source: derived from McConnell (1991)
* Note: Mandarin is not counted as a mother tongue for dialect speakers of Chinese

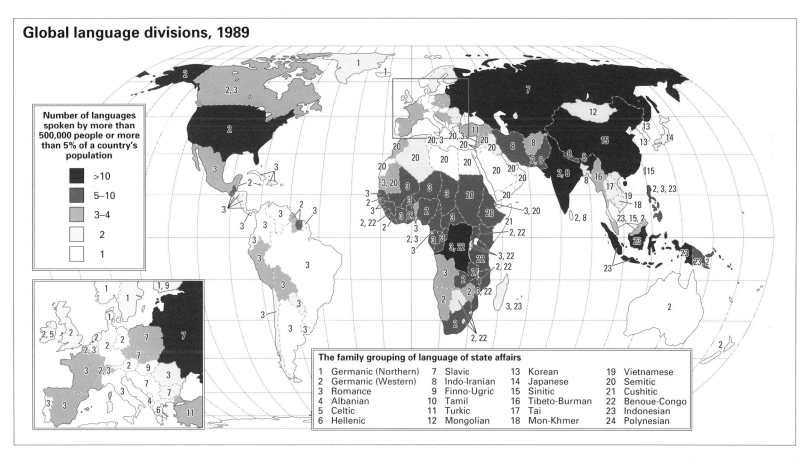

Figure 6.4 Global language divisions, 1989

of official uni- or bi-lingualism are interpreted as an indicator of state integrity and stability. Thus newly-emergent states are especially prone to downplay an increase in language diversity, to ignore selected language categories on census surveys, consciously to conflate into one meta-language group a number of diverse and distinct languages. Hindi, India's co-official language with English, and the only mass language able to claim Pan-Indian allegiance, has been particularly subject to such political manipulation since independence in 1947. As part of the centralising strategy of successive Indian governments separate languages such as Maithili and Bhojpuri have been marginalised and often included within the Hindi category (McConnell, 1991: 43).

In addition to government backing in spheres such as education, mass literacy programmes, the military, public services, media communications, the law and commerce, official languages can be boosted by whether or not they coincide with a religious function. Arabic, because of its diglossic situation (archaic but standardised literary form versus a fragmented spoken dialect situation), is a most important international language because of its integral affiliation with Islam. Indeed much of the early impetus for language standardisation, let alone the zeal for witness and conversion, came from the religious impulses of Christianity, Islam, Hinduism and Buddhism. In a very real way the current distribution of the world's official languages owes more to religiously-justified territorial conquest than it does to any other single contributory factor. Consequently, one should cross-reference Figure 6.4 with the ideological and religious divisions in this section for a more complete picture of the meaning which speaking, reading, or writing various languages may have in multilingual societies. The vast majority of the world's population is bi- or tri-lingual and often

specific languages are reserved for separate aspects of daily life such as family interaction, worship, commerce and officialdom. Code-switching by domain is a norm for many people; Figure 6.4 merely shows the official imprimatur of the state, which for many may be severely at odds with their daily, lived experience. Thus what is often referred to as 'language conflict' within multilingual societies is a shorthand for a much larger reality, namely inter-group competition for resources, for rights in education, religion, for participation, and for recognition. No wonder, then, that in the evolving state system of the past century, strident appeals to language defence and to ethno-linguistic unification have been so present in virtually all cases of national self-determination. And on independence itself, how often has the national language question generated a further round of conflict, mass violence and persistent negotiation as to who may legitimately speak which language(s) to whom and when! (Williams, 1988).

The abiding feature of the current linguistic scene is the increasing ability of selected global languages such as English, French, Spanish and Japanese to transcend traditional state boundaries and social functions and to appeal directly to more and more people in such diverse fields as science, mass entertainment, sport, technology and administration. As a few languages grow and spread, they pose a challenge to the hundreds of minority languages they threaten to displace (Williams, 1991). Multilingual proliferation does not necessarily involve the protection of threatened ethnolinguistic groups and those without a written, codified standardised form are most at risk of extinction in this forever-changing world. Nation may speak unto nation but in fewer and fewer tongues.

Further reading

Breton, R.J.L. (1991), *Geolinguistics: Language Dynamics and Ethnolinguistic Geography*, Ottawa: University of Ottawa Press.
McConnell, G. (1991), *A Macro-Sociolinguistic Analysis of Language Vitality*, Quebec: Les Presses de l'Université Laval.
Williams, C.H. (ed.) (1988), *Language in Geographic Context*, Clevedon: Multilingual Matters.
Williams, C.H. (ed.) (1991), *Linguistic Minorities: Society and Territory*, Clevedon: Multilingual Matters.

6.5 NATIONAL LANGUAGE DIVERSITY: INDIA
Robert W. Bradnock

India's linguistic diversity matches its sub-continental geographical scale (Figure 6.5). Although there are over 700 languages, the top 10 account for approximately 90% of the population. Given India's ancient but continuous cultural history and development, in which the classical language of Sanskrit was dominant, it is striking that most living Indian languages do not pre-date the 11th century.

Indian languages belong unequally to two language families. In the north Indo-Aryan languages, the easternmost of the Indo-European group, were brought in their earliest form by the waves of Indo-Aryan migrants who penetrated India from the north-west. They came to dominate the northern plains of the Indus and Ganges rivers. Indo-Aryan migrants encountered people whose speech belonged to the second and wholly distinct language family, the Dravidian group. These were gradually pushed southwards into peninsular India, and Dravidian languages are now confined almost exclusively to the four southern states, the exception of Brahui being found in Pakistan.

Indo-Aryan languages   Sanskrit evolved from the early Indo-Aryan languages of the 15th century BC into the classical form expressed in Pannini's grammar a thousand years later. The language of the Vedas, India's oldest religious literature, Sanskrit remained current among the educated until about AD 1000. Prakrit, a related Indo-Aryan language, had a number of regional forms, among them Pali. Dating from around the 4th century BC, Pali became the language of Buddhist scriptures and a major influence on south and south-east Asian Buddhism. Later, Persian was introduced as the language of Muslim consorts, and Hindi (spoken by over 300 million people) and Urdu (45 million in India) resulted from the fusion of the earlier Indo-Aryan language with later Persian influences. During the 19th century the hybrid language became known as Hindustani, which remains the lingua franca for much of north India. Locally, there are many related dialects, which shade into discrete languages on the margins of the northern Hindi heartland. The most important of these is Bengali, now known as Bangla in neighbouring Bangladesh, and spoken by a total of over 160 million people. One of the great languages of modern Indian literature, Bengali is closely related to Assamese (18 million) to the north and Oriya (28 million) to the south. Marathi (60 million) and Gujarati (40 million) lie to the south and south-west, while Panjabi (22 million) stretches across into Pakistan.

Dravidian languages   The oldest of the modern Dravidian languages is Tamil (55 million). With a classical literature dating from the early centuries AD, Tamil was the Indian language least influenced by Sanskrit. After the reorganisation of India's states on a predominantly linguistic basis from 1953, each Dravidian language has been dominant in its own state: Tamil in Tamil Nadu, Telugu in Andhra Pradesh (66 million), Kannada in Karnataka (342 million) and Malayalam in Kerala (30 million). While Telugu and Kannada took shape around AD 1000, Malayalam developed from its status as a Tamil dialect as late as the 14th century.

Scripts   The Emperor Ashoka's monumental inscriptions, dating from the 3rd century BC and written in the Brahmi script, are the earliest recorded writing directly linked to scripts in current use. Written from left to right and with the principle of having a separate symbol to represent each sound Brahmi was used with only minor modifications for both Indo-Aryan and Dravidian languages. It was the basis for the eleven indigenous scripts still in use across India. The most important is the Devanagari ('the script of the city of the gods'), used for Hindi and several related languages. Apart from the Roman script used for English, the most important exogenous script is the Perso-Arabic used for Urdu.

Further reading

Burrow, T. (1975), Ancient and modern languages, in: Basham, A.L. (ed.), *A Cultural History of India*, Delhi: Oxford University Press, 162–169.

Robinson, F. (ed.) (1989), *The Cambridge Encyclopedia of India, Pakistan, Bangladesh, Sri Lanka, Nepal, Bhutan and the Maldives*, Cambridge: Cambridge University Press.

Shackle, C. (ed.) (1985), *South Asian Languages: a Handbook*, London: School of Oriental and African Studies.

Schwartzberg, J.E. (1993), *An Historical Atlas of South Asia*, Chicago: Chicago University Press, 2nd ed.

Zograph, G.A. (1982), *Languages of South Asia: a Guide*, London: Routledge and Kegan Paul.

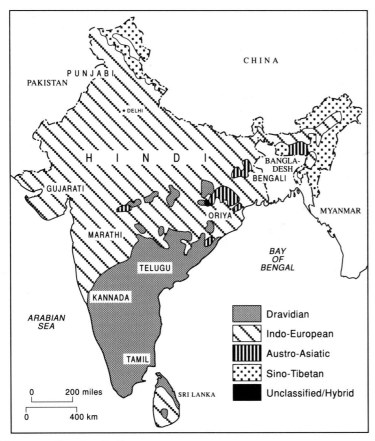

Figure 6.5 National language diversity: India

6.6 GLOBAL RELIGIONS
Jørgen S. Nielsen

The religious adherence of human communities is one which has regularly in history been a dimension of serious conflicts as well as of great moments in civilisation. Unfortunately, it is the conflicts which are more often remembered by the communities themselves. As the Cold War has ended, so the scope for local and regional tensions has resurfaced, and with that the role of religion as a factor in public and communal life. One need only refer to the Lebanese civil war, the rise of Hindu nationalism in India, the ethno-religious dimensions of relations among the states of the former Soviet Union and, of course, the conflicts in former Yugoslavia to underline the point.

It is hardly possible to show such dimensions on a small map of the distribution of the religions of the world. What Figure 6.6 can show, however, is the geographical areas in which the main religions find their popular, and thence often their cultural and potentially political base. Thus post-Cold War rhetoric on the part of both western and Muslim commentators about a new clash of civilisations may see possible geographical flash points on this map, as may centuries of mistrust between western and eastern Christianity.

It remains a fact that minority-majority situations cannot be shown on this map. A more detailed presentation of the complicated religious map of the Balkans would, in fairness, for example, have to be matched by ones for areas such as the countries bordering the eastern Mediterranean, those across the immediate sub-Saharan parts of Africa, parts of India and of south-east Asia. As one instance of this complexity, the distribution of different religious groupings in south Asia is illustrated in Section 6.7.

Further reading

Barrett, D. (1982), *World Christian Encyclopedia*, Oxford: Oxford University Press.

The Economist (1990), *The Economist Book of Vital World Statistics*, London: Hutchinson.

Mews, S. (ed.) (1989), *Religion in Politics: a World Guide*, London: Longman.

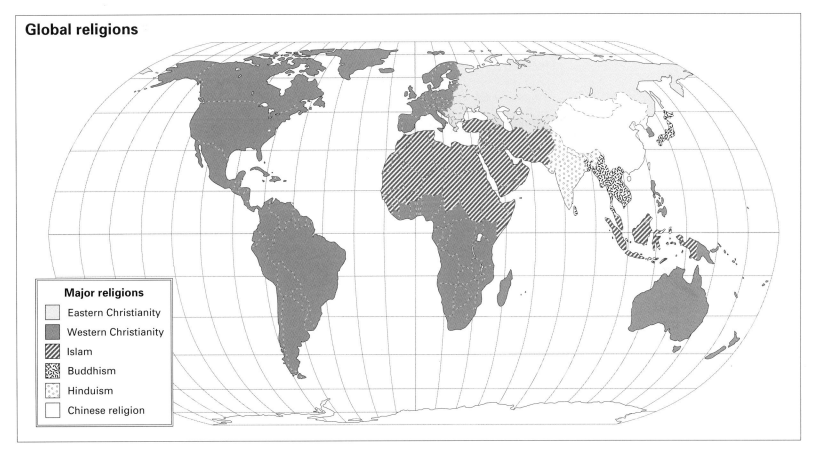

Figure 6.6 Global religions

6.7 REGIONAL RELIGIOUS DIVERSITY IN SOUTH ASIA
Robert W. Bradnock

South Asia is home to adherents of four of the world's major religions, Hinduism, Islam, Christianity and Buddhism, and to important regional religions, including Sikhism and Jainism (Figure 6.7). There are also very small communities of Jews and Zoroastrians, the latter originating in Persia but now found largely in India.

Hinduism, Sikhism, Buddhism and Jainism all originated within south Asia, while the distribution of Islam and Christianity reflects their external origin and relations. Alongside the religions which have formal structures of theistic belief (Islam, Christianity or Sikhism), or philosophical doctrine and social practice (Hinduism, Buddhism and Jainism), south Asia has millions of tribal peoples, some of whom remain animists.

Hinduism Indo-Aryans spread east and south across the sub-continent from the 15th century BC. Their orally transmitted hymns, finally written down as the Vedas by the 6th century BC, laid the basis for *Brahmanism*, the ancestor of modern Hinduism. The epic poems the *Mahabharata* and the *Ramayana* (8th–6th centuries BC) remain a living part of Hindu tradition.

Modern Hinduism has no creed or universal framework of beliefs, though core concepts such as *dharma* ('duty') and *karma* ('the effect of former actions') are widespread. Some Hindu philosophers stress an ultimate belief in one God, but popular Hinduism has many deities. Rivers and mountains are particularly sacred, and pilgrimage to holy places is central to Hindu worship. Hindu society, nominally conceived of as having four groups or *varna* (literally 'colour') is in practice divided into many regional and social sub-groups (*jati*, sometimes loosely translated as 'caste').

Islam Islam was brought to Sind by Arab navies in 711–12 AD. Arab traders made contact with south India and Sri Lanka, but the main expansion of Islam took place after the Turkish Afghan conquest of the Delhi region in 1192. Islamic cultural influence spread through the influence of a succession of Mughal rulers, from 1526 to 1707, though Muslims remained in a minority except in the north-west and north-east. Demands for a state for Muslims before Independence (1947) led to the creation of Pakistan. Up to 15 million Hindus, Muslims and Sikhs fled their homes and one million people were massacred. In 1991, 115 million of south Asia's Muslims lived in Pakistan, 105 million in Bangladesh and 100 million in India. Sunni Muslims are in the overwhelming majority throughout south Asia, though there are important Shi'i communities in Pakistan.

Minority religions

Buddhism and Jainism Siddharta Gautama, the Buddha (b. 563 BC) and Mahavir (b. 599 BC), the founders of Buddhism and Jainism respectively, were born within 100 km of each other to the north of Patna. While Jainism never became widely popular, Buddhism was spread across south Asia by the first great Indian Emperor, Asoka (r. 272–32 BC), himself a convert. Gradually absorbed on the Indian mainland by resurgent Hinduism, today Buddhism remains the dominant religion in Sri Lanka and important in Nepal and the Himalayan margins. Large-scale recent conversions of outcaste Hindus have swelled their numbers in India since the 1950s.

Christianity The third largest religious community, some of south Asia's Christians trace their origin to the arrival of St Thomas the Apostle in south India in AD 52. Most numerous in the south, south Asia's Christians today are roughly equally Protestant and Catholic.

Sikhs Founded by Guru Nanak (1469–1539), Sikhism developed on the Punjab plains of north India. With a belief in one God and a strong opposition to caste discrimination, Sikhs retain important aspects of Hindu philosophy. Partition led to the flight of Sikhs from Pakistan to India, and today the population is overwhelmingly concentrated in Punjab and neighbouring states.

Further reading

Brass, P.R. (1989), Politics in India, in: Robinson, F. (ed.) (1989), *The Cambridge Encyclopedia of India, Pakistan, Bangladesh, Sri Lanka, Nepal, Bhutan and the Maldives*, Cambridge: Cambridge University Press, 168–201.

Brass, P.R. (1990), *The Government and Politics of India*, Cambridge: Cambridge University Press.

Butler, D., Lahiri, A. and Roy, P. (1989), *India Decides: Indian Elections 1952–1989*, New Delhi: U.M. Books.

Hardgrave, R.L. and Kochanek, S. (1986), *India: Government and Politics in a Developing Nation*, Princeton: Princeton University Press, 4th ed.

Kohli, A. (1990), *Democracy and Discontent: India's Growing Crisis of Governability*, Princeton: Princeton University Press.

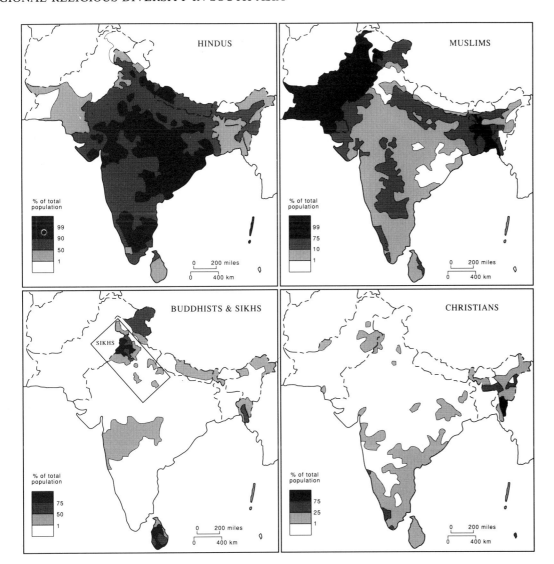

Figure 6.7 Regional religious diversity in south Asia

6.8 VOLUNTARY AID AGENCIES IN DEVELOPMENT

Martin Cottingham

A growing proportion of aid to developing countries is being channelled through non-government organisations (NGOs) as donor governments recognise the potential of small community projects to reach the poorest people. NGOs often have unrivalled access to local communities and the ability to support them directly and flexibly in ways which governments cannot.

The NGOs involved in Third World development fall into two main categories: indigenous groups set up in developing countries to tackle poverty locally, and organisations founded in industrialised countries to channel funds overseas. They range from vast international networks, such as the Red Cross and Red Crescent, to small projects providing a health clinic or school in a single Third World community.

Most of the biggest NGOs are in richer countries, where money is raised through a combination of public appeals and regular voluntary donations, reinforced by grants from government. In the United Kingdom two of the five biggest charities are overseas aid agencies. Aid through voluntary organisations in the United Kingdom amounted to £215 million in 1991, equivalent to over a tenth of the value of the British government's aid programme.

Church-based aid agencies such as Bread for the World (Germany), Catholic Relief Services (USA) and Christian Aid (United Kingdom) are among the longest established NGOs. Christian Aid, for example, set up in 1944 to help refugees in Europe in the wake of the Second World War, raised over £45 million in 1992/93 and now funds about 900 projects in 70 countries (Figure 6.8).

Most of its support comes from churchgoers, but its overseas work reaches well beyond church groups to support poor communities wherever the need is greatest, regardless of race or religion.

Like most European NGOs, Christian Aid spends the bulk of its income (44% in 1992/93) on long-term development work in the world's poorest nations. It funds agricultural support and technical training, primary health care, non-formal education, clean water initiatives and community organisation, helping poor families to increase their incomes and gain more control over their lives.

The emphasis is on strengthening the poor towards self-reliance by funding programmes devised and run by poor communities themselves. Many NGOs have learned the lessons of the 1960s and 1970s, when water pumps stood idle for want of locally available parts and expertise, and have adopted a more participatory approach. Local volunteers are trained for tasks as varied as teaching, pump maintenance and midwifery. Initial financial support is often provided in the form of low-interest or interest-free loans which are repaid at harvest time with a view to the funding agency's eventual withdrawal.

Besides these long-term projects, Christian Aid spent 31% of its 1992/93 income on emergencies and refugees, funding relief and rehabilitation for the victims of famine, war, ethnic conflict and natural disasters. In both relief and development the charity operates by funding local groups, employing no staff from the UK in developing countries.

The third broad area of Christian Aid's work is in campaigning, lobbying and education work in the UK (8% of income). As charity appeal follows charity appeal, more and more NGOs and their supporters are recognising that the needs of the Third World will never be met unless there is a concerted effort to tackle the root causes of poverty as well as treating its symptoms.

Christian Aid has run two-year campaigns on the issues of Third World debt and trade, aiming to show supporters and politicians how richer countries too often remove through interest repayments and trade restrictions far more than they invest through aid. By working more and more closely together in lobbying governments and encouraging concerned individuals to do likewise, NGOs throughout Europe are pressing for political change which will bring lasting benefits to poorer countries.

Further reading

OECD (Organisation for Economic Co-operation and Development) Development Centre (1992), *Directory of Non-Governmental and Development Organisations in OECD Member Countries*, Paris: Organisation for Economic Co-operation and Development.

Stubbs, L. (ed.) (1993), *The Third World Directory*, London: Directory of Social Change.

Vallely, P. (1992), *Promised Lands: Stories of Power and Poverty in the Third World*, London: Harper Collins.

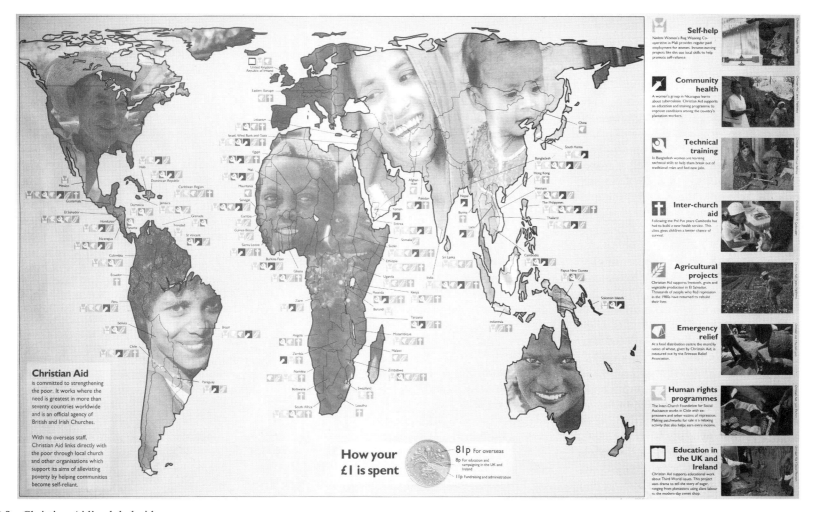

Figure 6.8 Christian Aid's global aid programme

6.9 CHRISTIAN AID PROJECTS IN INDIA
Eileen Maybin

With one of the highest concentrations of rural poor in the world, India is a priority country for Christian Aid's support to development work in Asia. A World Bank report in 1989 estimated that, of the 832.5 million people in India, 322.3 million people were living in poverty – the largest percentage of people living below the poverty line anywhere in the world. Poverty is still predominantly a problem for people living in the countryside where lack of access to land and resources leaves families struggling to eke out a living. A total of 46 million children in India were reported malnourished in the 1980–88 period.

Following independence in 1947, India opted for a 'mixed economy', providing for private and public investment and promoting a series of five-year plans which the government predicted would bring economic growth, self-reliance and social justice. While there has been significant achievement in the industrial sector and India now has the 12th largest Gross National Product (GNP) in the world with a wide manufacturing base, the policy of encouraging industrial growth to fuel development has rarely led to an improvement in the standard of living for the poor. It is the urban middle classes who have benefited from the type of development which makes consumer goods, medical care and education available to those with a comfortable income. The relative neglect of the agricultural sector has meant a decrease in its contribution to GNP while the number of people dependent on farming for a living is rising.

With India's foreign debt at more than US$ 70 billion in 1991, according to World Bank figures, the government headed by Narasimha Rao introduced new economic policies. In return for the sanctioning of IMF and World Bank loans, the government began to implement economic structural adjustment measures. However, the poor are particularly vulnerable to the rigorous effects of such measures which include spiralling inflation, increasing unemployment, deteriorating health and education services, falling wage levels and cuts in food subsidies.

In seeking to fulfil its commitment to strengthen the poor, Christian Aid supports partner organisations in India which run development projects addressing the situation of the very poorest and most oppressed. Target groups identified as in greatest need include the *dalits* (people of the lowest social stratification in the caste system), tribals, women, the landless, bonded labourers (many of whom are working to pay off parents' or grandparents' indenture because money-lenders cheat in the calculation of debt repayments) and child workers.

Christian Aid supports projects which tackle issues relating to gender, community health work, the environment, sustainable agriculture and the development of water resources. With the World Health Organisation predicting that AIDS could have reached epidemic proportions and be the major public health problem in India by the end of the century, work to raise awareness about HIV/AIDS is becoming increasingly important in health programmes and community education.

Christian Aid works predominantly in the poorest districts of Andhra Pradesh, Bihar, Karnataka, Madhya Pradesh, Maharashtra, Orissa, Tamil Nadu, Uttar Pradesh and West Bengal (Figure 6.9). Local development workers, appointed as Christian Aid *accompaniers*, visit partners to discuss the progress of projects and offer their skills or practical advice.

As the resources allocated for development programmes will never be sufficient, Christian Aid's Asia/Pacific Group undertakes advocacy work in Britain and Ireland through development education, fund-raising and publicity initiatives. Christian Aid materials use examples from India to show how macro-economic issues affect the poor. They encourage the public to support fairer systems of international trading and to lobby against projects of the international financial institutions which adversely affect the poor.

Further reading

Cleves Mosse, J. (1991), *India: Paths to Development*, Oxford: Oxfam Publications.
Economist Intelligence Unit (1993), *India, Nepal: Annual Survey of Political and Economic Background 1992–93*, London: Economist Intelligence Unit, 4–59.
Far Eastern Economic Review (1993), *Asia 1993 Yearbook: a Review of the Events of 1992*, Hong Kong: National Fair Ltd., 123–128.
Tully, M. (1991), *No Full Stops in India*, London: Viking.
Voluntary Health Association of India (1992), *State of India's Health*, New Delhi: Voluntary Health Association of India.

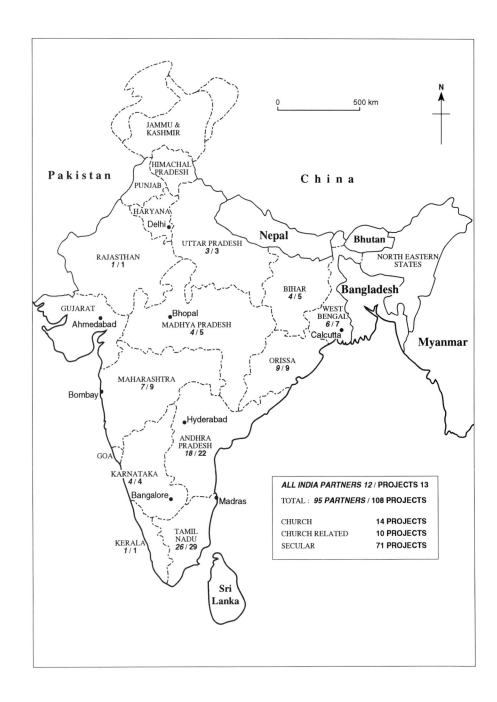

Figure 6.9   Indian States and Christian Aid
partners/projects (31 March 1993)

6.10 IDEOLOGIES OF DEVELOPMENT: UJAMAA

John Briggs

Ujamaa (literally meaning 'familyhood' in Kiswahili) was formally adopted as official policy in Tanzania in the Arusha Declaration of 1967. Ujamaa villages were introduced as 'rural economic and social communities where people live and work together for the good of all' (Nyerere, 1968: 348). In practice, the creation of successful ujamaa villages required: the relocation of the rural population of Tanzania into nucleated villages; the introduction of communal agricultural production; and the voluntary will of people to be involved. One of the major attractions of living and working in ujamaa villages was that considerable economies of scale could be achieved in both the production of crops and in the delivery of social service provision, especially health and education.

The process of creating such villages took place in three distinct phases. Phase 1 (1967–1970) was characterised by a totally voluntary movement by peasants to ujamaa villages, but only about half a million people moved (about 4% of Tanzania's population). In response, the government became more directly involved in 'encouraging' people to move during Phase 2 (1970–73). The population of selected regions of Tanzania was moved into new villages during this period, but, even so, only just over two million had moved by 1973. Between 1973 and 1976 (Phase 3), however, the remaining 10 million rural Tanzanians were moved, frequently by force. Significantly, they were moved to Development Villages, *not* Ujamaa Villages: that is, although they were still nucleated settlements, there was no longer a requirement for communal production to take place, the central element of the whole ujamaa philosophy.

The results of the ujamaa policy in Tanzania were mixed. By the mid-1970s, it was apparent that agricultural output was in decline, to the extent that Tanzania had to divert large sums of foreign exchange into importing large quantities of basic foodstuffs to avert famine. Village formation (especially in Phase 3) was highly centralist and dirigiste. Little explanation was given to the peasantry, and hence there was little support from the very people whom it was meant to benefit. The situation was not improved by the use of force in moving significant numbers of people to new villages. Moreover, there was only a limited amount of planning undertaken. Consequently, people arrived at new villages to find no housing ready for them. Not surprisingly, energies were put into providing the immediate needs of shelter provision for families, at the expense of preparing land for cultivation. Agricultural output was bound to be drastically affected.

Figure 6.10 illustrates an example from the Rufiji river valley, demonstrating the lack of ecological and economic understanding on the part of the planners. Before villagisation, the population was located in the valley floor, cultivating land by making use of the silty soils replenished each year by the annual Rufiji flood. This could be a hazardous way of life, in that in years of exceptionally high floods, loss of life could occur. Nevertheless, most residents considered it to be a worthwhile risk in that production levels were high, and they were close to their land, reducing travelling time to the fields and providing protection for crops from wildlife. The state decided that the best location for the new nucleated settlements was on the levee, away from the valley floor. This made sense in terms of the risks associated with the annual floods. However, it made no agricultural,

ecological or economic sense. The soils on the levee were very sandy and gravely, and hence of only limited fertility. Production levels plummeted. There were also severe water shortages, both for agricultural and domestic purposes. Some farmers tried to re-cultivate land on the valley floor, but journey-to-work times used up a significant part of the working day. Further, crops grown here were vulnerable to attack by wild animals, as people were no longer living by their land to offer some form of protection.

Today, there are no working ujamaa villages in Tanzania; indeed, the word 'ujamaa' has now disappeared from the Tanzanian political lexicon. Nevertheless, practically all the 8000 villages created between 1967 and 1973 continue to exist, albeit with private household production dominant. Although economically disastrous, Tanzania's villages have been socially successful, in that they have allowed the delivery of social services, especially rudimentary health care and universal primary education.

Further reading

Briggs, J. (1980), Rural policy in Tanzania since 1967: trends and issues, in: Simpson, E. (ed.), *The Rural-Agricultural Sector*, Newcastle upon Tyne: Department of Geography, Newcastle upon Tyne, on behalf of the Developing Areas Research Group, Institute of British Geographers, 9–25.

Coulson, A. (1982), *Tanzania: a Political Economy*, Oxford: Oxford University Press.

Hyden, G. (1980), *Beyond Ujamaa in Tanzania: Underdevelopment and an Uncaptured Peasantry*, London: Heinemann.

Nyerere, J.K. (1968), *Freedom and Socialism*, London: Oxford University Press.

Settlement and land-use in the Rufiji valley, east-central Tanzania.

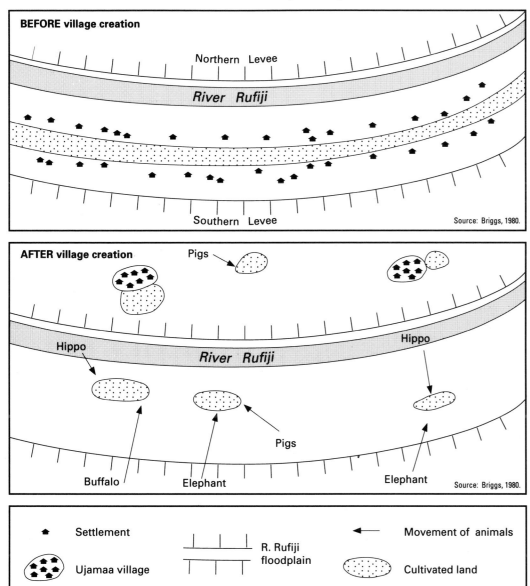

Figure 6.10 Settlement and land use in the Rufiji valley, east-central Tanzania

6.11 THE APARTHEID CITY
David Simon

The term 'apartheid city' denotes the unique and specific urban form developed in South Africa to comply with the dictates of apartheid ideology. Implemented by the National Party from 1948 onwards, this ideology was explicitly designed to perpetuate the political, economic and social supremacy of the country's white minority and their supposed racial purity.

This was achieved – at great human and financial cost – by depriving the majority of the population of free access to the bases for accumulating political, economic and social power and through the institutionalisation of racial segregation at all geographical scales. Official protestations that this meant 'separate but equal' opportunities were nothing short of a smokescreen for state-sponsored racial discrimination.

However, the Afrikaner nationalists were by no means the first South African government to invoke stereotyped constructions of race and culture as the basis of discriminatory state policy. Since the early years of this century, the state had enforced progressively stricter segregation through legislation including the 1913 and 1936 Land Acts and the Natives (Urban Areas) Consolidation Act of 1945. All of these discriminated blatantly against Africans in particular, restricting them to only 13% of the country's land, imposing the 'pass laws' as an institutionalised system of control over their migration from rural to urban areas, and confining them within segregated urban 'locations'. The typical South African urban form during this period, which was comparable to that pertaining in other colonial situations, is

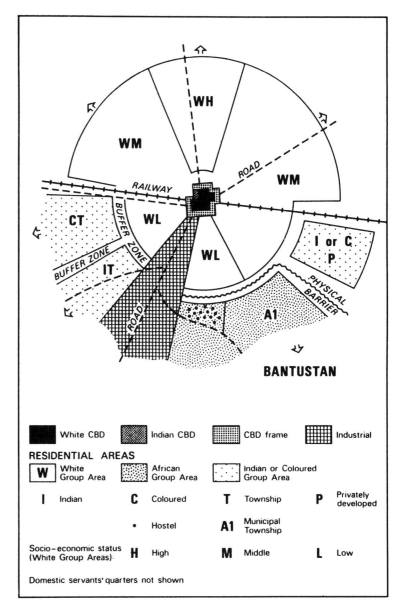

Figure 6.11a The original apartheid city model

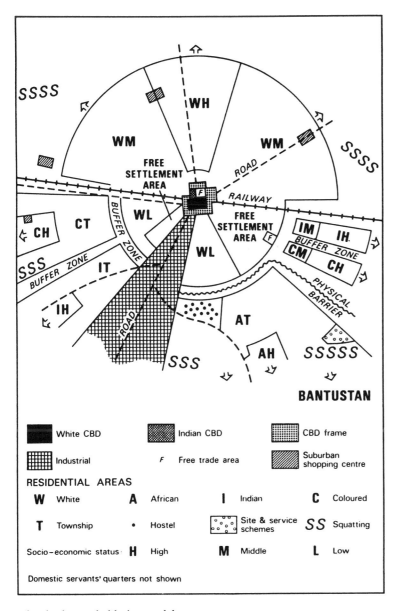

Figure 6.11b The modernised apartheid city model

known as the 'segregation city' to distinguish it from the structurally simplified version which was subsequently created under apartheid (Davies, 1981; Western, 1981; Simon, 1989, 1992).

The principal instrument for imposing urban apartheid was the Group Areas Act of 1950, as amended in 1966 and subsequently. This required members of all four 'race groups', as officially defined by the 1949 Population Registration Act, to live in separate urban segments known as Group Areas. Moreover, the urban morphology was to be restructured so as to minimise inter-racial contact outside the workplace, where highly articulated and discriminatory labour practices already maintained extreme social distance. These principles also required making provision for future urban growth at the urban fringe to occur radially from each Group Area (Figure 6.11a).

Inevitably, the process of imposing this regime on existing urban fabrics was complicated and protracted, involving bureaucratic investigations, pronouncements, local appeals and often heated conflicts between local and national state, the interests of various fractions of capital, and particular communities (Pirie, 1984). Altogether, over 860 000 people, the vast majority of them classified as 'coloured' and Asian, were forcibly removed from their homes over the period 1960–83 alone (Platzky and Walker, 1985). Except for whites, compensation was generally inadequate and the victims found themselves being relocated to new Group Areas on the urban periphery, often far from their workplaces, schools and social networks. The social costs and alienation generated by such uprootings have been immense.

During the 1980s, piecemeal reforms designed to remove the most individually hurtful aspects of apartheid, while maintaining the basic social structures and features, were introduced under

President P.W. Botha. In other words, the objective was to modernise rather than abolish apartheid. Such measures included the desegregation of hotels, cinemas and many other public facilities, the establishment of 'free trade areas' where racial exclusivity no longer applied to the conduct of business, and the implementation of site and service and squatter upgrading schemes to cater for the rapidly growing black population unable to find shelter in the already overcrowded townships. Permanently resident Africans were also accorded progressively longer leasehold and ultimately freehold rights in the townships. The pass laws were abolished in 1986 and replaced by a supposedly racially neutral policy of 'orderly urbanisation'. In reality, though, this was still aimed essentially at Africans. In 1989 a handful of 'free settlement areas', i.e. racially mixed Group Areas, were permitted. This amounted merely to recognition of the status quo, thereby attempting to arrest the 'greying' of other white suburbs. These features are all representative of the modernised apartheid city (Figure 6.11b).

Botha's successor as President, F.W. de Klerk, moved rapidly to unban and release political adversaries, dismantle apartheid legislation and usher in a new era in South African history. By mid-1991, the Reservation of Separate Amenities, Group Areas, Land, and Population Registration Acts had all been abolished, heralding the end of statutory apartheid. This, then, marks the end of the apartheid city as a legally enforced form, but its legacy will endure for many years irrespective of the nature of the post-apartheid order in South Africa. Already, rapid residential integration is occurring in some areas of large cities, and evidence of new class-based alliances within these areas is emerging.

Further reading

Davies, R.J. (1981), The spatial formation of the South African city, *GeoJournal* supplementary issue, **2**: 59–72.

Jeppie, S. and Soudien, C. (eds) (1990), *The Struggle for District Six: Past and Present*, Cape Town: Buchu Books.

Lemon, A. (ed.) (1991), *Homes Apart: South Africa's Segregated Cities*, London: Paul Chapman.

Pirie, G.H. (1984), Race zoning in South Africa: board, court, parliament, public, *Political Geography Quarterly*, **3**(3): 207–221.

Platzky, L. and Walker, C. (1985), *The Surplus People: Forced Removals in South Africa*, Johannesburg: Ravan.

Simon, D. (1989), Crisis and change in South Africa: implications for the apartheid city, *Transactions of the Institute of British Geographers*, new series **14**(2): 189–206.

Simon, D. (1992), Reform in South Africa and modernisation of the apartheid city, in: Drakakis-Smith, D. (ed.), *Urban and Regional Change in Southern Africa*, London: Routledge: 33–65.

Smith, D.M. (ed.) (1992), *The Apartheid City and Beyond*, London: Routledge.

Swilling, M., Humphries, R. and Shubane, K. (eds) (1991), *Apartheid City in Transition*, Cape Town: Oxford University Press.

Western, J. (1981), *Outcast Cape Town*, London: Allen and Unwin.

6.12 WORLD HERITAGE SITES
Gareth A. Jones

Heritage was formally placed on the development agenda with the setting up of the World Heritage Committee by UNESCO in 1972. The stated purpose of the Committee is to compile a list of the world's most outstanding historic monuments and natural sites so as to pressure national governments to devote resources for their maintenance. Although no funds are made directly available for this purpose from UNESCO, it is recognised that designation as a World Heritage site carries with it significant scope for attracting the increasing numbers of 'cultural tourists' (Hardoy and Gutman, 1991; Harrison, 1992).

Developing countries play an important part in the designation of world heritage. There are 358 separate heritage sites recognised by the World Heritage Committee (Figure 6.12): 191 (53.3%) are located in developing countries; 137 (38.2%) in Europe, North America and Australasia; 31 (8.6%) in the former Soviet Union and Soviet Bloc. Of the 358 sites, 260 are designated as cultural sites. These include Cuzco and Chan Chan (Peru), Damascus and Aleppo (Syria), and Shibam (Yemen). A further 84 are natural sites, for example, Iguazu National Park (Argentina), the Galapagos Islands (Ecuador) and the Serengeti and Kilimanjaro National Parks (United Republic of Tanzania), and 14 are mixed sites.

Not surprisingly, politics plays a key role – indeed understanding the procedure for heritage designation is an instructive exercise in the workings of international political relations. Partly for this reason, Europe provides the most significant number of sites (100), 27.9% of the total. However, the country with the most heritage

sites in the world until recently was India (19 sites), now joined by France (19 sites), and followed by Spain (17), the USA (16) and the UK (14). The next highest developing countries on the list are Mexico (9 sites) and Peru (8 sites). Clearly, both have been quick to recognise the advantages of site designation, possibly for its attractions to the tourist industry.

The imbalance in designation begins to multiply on closer examination. While Ethiopia and Egypt can claim a number of sites, seven and five respectively, as the centre of the world's earliest known civilisations – supporting a claim that Africa is the First World – Iraq has just one site (Hatra), Iran three and the Sudan has no recognised site although the pyramids at Meroe (Kush) would surely qualify. The absence of a heritage site might be interpreted as making a statement about the contribution of certain nations to world heritage. On occasion this absence is without apparent justification, other than the need for political sensitivity. Israel, for example, contributes no sites to the list, although Jerusalem is covered by Jordan. Similarly, Lhasa in Tibet, annexed by China, is absent. Less explicable, however, Easter Island is not present and Papua New Guinea provides no heritage site despite the wealth of anthropological information about the islands. Modern cultural heritage is also largely absent, the only example from the developing world being Brasilia (Dickenson, 1992).

Looking specifically at the distribution of sites among developing countries is useful. Until 1990, Asia appeared to be poorly represented despite the contribution of India. The recent inclusion of Thailand and Indonesia, however, has increased the total to 43 sites. China is also largely excluded – one of the world's oldest civilisations and one-fifth of the current global population provides just seven sites. Beyond such observations, however,

the regional distribution is largely equitable with North Africa and the Middle East contributing 49 sites, Latin America and the Caribbean 48 sites, and Africa 44 sites.

Apart from the natural sites, the designation of World Heritage sites in developing countries is predominantly urban. The impact which selection as a World Heritage site might have upon a city is difficult to ascertain and is under-researched (Dix, 1990). Nevertheless, a number of general patterns do emerge. First, there is a close association with national identity and continuity. Thus, sites of a glorious historical past, a 'golden age', will be conserved at the expense of symbolically more ambivalent locations. Equally, the creation of a national heritage may be a conscious effort to dispel 'historical amnesia' (Dickenson, 1992). In either case, the result may mean that the selected sites are geographically restricted (Figure 6.12).

The second pattern is the apparent selectivity with which heritage sites are proposed by national governments. In Brazil, for example, there appears to be an over-representation of religious monuments – some 40% of conserved buildings – suggesting the confirmation of a past in line with a Catholic religious orthodoxy (Dickenson, 1992; Vearncombe, 1981). The combination of these features suggests that what is preserved strongly reflects an elite definition of landscape. This may go so far as to reinterpret vernacular sites and package them for elite consumption. In Antigua, for example, the former slave halls of the port area have been converted into shopping malls for white tourists (Thomas, 1991). Lastly, it is increasingly understood that the definition of heritage sites will mean a changing social composition of the conserved area as pressure increases for the poor to be displaced in favour of a 'more dignified' array of elite land uses (Jones and Varley, 1994).

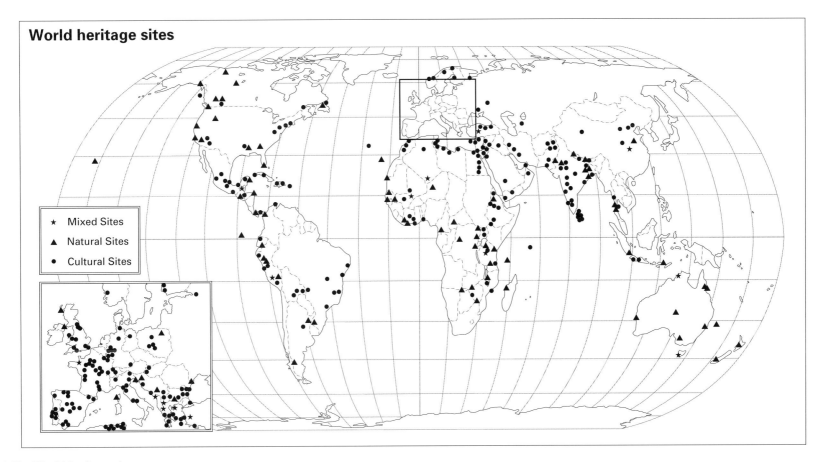

Figure 6.12 World heritage sites

Further reading

Dickenson, J. (1992), *The Past is a Foreign Country: a Case Study of Minas Gerais, Brazil*, Liverpool: Department of Geography, University of Liverpool, Liverpool Papers in Human Geography, new series, no. 3.

Dix, G. (1990), Conservation and change in the city, *Third World Planning Review*, **12**(4): 385–406.

Hewison, R. (1987), *The Heritage Industry*, London: Methuen.

Lowenthal, D. (1985), *The Past is a Foreign Country*, Cambridge: Cambridge University Press.

Bibliography

ACC/SCN (Administrative Committee on Co-ordination – Sub-Committee on Nutrition) (1989), *Update on the Nutrition Situation. Recent Trends in Nutrition in 33 Countries*, Geneva: ACC/SCN c/o World Health Organisation.

ACC/SCN (Administrative Committee on Co-ordination – Sub-Committee on Nutrition) in collaboration with IFPRI (International Food Policy Research Institute) (1992), *Second Report on the World Nutrition Situation. Volume 1: Global and Regional Results*, Geneva: ACC/SCN Secretariat c/o WHO; Washington DC: International Food Policy Research Institute.

Adams, M.E. (1990), Slow progress with integrated rural development programmes in Kenya's arid and semiarid lands, *Land Degradation & Rehabilitation*, **2**: 285–299.

Addus, A.A. (1989), Road transportation in Africa, *Transportation Quarterly*, **43**(3): 421–433.

Airey, A. (1985), Rural road improvements in Sierra Leone, *Singapore Journal of Tropical Geography*, **6**(2): 78–90.

Alexander, J. and Alexander, P. (1982), Shared poverty as ideology: agrarian relationships in colonial Java, *Man*, **17**: 597–619.

Allen, C. (1988), *The Hold Life Has: Coca and Cultural Identity in an Andean Community*, Washington DC: Smithsonian Institute.

Althusser, L. (1969), *For Marx*, Harmondsworth: Penguin.

Althusser, L. and Balibar, E. (1970), *Reading Capital*, London: New Left Books.

Amin, S.H. (1981), *International and Legal Problems of the Gulf*, London: Menas Press.

Amnesty International (1987), *USA: the Death Penalty*, London: Amnesty International.

Amnesty International (1989a), *When the State Kills*, London: Amnesty International.

Amnesty International (1989b), *Jamaica: the Death Penalty*, London: Amnesty International.

Amnesty International (1989c), *Religions and the Death Penalty*, London: Amnesty International.

Amnesty International (1989d), *Death Penalty: Facts and Figures*, London: Amnesty International.

Amnesty International (1991a), *Amnesty International Report 1991*, London: Amnesty International.

Amnesty International (1991b), *Parliamentary Arguments on Reintroducing the Death Penalty: the United Kingdom Debate, 1990*, London: Amnesty International, unpublished document ACT 50/06/91.

Amnesty International (1992a), *The Death Penalty: List of Abolitionist and Retentionist Countries (December 1991)*, London: Amnesty International, unpublished document ACT 50/01/92.

Amnesty International (1992b), *Death Sentences and Executions in 1991*, London: Amnesty International, unpublished document ACT 51/01/92.

Anderson, J.R. and Hazell, P.B.R. (1989), *Variability in Grain Yields*, Baltimore: Johns Hopkins University Press.

Anon. (1985), Peru's National Population Policy Law, *Population and Development Review*, **11**(4): 789–794.

Antipode (1984), Special issue. The Fourth World: a geography of indigenous struggles, *Antipode*, **16**(2).

Ariff, M. and Hill, H. (1985), *Export-oriented Industrialisation: the ASEAN Experience*, London: Allen and Unwin.

Arrighi, G. and Drangel, J. (1986) Semi-peripheral countries in the global economic and military order, in: Tuomi, H. and Varynen, R. (eds), *Militarization and Arms Production*, London: Croom Helm, 163–192.

Auty, R. (1979), Worlds within worlds, *Area*, **11**: 232–235.

Barbier, E.B. (1992), Community-based development in Africa, in: Swanson, T.M. and Barbier, E.B. (eds), *Economics for the Wilds: Wildlife, Wildlands, Diversity and Development*, London: Earthscan, 103–135.

Barham, B. *et al.* (1992), Nontraditional exports in Latin America, *Latin American Research Review*, **27**(2): 43–82.

Barker, R., Herdt, R.W. and Rose, B. (1985), *The Rice Economy of Asia*, Washington DC: Resources for the Future.

Barkin, D. (1993), *Distorted Development. Mexican Agriculture in the World Economy*, Boulder: Westview, 2nd ed.

Barnes, J., Burgess, J. and Pearce, D. (1992), Wildlife tourism, in: Swanson, T.M. and Barbier, E.B. (eds), *Economics for the Wilds: Wildlife, Wildlands, Diversity and Development*, London: Earthscan, 136–151.

Barnett, T. and Blaikie, P. (1992), *AIDS in Africa: its Present and Future Impact*, London: Belhaven.

Barnett, T.P. (1988), *Global Sea Level Change*, Washington DC: NOAA.

Barrett, D.B. (1982), *World Christian Encyclopedia*, Oxford: Oxford University Press.

Barry, R.G. and Chorley, R.J. (1987), Climatic classification, in: Barry, R.G. and Chorley, R.J., *Atmosphere, Weather and Climate*, London: Routledge, 411–427, 5th ed.

Barry, R.G. and Chorley, R.J. (1990), *Atmosphere, Weather and Climate*, London: Routledge, 6th ed.

Barwell, I., Edmonds, G.A., Howe, J.D. and Veen, J. de (1985), *Rural Transport in Developing Countries*, London: Intermediate Technology Publications.

Basham, A.L. (ed.) (1975), *A Cultural History of India*, Delhi: Oxford University Press.

Bauer, P. (1984), *Reality and Rhetoric*, London: Weidenfeld and Nicolson.

Bayliss-Smith, T. and Wanmali, S. (eds) (1984), *Understanding Green Revolutions: Agrarian Change and Development Planning in South Asia*, Cambridge: Cambridge University Press.

Beaton, G.H. (1989), Small but healthy? Are we asking the right question?, *Human Organization*, **48**(1): 31–37.

Beaton, G., Kelly, A., Kevany, J., Martorell, R. and Mason, J. (1990), *Appropriate Uses of Anthropometric Indices in Children*, Geneva: Administrative Committee on Co-ordination – Sub-Committee on Nutrition, State-of-the-Art Series Nutrition Policy Discussion Paper 7.

Beneria, L. (1992), Accounting for women's work: the progress of two decades, *World Development*, **20**(11): 1547–1560.

Bergesen, A. and Schoenberg, R. (1980), Long waves of colonial expansion and contraction, 1415–1969, in: Bergesen, A. (ed.), *Studies of the Modern World System*, London: Macmillan, 231–277.

Biro Pusat Statistik (1990), *Statistik Indonesia* (Statistical Year Book of Indonesia), Jakarta: Biro Pusat Statistik.

Biswas, M. and Pinstrup-Anderson, A. (1985), *Nutrition and Development*, Oxford: Oxford University Press.

Black, R. (1991), Refugees and displaced persons: geographical perspectives and research direction, *Progress in Human Geography*, **15**(3): 281–298.

Black, R. and Robinson, V. (eds) (1993), *Geography and Refugees: Patterns and Processes of Change*, London: Belhaven Press.

Blaikie, P. (1985), *The Political Economy of Soil Erosion in Developing Countries*, London: Longman.

Blaikie, P. and Brookfield, H. (1987), *Land Degradation and Society*, London: Methuen.

Bloomfield, P. (1992), Trends in global temperature, *Climatic Change*, **21**: 1–16.

Blum, R.H. (1981), Offshore money flows: a large dark number, *Journal of International Affairs*, **35**: 69–93.

Blumenfeld, J. (1991), *Economic Interdependence in Southern Africa: from Conflict to Co-operation?*, London: Pinter.

Bolt, B.A. (1988), *Earthquakes, a Primer*, New York: Freeman.

Bongaarts, J. (1985), The fertility inhibiting effects of the intermediate fertility variables, in: Shorter, F. *et al.* (eds) *Population Factors in Development Planning in the Middle East*, Cairo: Population Council, 152–169.

Booth, A. (1989), *Raising the Roof on Housing Myths*, London: Shelter.

Booth, A. (1992), Income distribution and poverty, in: Booth, A. (ed.), *The Oil Boom and After: Indonesian Economic Policy and Performance in the Soeharto Era*, Singapore: Oxford University Press, 323–362.

Boserup, E. (1965), *The Conditions of Agricultural Growth: the Economics of Agrarian Change under Population Pressure*, London: Allen & Unwin.

Boserup, E. (1981), *Population and Technology*, Oxford: Blackwell.

Bradbury, J. (1982), Some geographical implications of the restructuring of the iron ore industry, 1950–1980, *Tijdschrift voor Economische en Sociale Geografie*, **73**(5): 295–306.

Bradnock, R. (1984), Agricultural development in Tamil Nadu: two decades of land use and change at village level, in: Bayliss-Smith, T. and Wanmali, S. (eds), *Understanding Green Revolutions: Agrarian Change and Development Planning in South Asia*, Cambridge: Cambridge University Press, 136–152.

Bradshaw, M.J. (1993), *The Economic Effects of Soviet Dissolution*, London: Royal Institute of International Affairs.

Brandt, W.C. (1980), *North-South: a Programme for Survival*, London: Pan.

Brass, P.R. (1989), Politics in India, in: Robinson, F. (ed.), *The Cambridge Encyclopedia of India, Pakistan, Bangladesh, Sri Lanka, Nepal, Bhutan and the Maldives*, Cambridge: Cambridge University Press, 168–201.

Brass, P.R. (1990), *The Government and Politics of India*, Cambridge: Cambridge University Press.

Bremen Institute of Shipping Economics (1992), *Shipping Statistics*, Bremen: University of Bremen.

Breton, R.J.L. (1991), *Geolinguistics: Language Dynamics and Ethnolinguistic Geography*, Ottawa: University of Ottawa Press.

Bridges, R.C. (1985), Africa, Africans and the sea, in: Stone, J.C. (ed.), *Africa and the Sea*, Aberdeen: Aberdeen University African Studies Group, 14–26.

Briggs, J. (1978), Farmers' responses to planned agricultural development in the Sudan, *Transactions of the Institute of British Geographers*, **3**: 464–475.

Briggs, J. (1980), Rural policy in Tanzania since 1967: trends and issues, in: Simpson, E. (ed.), *The Rural-agricultural Sector*, Newcastle upon Tyne: Department of Geography, Newcastle upon Tyne for the Developing Areas Research Group, Institute of British Geographers, 9–25.

Brogan, P. (1992), *World Conflicts*, London: Bloomsbury.

Browett, J. (1981), On the development in development geography, *Tijdschrift voor Economische en Sociale Geografie*, **72**(3): 155–161.

Brown, G. and Henry, W. (1989), *The Economic Value of Elephants*, London: London Environmental Economics Centre, LEEC Discussion Paper 89–12.

Brown, L.R. (1975), *The Politics and Responsibility of the North American Breadbasket*, Washington DC: Worldwatch Institute, Worldwatch Paper 2.

Brzoska, M. and Ohlson, T. (1987), *Arms Transfer to the Third World 1971–85*, Oxford: Oxford University Press.

Burbach, R. and Flynn, P. (1980), *Agribusiness in the Americas*, New York: Monthly Review Press.

Burrow, T. (1975), Ancient and modern languages, in: Basham, A.L. (ed.), *A Cultural History of India*, Delhi: Oxford University Press, 162–169.

Butler, D., Lahiri, A. and Roy, P. (1989), *India Decides: Indian Elections 1951–1991*, New Delhi: U.M. Books.

Butterworth, D. and Chance, J. (1981), *Latin American Urbanization*, Cambridge: Cambridge University Press.

Byrne, R. (1992), Climatic change and the origins of agriculture, Paper presented to the IBG annual conference, Swansea, 7–10 January 1992.

CAAT (Campaign Against Arms Trade) (1990), *Death on Delivery: the Impact of the Arms Trade on the Third World*, London: Campaign Against Arms Trade.

Cahen, C. (1970), Quelques notes sur le déclin commerciale du monde musulman à la fin du moyen age, in: Cook, M.A. (ed.), *Studies in the Economic History of the Middle East*, Oxford: Oxford University Press, 31–36.

Cardoso, E. and Helwege, A. (1992), Below the line: poverty in Latin America, *World Development*, **20**(1): 19–38.

Carter, J. (1982), Wildlife species as an economic asset, in: *Proceedings of the Seminar on Environmental Conservation and Ecological Principles for Economic Development*, Gaborone: Department of Wildlife and National Parks, Republic of Botswana, 78–80.

Carter, J. (1983), Wildlife management areas, unpublished paper presented at Kalahari Conservation Society Conference, 'Which Way Botswana's Wildlife?', Gaborone, 15–16 April 1983.

Carter, R.N. and Prince, S.D. (1985), The effect of climate on plant distributions, in: Tooley, M.J. and Sheail, G.M. (eds) *The Climatic Scene*, London: George Allen and Unwin, 235–254.

Catrina, C. (1988), *Arms Transfers and Dependence*, London: Taylor and Francis.

Centre for Science and Environment, India (1989), The environmental problems associated with India's major cities, *Environment and Urbanization*, **1**(1): 7–15.

Chamberlain, M.E. (1985), *Decolonization*, Oxford: Blackwell.

Chambers, R. (1983), *Rural Development: Putting the Last First*, London: Longman.

Charney, J.I. and Alexander, L.M. (eds) (1993), *International Maritime Boundaries*, Dordrecht: Martinus Nijhoff.

Chaudhuri, K.N. (1985), *Trade and Civilisation in the Indian Ocean*, Cambridge: Cambridge University Press.

Chomsky, N. (1991), *Deterring Democracy*, London: Verso.

Cleary, D. (1991), *The Brazilian Rainforest: Politics, Finance, Mining and the Environment*, London: Economist Intelligence Unit, Special Report 2100.

Cleland, J. and Hobcroft, J. (eds) (1985), *Reproductive Change in Developing Countries*, Oxford: Oxford University Press.

Cleves Mosse, J. (1991), *India: Paths to Development*, Oxford: Oxfam Publications.

Coastal Zone Management Subgroup (1992), *Global Climate Change and the Rising Challenge of the Sea*, The Hague: Ministry of Transport, Public Works and Water Management.

Cobbe, J.H. (1980), Integration among unequals: the Southern African Customs Union and development, *World Development*, **8**(4): 329–336.

Cole, J. (1991), *The USSR in the 1990s: which Republic?*, Nottingham: Nottingham University Department of Geography, Working Paper 9.

Cole, Viscount (1989), General aviation – the developing world's indispensable transport, in: Heraty, M. (ed.), *Developing World Transport*, London: Grosvenor Press International, 325–327.

Cook, N. (1982), Population data for Indian Peru, *Hispanic American Historical Review*, **62**(1): 73–120.

Coquery-Vidrovitch, C. (1988), *Africa: Endurance and Change South of the Sahara*, Berkeley: University of California Press.

Corbridge, S. (1984), Agrarian policy and agrarian change in tribal India, in: Bayliss-Smith, T. and Wanmali, S. (eds), *Understanding Green Revolutions: Agrarian Change and Development Planning in South Asia*, Cambridge: Cambridge University Press, 87–108.

Corbridge, S. (ed.) (1993), *World Economy*, New York: Oxford University Press.

Corbridge, S. and Agnew J. (1991), The US trade and budget deficits in global perspective: an essay in geopolitical economy, *Society and Space*, **9**: 71–90.

Corbridge, S., Martin, R. and Thrift, N. (eds) (1994), *Money, Power and Space*, Oxford: Basil Blackwell.

Coulson, A. (1982), *Tanzania: a Political Economy*, Oxford: Oxford University Press.

Couper, A. (ed.) (1983), *Times Atlas of the Oceans*, London: Times Books.

Crone, D.K. (1993), States, elites and social welfare in Southeast Asia, *World Development*, **21**(1): 55–66.

Crone, G.R. (1968), *Maps and their Makers: an Introduction to the History of Cartography*, London: Hutchinson University Library, 4th ed.

Crone, G.R. (1978), *Maps and their Makers*, Folkestone: Dawson, 5th ed.

Cross, S. and Whiteside, A. (1993), *Facing up to AIDS: the Socio-economic Impact in Southern Africa*, London: Macmillan.

Crow, B. and Thomas, A. (1983), *Third World Atlas*, Milton Keynes: Open University Press.

Dalrymple, D. (1986), *Development and Spread of High-yielding Rice Varieties in Developing Countries*, Washington DC: USAID.

Davies, R.J. (1981), The spatial formation of the South African city, *GeoJournal* supplementary issue **2**: 59–72.

Davis, B. (1985), Maps on postage stamps as propaganda, *The Cartographic Journal*, **22**: 125–130.

Davis, R. (1979), *The Industrial Revolution and British Overseas Trade*, Leicester: Leicester University Press.

De Blij, H.J. and Muller, P.O. (1991), *Geography, Regions and Concepts*, New York: Wiley, 6th ed.

Dermigny, L. (1964), *Le Commerce à Canton au XVIIIe Siècle, 1719–1833*, Paris: SEVPEN.

Development Dialogue (1987), The Maseru seminar on 'Another development for SADCC countries': an agenda for action, *Development Dialogue*, **1987** (1): 74–111.

Dickenson, J. (1992), *The Past is a Foreign Country: a Case Study of Minas Gerais, Brazil*, Liverpool: Department of Geography, University of Liverpool, Liverpool Papers in Human Geography, new series, 3.

Dilke, O.A.W. (1985), *Greek and Roman Maps*, London: Thames and Hudson.

Dix, G. (1990), Conservation and change in the city, *Third World Planning Review*, **12**(4): 385–406.

Dixon, C. and Drakakis-Smith, D. (eds) (1993), *Economic and Social Development in Pacific Asia*, London: Routledge.

Dixon, J. and Sherman, P. (1990), *Economics of Protected Areas: a New Look at Benefits and Costs*, London: Earthscan.

Doganis, R. (1985), *Flying Off Course*, London: Allen & Unwin.

Doherty, J. (1983), Beyond dependency, *Professional Geographer*, **35**(1): 81–83.

Donaldson, P. and Tsui, A. (1990), The international family planning movement, *Population Bulletin*, **45**(3): 1–46.

Dowler, E.A. and Seo, S.O. (1985), Assessment of energy intake: estimates of food supply vs measurement of food consumption, *Food Policy*, **10**(3): 278–288.

Drakakis-Smith, D.W. (1984), Underdevelopment in the tropics: the case of North Australia, *Singapore Journal of Tropical Geography*, **5**(2): 125–139.

Drakakis-Smith, D. (1990), Is there still a Third World, Keele: Inaugural Lecture from the Chair of Development Studies, Keele University.

Drakakis-Smith, D. (1993) Is there still a Third World?, *Choros*, **1**: 1–21.

Drakakis-Smith, D. and Williams, S.W. (eds) (1983), *Internal Colonialism: Essays Around a Theme*, Edinburgh: Department of Geography, University of Edinburgh on behalf of the Developing Areas Research Group of the Institute of British Geographers, Monograph 3.

Drakakis-Smith, D., Doherty, J. and Thrift, N. (1987), Socialist development in the Third World, *Geography*, **72**: 333–362.

Dreze, J. and Sen, A. (1989), *Hunger and Public Action*, Oxford: Clarendon Press, WIDER Studies in Development Economics.

Drysdale, A.D. and Blake, G.H. (1985), *The Middle East and North Africa: a Political Geography*, New York: Oxford University Press.

Duncan, T.J. and Barnes, J.S. (1992), *Writing Worlds: Discourse, Text and Metaphor in the Representation of Landscape*, London: Routledge.

Economist Intelligence Unit (1990), *World Commodity Outlook, 1991 – Industrial Raw Materials*, London: Economist Intelligence Unit.

Economist Intelligence Unit (1993), *India, Nepal: Annual Survey of Political and Economic Background 1992–93*, London: Economist Intelligence Unit, 4–59.

Eden, M.J. (1990), *Ecology and Land Management in Amazonia*, London: Belhaven Press.

Ehrlich, P. and Ehrlich, A. (1969), *The Population Bomb*, New York: Ballantine.

El-Hakim, A.A. (1979), *The Middle Eastern States and the Law of the Sea*, Manchester: Manchester University Press.

Elliott, J. A. (1989), Soil Erosion and Conservation in Zimbabwe: Political Economy and the Environment, unpublished Ph.D. thesis, Loughborough University of Technology.

Elsom, D. (1992), *Atmospheric Pollution – a Global Problem*, Oxford: Blackwell.

Eltringham, S.K. (1984), *Wildlife Resources and Economic Development*, Chichester: Wiley.

Eltringham, S.K. (1992), Tropical wildlife resources, in: Furtado, J., Morgan, W.B., Pfafflin, J.R. and

Ruddle, K. (eds) (1992), *Tropical Resources: Ecology and Development*, Philadelphia: Harwood Academic, 97–114.

Enfield, D.B. and Luis, C.S. (1991), Low frequency changes in El Niño-Southern Oscillation, *Journal of Climate*, **4**: 1137–1146.

Ennew, J. (1986), *Mujercita y mamacita*: girls growing up in Lima, *Bulletin of Latin American Research*, **5**(2): 49–66.

Ennew, J. and Milne, B. (1989), *The Next Generation: Lives of Third World Children*, London: Zed.

Erasmus, J. *et al.* (1991), *South Africa: an Interregional Profile*, Midrand: Development Bank of South Africa.

Estes, R. (1988), Towards a quality of life index, in: Norwine, J. and Gonzalez, A. (eds), *The Third World: States of Mind and Being*, London: Unwin Hyman, 23–36.

Esteve, G. (1992), Development, in: Sachs, G. (ed.), *The Development Dictionary*, London: Zed Books, 6–25.

European Commission (1986), Europe as seen by Europeans: European polling 1973–86, *European Documentation*, 1986/4.

European Commission (1993), Reform issues in the former Soviet Union, *European Economy*, **79**.

Ezeife, P.C. (1984), The development of the Nigerian transport system, *Transport Reviews*, **4**(4): 305–30.

Fair, T.J.D. (1982), *South Africa: Spatial Frameworks for Development*, Cape Town: Juta.

Fairplay Publications (annual), *World Shipping Statistics*, Coulsdon: Fairplay.

FAO (Food and Agriculture Organization of the United Nations) (annual), *Production Yearbook*, Rome: Food and Agriculture Organization of the United Nations.

FAO (Food and Agriculture Organization of the United Nations) (annual), *Trade Yearbook*, Rome: Food and Agriculture Organization of the United Nations.

FAO (Food and Agriculture Organization of the United Nations) (various years), *The State of Food and Agriculture*, Rome: Food and Agriculture Organization.

FAO (Food and Agriculture Organization of the United Nations) (1979), *A Provisional Methodology for Soil Degradation Assessment. FAO/UNEP/UNESCO Report with Mapping of Soil Degradation of Africa North of the Equator and the Middle East*, Rome: Food and Agriculture Organization.

FAO (Food and Agriculture Organization) (1985), *The Fifth World Survey*, Rome: FAO.

FAO (Food and Agriculture Organization of the United Nations) (1990), *The conservation and rehabilitation of African lands*, Rome: Food and Agriculture Organization.

FAO/WHO (Food and Agriculture Organization/ World Health Organisation) (1992a), *Nutrition and Development: a Global Assessment*, Rome: FAO/WHO, International Conference on Nutrition.

FAO/WHO (Food and Agriculture Organization/ World Health Organisation) (1992b) *Food and Nutrition at the Turn of the Millenium: Maps Produced by FAO/WHO Joint Secretariat for the International Nutrition Conference, Rome, December 1992*, Rome: FAO/WHO.

Far Eastern Economic Review (1993), *Asia 1993 Yearbook: a Review of the Events of 1992*, Hong Kong: National Fair Ltd., 123–128.

Fargues, P. (1989), The decline of Arab fertility, *Population*, **44**: 147–174.

Farmer, B.H. (1993), *An Introduction to South Asia*, London: Routledge, 2nd ed.

Feder, G. (1987), Land ownership security and farm productivity: evidence from Thailand, *Journal of Development Studies*, **24**(1): 16–30.

Feder, G., Onchan, T., Chalamwong, Y. and Hongladarom, C. (1988), *Land Policies and Farm Productivity in Thailand*, Baltimore: Johns Hopkins University Press.

Findlay, A. (1985), Migrants' dreams and planners' nightmares, *Cities*, **2**: 331–339.

Findlay, A. (1987), *The Role of International Labour Migration in the Transformation of an Economy*, Geneva: International Labour Office, International Migration for Employment Working Paper, 35.

Findlay, A. (1994), *The Arab World*, London: Routledge.

Findlay, A. and Findlay, A. (1987), *Population and Development in the Third World*, London: Routledge.

Foeken, D. (1982), Explanation for the partition of sub-Saharan Africa, 1881–1900, *Tijdschrift voor Economische en Sociale Geografie*, **73**: 138–148.

Forbes, D. (1984), *The Geography of Underdevelopment*, London: Croom Helm.

Forbes, D. and Thrift, N. (1987), *The Socialist Third World*, Oxford: Blackwell.

Foreign and Commonwealth Office (1989), *Transport Routes of the Frontline States, Malawi and Zaire*, London: Africa Section, Research Department, Foreign and Commonwealth Office.

Forster-Sutton, S., Thornley, C.S. and Hyde-Clarke, M. (1962), *Report of the Regional Boundaries Commission*, London: HMSO (Cmnd 1899).

Fournier, F. (1960), *Climat et Erosion*, Paris: Presses Universitaires de France.

Fox, R.C. (1991), *Ethnic Distributions in Colonial and Postcolonial Kenya*, Pretoria: Human Sciences Research Council.

Frank, A.G. (1969), *Capitalism and Underdevelopment in Latin America*, New York: Monthly Review Press.

Freeman, M. (1991), *Atlas of the World Economy*, London: Routledge.

Fryer, D.W. (1987), The political geography of international lending by private banks, *Transactions of the Institute of British Geographers*, **12**: 413–432.

Furley, P. (1993), Tropical moist forests: transformation or conservation?, in: Roberts, N. (ed.), *The Changing Global Environment*, Oxford: Basil Blackwell.

Furtado, J., Morgan, W.B., Pfafflin, J.R. and Ruddle, K. (eds) (1992), *Tropical Resources: Ecology and Development*, Philadelphia: Harwood Academic.

Gade, D. and Escobar, M. (1982), Village settlement and the colonial legacy in Southern Peru, *Geographical Review*, **72**(4): 430–449.

Galtung, (1971), A structural theory of imperialism, *Journal of Peace Research*, **8**: 81–117.

Gamini, G. (1992), Shining Path rebels lose control of stronghold to army, *The Times*, May 29: 10.

Gardiner, R. (1992), *The Shipping Revolution*, London: Conway Maritime.

Geeraerts, G. (1991), Basic research on war: theoretical need and practical relevance, *Bulletin of Peace Proposals*, **22**(3): 346–552.

George, S. (1988), *A Fate Worse than Debt*, Harmondsworth: Penguin.

Giddens, A. (1979), *Central Problems in Social Theory: Action, Structure and Contradiction in Social Analysis*, London: Macmillan.

Gidwitz, B. (1980), *The Politics of International Air Transport*, Lexington: DC Heath.

Gilbert, A.G. (1992), *An Unequal World*, Walton-on-Thames: Thomas Nelson.

Gilbert, A. and Goodman, D.E. (1976), Regional income disparities in development, in: Gilbert, A. (ed.), *Development Planning and Spatial Structure*, New York: Wiley, 113–142.

Gilbert, A.G. and Gugler, J. (1982), *Cities, Poverty and Development: Urbanization in the Third World*, Oxford: Oxford University Press.

Gilbert, A.G. and Varley, A. (1991), *Landlord and Tenant: Housing the Poor in Urban Mexico*, London: Routledge.

Ginsburg, N., Osborne, J. and Blank, G. (1986), *Geographic Perspectives on the Wealth of Nations*, Chicago: Department of Geography, University of Chicago.

Glacken, C.J. (1967), *Traces on the Rhodian Shore: Nature and Culture in Western Thought from Ancient Times to the End of the Eighteenth Century*, Berkeley and Los Angeles: University of California Press.

Glantz, M.H. and Katz, R.W. (1986), Drought as a constraint to development in sub-Saharan Africa, *Ambio*, **6**: 334–339.

Glantz, M.H., Katz, R.W. and Nicholls, N. (1991), *Teleconnections: Linkages between ENSO, World-wide Climate Anomalies and Societal Impacts*, Cambridge: Cambridge University Press.

Glassner, M.I. (1992), *Political Geography*, New York: John Wiley.

Gold, E. (1981), *Maritime Transport*, Lexington: D.C. Heath.

Goldgeier, J.M. and McFaul, M. (1992), A tale of two worlds: core and periphery in the post-cold war era, *International Organisation*, **46**(2): 467–491.

Gonzales, E. (1984), *Economía de la Comunidad Campesina*, Lima: Instituto de Estudios Peruanos.

Gonzalez, A. (1988), Indexes of socio-economic development, in: Norwine, J. and Gonzalez, A. (eds) *The Third World: States of Mind and Being*, London: Unwin Hyman, 37–49.

Gonzalez de la Rocha, M. (1988), Economic crisis, domestic reorganization and women's work in Guadalajara, Mexico, *Bulletin of Latin American Research*, **7**(2): 207–224.

Goodland, R. (1985), Brazil's environmental progress in Amazonian development, in: Hemming, J. (ed.), *Change in the Amazon Basin*, Manchester: Manchester University Press, volume 1, 5–35.

Goodman, D. and Hall, A. (eds) (1990), *The Future of Amazonia: Destruction or Sustainable Development*, London: Macmillan.

Gould, P.R. (1969), Problems of space preference measures and relationships, *Geographical Analysis*, **1**: 31–44.

Gould, P.R. and White, R. (1974), *Mental Maps*, Harmondsworth: Penguin.

Gould, W.T.S. (1988), Government policies and international migration of skilled workers in Sub-Saharan Africa, *Geoforum*, **19**(4): 433–445.

Gould, W.T.S. (1993), *People and Education in the Third World*, Harlow: Longman.

Gray, A. (ed.) (1993), *World Health and Diseases*, Buckingham: Open University Press, OU Health and Disease Series, 3.

Green, D. (1991), *Faces of Latin America*, London: Latin America Bureau.

Green, R.H. (1991), *Reduction of Absolute Poverty: a Priority Structural Adjustment*, Brighton: Institute of Development Studies, Discussion Paper 287.

Gregory, D. and Urry, J. (eds) (1985), *Social Relations and Spatial Structures*, Basingstoke: Macmillan.

Griffin, K. (1991), Foreign aid after the Cold War, *Development and Change*, **22**: 645–685.

Grigg, D. (1974), *The Agricultural Systems of the World*, Cambridge: Cambridge University Press.

Grigg, D. (1982), *The Dynamics of Agricultural Change*, Cambridge: Cambridge University Press.

Grigg, D. (1984), *An Introduction to Agricultural Geography*, London: Hutchinson.

Grimal, H. (1978), *Decolonization: the British, French, Dutch and Belgian Empires 1919–1963*, London: Routledge and Kegan Paul.

Guma, X.P. (1987), The revised Southern African Customs Union Agreement: an appraisal, *South African Journal of Economics*, **58**(1): 63–73.

Haakonson, J.M. (1979), *Survey of the Fishing Co-operatives for Resettled Nomads in Somalia*, Montreal: Report Prepared for the Somali Democratic Republic, Ministry of Fisheries by the Food and Agriculture Organisation of the United Nations.

Hallett, R. (1970), *Africa to 1875*, Ann Arbor: University of Michigan Press.

Hallett, R. (1974), *Africa since 1875*, Ann Arbor: University of Michigan Press.

Halliday, F. (1986), *The Making of the Second Cold War*, London: Verso.

Hancock, G. (1989), *Lords of Poverty*, London: Macmillan.

Hardgrave, R.L. and Kochanek, S. (1986), *India: Government and Politics in a Developing Nation*, Princeton: Princeton University Press, 4th ed.

Hardoy, J.E. and Gutman, M. (1991), The role of municipal government in the protection of historic centres in Latin American cities, *Environment and Urbanization*, **3**(1): 96–108.

Hardoy, J.E. and Satterthwaite, D. (1989), *Environmental Problems in Third World Cities: a Global Issue Ignored?*, London: International Institute for Environment and Development.

Hardy, C. (1987), The prospects for growth and structural change in southern Africa, *Development Dialogue*, **1987**(2): 33–58.

Hargreaves, J.D. (1984), The Berlin West Africa Conference. A timely centenary?, *History Today*, **34** (Nov.): 16–22.

Harloe, M. (1985), *Private Rented Housing in the US and Europe*, London: Croom Helm.

Harris, O. (1980), *Latin American Women*, London: Minority Rights Group Report.

Harrison, D. (1992), *Tourism and the Less Developed Countries*, London: Pinter.

Harrison, P. (1987), *The Greening of Africa*, London: Paladin.

Harrison, P. (1993), *The Third Revolution: Population, Environment and a Sustainable World*, Harmondsworth: Penguin.

Harriss, J. and Harriss, B. (1979), Development studies, *Progress in Human Geography*, **3**: 576–584.

Harvey, D. (1989), *The Condition of Postmodernity: an Enquiry into the Origins of Cultural Change*, Oxford: Basil Blackwell.

Hashemite Kingdom of Jordan (1990), *Survey of Household Fertility*, Amman: DHS/Department of Statistics, Hashemite Kingdom of Jordan.

Hayami, Y. and Kikuchi, M. (1981), *Asian Village Economy at the Crossroads: an Economic Approach to Institutional Change*, Tokyo: University of Tokyo Press.

Hayter, T. (1989), *Exploited Earth: Britain's Aid and the Environment*, London: Earthscan.

Hecht, S. and Cockburn, A. (1990), *The Fate of the Forest*, London: Penguin Books.

Hechter, M. (1983), Internal colonialism revisited, in: Drakakis-Smith, D.W. and Williams, S.W. (eds) (1983), *Internal Colonialism: Essays Around a Theme*, Edinburgh: Department of Geography, University of Edinburgh on behalf of the Developing Areas Research Group of the Institute of British Geographers, 28–40.

Heldt, B. (1992), *States in Armed Conflict 1990, 1991*, Uppsala: Department of Peace and Conflict Resolution, Uppsala University.

Helburn, N. (1957), The bases for a classification of world agriculture, *Professional Geographer*, **9**: 2–7.

Henderson, J. (1989), *The Globalisation of High-Technology Production*, London: Routledge.

Henderson-Sellers, A. and Robinson, P.J. (1986), *Contemporary Climatology*, New York: Longman Scientific and Technical.

Henige, D.P. (1970), *Colonial Governors from the Fifteenth Century to the Present*, Madison: University of Wisconsin Press.

Hess, A.C. (1970), The creation of the Ottoman seaborne empire in the age of oceanic discoveries, 1453–1525, *American Historical Review*, **75**: 892–919.

Hewison, R. (1987), *The Heritage Industry*, London: Methuen.

Hill, H. (1992), Regional development in a boom and bust petroleum economy: Indonesia since 1970, *Economic Development and Cultural Change*, **40**(2): 351–379.

Hill, R.D., Owen, N.G. and Roberts, E.C. (eds) (1991), *Fishing in Troubled Waters: Territorial Claims in the South China Sea*, Hong Kong: Centre of Asian Studies, University of Hong Kong.

Hills, J. (1990), The telecommunication rich and poor, *Third World Quarterly*, **12**(2): 71–90.

Hobsbawm, E.J. (1987), *The Age of Empire, 1875–1914*, London: Guild.

Holdridge, L.R. (1947), Determination of world plant formations from simple climatic data, *Science*, **105**: 367–368.

Holdridge, L.R. (1964), *Life Zone Ecology*, San José, Costa Rica: Tropical Science Centre.

Hollist, W.L. and Tullis, F.L. (eds) (1987), *Pursuing Food Security: Strategies and Obstacles in Asia, Africa, Latin America and the Middle East*, Boulder: Lynne Rienner.

Hotelling, H. (1929), Stability in competition, *Economic Journal*, **39**(3): 41–57.

Houghton, J.T., Callendar, B.A. and Varney, S.K. (eds) (1992), *Climate Change 1992: the Supplementary Report to the IPCC Scientific Assessment*, Cambridge: Cambridge University Press.

Howard, M.C. and King, J.E. (eds) (1976), *The Economics of Marx: Selected Readings of Exposition and Criticism*, Harmondsworth: Penguin.

Howe, G.M. (ed.) (1977), *A World Geography of Human Diseases*, London: Academic Press.

Howitt, R. (1990), A different Kimberley: Aboriginal marginalization and the Argyle diamond mine, *Geography*, **74**(3): 232–238.

Hoyle, B.S. (1988), *Transport and Development in Tropical Africa*, London: John Murray.

Hoyle, B.S. and Knowles, R.D. (1992), *Modern Transport Geography*, London: Belhaven.

Huddleston, B. (1990), FAO's overall approach and methodology for formulating national food security programmes in developing countries, *IDS Bulletin*, **21**(3): 72–80.

Hulme, M., Marsh, R. and Jones, P.D. (1992a), Global changes in a humidity index between 1931–60 and 1961–90, *Climate Research*, **2**: 1–22.

Hulme, M., Wigley, T.M.L., Jiang, T., Zhao, Z-C., Wang, F., Ding, Y., Leemans, R. and Markham, A. (1992b), *Climate Change due to the Greenhouse Effect and its Implications for China*, Gland: WWF International.

Huppi, M. and Ravallion, M. (1991), The sectoral structure of poverty during an adjustment period: evidence for Indonesia in the mid–1980s, *World Development*, **19**(12): 1653–1678.

Hyden, G. (1980), *Beyond Ujamaa in Tanzania: Underdevelopment and an Uncaptured Peasantry*, London: Heinemann.

ICOMOS (International Council on Monuments and Sites) (1991), *World Heritage List*, London: International Council on Monuments and Sites.

IFAD (International Fund for Agricultural Development) (1992), *Soil and Water Conservation in Sub-Saharan Africa. Towards Sustainable Production by the Rural Poor. A Report Prepared by the Centre for Development Cooperation Services, Free University, Amsterdam*, Rome: International Fund for Agricultural Development.

Ilbery, B.W. (1985), *Agricultural Geography: a Social and Economic Analysis*, Oxford: Oxford University Press.

ILO (International Labour Office) (1990), *Year Book of Labour Statistics*, Geneva: International Labour Office.

ILO (International Labour Office) (1992), *World Labour Report*, Geneva: International Labour Office.

IMF (International Monetary Fund) (1991), *International Financial Statistics Yearbook 1990*, Washington DC: International Monetary Fund.

İnalcık, H. (1973), *The Ottoman Empire: the Classical Age 1300–1600*, London: Weidenfeld and Nicolson.

International Civil Aviation Organisation (monthly), monthly statistics *International Civil Aviation Organisation Journal*.

International Civil Aviation Organisation (annual), annual statistics, *International Civil Aviation Organisation Journal*.

International Road Federation (1991), *World Road Statistics*, Geneva: International Road Federation.

IRRI (International Rice Research Institute) (1994), *IRRI Rice Facts*, Philippines: International Rice Research Institute.

IPCC (Intergovernmental Panel on Climatic Change) (1990), *Climatic Change: the IPCC Scientific Assessment*, Cambridge: Cambridge University Press.

IPCC (Intergovernmental Panel on Climatic Change) (1992), *Climatic Change 1992: the Supplementary Report to the IPCC Scientific Assessment*, Cambridge: Cambridge University Press.

Islamoğlu, H. and Faroqhi, S. (1979), Crop-patterns and agricultural production trends in sixteenth-century Anatolia, *Review*, **2**: 401–436.

IUCN (International Union for the Conservation of Nature) (1989), *The IUCN Sahel Studies*, Gland: International Union for the Conservation of Nature.

James, W.P.T. and Schofield, E.C. (1990), *Human Energy Requirements: a Manual for Planners and Nutritionists*, Oxford: Oxford University Press by arrangement with FAO.

Janzen, J. (1984), Nomadismus in Somalia, *Afrika-Spektrum*, **19**(2): 149–171.

Janzen, J. (1986), The process of nomadic sedentarisation – distinguishing features, problems and consequences for Somali development policy, in: Conze, P. and Labahn, T. (eds), *Agriculture in the Winds of Change*, Saarbrücken: EPI-Dokumentation 2, 73–91.

Jeppie, S. and Soudien C. (eds) (1990), *The Struggle for District Six: Past and Present*, Cape Town: Buchu Books.

Johnston, R. (1989), The individual and the world-economy, in: Johnston, R.J. and Taylor, P.J. (eds), *World in Crisis*, Oxford: Blackwell, 205–226.

Johnston, R.J. (1987), The minority problem in a multicultural world, *Geography Review*, September: 23–28.

Johnston, R.J., O'Loughlin, J. and Taylor, P.J. (1987), The geography of violence and premature death, in: Vayrynen, R. (ed.), *The Quest for Peace*, London: Sage, 241–295.

Jones, G.A. and Varley, A. (1994), The contest for the city centre: street traders versus buildings, *Bulletin of Latin American Research*, **13** (1): 27–44.

Jones, H. (1990), *Population Geography*, London: Paul Chapman.

Jones, P.D. and Briffa, K.R. (1992), Global surface air temperature variations: part I the instrumental period, *Holocene*, **2**: 174–188.

Jones, P.D., Wigley, T.M.L. and Farmer, G. (1991), Marine and land temperature data sets: a comparison and looks at recent trends, in: Schlesinger, M.E. (ed.), *Greenhouse-gas-induced Climatic Change: a Critical Appraisal of Simulations and Observations*, Amsterdam: Elsevier, 153–172.

Jones, R.C. (1978), Myth maps and migration in Venezuela, *Economic Geography*, **54**: 75–91.

Jowett, A.J. (1989), *China's One Child Programme*, Glasgow: University of Glasgow, Applied Population Research Unit Discussion Paper 89/3.

Kabeer, N. (1991), Gender dimensions of rural poverty: analysis from Bangladesh, *Journal of Peasant Studies*, **18**(2): 241–262.

Keely, C. and Tran, B. (1989), Remittances from labour migration, *International Migration Review*, **87**: 500–525.

Keen, D. (1992), *Refugees: Rationing the Right to Life. The Crisis in Emergency Relief*, London: Zed Press.

Kemp, J. (1981), Legal and informal land tenures in Thailand, *Modern Asian Studies*, **15**(1): 1–23.

Kendall, L.C. (1986), *The Business of Shipping*, Maryland: Centreville, Cornell Maritime.

Kennedy, E. and Peters, P. (1992), Household food security and child nutrition: the interaction of income and gender of household head, *World Development*, **20**(8): 1077–1086.

Kennedy, T.L. (1988), *Transport in Southern Africa*, Johannesburg: South African Institute of International Affairs.

Kent, R.B. (1986), National atlases: the influence of wealth and political orientation on content, *Geography*, **71**(2): 122–130.

Kidron, M. and Segal. R. (1981), *The State of the World Atlas*, London: Pan.

Kidron, M. and Segal. R. (1984), *The New State of the World Atlas*, London: Pan.

Kimmel, M.S. (1990), *Revolution, a Sociological Interpretation*, Cambridge: Polity Press.

King, R. (1990), *Visions of the World and Language of Maps*, Dublin: Department of Geography, Trinity College Dublin, Trinity Papers in Geography, 1.

King, R. and Vujakovic, P. (1989) Peters Atlas: a new era of cartography or publisher's con-trick?, *Geography*, **74**(3): 247–254.

Knox, P. and Agnew, J. (1989), *The Geography of the World Economy*, London: Routledge.

Kohli, A. (1990), *Democracy and Discontent: India's Growing Crisis of Governability*, Princeton: Princeton University Press.

Kumar, U. (1990), Southern African Customs Union and BLS-countries (Botswana, Lesotho and Swaziland), *Journal of World Trade*, **24**(3): 31–53.

Kurian, G (ed.) (1992), *Atlas of the Third World*, New York: Facts on File, 2nd ed.

Labahn, T. (1982), Nomadenansiedlungen in Somalia, in: Scholz, F. and Janzen, J. (eds), *Nomadismus – Ein Entwicklungsproblem?*, Berlin: Abhandlungen des Geographisches Instituts – Anthropogeographie 33, 81–95.

Lancaster, C. (1992), The Lagos Three: economic regionalism in sub-Saharan Africa, in: Harbeson, J.W. and Rothchild, D. (eds), *Africa in World Politics*, Boulder: Westview, 249–267.

Laquain, A. (1983), *Basic Housing; Policies for Urban Sites, Services and Shelter in Developing Countries*, Ottawa: International Development Research Center.

Larson, R.L., Pitman III, W.C., Golovchenko, X., Cande, S.C., Dewey, J.F., Haxby, W.F. and LaBrecque, J.L. (1985), *The Bedrock Geology of the World*, New York: W.H. Freeman.

Lau, K.M. and Sheu, P.J. (1988), Annual cycle, quasi-biennial oscillation, and Southern Oscillation in global precipitation, *Journal of Geophysical Research Series D*, **93**: 10975–10988.

Leatherby, J. (1989), The millions forced to flee, *Geographical Magazine*, December: 14–19.

Leemans, R. (1990), *Possible Changes in Natural Vegetation Patterns Due to Global Warming*, Laxenburg, Austria: International Institute for Applied Systems Analysis, Biosphere Dynamics Project (Publication No. 108).

Legates, D.R. and Willmott, C.J. (1989), Global air temperature and precipitation digital data, in: *Global Ecosystems Database*, Boulder: NOAA/NGDC.

Legates, D.R. and Willmott, C.J. (1990a), Mean seasonal and spatial variability in global surface air temperature, *Theoretical and Applied Climatology*, **41**: 11–21.

Legates, D.R. and Willmott, C.J. (1990b), Mean seasonal and spatial variability in gauge-corrected global precipitation, *International Journal of Climatology*, **10**: 111–127.

Legates, D.R. and Willmott, C.J. (1992), Monthly Average Surface Air Temperature and Precipitation. Digital Raster Data on a 30 minute Geographic (lat/long) 360 × 720 grid, in: *Global Ecosystems Database Version 1.0: Disc A*, Boulder, Colorado: NOAA Geophysical Data Center.

Leggett, J., Pepper, W.J. and Swart, R.J. (1992), Emissions scenarios for the IPCC: an update, in: Houghton, J.T., Callendar, B.A. and Varney, S.K. (eds), *Climate Change 1992: the Supplementary Report to the IPCC Scientific Assessment*, Cambridge: Cambridge University Press, 75–95.

Lehmann, D. (ed.) (1982), *Ecology and Exchange in the Andes*, Cambridge: Cambridge University Press.

Leinbach, T.R. (1975), Transportation and the development of Malaya, *Annals of the Association of American Geographers*, **65**: 270–282.

Lemon, A. (1976), *Apartheid: a Geography of Separation*, Farnborough: Saxon House.

Lemon, A. (1987), *Apartheid in Transition*, Aldershot: Gower.

Lemon, A. (ed.) (1991), *Homes Apart: South Africa's Segregated Cities*, London: Paul Chapman.

Leo, C. (1984), *Land and Class in Kenya*, Toronto: University of Toronto Press.

Lightfoot, P. and Fuller, T. (1983), Circular rural-urban movement and development planning in northeast Thailand, *Geoforum*, **14**: 277–287.

Lipton, M. (1977), *Why Poor People Stay Poor: a Study of Urban Bias in World Development*, London: Temple Smith.

Lipton, M. and Longhurst, R. (1989), *New Seeds and Poor People*, London: Unwin Hyman.

Logan, B.I. (1990), An assessment of the Transfer of Knowledge through Expatriate Nationals (TOKTEN) programme in sub-Saharan Africa, *Applied Geography*, **10**(2): 223–236.

Loh, C. (1993), The rights stuff, *Far Eastern Review*, July 8: 15.

Long, R.G. (1948), Volta Redonda: symbol of maturity in industrial progress in Brazil, *Economic Geography*, **24**: 149–54.

Lowenthal, D. (1985), *The Past is a Foreign Country*, Cambridge: Cambridge University Press.

Luard, E. (1988), *The Blunted Sword: the Erosion of Military Power in Modern World Politics*, London: Tauris.

Lugo, A.E. (1990), Development, forestry, and environmental quality in the eastern Caribbean, in: Beller, W., d'Ayal P., and Hein, P. (eds), *Sustainable Development and Environmental Management of Small Islands*, Carnwath: Parthenon Publishing, 317–342.

Luxmoore, R. and Swanson, T.M. (1992), Wildlife and wildland utilization and conservation, in: Swanson, T.M. and Barbier, E.B. (eds), *Economics for the Wilds: Wildlife, Wildlands, Diversity and Development*, London: Earthscan, 170–194.

Maasdorp, G. (1992), Economic co-operation in Southern Africa: prospects for regional integration, *Conflict Studies* **253**.

Mabogunje, A.L. (1980), *The Development Process: a Spatial Perspective*, London: Hutchinson.

MacArthur, R.H. (1972), *Geographical Ecology*, New York: Harper & Row.

MacPhee, C.R. and Hassan, M.K. (1990), Socio-economic determinants of Third World professional immigration to the United States: 1972–87, *World Development*, **18**(8): 1111–1118.

MacPherson, S. (1987), *Five Hundred Million Children: Poverty and Child Welfare in the Third World*, Sussex: Wheatsheaf Books.

Maling, D. (1974), A minor modification of the cylindrical equal-area projection, *Geographical Journal*, **140**: 599–600.

Malthus, T. (1798), *Essay on the Principle of Population*, London.

Mangin, W. (1967), Latin American squatter settlements: a problem and a solution, *Latin American Research Review*, **2**: 65–98.

Mann, J., Tarantola, D.J.M. and Netter, T.W. (eds) (1992), *AIDS in the World*, London: Harvard University Press.

Mantran, R. (ed.) (1989), *Histoire de l'Empire Ottoman*, Paris: Fayard.

Martin, M.F. (1990), Bias and inequity in rural incomes in post-reform China, *Journal of Peasant Studies*, **17**(2): 273–287.

Martin, R.J. (1983), Upgrading, in: Skinner, R.J. and Rodell, M.J. (eds), *People, Poverty and Shelter: Problems of Housing in Developing Countries*, London: Methuen, 53–79.

Martorell, R. (1985), Child growth retardation: a discussion of its causes and its relationship to health, in: Blaxter, K. and Waterlow, J.C. (eds), *Nutritional Adaptation in Man*, London and Paris: John Libbey.

Martyn, D. (1992), *Climates of the World*, Amsterdam: Elsevier, Developments in Atmospheric Science, 18.

Marx, K. (1976), *Capital Volume 1*, Harmondsworth: Penguin.

Massey, D. (1973), Towards a critique of industrial location theory, *Antipode*, **5**: 33–39.

Massey, D. (1984), *Spatial Divisions of Labour: Social Structures and the Geography of Production*, New York: Methuen.

Mauldin, W.P. and Ross, J. (1991), Family planning programs, efforts and results, 1982–89, *Studies in Family Planning*, **22**: 350–367.

Maxwell, S, (1990), Food security for developing countries: issues and options, *IDS Bulletin*, **21**(3): 2–13.

Maxwell, S. (ed.) (1990), Food security in developing countries, *IDS Bulletin*, **21**(3).

Mazrui, A.A. (1986), In search of self-reliance: capitalism without winter, in: Mazrui, A.A. (ed.), *The Africans: a Triple Heritage*, London: Guild Publishing, 213–239.

McAuley, A. (1991), The economic consequences of Soviet disintegration, *Soviet Economy*, 7: 189–214.

McConnell, G. (1991), *A Macro-sociolinguistic Analysis of Language Vitality*, Quebec: Les Presses de l'Université Laval.

McGlashen, N.D. and Blunden J.R. (eds) (1983), *Geographical Aspects of Health*, London: Academic Press.

McGregor, D.F.M. and Barker, D. (1991), Land degradation and hillside farming in the Fall River basin, Jamaica, *Applied Geography*, 11: 143–156.

Meadows, D. *et al.* (1972), *The Limits to Growth*, Washington DC: Potomac Associates.

Mehmet, O. (1986), *Development in Malaysia: Poverty, Wealth and Trusteeship*, London: Croom Helm.

Mellor, J.W. (1988), Global food balances and food security, *World Development*, 16(9): 997–1011.

Merriam, A. (1988), What does 'Third World' mean?, in: Norwine, J. and Gonzalez, A. (eds), *The Third World: States of Mind and Being*, Boston: Unwin Hyman, 15–22.

Mews, S. (ed.) (1989), *Religion in Politics: a World Guide*, London: Longman.

Michel, A.A. (1967), *The Indus Rivers*, New Haven: Yale University Press.

Milliman, J.D., Broadus, J.M. and Gable, F. (1989), Environmental and economic implications of rising sea level and subsiding deltas: the Nile and Bengal examples, *Ambio*, 18: 340–345.

Mills-Tettey, R. (1986), New Bussa: the township and resettlement scheme, *Third World Planning Review*, 8: 31–50.

Ministry of Foreign Affairs, Jerusalem (1985), *Facts about Israel*, Jerusalem: Ministry of Foreign Affairs.

MOAC (Ministry of Agriculture and Co-operatives) (1990), *Agricultural Statistics of Thailand, Crop Year 1989/90*, Bangkok: Ministry of Agriculture and Co-operatives.

Mohamed, A.F. and Touati, J. (1991), *Sedentarisierung von Nomaden – Chancen und Gefahren einer Entwicklungsstrategie am Beispiel Somalias*, Saarbrücken: Bielefeld Studies on the Sociology of Development, 48.

Momsen, J. and Townsend, J. (1987), *Geography of Gender in the Third World*, London: Hutchinson.

Monkhouse, F.J. and Wilkinson, H.R. (1963), *Maps and Diagrams*, London: Methuen, 2nd ed.

Monmonier, M. (1991), *How to Lie with Maps*, Chicago: University of Chicago Press.

Morgan, D. (1979), *Merchants of Grain*, London: Weidenfeld and Nicolson.

Morris, M.D. (1979), *Measuring the Condition of the World's Poor*, Washington DC: Pergamon.

Mortimore, M.J. (1989), *Adapting to Drought: Farmers, Famines and Desertification in West Africa*, Cambridge: Cambridge University Press.

Mosley, P., Toye, P. and Harrigan, J. (1991), *Aid and Power. The World Bank and Policy-based Lending*, London: Routledge.

Mountjoy, A. (1980), Worlds without end, *Third World Quarterly*, 2(4): 753–757.

Muir, K. (1989), The potential role of indigenous resources in the economic development of arid environments in sub-Saharan Africa: the case of wildlife utilization in Zimbabwe, *Society and Natural Resources*, 2: 307–318.

Murra, J. (1956), The Economic Organisation of the Inca State, unpublished Ph.D. thesis, University of Chicago.

Murray, J.S. (1987), The map is the message, *Geographical Magazine*, 46(8): 237–241.

Mwase. N. (1987), Zambia, the TAZARA and the alternative outlets to the sea, *Transport Reviews*, 7(3): 191–206.

Myers, N. (1989), *Deforestation Rates in Tropical Forests and their Climatic Implications*, London: Friends of the Earth Publication.

Myers, R. (1992), *The Twelve who Survive: Strengthening Programmes of Early Childhood Development in the Third World*, London: Routledge in co-operation with UNESCO for The Consultative Group on Early Childhood Care and Development.

Najafizadeh, M. and Mennerick, L.A. (1988), Worldwide educational expansion from 1950 to 1980: the failure of the expansion of schooling in Developing Countries, *The Journal of Developing Areas*, 22(2): 333–358.

Naveau, J. (1989), *International Air Transport in a Changing World*, London: Nijhoff.

Naylor, R.T. (1987), *Hot Money and the Politics of Debt*, London: Unwin Hyman.

Nebenzahl, K. (1990), *Maps from the Age of Discovery: Columbus to Mercator*, London: Times Books.

Newell, C. (1988), *Methods and Models of Demography*, London: Belhaven.

Nijman, J. (1992), The political geography of the post cold war world, *The Professional Geographer*, 44: 1–3.

Nitz, H.-J. (ed.) (1993), *The Early Modern World–System in Geographical Perspective*, Stuttgart: Franz Steiner Verlag.

North, F.K. (1985), *Petroleum Geology*, London and Sydney: Allen and Unwin.

Norwine, J. and Gonzalez, A. (1988), *The Third World: States of Mind and Being*, London: Unwin Hyman.

Nyerere, J.K. (1968), *Freedom and Socialism*, London: Oxford University Press.

OECD (Organisation for Economic Cooperation and Development) (annual), *Maritime Transport*, Paris: Organisation for Economic Cooperation and Development.

OECD (Organisation for Economic Cooperation and Development) (1990), *National Policies and Agricultural Trade*, Paris: Organisation for Economic Cooperation and Development.

OECD (Organisation for Economic Cooperation and Development) (1991), *Agricultural Policies, Markets and Trade: Monitoring and Outlook*, Paris: Organisation for Economic Cooperation and Development.

OECD (Organisation for Economic Co-operation and Development) Development Centre (1992), *Directory of Non-Governmental and Development Organisations in OECD Member Countries*, Paris: Organisation for Economic Co-operation and Development.

Oldeman, L.R., Hakkeling, R.T.A. and Sombroek, W.G. (1990), *World Map on the Status of Human-induced Soil Degradation. At a Scale of 1:10 Million with Explanatory Note*, Wageningen: International Soil Reference and Information Centre.

Oliver, R. (ed.) (1977), *The Cambridge History of Africa*, Cambridge: Cambridge University Press.

Omiunu, F. (1987), Transport policy for the ECOWAS sub-region, *Transport Reviews*, 7(4): 327–340.

Omran, A. (1971), The epidemiologic transition, *Millbank Memorial Fund Quarterly*, 19: 509–538.

Orlansky, D. and Dubrovsky, S. (1978), *The Effects of Rural-Urban Migration on Women's Role and Status in Latin America*, Paris: United Nations Economic, Social and Cultural Organisation.

Owen, W. (1987), *Transportation and World Development*, Baltimore: Johns Hopkins University Press; London: Hutchinson.

Packard, R.M. and Epstein, P. (1991), Epidemiologists, social scientists, and the structure of medical research on AIDS in Africa, *Social Science and Medicine*, 33(7): 771–794.

Panos Institute (1992), *The Hidden Costs of AIDS: the Challenge of HIV to Development*, London: Panos.

Papps, I. (1992), Women, work and well-being in the Middle East: an outline of the relevant literature, *Journal of Development Studies*, 28(4): 595–615.

Paranjpye, V. (1990), *High Dams on the Narmada*, New Delhi: India National Trust for Art and Cultural Heritage (Intach).

Parnwell, M. (1993), *Population Movements in the Third World*, London: Routledge.

Parry, M.L., Carter, T.R. and Konijn, N.T. (eds), (1988), *The Impact of Climatic Variations on Agriculture, Vol. 2: Assessments in Semi-Arid Regions*, Dordrecht: Kluwer Academic Publishers.

Parry, R.B. (1987), The state of world mapping, in: Parry, R.B. and Perkins, C.R. (eds), *World Mapping Today*, London: Butterworths, 6–14.

Paskett, C.J. and Philcotete, C-E. (1990), Soil Conservation in Haiti, *Journal of Soil and Water Conservation*, 45: 457–459.

Patterson, S. (1986), *World Bauxite Resources*, Washington DC: United States Geological Survey, Professional Paper, 1076.

Payer, C. (1985), Repudiating the past, *NACLA: Report on the Americas*, March/April: 14–24.

Payne, G.K. (ed.) (1984), *Low-income Housing in the Developing World: the Roles of Sites and Services and Settlement Upgrading*, Chichester: Wiley.

Payne, P.R. (1990), Measuring malnutrition, *IDS Bulletin*, 21(3): 14–30.

Pelletier, D.L. (1991), *Relationship Between Child Anthropometry and Mortality in Developing Countries: Implications for Policy, Programs and Future Research*, Cornell: Cornell Food and Nutrition Policy Program, Monograph 12.

Perry, M. (1991), The Singapore growth triangle: state, capital and labour at a new frontier in the world economy, *Singapore Journal of Tropical Geography*, 12: 25–46.

Peters, A. (1983), *The New Cartography*, New York: Friendship Press.

Peters, A. (1989) *Peters' Atlas of the World*, Harlow: Longman.

Peters, C.M., Gentry, A.H. and Mendelsohn, R.O. (1989), Valuation of an Amazonian rainforest, *Nature*, 339: 655–656.

Petroconsultants S.A., Geneva (1986), *World sedimentary basins*, map at scale of 1:23 million.

Phillips, D. (1988), *The Epidemiological Transition in Hong Kong*, Hong Kong: University of Hong Kong, Centre for Asian Studies Occasional Papers, 75.

Pickles, J. (1988), Recent changes in regional policy in South Africa, *Geography*, 73(3): 233–239.

Pickles, J. and Weiner, D. (1991), Rural and regional restructuring of Apartheid: ideology, development policy and the competition for space, *Antipode*, 23(1): 2–32.

Pierce, J.T. (1990), *The Food Resource*, London: Longman.

Pirie, G.H. (1982), The decivilizing rails; railways and underdevelopment in southern Africa, *Tijdschrift voor Economische en Sociale Geografie*, 73(4): 221–228.

Pirie, G.H. (1984), Race zoning in South Africa: board, court, parliament, public, *Political Geography Quarterly*, 3(3): 207–221.

Pirie, G.H. (1993), Slaughter by steam: railway subjugation of ox wagon transport in the eastern Cape and Transkei, 1886–1910, *International Journal of African Historical Studies*, 26(2): 319–343.

Planning Institute of Jamaica (1992), *Economic and Social Survey: Jamaica 1991*, Kingston, Jamaica: Planning Institute of Jamaica.

Platzky, L. and Walker, C. (1985), *The Surplus People: Forced Removals in South Africa*, Johannesburg: Ravan.

Population Crisis Committee (1993), *An Index of Human Suffering*, Washington DC: Population Crisis Committee.

Population Reference Bureau (1991), *1991 World Population Data Sheet*, Washington DC: Population Reference Bureau.

Porteus, J.D. (1973), The company state: a Chilean case study, *Canadian Geographer*, 17: 113–126.

Posey, D. and Balee, W. (eds) (1989), Resource management in Amazonia: indigenous and folk strategies, *Advances in Economic Botany*, 7: 1–240.

Post, K. and Wright, P. (1989), *Socialism and Underdevelopment*, London: Routledge.

Potter, R.B. (1983), *Spatial Perceptions and Physical Development Planning in Trinidad and Tobago*, London: Department of Geography, Bedford College, University of London, Papers in Geography, 15.

Potter, R.B. (1985), *Urbanisation and Planning in the Third World: Spatial Perceptions and Public Participation*, London: Croom Helm; New York: St Martin's Press.

Potter, R.B. (1986), Housing upgrading in Barbados: the Tenantries programme, *Geography*, 71: 255–257.

Potter, R.B. (1992), *Urbanisation in the Third World*, Oxford: Oxford University Press.

Potter, R.B. and Unwin, T. (1988), Developing areas research in British geography, *Area*, 20(2): 121–126.

Potter, R.B. and Unwin, T. (1989), *The Geography of Urban-Rural Interaction in Developing Countries: Essays for Alan B. Mountjoy*, London: Routledge.

PREALC (Oficina Internacional de Trabajo-PRE-América Latina y Caribe) (1985), *Antecedentes para el Análisis del Trabajo de los Menores. Tres Estudios: América Latina, Costa Rica y Brasil*, Santiago: OIT-PREALC.

Prescott, J.R.V. (1985), *The Maritime Political Boundaries of the World*, London: Methuen.

Prescott-Allen, R. and Prescott-Allen, C. (1982), *What's Wildlife Worth?*, London: Earthscan.

Preston, D. (1987), Population mobility and the creation of new landscapes, in: Preston, D. (ed.), *Latin American Development: Geographical Perspectives*, London: Longman, 229–259.

Prior, F.L. (1990), Changes in income distribution in poor agricultural nations: Malawi and Madagascar, *Economic Development and Cultural Change*, 39(1): 23–45.

Radcliffe, S.A. (1986), Women's Lives and Peasant Livelihood Strategies. A Study of Migration in the Peruvian Andes, unpublished Ph.D. thesis, University of Liverpool.

Radcliffe, S.A. (1990a), Marking the boundaries between the community, the state and history, *Journal of Latin American Studies*, 22(3): 575–594.

Radcliffe, S.A. (1990b), Between hearth and labor market: the recruitment of peasant women in the Andes, *International Migration Review*, 24(2): 229–249.

Radcliffe, S.A. (1992), Mountains, maidens and migration: gender and mobility in Peru, in: Chant, S. (ed.), *Gender and Migration in Developing Countries*, London: Belhaven, 30–48.

Rampino, M. (1992), Volcanic Hazards, in: Brown, G.C. *et al.* (eds.), *Understanding the Earth a New Synthesis*, Cambridge: Cambridge University Press, 506–522.

Rao, K.L. (1979), *India's Water Wealth*, New Delhi: Orient Longman.

Redclift, M. (1984), *Development and the Environmental Crisis: Red or Green Alternatives?*, London: Methuen.

Regan, C., Sinclair, S. and Turner, M. (1988), *Thin Black Lines: Political Cartoons and Development Education*, Birmingham: Development Education Centre.

Reichardt, M. and Duncan, D. (1990), Rail transport and the political economy of Southern Africa, 1965–1980, *Africa Insight*, 20(2): 100–110.

Renner, R. (1992), Creating sustainable employment in industrial countries, in: Brown, L.R. (ed.), *State of the World*, London: Earthscan, 138–154.

Republic of Kenya (1981), *Kenya Population Census 1979, Volume 1*, Nairobi: Central Bureau of Statistics.

Rhind, D. (1993), Maps, information and geography: a new relationship, *Geography*, 78(2):150–160.

Richards, P. (1985), *Indigenous Agricultural Revolution*, London: Hutchinson.

Richardson, B.H. (1992), *The Caribbean and the Wider World, 1492–1992*, New York: Cambridge University Press.

Richardson, H. (1989), The big, bad city: mega-city myth, *Third World Planning Review*, 11: 355–372.

Rigg, J. (1986), The Chinese agricultural middleman in Thailand: efficient or exploitative?, *Singapore Journal of Tropical Geography*, 7(1): 68–79.

Rigg, J. (1989), The new rice techology and agrarian change: guilt by association?, *Progress in Human Geography*, 13(3): 374–399.

Roberts, S. (1994), Fictitious capital, fictitious spaces?: the geography of offshore financial flows, in: Corbridge, S., Martin, R. and Thrift, N. (eds), *Money, Power and Space*, Oxford: Basil Blackwell.

Robinson, A.H. (1990), Rectangular world maps – no!, *Professional Geographer*, 42(1): 101–104.

Robinson, F. (ed.) (1989), *The Cambridge Encyclopedia of India, Pakistan, Bangladesh, Sri Lanka, Nepal, Bhutan and the Maldives*, Cambridge: Cambridge University Press.

Robinson, G.M. (1990), *Conflict and Change in the Countryside*, London: Belhaven Press.

Rodney, W. (1972), *How Europe Underdeveloped Africa*, Dar es Salaam: Tanzania Publishing House.

Ropelewski, C.F. and Halpert, M.S. (1987), Global and regional scale precipitation patterns associated with the El Niño/Southern Oscillation, *Monthly Weather Review*, 115: 1606–1626.

Ross, H. and Drakakis–Smith, D.W. (1983), Socio-spatial aspects of Australian Aboriginal underdevelopment, *Geoforum*, 14(3): 325–332.

Ross, J. and Frankenberg, E. (1993), *Findings from Two Decades of Family Planning Research*, New York: Population Council.

Ross, J., Mauldin, W.P., Green, S. and Cooke, E. (1992), *Family Planning and Child Survival Programs*, New York: Population Council.

Rostow, W.W. (1960), *The Stages of Economic Growth*, Cambridge: Cambridge University Press.

Rowell, D.P., Folland, C.K., Maskell, K., Owen, J.A. and Ward, M.N. (1992), *Geophysical Research Letters*, 19: 905–908.

Ruddiman, W.F., and Kutzbach, J.E. (1991), Plateau uplift and climatic change, *Scientific American*, March: 43– 48.

Saarinen, T.F. (1988), Centering of mental maps of the world, *National Geographic Research*, 4(1): 112–127.

Sachs, G. (1992), One world, in: Sachs, G. (ed.), *The Development Dictionary*, London: Zed Books, 102–115.

Sachs, G. (ed.) (1992), *The Development Dictionary*, London: Zed Books.

SADCC (Southern African Development Co-ordination Conference) (annual), *Progress Report*, Luanda: SADCC.

Sallnow, M. (1987), *Pilgrims of the Andes: Regional Cults in Cusco*, Washington DC: Smithsonian Institute.

Salt, J. (1989), A comparative overview of international trends and types, 1950–80, *International Migration Review*, 87: 431–456.

Schneider, C. and Wallis, B. (eds) (1988), *Global television*, New York: Wedge Press.

Scholz, F. (ed.) (1991), *Nomaden, Mobile Tierhaltung. Zur gegenwärtigen Lage von Nomaden und zu den Problemen und Chancen mobiler Tierhaltung*, Berlin: Das Arabische Buch.

Scholz, F. (ed.) (1992), *Nomadismus/Bibliographie*, Berlin: Das Arabische Buch.

Schwartzberg, J.E. (1993), *An Historical Atlas of South Asia*, Chicago: Chicago University Press, 2nd ed.

Scott, A. (1985), The semi-conductor industry in South East Asia: organisation, location and international division of labour, *Regional Studies*, 21(2): 143–160.

Seager, J. and Olson, A. (1986), *Women in the World: an International Atlas*, London: Pan Books.

Shackle, C. (ed.) (1985), *South Asian Languages: a Handbook*, London: School of Oriental and African Studies.

Sheng, T.C. (1972), A treatment-oriented land capability classification scheme for hilly marginal lands in the humid tropics, *Journal of the Science Research Council of Jamaica*, 3: 93–112.

Sheng, T.C. (1981), The need for soil conservation structures for steep cultivated slopes in the humid tropics, in: Lal, R. and Russell, E.W. (eds), *Tropical Agricultural Hydrology*, Chichester: John Wiley, 357–372.

Sicular, D.T. (1991), Pockets of peasants in Indonesian cities: the case of scavengers, *World Development*, 19(2–3): 137–162.

Sidaway, J.D. (1991), Contested terrain: transformation and continuity of the territorial organisation in Post-Independence Mozambique, *Tijdschrift voor Economische en Sociale Geografie*, 82(5): 367–376.

Sidaway, J.D. (1992), Mozambique: destabilisation, state, society and space, *Political Geography*, 11(3): 239–258.

Sidaway, J.D. and Simon, D. (1990), Spatial policies and uneven development in the Marxist-Leninist states of the Third World, in: Simon, D. (ed.), *Third World Regional Development*, London: Paul Chapman, 24–38.

Sill, M. (1992), Cultivating a new system, *Geographical Magazine*, 64(5): 45–50.

Simon, D. (1989), Crisis and change in South Africa: implications for the apartheid city, *Transactions of the Institute of British Geographers*, new series 14(2): 189–206.

Simon, D. (1991), Namibia in southern Africa: the regional implications of independence, *Tijdschrift voor Economische en Sociale Geografie*, **82**(5): 377–387.

Simon, D. (1992), Reform in South Africa and modernisation of the apartheid city, in: Drakakis-Smith, D. (ed.), *Urban and Regional Change in Southern Africa*, London: Routledge, 33–65.

Sinha, B. and Bhatia, R. (1984), *Economic Appraisal of Irrigation Projects in India*, New Delhi: Agricole Publishing.

SIPRI (Stockholm International Peace Research Institute) (annual), *World Armaments and Disarmament Yearbook*, Oxford: Oxford University Press.

Sivard, R.L. (1985), *Women – a World Survey*, Washington DC: World Priorities.

Skinner, R.J. and Rodell, M.J. (eds) (1983), *People, Poverty and Shelter: Problems of Housing in the Third World*, London: Methuen.

Skocpol, T. (1979), *States and Social Revolutions*, Cambridge: Cambridge University Press.

Slater, D. (1989), *Territory and State Power in Latin America: the Peruvian Case*, London: Macmillan.

Small, M. and Singer, J.D. (1982), *Resort to Arms, International and Civil Wars 1816–1980*, Beverley Hills, Sage.

Smith, D.M. (1985), *Apartheid in South Africa*, Cambridge: Cambridge University Press.

Smith D.M. (ed.) (1982), *Living Under Apartheid: Aspects of Urbanization and Social Change in South Africa*, London: George Allen & Unwin.

Smith D.M. (ed.) (1992), *The Apartheid City and Beyond*, London: Routledge.

Smith, G. (1993), Ends, geopolitics and transitions, in: Johnston, R.J. (ed.), *The Challenge for Geography. A Changing World: a Changing Discipline*, Oxford: Blackwell, 76–99.

Smith, J.A. (1989) Transport and marketing of horticultural crops by communal farmers in Harare, *Geographical Journal of Zimbabwe*, **20**: 1–14.

Smith, M. McLoughlin, J., Large, P. and Chapman, R. (1985), *Asia's New Industrial World*, London: Methuen.

Smith, N. (1982). Theories of underdevelopment, *Professional Geographer*, **34**(3): 332–337.

Smith, N. (1989), Uneven development and location theory: towards a synthesis, in Peet, R. and Thrift, N. (eds), *New Models in Geography: the Political-Economy Perspective, Volume 1*, London: Unwin Hyman, 142–163.

Smith, R.W. (1986), *Exclusive Economic Zone Claims: Analysis and Primary Dcouments*, Dordrecht: Martinus Nijhoff.

Sofer, M. (1993), Uneven regional development and internal labour migration in Fiji, *World Development*, **21**(2): 301–310.

Somali Democratic Republic (1977), *Objectives and Policy of the Resettlement*, Mogadishu: Settlement Development Agency (SDA).

Sopher, D.E. (1975), The geographic patterning of culture in India, in: Sopher, D.E. (ed.), *The Discovery of India*, Boulder: Westview Press, 289–326.

Starkie, D. (1982), *The Motorway Age*, Oxford: Pergamon.

Stavenhagen, R. (1986), Ethnodevelopment: a neglected dimension in development thinking, in: Anthorpe, R. and Krahl, A. (eds), *Development Studies: Critique and Renewal*, Leiden: E.J. Brill, 21–39.

Stavrianos, L.S. (1981), *Global Rift: the Third World Comes of Age*, New York: William Morrow.

Steensgard, N. (1974), *The Asian Trade Revolution of the Seventeenth Century*, Chicago: Chicago University Press.

Stewart, F. (1985), *Planning to Meet Basic Needs*, London: Macmillan.

Stickler, P.J. (1990), Invisible towns: a case study in the cartography of South Africa, *GeoJournal*, **22**(3): 329–333.

Stone, I. (1984), *Canal Irrigation in British India*, Cambridge: Cambridge University Press.

Strabo (1949), *The Geography of Strabo*, London: Heinemann.

Strakhov, N.M. (1967), *Principles of Lithogenesis, Volume 1*, Edinburgh: Oliver and Boyd.

Stubbs, L. (ed.) (1993), *The Third World Directory*, London: Directory of Social Change.

Sundrum, R.M. (1990), *Income Distribution in Less-developed Countries*, London: Routledge.

Swanson, T.M. and Barbier, E.B. (eds) (1992), *Economics for the Wilds: Wildlife, Wildlands, Diversity and Development*, London: Earthscan.

Swilling, M., Humphries, R. and Shubane, K. (eds) (1991). *Apartheid City in Transition*, Cape Town: Oxford University Press.

Tamayo, J. (1981), *Historia Social del Cuzco Republicano*, Lima: Editorial Universo.

Taneja, N.K. (1989), *Introduction to Civil Aviation*, Lexington: DC Heath.

Tarrant, J. (1974), *Agricultural Geography*, Newton Abbot: David and Charles.

Tarrant, J.R. (1985), A review of international food trade, *Progress in Human Geography*, **9**(2): 235–254.

Tata, R. and Schultz, R. (1988), World Variations in human welfare, *Annals of the Association of American Geographers*, **78**(4): 580–593.

Taylor, P.J. (1986), An exploration into world-systems analysis of political parties, *Political Geography Quarterly*, **5** (supplement): 5–20.

Taylor, P.J. (1990), Extending the world of electoral geography, in: Johnston, R.J., Shelley, F.M. and Taylor, P.J. (eds), *Developments in Electoral Geography*, London: Routledge.

Taylor, P. (1993a), Geopolitical world orders, in: Taylor, P.J. (ed.), *Political Geography of the Twentieth Century, a Global Analysis*, London: Belhaven, 33–61.

Taylor, P.J. (1993b), *Political Geography: World-Economy, Nation-State, and Locality*, London: Longman; New York: Wiley, 3rd ed.

Tecke, B. (1985), Determinants of child survival, in Shorter, F. *et al.* (eds), *Population Factors in Development Planning in the Middle East*, Cairo: Population Council, 137–150.

Teidemann, H. (1991), *Catalogue of Earthquakes and Volcanoes*, Zurich: Swiss Reinsurance Co.

Teklu, T., von Braun, J. and Zaki, E. (1991), *Drought and Famine Relationships in Sudan: Policy Implications*, Washington DC: International Food Policy Research Institute, Research Report 88.

The Banker (1992), Global gamble, *The Banker*, February: 8–17.

The Economist (1988) *The Economist Book of Vital World Statistics: a Complete Guide to the World in Figures*, London: Hutchinson.

The Economist (1990) *The Economist Book of Vital World Statistics: a Complete Guide to the World in Figures*, London: Hutchinson.

The Economist (1992a), Environmental imperialism, *The Economist*, 15th February: 86.

The Economist (1992b), Third World debt: the disaster that didn't happen, *The Economist*, 12th September: 23–26.

Third Word Quarterly (1992), Special issue: rethinking socialism, *Third World Quarterly*, **13**(1).

Thomas, B.L. (1990), The Spratly Islands imbroglio: a tangled web of conflict, in: Grundy-Warr, C.E.R. (ed.), *International Boundaries and Boundary Conflict Resolution*, Durham: International Boundaries Research Unit, 413–428.

Thomas, G.A. (1991), The gentrification of paradise: St. John's, Antigua, *Urban Geography*, **12**(5): 469–487.

Thrift, N. (1990), The geography of international economic disorder, in: Johnston, R.J. and Taylor, P.J. (eds), *A World in Crisis: Geographical Perspectives*, Oxford: Blackwell, 16–78.

Tickner, R. (1991), *Social Justice for Indigenous Australians*, Canberra: Australian Government Publications Service, Budget Papers, 7.

Tilling, R.L. and Lipman, P.W. (1993), Lessons in reducing volcano risk, *Nature*, **364**: 277–280.

Timberlake, L. (1985), *Africa in Crisis: the Causes, Cures of Environmental Bankruptcy*, London: Earthscan.

Toit, R. du (1985), A middle way for wildlife parks, *New Scientist*, **105**: 33–36.

Tsemenyi, B.M. (1988), The exercise of coastal state jurisdiction over EEZ fisheries resources: the South Pacific practice, *Ambio*, **17**(4): 255–258.

Tully, M. (1991), *No Full Stops in India*, London: Viking.

Turner, A. (ed.) (1980), *The Cities of the Poor: Settlement Planning in Developing Countries*, London: Croom Helm.

Turner, J. (1967), Barriers and channels for housing development in modernising countries, *Journal of the American Institute of Planners*, **33**: 167–181.

Ulmishek, G.F. and Klemme, H.G. (1990), *Depositional Controls, Distribution and Effectiveness of World's Petroleum Source Rocks*, US Geological Survey Bulletin, no. 1931.

UN Population Division (1990), *Global Population Policy Data Base 1989*, New York: United Nations, Population Policy Paper 28, ST/ESA/SER.R/99.

UNDP (United Nations Development Programme) (annual), *Human Development Report*, New York: Oxford University Press for UNDP.

UNDP (United Nations Development Programme) (1991), *Human Development Index*, Oxford: Oxford University Press.

UNEP (United Nations Environment Programme) (1991) *Urban Air Pollution, ENEP/GEMS Environment Library No. 4*, Nairobi: United Nations Environment Programme.

UNEP (United Nations Environment Programme) (1992) *Urban Air Pollution in Megacities of the World*, Oxford: Blackwell.

UNEP/UNICEF (United Nations Environment Programme/United Nations Children's Fund) (1990), *The State of the Environment 1990: Children and the Environment*, New York: United Nations Environment Programme/United Nations Children's Fund.

UNESCO (United Nations Economic, Social and Cultural Organisation) (1975), *Gross Sediment Transport into the Oceans*, Paris: United Nations Economic, Social and Cultural Organisation/International Association of Hydrological Sciences.

UNESCO (United Nations Economic, Social and Cultural Organisation) Commission for the Geological Map of the World (1976), *Atlas Géologique du Monde*, Paris: United Nations Economic, Social and Cultural Organisation.

UNICEF (United Nations Children's Fund) (1990a), *Children and Development in the 1990s: a UNICEF Sourcebook*, New York: United Nations Children's Fund.

UNICEF (1990b), *Infancia, Adolescencia y Control Social en América Latina, Primer Informe Proyecto de Investigación Desarrollo de los Tribunales de Menores en Latinoamérica: Tendencias y Perspectivas*, Buenos Aires: Ediciones Depalma.

UNICEF (United Nations Children's Fund) (1992), *The State of the World's Children 1992*, Oxford: Oxford University Press for United Nations Children's Fund.

United Nations (annual), *Statistical Yearbook*, New York: United Nations.

United Nations (1983) *The Law of the Sea: Official Text of the U.N. Convention on the Law of the Sea*, London: Croom Helm.

United Nations (1987), *Women's Economic Participation in Asia and the Pacific*, Bangkok: ESCAP.

United Nations (1989), *Demographic Yearbook*, New York: United Nations.

United Nations (1990), *Debt: a Crisis for Development*, New York: United Nations.

United Nations (1991), *The World's Women 1970–1990, Trends and Statistics*, New York: United Nations.

United Nations (1992), *Law of the Sea Bulletin 20*, New York: United Nations Office of Legal Affairs.

United Nations Industrial Development Organisation (1992), *Handbook of Industrial Statistics, 1992*, Vienna: United Nations Industrial Development Organisation.

United States Geological Survey (1990), *Earthquakes with Magnitudes >5.0*, World Seismicity Map, Washington DC: USGS Earthquake Information Center.

Unwin, T. (1983), Perspective on 'Development' – an introduction, *Geoforum*, **14**(3): 235–241.

Unwin, T. (1988), Boserup revisited?, in: Blaikie, P. and Unwin, T. (eds), *Environmental Crises in Developing Countries*, Egham: Developing Areas Research Group of the Institute of British Geographers, Monograph, 5, 111–124.

Unwin, T. (1992), *The Place of Geography*, Harlow: Longman.

US Committee for Refugees (1993), *World Refugee Survey 1992*, Washington DC: US Committee for Refugees.

US Department of State (1981), *Limits in the Seas No 94, The Persian Gulf*, Washington DC: US Department of State.

US Department of State (1990), *Limits in the Seas No. 108, Maritime Boundaries of the World*, Washington DC: US Department of State.

US Arms Control and Disarmament Agency (1991), *World Military Expenditure and Arms Transfers*, Washington DC: US Government Printing Office.

Vallely, P. (1992), *Promised Lands: Stories of Power and Poverty in the Third World*, London: Harper Collins.

Van den Berghe, P. and Primov, G. (1977), *Inequality in the Peruvian Andes: Class and Ethnicity in Cuzco*, Columbia: University of Missouri Press.

Vayrynen, R. (1983), Semiperipheral countries in the global economic and military order, in: Tuomi, H. and Vayrynen, R. (eds), *Militarization and Arms Production*, London: Croom Helm, 163–192.

Vearncombe, R. (1981), Architectural conservation in

Minas Gerais, Brazil, *Third World Planning Review*, **3** 297–312.

Voluntary Health Association of India (1992), *State of India's Health*, New Delhi: Voluntary Health Association of India.

Vos, A. de (1977), Game as food: a report on its significance in Africa and Latin America, *Unasylva*, **29**(116): 2–12.

Vujakovic, P. (1987), Monitoring extensive 'buffer zones' in Africa: an application for satellite imagery. *Biological Conservation*, **39**: 195–208.

Vujakovic, P. (1989), Mapping for world development, *Geography*, **74**(2): 97–105.

Vujakovic, P. (1990), Comic cartography: maps in cartoons, *Geographical Magazine*, **62**(2): 22–26.

Wagner, P.A. (1990), Literacy assessment in the Third World: an overview and proposed schema for survey use, *Comparative Education Review*, **34**(1): 112–138.

Walker, R. and Storper, M. (1983), Capital and industrial location, *Progress in Human Geography*, **5**: 473–509.

Wallerstein, I. (1974, 1980a, 1989), *The Modern World System*, New York and London: Academic Press, 3 volumes.

Wallerstein, I. (1976), Semi-peripheral countries and the contemporary world crisis, *Theory and Society*, **3**: 341–384.

Wallerstein, I. (1980), Imperialism and development, in: Bergesen, A. (ed.), *Studies of the Modern World-System*, London: Macmillan, 128–145.

Warren, A. and Khogali, M. (1992), *Assessment of Desertification and Drought in the Sudano-Sahelian Region, 1985–1991*, New York: United Nations Sudano-Sahelian Office, United Nations Development Programme.

Warrick, R.A., Barrow, E.M. and Wigley, T.M.L. (1993), *Climate and Sea Level Change*, Cambridge: Cambridge University Press.

Watts, D. (1987), *The West Indies: Patterns of Development, Culture and Environmental Change Since 1492*, Cambridge: Cambridge University Press.

Watts, M.J. (1993), Development 1: power, knowledge, discursive practice, *Progress in Human Geography*, **17**(2): 257–272.

Webb-Vidal, A. (1992), The shrimp cocktail's hidden sting, *Geographical Magazine*, **64**(8): 16–20.

Weber, A. (1929), *Theory of the Location of Industries*, Chicago: University of Chicago Press.

Western, J. (1981), *Outcast Cape Town*, London: Allen and Unwin.

White, G. and Murray, R. (1983), *Revolutionary Socialist Development in the Third World*, Brighton: Wheatsheaf Books.

Whittaker, R.H. (1975), *Communities and Ecosystems*, New York: Macmillan, 2nd ed.

Whittlesey, D. (1936), Major agricultural regions of the earth, *Annals of the Association of American Geographers*, **26**: 199–240.

WHO (World Health Organisation) (1990), *International Water and Sanitation Decade 1981–1990: Decade Assessment*, Geneva: WHO.

Wigley, T.M.L. and Raper, S.C.B. (1991), Detection of the enhanced greenhouse effect on climate, in: Jäger, J. and Ferguson, H.L. (eds), *Climate Change: Science, Impacts and Policy*, Cambridge: Cambridge University Press, 232–242.

Wigley, T.M.L. and Raper, S.C.B. (1992), Implications of revised IPCC emissions scenarios, *Nature*, **357**, 293–300.

Williams, C.H. (ed.) (1988), *Language in Geographic Context*, Clevedon: Multilingual Matters.

Williams, C.H. (ed.) (1991), *Linguistic Minorities: Society and Territory*, Clevedon: Multilingual Matters.

Woodward, F.I. (1987), *Climate and Plant Distribution*, Cambridge: Cambridge University Press.

World Bank (1986), *Poverty and Hunger. Issues and Options for Food Security in Developing Countries*, Washington DC: The International Bank for Reconstruction and Development/The World Bank.

World Bank (1988), *Education in Sub-Saharan Africa: Policies for Adjustment, Revitalization and Expansion*, Washington DC: The World Bank.

World Bank (1989a), *Social Indicators of Development 1989*, Baltimore: The Johns Hopkins University Press.

World Bank (1989b), *Sub-Saharan Africa: from Crisis to Sustainable Growth. A Long-term Perspective Study*, Washington DC: World Bank.

World Bank (1989c), *World Development Report*, New York: Oxford University Press.

World Bank (1991), *Urban Policy and Economic Development. An Agenda for the 1990s*, Washington DC: World Bank, Policy Paper.

World Bank (1992a), *Universities and Africa: Strategies for Stabilisation and Revitalisation*, Washington DC: The World Bank.

World Bank (1992b), *World Development Report 1992. Development and the Environment*, New York: Oxford University Press.

World Bank (1993), *Statistical Handbook 1993: States of the Former USSR*, Washington DC: World Bank, Studies of Economies in Transformation.

World Bank (annual since 1946), *Annual Report*, Washington DC: The World Bank.

World Bank (annual since 1978), *World Development Report*, New York: Oxford University Press for The World Bank.

World Development (1991), Special issue – adjustment with growth and equity, *World Development*, **19**(11).

World Resources Institute and International Institute for Environment and Development (1988), *World Resources 1988–89*, New York: Basic Books.

Worsley, P. (1964), *The Third World*, London: Weidenfeld & Nicolson.

Worsley, P. (1979) How many worlds?, *Third World Quarterly*, **1**(2): 100–108.

WRI (World Resources Institute) (1990), *World Resources 1990–1991: a Guide to the Global Environment*, Oxford: Oxford University Press, World Resources Institute/United Nations Environment Programme/United Nations Development Programme.

Zograph, G.A. (1982), *Languages of South Asia: a Guide*, London: Routledge and Kegan Paul.

Appendix: Sources for Figures and Tables

Figures

0.1 State names and boundaries, July 1993
Source: MAPINFO (map); Times Atlas (names)

1.1 Conventional projections of the world
Source: author

1.2 Sino-centric 'turnabout' cartogram of world population 1991
Source: adapted and redrawn from De Blij, H.J. and Muller, P.O. (1991)

1.3 Rumold Mercator's 2-hemisphere map of the world, 1587
Source: Mercator, *Atlas*, 1595

1.4 The Ottoman Empire, *c.* 1520
Source: author

1.5 Elements of the world economy, *c.* 1780
Source: author

1.6a Number of colonies, 1500–1950
Source: author

1.6b Colonial development
Source: author

1.7 Imperialism
Source: author

1.8a European colonisation of Africa, 1880
Source: author

1.8b The extent of European colonisation in Africa, 1914
Source: author

1.8c Dates of independence of African states
Source: author

1.9 Decolonisation
Source: author

1.10 The Third World and the North-South divide
Source: author

1.11a GNP per capita, 1990
Source: World Bank, *World Development Report* (1991)

1.11b Trends in regional inequalities in Thailand
Source: derived from data from National Statistical Office, Bangkok

1.12a The stability of countries in the core, semi-periphery and periphery
Source: after Arrighi and Drangel (1986)

1.12b The world system
Source: author

1.13a PQLI map of the world
Source: after Morris (1979)

1.13b Political freedom and civil rights
Source: derived from Population Crisis Committee (1993)

2.1 Bedrock geology
Source: adapted from Larson *et al.* (1985)

2.2a Outline of plate tectonic mechanism
Source: author

2.2b Simplified distribution of major tectonic plates and their relationship to earthquakes, volcanoes and zones of elevated topography
Source: partly derived from Teidemann (1991)

2.3 Distribution of world sedimentary basins and hydrocarbon resources
Source: derived from map of *World sedimentary basins* produced by Petroconsultants S.A., Geneva (1986), scale 1:23 million

2.4a Global temperature
Source: data derived from Legates, D.R. and Willmott, C.J. (1992)

2.4b Global precipitation
Source: data derived from Legates, D.R. and Willmott, C.J. (1992).

2.5 Precipitation variability index
Source: author

2.6a Temperature seasonality index
Source: author

2.6b Precipitation seasonality index
Source: author

2.6c Annual cycle of precipitation at three contrasting African stations: Niamey (Niger), Nairobi (Kenya) and Harare (Zimbabwe), 1951–80
Source: author

2.7a Regions showing consistent ENSO-related precipitation anomalies
Source: redrawn from Ropelewski and Halpert (1987)

2.7b Annual rainfall anomalies in the Sahel, 1900–92
Source: author

2.8a Global-mean surface air temperature, 1854 to 1992
Source: P.D. Jones, Climatic Research Unit, University of East Anglia (pers. comm.)

2.8b Annual surface air temperature change, 1931–1960 and 1961–1990
Source: Hulme *et al.* (1992a)

2.9a Estimated global-mean sea level, 1880–2100
Source: redrawn and amended from Barnett (1988) and Wigley and Raper (1992)

2.9b Relative contributions to sea level rise
Source: Hulme *et al.* (1992b)

2.10a Holdridge Life Zones, southern
Source: derived from Leemans (1990)

2.10b Holdridge Life Zones, northern
Source: derived from Leemans (1990)

2.11a The Amazon forest
Source: author

2.11b Rates of deforestation
Source: modified from Myers (1989)

2.12a Suspended sediment yields in South America: a comparison of published estimates by three authors
Source: based on UNESCO (1975), Fournier (1960) and Strakhov (1967)

2.12b Simplified extract of Global Assessment of Soil Degradation map for South America
Source: Oldeman et al. (1990) and ISRIC, Wageningen/UNEP, Nairobi

2.13a Small island size and amphibian and reptile species diversity
Source: after MacArthur (1972)

2.13b Grand Cayman, Caribbean: land below six metres at risk from sea level rise and increased storminess
Source: derived from DOS map of Grand Cayman

2.14a Jamaica
Source: author

2.14b Integrated soil conservation strategies for steeply-sloping tropical hillsides
Source: after Sheng (1972)

2.15a Soil erosion in Svosve, 1947
Source: author

2.15b Soil erosion in Svosve, 1981
Source: author

2.16a The command areas of major irrigation schemes in India
Source: author

2.16b The irrigation schemes in the Punjab
Source: author

2.17 Average annual suspended particulate matter (SPM) concentrations at monitoring stations within selected cities
Source: Global Environmental Monitoring System (1991) GEMS/AIR Annual Data Summary, January 1991. Monitoring and Assessment Research Centre, King's College London, University of London.

3.1 Population density, 1991
Source: derived from Population Reference Bureau (1991)

3.2a Population doubling times
Source: derived from Population Reference Bureau (1991)

3.2b Population in India
Source: derived from Findlay and Findlay (1987)

3.3a Total fertility rates
Source: derived from Population Reference Bureau (1991)

3.3b Age-specific fertility, Jordan
Source: derived from Hashemite Kingdom of Jordan (1990)

3.4 Strength of family planning programmes in less developed countries, 1989
Source: data derived from Mauldin and Ross (1991)

3.5a Life expectancy at birth (years), 1990
Source: derived from Population Reference Bureau (1991)

3.5b Infant Mortality Rates in Africa
Source: derived from Population Reference Bureau (1991)

3.6 Under-five survival rates, 1990
Source: derived from data in UNICEF (1992)

3.7 The place of children in Latin America
Source: derived from data in UNICEF (1992)

3.8 Urban population as a percentage of population, 1990
Source: derived from Population Reference Bureau (1991)

3.9 Percentage of one-year-old children fully immunised against diptheria, pertussis and tetanus, 1989–90
Source: derived from data in UNICEF (1992)

3.10a Percentage of population without access to safe water, 1988–90
Source: derived from data in UNICEF (1992)

3.10b Percentages of urban and rural populations with access to safe water, 1988–1990
Source: derived from data in UNICEF (1992)

3.11a Average daily energy supply per person (1988–90)
Source: FAO/WHO (1992b)

3.11b Prevalence of underweight pre-school children in developing countries, 1990
Source: ACC/SCN (1992)

3.11c Child growth data, Sudan
Source: derived from Teklu et al. (1991)

3.11d Geographical distribution of xerophthalmia, 1987
Source: ACC/SCN (1992)

3.12a Proportion of rural population below the poverty line, 1980–88
Source: data derived from United Nations Development Programme, Human Development Report (1991: 158–159)

3.12b Proportion of population below the poverty line, classified by income and urban/rural status, 1977–86
Source: data derived from United Nations Development Programme, Human Development Report (1991: 158–159)

3.13a Share of income by top 20% of households, various years, 1978–89
Source: data derived from World Bank (1992b: 276–277)

3.13b Share of income by bottom 20% of households, by world region, 1978–89
Source: data derived from World Bank (1992b: 276–77)

3.14 Household income distribution in Indonesia
Source: data derived from Biro Pusat Statistik (1990: 41, 554–555)

3.15a Labour force participation by women, 1989
Source: data derived from World Bank (1989a: 218–219)

3.15b Total and female labour force participation, classified by income
Source: data derived from World Bank (1989a: 218–219)

3.16 Tenancy types
Source: author

3.17 Colombia: housing tenure for major cities, 1985
Source: author

3.18a The interrelations between settlements, space preferences, migration paths and policy space
Source: Potter (1985)

3.18b Space preferences in Trinidad and Tobago
Source: redrawn from Potter (1983: 23, 27)

3.19 Perception of natural resources and their use, Nubian Desert, south-eastern Egypt
Source: author

3.20a Percentage of riceland planted to modern varieties of rice, 1990
Source: derived from IRRI (1994)

3.20b Modern varieties, geology and the Tribal peoples of Bihar, India
Source: after Corbridge (1984)

3.21a Adult literacy rate, 1985
Source: data derived from World Bank, *World Development Report* (1991: 204–205)

3.21b Female literacy rate as a percentage of male rate in sub-Saharan Africa, Middle East/north Africa and Asia
Source: data derived from World Bank, *World Development Report* (1991: 204–205)

3.22a Total and girls' enrolment ratios, (a) primary and (b) secondary levels, 1965–88
Source: data derived from World Bank, *World Development Report* (1991: 260–261)

3.22b Secondary enrolment, 1988
Source: data derived from World Bank, *World Development Report* (1991)

3.23 Percentage in tertiary education, 1988
Source: World Bank, *World Development Report* (1991)

3.24 Rural settlement in part of Cuzco Department, Peru
Source: author

3.25 Myanmar: main ethnic groups
Source: Mehmet (1986)

3.26 The spread of HIV in Owambo, northern Namibia
Source: author

4.1 Crop production systems
Source: author

4.2 Staple food crops
Source: author

4.3a Non-EC fruit and vegetables, Sainsbury's Moortown, Leeds, 10 November 1993
Source: author

4.3b Exports of fresh poultry, 1991
Source: FAO, *Trade Yearbook* (1992)

4.4a Agricultural calendar in central Kenya and monthly rainfall totals, Nairobi
Source: Kenya Meteorological Service

4.4b Annual rainfall totals for Baydhabo, Somalia
Source: information from Somali Government Printer

4.5a Thailand: rented land as a percentage of total farm land, 1988
Source: MOAC (1990)

4.5b Thailand: rented land and rice yields, by region
Source: MOAC (1990)

4.5c Security of land ownership and productivity
Source: adapted from Feder *et al.* (1988)

4.6a Daily per capita calorie supply for middle and low income countries, 1974 and 1989
Source: data derived from World Bank, *World Development Report* (1991)

4.6b Cereal imports as a proportion of cereal production
Source: data derived from FAO, *Trade Yearbook* (1990)

4.6c Cereal imports and cereal food aid for middle and low income countries, 1974 and 1989
Source: data derived from World Bank, *World Bank Development Report* (1991)

4.7a Growth of world cereal trade, 1960–90
Source: data derived from FAO, *Trade Yearbooks* (various years)

4.7b Share of world cereal trade by region, 1989
Source: data derived from FAO, *Trade Yearbook* (1990)

4.7c The five major wheat exporters, 1989–1990
Source: data derived from World Wheat Council, unpublished statistics

4.8 Labour force as a percentage of population
Source: ILO, *World Labour Report* (1992)

4.9 Percentage of GDP contributed by manufacturing industry, 1990
Source: data derived from World Bank (1992b), *World Development Report*.

4.10 The South-east Asia growth triangle
Source: information from Baring Securities, Hong Kong (1992)

4.11a The location of company towns in Brazil
Source: author

4.11b Layout of the company mining town of Carajás, Pará
Source: author

4.12a Iron ore movements, 1990
Source: author based on OECD (1990)

4.12b Bauxite, alumina trade, 1990 and aluminium production, 1987
Source: author based on OECD (1990)

4.12c Phosphate production and trade, 1990
Source: author based on OECD (1990)

4.13a Density of world road networks, 1989
Source: derived from International Road Federation (1991), *World Road Statistics*.

4.13b Surface quality of world road networks, 1989
Source: derived from International Road Federation (1991), *World Road Statistics*.

4.13c Roads in commercial farming and communal farming areas in Mashonaland, Zimbabwe
Source: derived from contemporary maps and Provincial development plans for Mashonaland

4.13d The motorway network in Europe, 1991
Source: derived from contemporary maps and data from the International Road Federation

4.13e Roads in the Economic Community of West African States
Source: derived from contemporary maps and data from Ministries of Transport of member states

4.14 The rail network in southern and central Africa
Source: author

4.15a Development of world fleet by ship type, 1971–90
Source: data derived from OECD (1991)

4.15b Ship registration by principal flags
Source: data derived from OECD (1991)

4.15c Ship registration by economic grouping
Source: data derived from OECD (1991)

4.16a Growth of air transport, 1971–90
Source: International Civil Aviation Organisation (1991)

4.16b Regional contrasts in development of air transport
Source: International Civil Aviation Organisation, annual statistics (1991)

4.16c Regional distribution of scheduled air traffic
Source: International Civil Aviation Organisation, annual statistics (1991)

4.17 Proportion of national population living in the largest city, *c.* 1980
Source: United Nations (1989) *Demographic Yearbook*

4.18a Low-income housing in Third World cities
Source: Potter, R.B. (1992: 32)

4.18b Housing upgrading
Source: adapted from Turner, A. (ed.) (1980)

4.19 World Bank lending by type and sector, 1980, 1984, 1988, 1991
Source: World Bank *Annual Reports*

4.20 Foreign debt, 1989
Source: data derived from *World Bank* (1989c)

4.21 The global financial system
Source: author

4.22 Brain drain migrants to the USA: major Third World sources
Source: data derived from MacPhee and Hassan (1990)

4.23a Net remittances from international migration, 1988
Source: data derived from IMF (1991)

4.23b Ratio of remittances to exports for the six countries of the world most dependent on remittances
Source: IMF (1991)

4.24 Outmigration from Kallarayan, southern Peru
Source: author

4.25a TVs per 1000 inhabitants, 1988
Source: data derived from United Nations, *Statistical Yearbook* (1992: 203–215)

4.25b TVs and radios per 1000 inhabitants, classified by income, 1988
Source: data derived from United Nations, *Statistical Yearbook* (1992: 203–215), and World Bank, *World Development Report* (1992: 218–219)

4.26 Wildlife exploitation: the harvest of the seas
Source: author

4.27 Botswana: Wildlife Management Areas
Source: derived from Carter, J. (1983)

4.28 Net disbursement of Official Development Assistance (ODA) from all sources
Source: author

5.1a Positions on UN resolution 678, November 29th 1990, and formal geopolitical alliances, September 1993
Source: author

5.1b Emergent geo-economic blocs
Source: author

5.2a Membership of the SACU and SADCC/SADC
Source: author

5.2b Membership of the PTA
Source: author

5.3 Political stability
Source: author

5.4 Warfare since 1945
Source: author

5.5 The arms trade 1985–90
Source: author

5.6a The death penalty: abolished for all crimes, and for ordinary crimes only (December 1991)
Source: Amnesty International (1992a)

5.6b The death penalty: abolished de facto and retained (December 1991)
Source: Amnesty International (1992a)

5.7a Social revolutions since the Russian revolution producing radical regimes
Source: author

5.7b The extent of FRELIMO insurgency in 1974
Source: author

5.7c Geostrategic situation in Mozambique in 1990
Source: author

5.8 GNP per capita (1990) versus population increase (per 1000 pop.) (1989) in states of the former Soviet Union
Source: data derived from Goskomstat SSSR

5.9 Refugees worldwide
Source: US Committee for Refugees (1993)

5.10 Resettlement schemes for nomads: the case of Somalia
Source: author; Resettlement Project Office, Cadale, 1982; Settlement Development Agency, Muqdishu, 1982.

5.11 Party systems
Source: author

5.12 Indian Lok Sabha elections, 1977, 1984 and 1991
Source: author

5.13 The 200 nautical mile exclusive economic zone (EEZ) and progress towards ratification of the historic 1982 UN Convention on the Law of the Sea
Source: author

5.14 Maritime boundary agreements and potential maritime boundaries in the Gulf
Source: adapted from US Department of State (1981)

5.15 Geopolitics of the Spratly Islands in the South China Sea
Source: derived from Thomas (1990)

5.16a Kenya: Arid and Semiarid Administrative Districts
Source: compiled by author from various sources; GIS cover based on Survey of Kenya (1980), *1:1M (Special), Kenya, Administrative Boundaries*, Nairobi: Survey of Kenya, and Survey of Kenya (1987), *SK81C Kenya 1:1M Edition 5, Kenya, Parliamentary Constituencies*, Nairobi: Survey of Kenya.

5.16b Kenya: Parliamentary returns (Rural Constituencies) Multi-Party Elections December 1992
Source: compiled by author from various sources; GIS cover based on Survey of Kenya (1980), *1:1M (Special), Kenya, Administrative Boundaries*, Nairobi: Survey of Kenya, and Survey of Kenya (1987), *SK81C Kenya 1:1M Edition 5, Kenya, Parliamentary Constituencies*, Nairobi: Survey of Kenya.

5.17a South Africa: political and administrative regions
Source: compiled by author from various sources. GIS cover based on Republic of South Africa, Magisterial District Map, April, 1989, Scale 1:2 500 000.

5.17b Regional contribution to Gross Geographical Product, 1989: agriculture, hunting, forestry and fishing; mining and quarrying; and manufacturing.
Source: data derived from Erasmus, J. *et al.* (1991)

6.1 Propaganda cartography: Israeli and Arab populations
Source: adapted from Ministry of Foreign Affairs (Jerusalem) (1985)

6.2a   Maps in political graphics: the Iraqi invasion of Kuwait
Source: International Boundaries Research Unit, Durham University

6.2b   The European Community: the accession of Spain and Portugal
Source: redrawn from European Commission (1986), Europe as seen by Europeans: European polling 1973–86, *European Documentation*, 1986/4.

6.3   Aboriginal populations in Australia
Source: author

6.4   Global language divisions, 1989
Source: author

6.5   National language diversity: India
Source: author

6.6   Global religions
Source: author

6.7   Regional religious diversity in south Asia
Source: author

6.8   Christian Aid's global aid programme
Source: Christian Aid

6.9   Indian States and Christian Aid partners/projects (31 March 1993)
Source: Christian Aid

6.10   Settlement and land use in the Rufiji valley, east-central Tanzania
Source: Briggs (1980)

6.11a The original apartheid city model
Source: Simon (1992)

6.11b The modernised apartheid city model
Source: Simon (1992)

6.12   World heritage sites
Source: author based on ICOMOS (1991)

Tables

1.7   Resistance to imperialism in the 19th century
Source: derived from Small and Singer (1982)

1.11   Poverty and income distribution in Thailand
Source: data from National Statistical Office, Thailand

1.12   Vayrynen's semi-periphery
Source: after Vayrynen (1983)

1.13   Socio-economic development indices for selected countries
Source: Drakakis-Smith (1993), UNDP (1991), World Bank Development Report (1990)

2.3   Global hydrocarbon reserves and production
Source: derived from *Oil and Gas Journal* (1993, **91** (52): 41–45)

2.5   Examples of annual precipitation variability for three selected stations illustrating low, moderate and high precipitation variability regimes
Source: author

2.14a Environmental management of humid tropical hillsides
Source: Planning Institute of Jamaica (1992)

2.14b Average mean dry soil loss, yams under soil conservation treatments
Source: data derived from unpublished statistics, Soil Conservation Division, Kingston, Jamaica

2.15   Change in the nature and extent of soil erosion (hectares) in Svosve 1947–81
Source: Elliott (1989)

3.3   Government views of fertility levels in developing countries
Source: calculated from data in Population Reference Bureau (1991)

3.11   Three anthropometric indices providing different information about growth, all of which are sometimes used synonymously with 'malnutrition'
Source: author

3.12   Total population below the poverty line, 1977–86
Source: UNDP, *Human Development Report* (1990)

3.13   Ratio of income of top 20% of households to bottom 20%, 1980–87
Source: UNDP, *Human Development Report* (1991: 152–153, 186)

3.14   The distribution of the urban and rural poor in Indonesia, 1969/70–1987
Source: Booth (1992: 347)

3.20   Social influences, scale and the adoption of new rice technology
Source: Bradnock (1984), Hayami and Kikuchi (1981), and Barker *et al.* (1985)

3.23a Unit costs of public education as percentage of per capita GNP
Source: World Bank (1988: 75)

3.23b Percentage of age group enrolled in Higher Education, 1965 and 1988
Source: World Bank, *World Development Report* (1991: 261)

3.25   Malaysia: employment and ethnicity
Source: Mehmet (1986)

4.5   Land documentation in Thailand
Source: Feder *et al.* (1988)

4.6   World cereal production and year-end stocks
Source: FAO, *Production Yearbooks* (various years); FAO, *State of Food and Agriculture* (various years)

4.7a   Agricultural trade, 1989
Source: FAO, *Trade Yearbook* (1990)

4.7b   Importance of agricultural trade
Source: FAO, *Trade Yearbook* (1990)

4.7c   World net grain trade (positive numbers denote exports)
Source: Brown (1975), FAO *Production Yearbooks* (various dates)

4.8a   The structure of employment and level of development
Source: UNDP, *Human Development Report* (1993)

4.8b   Percentage contribution of manufacturing, 1990
Source: World Bank, *World Development Report* (1992)

4.10   Growth of the Asian NICs, annual average percentage rates
Source: World Bank, *World Development Report* (various years); *Industry of Free China* (various years)

4.12a Iron ore production and consumption, 1988 (million tonnes)
Source: *The Economist* (1990)

4.12b World bauxite reserves (million metric tonnes)
Source: Patterson (1986)

4.19a IBRD voting power, 1976 and 1991, selected countries: percentage of total votes in Executive Council
Source: World Bank, *Annual Reports* (1976, 1991)

4.19b IBRD and IDA loans, 1945–76, 1982 and 1991
       by region (US$ millions)
       Source: World Bank, *Annual Reports* (1976,
       1982, 1991)
4.20   The world's largest debtors in 1988
       Source: *The Economist* (1988)
4.23   The world's most migrant dependent states
       Source: derived from International Monetary
       Fund (1991)
5.8a   Socio-economic characteristics of the republics
       of the former Soviet Union 1989
       Source: Goskomstat SSSR (1990),
       Demograficheskiy ezhegodnik SSSR 1990,
       Moscow: Finansy i statistika; Goskomstat
       SSSR (1991a), *Narodnoye khozyaystvo SSSR v
       9190g*, Moscow: Finansy i statistika;
       Goskomstat SSSR (1991b), *Soyuzniye
       respubliki: osnovnyye ekonomischeskiye i
       sotsial'nyye pokazateli*, Moscow:
       Informatsionno-izadetel'skiy tsentr Goskomstat
       SSSR
5.8b   Economic development of the post-Soviet
       republics in 1991
       Source: World Bank (1993)
5.16a 1992 Multi-party elections: tribal support
       (number of seats won) for political parties
       Source: compiled by author
5.16b 1992 Multi-party elections: provincial voting
       (%) for main presidential candidates
       Source: compiled by author
5.17   Socio-economic indices, development regions
       1989
       Source: Erasmus, J. *et al.* (1991)
6.3   Selected ratios for Aboriginal/non-Aboriginal
       populations
       Source: Tickner (1991)
6.4   Global languages ranked in importance
       Source: derived from McConnell (1991)

Index